John Duke McFaden

Our Bible, Our Church and Our Country..

John Duke McFaden

Our Bible, Our Church and Our Country..

ISBN/EAN: 9783337171841

Printed in Europe, USA, Canada, Australia, Japan

Cover: Foto ©Lupo / pixelio.de

More available books at **www.hansebooks.com**

OUR BIBLE, OUR CHURCH

AND

1889.

TO MY FATHER, WHO TAUGHT ME FROM

"OUR BIBLE;"

TO MY MOTHER, WHO LED ME TO

"OUR CHURCH;"

TO MY BROTHERS AND SISTERS, WHO MADE ME THINK

"OUR COUNTRY"

A GOODLY HERITAGE,

THIS BOOK IS AFFECTIONATELY DEDICATED.

THE AUTHOR'S PRELUDE.

IT is customary, in all well-regulated families, to say grace before meals, and, having provided so many good things for your enjoyment, it is right that I should offer a prelude before you partake of them.

OUR BIBLE.

THERE is no book like the Bible. It has God for its author and a world's salvation for its object; hence it was absolutely essential for the safety and happiness of the human race. Nature was not sufficient as a guide: it needed a supplement; God gave us a revelation.

You have probably visited the gallery of art in Washington City. If so, you have looked upon that noble piece of marble, "The Greek Slave," standing before it. You ask from whence it came, and why it is there, but you cannot get one idea by asking it questions. Its ears are deaf and its lips are dumb. It is beautiful, but cold and silent.

You purchase a catalogue, and in it you read that the piece of marble called "The Greek Slave" was made by an artist named Powers, and was purchased for the gallery of art, where it has been admired by thousands, and so you learn from the catalogue all the facts about the piece of marble.

"The Greek Slave" represents Nature, the catalogue represents Revelation. One is essential to the correct understanding of the other.

Nature is filled with beautiful paintings and wonderful formations, but all the beauties and wonders of nature are silent as to their author and object until supplemented by revelation.

Look at the rainbow as it spans the art gallery of the sky—what a beautiful piece of work! You want to learn something about its object, but you might stand and ask it questions until doomsday and get no information. It is only when you pick up the divine catalogue that you have revealed the object of the rainbow: "I do set my bow in the cloud, and it shall be for a token of a covenant between me and the earth."

Stand by the coffin of your loved one; the deep undercurrent of the heart seeks for a solution of the mystery men call death. The sun may be shining, the birds may be singing, the flowers may be blooming, the fountain may be sparkling, and all nature may be aglow; but nature through all her various manifestations cannot satisfy your mind nor comfort your heart.

Go to revelation; read such words as those of John: "And I heard a voice from heaven, saying unto me, write; Blessed are the dead which die in the Lord from henceforth: yea, saith the Spirit, that they may rest from their labors: and their works do follow them." Then you have: "Beauty for ashes, the oil of joy for mourning, the garment of praise for the spirit of heaviness." Revelation only enables you to appreciate the words of the Master: "Let not your heart be troubled, neither let it be afraid."

The Bible, being a supplement to Nature and essential to our nature, should be honestly used and practically followed. Many people have very fine Bibles, but they are not used; they are for visitors to look at, not for home-folks to handle. Such a state of affairs should not exist.

The captain studies his chart and examines his compass, and is able to direct his vessel in the right direction. The Bible is our chart and compass—its needle points toward Christ, the pole-star of the soul's universe; hence it should be studied, so that the bark of life can be kept from the breakers and guided into the gulf-stream of eternity.

The Bible should be used honestly. Over a door in London are the words: "All kinds of twisting and turning done here." Over the doors of many Bible-readers might be written the words: "All kinds of intellectual twisting and turning done here." Martin Luther said: "We should not bend the Bible to suit us, but let the Bible bend us, and so give it credit for knowing more than we do."

Use the Bible, use it right, and hold to it through life.

A preacher and his wife had occasion to leave their two little children with the nurse during the afternoon; the nurse also left and the two little ones were left alone. When evening came they were fearful. It was dark when the parents returned; they found the boy and girl on the steps with their hands on the Bible, which was between them. When fear seized them, they went into the parlor, got down the large family Bible, dragged it out on the steps, and put their little hands upon it. They said they were not afraid as long as they kept their hands upon the Bible.

The object of this book is to get your hands on the Bible; there you are safe. Depart from its teachings and you are in danger. Let us also hide it in our hearts, and practise its precepts in our lives.

OUR CHURCH.

If there is no book like the Bible, neither is there any organization like the Church. No doubt there were other boats in Noah's day, but there was no boat like the Ark. It successfully carried its passengers to the salvation mountain, where they met God and were circled by a rainbow.

By the term "Our Church," I have reference to all whose wills are in subjection to the will of God. All such are members of the church militant. The Master said: "Whosoever doeth the will of my Father, the same is my brother, my sister, my mother." This passage makes every doer of God's will a member of God's family, and places every woman on equality with the Virgin Mary, whom some place above every other woman.

There is but one church; Christ is its head. A perfect

head must not have two bodies; such a formation would be a monstrosity; hence there is but one body for the one head, and this body forms the family of God. Paul refers to the oneness of the church in Christ when he says: "Of whom the whole family in heaven and earth is named." The Head himself said: "One is your Master, even Christ, and all ye are brethren."

The object of the church is the world's salvation, physical, intellectual and spiritual. For this object Christ came into the world and worked the plan of salvation, and his body should continue the work and seek and save the lost. Any organization failing to have for its object the world's salvation cannot accomplish the object for which Christ died.

Some people seem to act as though they thought the church a mutual admiration society, organized especially for their benefit, and run on the "you tickle me and I will tickle you" principle; such individuals are an obstacle to success. They must be converted before they can help strengthen the brethren.

The church should be freed from all dead growth. Nature is more prolific if assisted by pruning. The dead growth must be removed, if the vital force would accomplish its object. The church often has an accumulation of dead growth, and if success would be sure, there must be more or less pruning. The sap power of Christianity must flow through clear channels if it would be successful in its operations. Dead ideas and worn-out theories have no right to impede the progress of Christ.

On one occasion a man detected an unpleasant odor, and it became worse; he consulted his physician, took medicine, but the trouble grew worse. It was supposed the offensive odor was the result of some disease. Matters went so far that preparations were made for death, when a dead mouse was found in the lining of the man's coat. The mystery being explained, the man's appetite returned and his health was restored, as was also his happiness.

There are many organizations having about them that which is offensive; consequently people condemn the society and talk against Christianity. But the trouble is not with Christ, nor the principle of Christianity, nor the Bible, nor the church as an organization, but some humanism, worldlyism, sinism has crawled in, and that "ism" is the trouble. Shake the coat, and throw the mouse away, and you will be healthy and happy.

The church should seek to be attractive. Nature is attractive, Grace is attractive, and the organization that attempts to develop Nature by Grace should do the work in an attractive manner. There was a time when two sticks at each end of a slab would do for a pew, and two laths tacked together with candles fastened at each end with hot tallow would do for a chandelier, but that time has gone by. People in the present day have more attractive homes than those in other days had, and they should seek attraction in the church, and thus have harmony between the home and church.

One element of Christian attractiveness—aside from the neatly-built and well-arranged house—is spiritual sociability. The church that is not social is on the dead line. A lady told me she had visited a church for two years, and in all that time no one had taken her by the hand. This may have been an extreme case, but there is too much of this lack of the social principle. There is a great deal of religion in a good honest shake of the hand. The gospel of the elbow is a good gospel; not only to preach, but to practise.

The preacher is often expected to do all this work. While the pews are frozen solid, the pulpit is expected to be on fire. It is true the preacher should manifest the social principle, but the pew should not be behind him in such manifestation. The members of a church can make the visitor have a home-like feeling that the preacher, no matter how friendly he may be, cannot make them have. The pulpit has a work; the pew also has a work; and the work of pulpit and pew tend in the same direction, viz., to seek and save the lost, and then develop the saved for work in time and happiness in heaven.

There is one element of a successful church not to be overlooked—CARE FOR THE YOUNG. If a church would grow and become strong and exert an influence for good, the young must be cared for; they are not only the hope but the strength of the church. Our nation recognizes the principle, and has her West Point. Every church should have a training-school for the young. Literary men recognize the principle and spend millions of dollars yearly in literature for the young; the church should never be behind the world in feeding the minds of the young. As the wise men took their best gifts to Christ, let us take our best offerings—the young—to Him who said: "Suffer little children to come unto me and forbid them not, for of such is the kingdom of heaven."

OUR COUNTRY.

How true are the words of David, and how applicable to our own land! "The lines are fallen unto me in pleasant places; yea, I have a goodly heritage." There is no land like the land we live in. It is great in many respects.

Our country is great in the extent of her territory. From the Pacific on the west to the Atlantic on the east, and from the Lakes on the north to the Gulf on the south is a vast extent of territory, inhabited by teeming millions who are working out the object of their creation.

Our country is great in her natural resources. There are veins of coal, wells of oil, fountains of gas, mines of gold, and silver, and copper—lodes of lead. God has not only led us into a great land, but he has put in it the material by which it can be used and made goodly. In a few years one hundred millions will be the number of inhabitants, and they will be just as well cared for then as the sixty millions are now.

Our country is great in her beautiful scenery. No American need visit Europe to look on beautiful scenery; we have it here, in beauty unsurpassed. This land has within its borders the skies of Italy, the glow of Spain, the ruggedness of Switzerland, and the pictured beauty of England, stamped with its own originality. Visit romantic Harper's Ferry, sublime Niagara, the wonderful Yosemite, and a thousand places where you can see the foot-prints and finger-marks of the great Jehovah; and seeing them you say: "This is none other but the house of God, and this is the gate of heaven."

Our country is great in the fundamental principles of her government. Life, liberty and the pursuit of happiness form a triangle which, struck by honest hearts, makes music rich enough for angelic ears. This triune bond of union touches mankind at the physical, intellectual and spiritual corners of life, and enables him to appreciate his Maker who said: "Let us make man in our own image." Where can man so enjoy life, breathe the air of liberty and unrestrained pursue his happiness, as in this country, the land of the free and the home of the brave?

Our country offsets the tower of Babel; there the people were of one speech and language, but God visited and confused them, and they were divided and scattered. From that tower young nations went forth in every direction; but into our country all nations are pouring their strong bodies, bright minds and brave hearts; and here, these men from all climes are being welded into one great, mighty, omnipotent nation—the light-house of the world, the guide of humanity, the index-finger pointing to the triumph of principle over policy. Babel meant scatteration, America means concentration for God and humanity.

These assertions are facts, recognized by the brightest minds of earth. Stoughton said: "God sifted a whole nation that he might send choice grain over into this wilderness." Klopstock said: "By the rivers of America light beams forth to the nations." Judge Gied said: "Who would not be an American citizen and claim a home in these United States!" Good old Father Taylor said: "I have travelled far, and have seen the best of all the countries of this world, and there is but one United States of America in the world."

If our country is God's creation, it should be so developed as to promote God's glory. This can be accomplished by repudiating sin and exalting righteousness, for "righteousness exalteth a nation; but sin is a reproach to any people." To this end let all religious societies and all political associations "make a chain: for the land is full of bloody crimes, and the city full of violence." Our nation started with an open Bible and a free church; let her so continue. As Bancroft says: "The maturity of the nation is but a continuation of its youth," and we all know that in a union of hands and hearts for a pure object there is strength.

Our country, to develop purity, must take the youth as she finds them, and make them what they ought to be. Let them be taught to obey the Bible, reverence the church, defend the Sabbath and love their country. Blend their bodies, minds and spirits, and teach them patriotism. Over every school-house let the stars and stripes float, and days be set apart especially for the purpose of impressing them with the greatness of our land, the glory of truth, the triumphs of righteousness and the goodness of God, keeping before them, first, last and all the time, the great fact taught by Washington: "While just government protects all in their religious rights, true religion affords to government its surest support."

Our country, great and glorious, should not be regarded with indifference. Well says James A. Garfield: "Shall we regard with indifference the great inheritance which cost our sires their blood, because we find in their gift an admixture of imperfection and evil? Surely there is good enough in the contemplation of which every patriotic heart may say: 'God bless my own, my native land!'"

Let every citizen do the duty lying nearest him or her, and it can ever be said: "God reigns, and the government at Washington still lives."

> Let the noble motto be,
> "God, the country, liberty!"
> Planted on religion's rock,
> Thou shalt stand in every shock.
>
> Laugh at danger far or near;
> Spurn at baseness, spurn at fear;
> Still with persevering might
> Speak the truth and do the right.

So shall Peace—a charming guest—
Dove-like in thy bosom rest,
So shall Honor's steady blaze
Beam upon thy closing days.

Happy if celestial favor
Smile upon the high endeavor;
Happy if it be thy call
In the holy cause to fall.

Trusting that "Our Bible, Our Church and Our Country" may lead the mind of the reader into green pastures and beside still waters, and enable you to say, "I will dwell in the house of the Lord forever," I am

Yours for the world's salvation.
John Duke McFaden.

LIST OF CONTENTS.

OUR BIBLE.

		PAGE
OUR BIBLE	*Dennis*	33
THE BIBLE	*Schaff*	34
ARGUMENT FOR ITS PURITY	*Protestant*	36
INDEPENDENT OF OTHER BOOKS	*Gilfillan*	37
SUPERIORITY OF THE BIBLE	*De Vere*	41
SOURCE OF ALL GOOD	*Webster*	41
ABROAD IN THE WORLD	*Stockton*	42
MORAL POWER OF THE BIBLE	*Chamberlain*	51
INSPIRATION OF THE BIBLE	*Dryden*	55
PROOF OF INSPIRATION	*Stockton*	56
INDISPENSABLE TO CHRISTIANS	*Rousseau*	59
THE BIBLE PROVES ITSELF	*Savage*	60
PRESERVATION OF SCRIPTURE	*Horne*	62
ITS PRESERVATION A STANDING MIRACLE	*Gumley*	64
THE SURVIVAL OF THE FITTEST	*Talmage*	67
SURVIVES FRIENDS AND FOES	*Rogers*	69
THE PYRAMID AMONG BOOKS	*Gibbons*	70
THE MARVEL OF THE AGES	*Storrs*	70
CHIEF REASON FOR BEING	*Whitman*	73
CITADEL OF CHRISTIAN FAITH	*Leech*	74
THE HOPE OF HUMAN PROGRESS	*Seward*	76
TEACHINGS OF THE BIBLE	*Pollok*	77
WISDOM OF BELIEVING THE BIBLE	*Coles*	80
OF INTEREST TO ALL	*Stockton*	86
A MANY-SIDED BOOK	*Storrs*	89
ADAPTED TO ALL CLASSES	*Guthrie*	92

CONTENTS.

		PAGE
A Mother's Gift—The Bible	*Anonymous*	93
A Book for Children	*Parker*	94
Three Bibles	*Evans*	95
The Old Family Bible	*Anonymous*	98
Study the Scriptures	*Locke*	101
The Picture Bible	*Freiligrath*	102
The Leadership of the Bible	*Spring*	104
Influence on Modern Authors	*Gilfillan*	108
Test the Influence of Scripture	*Gilfillan*	119
Reaches the Greatest Depth	*Coleridge*	120
The Bible in the School	*Halsey*	121
The Bible the Best Classic	*Grimke*	124
Understanding the Bible	*Moody*	126
A Remedy for Doubts	*Stanley*	128
Value of the Bible	*Whittier*	130
The Bible and Civilization	*Leech*	130
Women and the Bible	*Edwards*	132
One of the Sweet Old Chapters	*Advocate*	134
The Blessings of the Bible	*Evans*	135
But One Book	*McArthur*	138
One Bible Enough	*Stockton*	140
The Book Worth All	*Newton*	141
The Glory of the Bible	*World*	141
Christ in the Bible	*Graham*	142
The Bible God's Light	*Wadsworth*	143
The Fountain of Eloquence	*Ames*	144
Blessed Bible	*Palmer*	145
The Foundation of Nations	*Emperor William*	145
The Bible and Science	*Pentecost*	146
Science and the Bible	*Shaftesbury*	147
Striking the Bible	*Talmage*	148
The Rock of our Republic	*Jackson*	149
Resistance to the Bible	*Evans*	150
From the Author of Nature	*Origen*	151
Why Men Hate the Bible	*Hastings*	152

CONTENTS.

WHO REJECT THE BIBLE	Davies	154
EFFECTS OF DESTROYING THE BIBLE	Guard	155
OUR ANSWER TO THE SKEPTIC	Manship	157
OUR ONLY SOLACE IN DEATH	Robinson	157
A BOOK FOR A DYING PILLOW	Cook	158
THE BIBLE PRECIOUS	Fawcett	159
A PARADISE OF DELIGHTS	Chrysostom	159
THE SHEET ANCHOR OF LIBERTY	Grant	160
THE MYSTERY OF MYSTERIES	Scott	160

OUR CHURCH.

OUR CHURCH	Dennis	163
CHARACTER OF THE CHURCH	Stockton	164
SPIRITUALITY OF THE CHURCH	Ames	165
THE REVIVAL NEEDED	Advocate	169
A FOE TO THE CHURCH	Advocate	172
THE CHURCH IN THE WORLD	Anonymous	174
THE WORLD FEARS THE CHURCH	John Milton	174
THE CHURCH A BRIDE	Neal	175
THE CHURCH CHRIST'S BRIDE	Spurgeon	175
PURITY OF THE CHURCH	Baxandale	176
THE SHINING CHURCH	Olin	177
A PLACE FOR ACHING HEARTS	Cuyler	178
A GLORIOUS CHURCH	Christian	179
HISTORY OF THE PRIMITIVE CHURCH	Gibbon	181
THE CHURCH STILL UNFLINCHING	Hurst	194
STRENGTHENED BY PERSECUTION	Guthrie	195
LOVE FOR THE CHURCH	Dwight	195
THE CHURCH INDISPENSABLE	Washington	196
THE CROSS AND CROWN	Richards	196
THE MOTHER OF ALL GOOD	Marvin	197
THE WORLD WITHOUT THE CHURCH	Black	197
OBJECT OF THE CHURCH	Beecher	199

CONTENTS.

		PAGE
BUSINESS OF THE CHURCH	Cook	199
WHAT THE CHURCH MUST DO	Simpson	200
SPECIFIC WORK OF THE CHURCH	Christian	200
THE CHURCH SEEKS THE LOST	Bidwell	202
THE CHURCH AGGRESSIVE	Guard	203
WHAT THE CHURCH HAS ACCOMPLISHED	Farrar	203
THE CHURCH A LEADER	Abbott	204
THE CHURCH TO BE UNIVERSAL	Gilfillan	208
ONENESS OF CHRISTIANITY	Stockton	210
SPREAD OF THE CHURCH	Anonymous	212
NUMERICAL PROGRESS OF THE CHURCH	Ellicott	213
A NEW LITERATURE	Barnes	214
THE FOUNTAIN OF SONG	Hastings	215
THE ONE CHURCH	Gould	220
THE CHURCH WILL LIVE	Perry	221
TRUE CENTRE OF THE CHURCH	Christian	222
PERPETUITY OF THE CHURCH	Mason	223
THE CHURCH IMMOVABLE	Coxe	225
CHRISTIANITY A FINALITY	Williard	225
THE CHURCH	Burr	226
THE CHURCH GOD'S HOUSE	McFaden	227
THE HOUSE OF GOD A REFUGE	Edmeston	229
THE CHURCH IN THE HOUSE	Anonymous	230
THE VERDICT FOR CHRISTIANITY	Gibson	231
PICTURE OF FAMILY WORSHIP	Burns	232
THE MISSION OF THE CHURCH	Hall	233
THE CHURCH AND THE CHILDREN	Stoddard	234
EVERY FAMILY A CHURCH	Arnot	239
THE FAMILY A NURSERY	Mason	239
THE YOUNG FOR CHRIST	Simpson	239
COMING INTO THE CHURCH	Anonymous	240
THE CHURCH AND TEMPERANCE	Newman	243
THE MARK ON THE SHEEP	Thompson	247
THE CHURCH TO SAVE AMERICA	Cook	248
OUR COUNTRY'S SAFEGUARD	Webster	248

		PAGE
KEEP CHURCH AND STATE SEPARATE	Grant	249
TRUE TEST OF A CHURCH	Advocate	249
A CHRISTIAN	Union	253
WHAT CONSTITUTES A CHRISTIAN	Hopfner	254
THE CHRISTIAN THE WORLD'S BIBLE	Christlieb	254
CHRISTIAN SYSTEM OF CHRONOLOGY	Bidwell	256
HAND OF GOD IN MODERN MISSIONS	Pierson	264
HEADQUARTERS OF THE CHURCH	Christian	265
A CALL FOR WORKERS	Anderson	266
CHRIST'S CHURCH SHOULD LOOK UP	Taylor	267
SOUL-HUNGER OF THE CHURCH	Baker	269
THE CHURCH WATCHING	Downton	271
THE CHURCH WAITING	Bonar	272
THE LAST TESTIMONY	Melvill	273
NOT A WIFE OF PLEASURE	Arrowsmith	274
WATCHWORD OF THE CHURCH	Irving	275
THE CHURCH TRIUMPHANT	Toplady	277
WHERE THE CHURCH IS	Pressense	279
GOD IN THE CHURCH	Union	280
JOYS OF THE CHURCH TRIUMPHANT	Baxter	283
THE SPIRITUAL TEMPLE	Anonymous	285
THE UNREVEALED CHURCH	Chaplin	287
THE BLESSINGS OF ZION	Isaiah	289

OUR COUNTRY.

OUR COUNTRY	Dennis	293
AMERICA	Phillips	294
AMERICA THE OLD WORLD	Agassiz	296
WHERE TO ANCHOR POLITICS	Farrar	302
THE DISCOVERY OF AMERICA	Irving	303
GOD'S HAND IN THE DISCOVERY	Simpson	309
THE COLONIZATION OF AMERICA	Prescott	311
OUR NATIVE LAND	Dwight	315

CONTENTS.

		PAGE
Much Good in the Land	Garfield	315
First in War, etc.	Lee	315
Love of Country	Holt	316
A Product of Christianity	Republican ...	317
Our Country a Household	Whipple	318
What is our Country	Baker	320
The Old Thirteen	Brooks	320
Hymn to Washington	Pierpont	321
Not a Cent for Tribute	Pinckney ...	322
The Birthday of Washington	Choate	323
A Good Place to Live In	Scott	324
The Character of Washington	Anonymous ...	325
An Epitaph on Washington	Washington ...	326
The Land of our Birth	Anonymous ...	327
History of the Declaration	Parton	328
Independence Bell, July 4, '76	Garland	332
Liberty	Addison	335
The Fourth of July	Pierpont	335
Our Natal Day	Choate	336
Liberty in America	Moore	337
Spirit of Liberty	Webster	338
America vs. Europe	Gibbon	339
The Flower of Liberty	Holmes	340
Liberty Still Lives	Lear	341
Liberty and Greatness	Legare	343
Independence	Thomson ...	344
Three Bulwarks of Liberty	Century	345
Union Linked with Liberty	Jackson	345
Importance of the Union	Webster	347
We are One People	Whittier	348
The Union and its Results	Everett	349
What we Owe to the Union	Stephens	352
But One United States	Taylor	354
The Whole Union	Prentiss	355
The True Glory of America	Mellen	355

CONTENTS.

		PAGE
PATRIOTISM	Scott	357
FREEDOM AND PATRIOTISM	Dewey	358
THE IMMORTALITY OF PATRIOTS	Everett	361
SHRINES OF PATRIOTISM	Collins	363
RESPONSIBILITY OF OUR COUNTRY	Madison	363
THE GROWTH OF FREEDOM	Worst	364
SITUATION OF AMERICA	Webster	365
OUR COUNTRY'S DEFENCE	Webster	366
OUR REPUBLIC TRIUMPHANT	Sumner	367
TRUE RELIGION SUPPORTS GOVERNMENT	Washington	367
BLESSINGS OF A FREE GOVERNMENT	Ward	368
TAKE CARE OF OUR GOVERNMENT	Collyer	369
PUBLIC VIRTUE	Clay	371
FIRST, LAST, AND ALWAYS	Whipple	373
THE REPUBLIC GOD'S CREATION	Fulton	374
NATIONAL GUARDS	Ingersoll	375
OUR COUNTRY	Smith	380
OUR NATIONAL BANNER	Everett	381
HISTORY OF OUR FLAG	Putnam	382
THE AMERICAN FLAG	Drake	384
GOD BLESS THE FLAG	Simpson	386
OUR FLAG A POWER	Birkins	386
GUARDIAN OF HUMANITY	Kossuth	387
THE STAR-SPANGLED BANNER	Key	388
THE UTOPIA OF CHRISTIANITY	Gulliver	389
CHRIST WATCHES THE BALLOT-BOX	West	389
OUR CONSTITUTION WITHOUT PARALLEL	Langston	390
ORIGIN OF OUR CONSTITUTION	Webster	390
THE CONSTITUTION	Bryant	398
THE POSITION OF OUR FLAG	Simpson	399
AMERICAN CITIZENSHIP	Lossing	399
THE DUTY OF AMERICAN CITIZENSHIP	Webster	402
THE ARK OF AMERICA	Holland	403
DUTY TO THE STATE	More	404
THE BALLOT-BOX	Chapin	405

		PAGE
CHOICE GRAIN FOR AMERICA	Stoughton	406
THE SAFEGUARD OF THE REPUBLIC	Blaine	406
POOR VOTERS ON ELECTION DAY	Whittier	407
CHANGES OF A CENTURY	Smith	408
A CENTURY'S PROGRESS	Abbott	410
INTELLECTUAL PROGRESS OF A CENTURY	Ward	414
THE EMBLEM OF OUR COUNTRY	Wilson	416
THE AMERICAN EAGLE	Telegraph	419
AMERICAN HISTORY	Verplanck	420
THE COUNTRY OF HOMES	Cuyler	422
AMERICA THE LAND	Byron	423
AMERICAN SCENERY	Willis	424
THE PRAIRIES	Bryant	428
A VISIT TO THE YOSEMITE	Guard	432
DESCRIPTION OF NIAGARA FALLS	Anonymous	439
PAUL JONES AND THE NAVY	Murdoch	441
HAIL, COLUMBIA	Hopkinson	447
OUR COUNTRY'S GREATEST GLORY	Whipple	449
IDEAS THE LIFE OF A PEOPLE	Curtis	451
THE TRUE BASIS OF LIBERTY	Choate	453
OUR NATION STARTED RIGHT	Guard	454
THE SEED CORN OF THE REPUBLIC	Cuyler	455
MISSION OF AMERICA	Dwight	456
OPENING OF THE CENTENNIAL	Ridpath	457
CENTENNIAL HYMN	Whittier	461
GREETING TO AMERICA	Brehmer	462
OUR FUTURE GREATNESS	Guard	463
AMERICA HAS A FUTURE	Cantwell	465
DESTINY OF AMERICA	Berkeley	466
FREEDOM'S GRAND REVIEW	Delong	467
THE LIGHT-HOUSE OF NATIONS	Klopstock	470
DECLARATION OF INDEPENDENCE	Jefferson	471
OUR GOVERNMENT—ITS ADMINISTRATION		476
A PARTING WORD	Bartlett	480

AUTHORS QUOTED.

A

	PAGE
Arnot, Dr.	239
Ames, G. W.	165
Ames, Fisher	144
Abbott, Lyman	204
Abbott, John S. C.	410
Anderson, Mrs.	266
Addison, Joseph	335
Arrowsmith, Dr.	224
Advocate, Christian	134, 249
Advocate, Central Christian	169
Advocate, Western Christian	172

B

Burr, Dr.	226
Black, Judge	197
Byron, Lord	423
Bryant, W. C.	389, 428
Burns, Robert	232
Blaine, James G.	406
Birkins, Rev. H. H.	386
Brehmer, Frederica	462
Beecher, H. W.	199
Bidwell, Rev. I. G.	202, 256
Barnes, Albert	214
Baxter, Richard	283
Bonar, Horatinus	272
Baker, Senator	320
Baker, Sheridan	269

	PAGE
Brooks, Charles Timothy	320
Berkeley, George	466
Bartlett, Wm. A., D. D.	480
Baxandale, Rev. J.	176

C

Coleridge	120
Coles, George	80
Choate, Rufus	453, 323, 336
Cook, Joseph	158, 199, 248
Cantwell, Edward	465
Christian, The	200, 222, 265
Cuyler, T. L., D. D.	178, 422, 455
Chaplin, S. A.	287
Chapin, E. H.	405
Clay, Hon. Henry	371
Collins, William	363
Coxe, A. Cleveland	225
Chrysostom, Father	159
Chamberlain, Dr. Jacob	51
Curtis, George W.	451
Collyer, Rev. Robert	369
Christlieb, Prof. Theo.	254

D

Dryden, John	55
Dwight, John S.	315
Dwight, Timothy	161, 195, 456
David, The King	31, 291

(27)

AUTHORS QUOTED.

Dewey, Orville 358
Delong, Hon. C. E. 470
Dounton, Henry 271
De Vere, Sir Aubrey . . . 41
Davies, James Hamilton . . . 154
Dennis, Amanda Elizabeth 33, 163, 293

E

Evans, Herbert . . 95, 135, 150
Edwards, Tryon 132
Edmeston, James 229
Ellicott, C. J. 213
Everett, Edward 349, 361
Everett, Alex. H. 381

F

Fawcett, John 159
Farrar, Canon 203, 302
Freiligrath, Ferdinand . . . 102
Fulton, Justin D., D. D. . . . 374

G

Grinke 124
Grant, U. S. 160, 249
Graham, H. 142
Guard, Rev. Thomas 155, 203, 432, 454, 463
Guthrie, Thomas . . 92, 195
Gibbon, Edward 181
Gibbons, Archbishop . . 70, 339
Gibson, Chief-Justice . . . 231
Gumley, J. Stewart 64
Gilfillan, George . 37, 108, 119, 208
Garfield, James A. 315
Gulliver, Rev. John P. . . . 389
Garland, Speaker 335
Gould, Sabine Baring . . . 220

H

Hopfner 254
Horne, Thomas 62
Hurst, Bishop 194
Hall, John, D. D. 233
Holt, Hon. Joseph 216
Hastings, H. L. 152, 215
Henry, Patrick 362
Holland, Rev. R. A. . . . 403
Hopkinson, Joseph 447
Holmes, Oliver Wendell . . 340
Hasey, Le Roy J., D. D. . . . 121

I

Irving, Edward 275
Irving, Washington 303
Ingersoll, Edward P., D. D. . . 375
Isaiah, The Prophet 289

J

Jefferson, Thomas 471
Jackson, Andrew . . . 149, 345

K

Klopstock 470
Kossuth, Louis 387
Key, Francis Scott 388

L

Locke, John 101
Leech, S. V., D. D. . . . 74, 132
Lincoln, Abraham 455
Lee, Gen. Henry 315
Lear, Hon. George 343
Legare, Hugh Swinton . . . 344
Lossing, Benson J., LL. D. . . 399
Langston, Prof. John Mercer . 390

M

Mason, Dr. 223
Mason, J. M. 239

AUTHORS QUOTED. 29

	PAGE		PAGE
Moody, D. L.	126	Rogers, Henry	69
Melvill, Henry	273	Robinson, Charles S.	157
Manship, Andrew	157	Richards, W. C.	196
Milton, John	174	Ridpath, John Clark	457
Marvin, Bishop	197	Republican, Springfield	317
Moore, Thomas	337		
More, Hannah	404		

S

Magazine, Century	345	Stoughton	406
Mellen, Greenville	355	Simpson, Bishop	200, 239, 309, 399
Madison, James	363	Sumner, Charles	367, 464
Murdock, James E.	441	Schaff, Phillip	34
McFaden, Rev. J. A.	227	Storrs, R. S.	70, 89
MacArthur, R. S., D. D.	138	Seward, W. H.	76

N

		Spring, L. W.	104
		Stoddard, W. P.	234
Newton, John	141	Spurgeon, Charles	175
Neal, Alice B.	175	Scott, George R.	324
Newman, Bishop	247	Scott, Sir Walter	160, 358

O

		Savage, Minot F.	60
Olin, Stephen	177	Stockton, Thomas H.	42, 56, 86, 140, 164, 210
Origen, Father	151		
		Stanley, Arthur P.	128

P

		Stephens, Hon. A. H.	352
Pressence	279	Smith, Samuel F.	380
Paul, The Apostle	161	Smith, Judge I. W.	408
Parton, James	328	Simpson, Samuel L.	386
Pierpont, John	321, 335	Shaftesbury, Earl of	147
Pollok, Robert	77, 162		
Phillips, Charles	294	T	
Parker, Theodore	94		
Pinckney, Cotesworth	322	Thompson, Dr.	247
Palmer, Phœbe	145	Taylor, D. T.	267
Perry, John T.	221	Taylor, Father	354
Pentecost, George F.	146	Tocqueville, De	418
Prentiss, S. S.	355	Thomson, James	344
Pierson, Rev. Arthur T.	265	Talmage, DeWitt	67, 148
Protestant Methodist	36	Toplady, Augustus Montague	277
Prescott, William Hickling	311	Telegraph, Southern Religious	419
Putnam, Rev. Alfred P.	382		

U

R

		Union, Baptist	253
Rousseau	59	Union, Christian	280

V

Verplanck, Gulian C. 420

W

Wilson 416
Willis, N. P. 424
Watts, Isaac 161
Whipple, Bishop . 318, 373, 449
Webster, Daniel . 41, 248, 338, 347, 365, 366, 390, 402
Whitman, Walt 73
World, Christian 141
Wadsworth, Charles 143
Washington, George . . 196, 367
Washington, Judge 326
Williard, G. W. 225
Whittier, John G. . 130, 348, 408, 461
Worst, John H. 364
West, Mary Allen 389
Ward, Gen. Durbin . . . 368, 415
William, Emperor of Germany . 145

OUR BIBLE.

"WHAT glory gilds the sacred page,
　　Majestic like the sun!
It gives a light to every age,
　　It gives but borrows none."

The word of the Lord is perfect, converting the soul. Psa. xix. 7.

OUR BIBLE.

THIS blessed book I'd rather own
    Than all the gold and gems
That e'er in monarchs' coffers shone,
    Than all their diadems.
Nay, were the whole sea one chrysolite,
    The earth a golden ball,
And diamonds all the stars of night,
    This book were worth them all.
Here He who died on Calvary's tree
    Hath made that promise blest,
Ye weary, heavy laden, come to me
    And I will give you rest.
A bruised reed I will not break,
    A contrite heart despise,
My burden's light, and all who take
    My yoke shall win the prize."

OUR BIBLE.

[WRITTEN EXPRESSLY FOR THIS WORK BY AMANDA ELIZABETH DENNIS.]

O GLORIOUS GIFT of Love Divine!
What heart can seek for surer sign
  Of love's divine completeness?
We lift our tender, rev'rent eyes,
And fold our palms in thankful guise
  For thine untold repleteness.

Athrong the dust of ages gone,
Thine everlasting truths shine on,
  Unchanged, undimmed, unfaded;
Along the passing years' swift flight,
In lett'rings of immortal light,
  They gleam, untouched, unshaded.

Our deepest anguish finds a balm,
Our wildest storm a blessed calm,
  Our dearest hopes fruition;
Our fondest hopes are blent with praise,
And dear rest crowns the weariest days
  Beneath thy sweet tuition.

O glorious Book! O Gift Divine!
No earthly love shall live like thine,
  By gloom of years unshaded;
Thy truths shall gild forevermore
Faith's "Promised Land," life's "Farther Shore,"
  When *earthly* things have faded.

THE BIBLE.

THE Bible is the book of life, written for the instruction and edification of all ages and nations. No man who has felt its divine beauty and power would exchange this one volume for all the literature of the world. Eternity alone can unfold the extent of its influence for good.

The Bible, like the person and work of our Saviour, is theanthropic in its character and aim. The eternal personal word of God was made flesh, and the whole fulness of the Godhead and of sinless manhood were united in one person forever. So the spoken word of God may be said to have become flesh in the Bible.

It is, therefore, all divine, and yet all human, from beginning to end: through the veil of the letter we behold the glory of the eternal truth of God. The divine and human in the Bible sustain a similar relation to each other, as in the person of Christ: they are unmixed, yet inseparably united, and constitute but one life, which kindles life in the heart of the believer.

Viewed merely as a human or literary production, the Bible is a marvellous book, and without a rival. All the libraries of theology, philosophy, history, antiquities, poetry, law and policy would not furnish material enough for so rich a treasure of the choicest gems of human genius, wisdom and experience.

It embraces works of about forty authors, representing the extremes of society, from the throne of the king to the boat of the fisherman. It was written during a long period of sixteen centuries, on the banks of the Nile, in the desert of Arabia, in the land of promise, in Asia Minor, in classical Greece, and in imperial Rome: it commences with the creation and ends with the final glorification, after describing all the intervening stages in the Revelation of God and the spiritual development of man; it uses all forms of literary composition; it rises to the highest heights and descends to the lowest depths of humanity. It measures all states and conditions of life; it is acquainted with every grief and every woe; it touches every chord of sympathy; it contains the spiritual biography of every human heart; it is suited to every class of society, and can be read with the same interest and profit by the king and the beggar, by the philosopher and the child; it is as universal as the race, and reaches beyond the limits of time into the boundless regions of eternity.

Even this matchless combination of human excellencies point to its divine character and origin, as the absolute perfection of Christ's humanity, as an evidence of his divinity; but the Bible is first and last a book of religion: it presents the only true, universal and absolute religion of God, both in its preparatory process or growth under the dispensation of the law and the promise, and in its completion under the dispensation of the gospel. A religion which is intended ultimately to absorb all the other religions of the world, it speaks to us as immortal beings on the highest, noblest and most important themes which can challenge our attention, and with an authority that is absolutely irresistible and overwhelming. It can instruct, edify, warn, terrify, appease, cheer and encourage as no other book. It seizes man in the hidden depths of his intellectual and moral constitution and goes to the quick of the soul, to that mysterious point where it is connected with the unseen world and with the great Father of spirits.

It acts like an all-penetrating and all-transforming leaven upon every faculty of the mind and every emotion of the heart. It enriches the memory; it elevates the reason; enlivens the imagination; it directs the judgment; it moves the affections; it controls the passions; it quickens the conscience; it strengthens the will. It kindles the sacred flame of faith, hope, charity; it purifies, ennobles, sanctifies the whole man, and brings him into living union with God. It cannot only enlighten, reform and improve, but regenerate and create anew, and produce effects which lie far beyond the power of human genius.

It has light for the blind, strength for the weak, food for the hungry, drink for the thirsty; it has a counsel in precept or example for every relation of life, a comfort for every sorrow, a balm for every wound. Of all the books in the world the Bible is the only one of which we never tire, but which we admire and love more and more in proportion as we use it.

Like the diamond, it casts its lustre in every direction; like a torch, the more it is shaken the more it shines; like a healing herb, the harder it is pressed the sweeter is its fragrance.—*Philip Schaff.*

THERE is one argument for the purity and divinity of the Bible more potent and unanswerable than all the evidences that have ever been collated—it is universally hated by bad men.—*The Methodist Protestant.*

THE BIBLE INDEPENDENT OF ALL OTHER BOOKS.

IN relation to other books, the Bible occupies a peculiar and solitary position. *It is independent* of all others; it imitates no other books; it copies none; it hardly alludes to any other, whether in praise or blame, and this is nearly as true of its later portions, when books were common, as of its earlier, when books were scarce. It proves thus its originality and power. Mount Blanc does not measure himself with Jura, does not name her, nor speaks save when in thunder he talks to her of God. *Then* only, too, does she

> "Answer from her misty shroud,
> Back to the joyous Alps."

John never speaks of Plato, nor Paul of Demosthenes, nor Jesus of any writer, save Moses and the Prophets. In those great heights, you feel, blowing round your temples and stirring your hair, the free, original, ancient Breath of the upper world, unconventional, unmixed, and irresistible as the mountain tempest.

It is a book *unlike* all others—the points of difference being these, among many more: First. There is a certain grand unconsciousness, as in Niagara, speaking now in the same tone to the tourists of a world, as when she spoke to the empty wilderness and the silent sun; as in the Himalayan hills, which cast the same looks of still sovereignty over an India unpeopled after the Deluge, as over an India the hive of sweltering nations. Thus burst forth cries of

Nature, the voices of the Prophets, and thus do their eyes from the high places of the world overlook all the earth. You are aware again, in singular union with this profound unconsciousness and simplicity, of a knowledge and insight equally profound. It is as though a child should pause amid her play, and tell you the secrets of your heart, and the particulars of your after history. The bush beside your path suddenly begins to sigh forth an oracle in "words unutterable." That unconscious page seems like the wheel in Ezekiel's vision, to be "full of eyes," and open it wherever you may, you start back in surprise or terror, feeling "this book knows all about us;" it eyes us meaningly; it is a "discerner of the thoughts and intents of our hearts." Those herdsmen, vinedressers, shepherds, fishermen, and homeless wanderers are coeval with all time, and see the end from the beginning.

You perceive again the presence of a high and holy purpose pervading the book, which is to trace and promulgate the existence of certain spiritual laws, originally communicated by God, developed in the history of a peculiar people, illustrated by the ruin of nations, proclaimed in a system of national religion and national poetry, and at last sealed, cemented, and spread abroad through the blood and Gospel of One who had always been expected, and who at last arrived, the Christ promised to the Fathers. It is this which renders the Bible, in all its parts, religious and holy; casts over its barest portions such an interest as the shadow of the Fiery Pillar gave to the sand and shrubs over which it passed, makes what otherwise appear trifles, great as trappings of Godhead, and extracts from fiction and fable, from the crimes of the evil and the failings of the good, aid to its main object, and illustrations of its main principles.

You find yourselves again in the presence of a "true thing." We hear of the spell of fiction, but a far stronger spell is that of truth; indeed, fiction derives its magic from the quantity of truth it contrives to disguise. In this book you find truth occasionally, indeed, concealed under the garb of allegory and fable, but frequently in a form as naked and majestic as Adam when he rose from the green sward of Eden. "This is true!" we exclaim, "were all else a lie." Here we have found men earnest as the stars, speaking to us in language which, by its very heat, impetuosity, unworldliness, fearlessness, almost if not altogether imprudence, severity, and grandeur, proves itself *sincere*, if there be sincerity in earth or in heaven.

Once more, the Bible, you feel, answers a question which other books cannot. This—the question of questions, the question of all ages—is, in our vernacular and expressive speech, "What shall I do to be *saved?*" "How shall I be peaceful, resigned, holy, and hopeful here, and how happy hereafter, when this cold cloak—the body—has fallen off from the bounding soul within?" To this, the "Iliad" of Homer, the plays of Shakespeare, the "Celeste Mechanique" of La Place, and the works of Plato, return no proper reply. To this immense query the book has given an answer which may theoretically have been interpreted in various ways, but which, as a practical truth, he who runs may read; which has satisfied the souls of millions; which none ever repented of obeying, and on which many of the wisest, the most learned, the most slow of heart to believe, as well as the ignorant and simple-minded, have at last been content to lean their living confidence and their dying peace.

The book we are thus justified in proclaiming to be *superior* to all other books that have been, or are, or shall ever be on earth. And this, not that it forestalls coming books, or includes all their essential truths within it; not that in polish, art, or instant effect, it can be exalted above the written masterpieces of human genius—what comparison in elaboration, any more than what comparison in girth and greatness, between the cabinet and the oak—but it is, that the Bible, while bearing on its summit the hues of a higher heaven, over-topping with ease all human structures and aspirations—in earth, but not of it—communicating with the omniscience, and recording the acts of the omnipotence of God—is at the same time the Bible of the poor and lowly, the crutch of the aged, the pillow of the widow, the eye of the blind, the "boy's own book," the solace of the sick, the light of the dying, the grand hope and refuge of simple, sincere, and sorrowing spirits—it is *this* which at once proclaims its unearthly origin, and so clasps it to the great common heart of humanity, that the extinction of the sun were not more mourned than the extinction of the Bible, or than even its receding from its present pride of place. For, while other books are planets shining with reflected radiance, this book, like the sun, shines with ancient and unborrowed ray.

Other books, to their loftiest altitudes, spring from earth; this book looks down from heaven high, other books appeal to understanding or fancy; this book to conscience and to faith. Other books seek our attention; this book demands it: it speaks with authority, and not as the scribes. Other books guide gracefully along the earth, or onwards to the mountain summits of the ideal; this, and this alone, conducts up the awful abyss which leads to heaven.

Other books, after shining their little season, may perish in flames, fiercer than those which destroyed the Alexandrian

Library; this must, in essence, remain pure as gold, but unconsumable as asbestos in the general conflagration.

Other books may be forgotten in a universe where suns go down and disappear like bubbles in the stream; the memory of this book shall shine as the brightness of that eternal firmament and those higher stars which are for ever and ever.—*George Gilfillan*

SUPERIORITY OF THE BIBLE.

LET those, who will, hang rapturously o'er
    The flowing eloquence of Plato's page,
Repeat, with flashing eye, the sounds that pour
    From Homer's verse as with a torrent's rage;
Let those, who list, ask Tully to assuage
Wild hearts with high-wrought periods, and restore
    The reign of rhetoric, or maxims sage
    Winnow from Seneca's sententious lore.
Not these, but Judah's hallowed bards, to me
    Are dear; Isaiah's noble energy;
    The temperate grief of Job; the artless strain
Of Ruth and pastoral Amos; the high songs
    Of David, and the tale of Joseph's wrongs,
    Simply pathetic, eloquently plain.
                          —*Sir Aubrey De Vere.*

IF anything I have ever said or written deserves the feeblest encomiums of my fellow-countrymen, I have no hesitation in declaring that for their partiality I am indebted, solely indebted, to the daily and attentive perusal of the Holy Scriptures, the source of all true poetry and eloquence, as well as of all good and all comfort.—*Daniel Webster.*

THE BIBLE IS NOW ABROAD IN ALL THE WORLD.

THE BIBLE *is now abroad in all the world*—so fairly and fully exposed that it can never again be concealed. There have been times, both before and since its completion, when in part or in whole, it was withdrawn from society and almost forgotten. Prior to the restoration of the law by Ezra it appears that the most of the books of the Old Testament had well-nigh perished. Under Antiochus Epiphanes all of them were ordered to be destroyed, and such persons as secreted any of them were doomed to death. Under Dioclesian an edict was issued requiring the whole Bible to be burnt throughout the whole Roman Empire—on which occasion myriads of Christians preferred death with the book to life without it. Finally, the church itself—that is, the Apostate Church—after long-continued neglect or abuse of the Scriptures, and consequent increasing corruption, formally forbade their use to the laity, and still more strictly prohibited the translation of them into the vulgar tongue. What was forbidden to the laity soon became useless to the clergy; and so, before the age of Luther, the Bible had nearly vanished from all observation.

But those times have passed, never, we trust, to be renewed. The book is abroad in all the world. Protestant Christendom is filled with it, from centre to circumference. Around all the borders of Romanism its voice is heard, like the trumpet of the resurrection. The out-posts of Mohammedanism and Paganism are all startled by the same awakening music. And, "whether they will hear or whether they will forbear," it is plain that, ere long, all mankind must acknowledge its presence and its power.

See! the sensible form in which it appears includes a vast variety of modifications. As a book, it exists, of course, either in manuscript or in print, and its records are either originals or versions.

It is a remarkable fact, that not a single autograph of the Holy Scriptures is known to be in existence. On the other hand, it is at least possible that not a single autograph has been destroyed. And it is a pleasant thought, that he who lived from the beginning, and yet once "was dead;" whose body lay in the grave, and whose soul entered the place of spirits; who is now "alive forever more," and has "the keys of hell and of death," of *hades* and of the grave; who carries these keys at his girdle, and hands them at his will to Latrobe, or Layard, or any of his servants, to open the galleries where he has treasured the historic memorials of his reign and confirmations of his word, may some time direct the unlocking of a chamber within which shall be found the *real* originals of the Bible in unimpaired preservation.

Meantime, the study of the extant manuscripts, especially of the accepted originals, both Hebrew and Greek, must be exceedingly interesting to those who are thoroughly qualified to pursue it. Even their external history is full of interest: their number and age, the materials on which and with which they were prepared, the extraordinary care which was taken to make them accurate, and, in many instances, most richly beautiful, the veneration with which they were preserved, the costly collections and laborious collations of them, their comparative critical reputation and influence, their present local distribution and accessibleness; these, and other points, might well claim, and would amply reward, attention. It is enough, however, for the occasion to compile the following particulars:

The Hebrew manuscripts are of two classes, *sacred* and *common*, or, synagogue rolls and private copies. "The synagogue rolls are uniform, hardly differing one from another, written on the skins of clean animals, prepared for the particular use of the synagogue by a Jew." The private copies "are in different forms—folio, quarto, octavo, duodecimo—and their material is mostly parchment, sometimes eastern paper, and even common paper." Both kinds of course were wrought with extraordinary care; but of the former it may be said that it is almost impossible to exaggerate the pains that were taken to secure their accuracy and sanctity. As would be expected, the more ancient they are the more rare they are. Dr. Kennicott is said to have collated six hundred and thirty, and De Rossi more than four hundred, the two "upwards of eleven hundred." Of Dr. Kennicott's, fifty-one were supposed to be from six to eight hundred years old, and a hundred and seventy-four from four hundred and eighty to five hundred and eighty years old. Of De Rossi's, some were said to be of the seventh or eighth century, which would make them now eleven or twelve hundred years old. A more reliable current authority, however, not long since declared that, so far "as certainty is concerned," the "oldest Hebrew MS. at present known belongs to A. D. 1106," making it now seven hundred and fifty-one years old. And yet the same authority more recently alludes to another collation "by Pinner, at Odessa," resulting in the discovery of *one* MS. of the sixth century (580), two of the ninth, and two of the tenth—the oldest, if correctly represented, being twelve hundred and seventy-seven years old. From these dates they multiply to their whole present number—those which have been produced since the fifteenth century being reported as "very numerous."

The Greek MSS., the accepted originals of the New Testament, are older than the Hebrew. Their materials are vellum or paper. In the oldest of them there are none of our common divisions, but words and sentences flow on in unbroken lines of capital letters. In a brief list which I have examined, one is attributed to the fourth century, two are ascribed to the fifth, five to the sixth, six to the seventh, three to the eighth, and eight to the ninth—the earliest of them, therefore, being some fifteen hundred years old, and the latest about a thousand.

Similar brief notice might be taken of the ancient *versions*—whether Greek, Oriental, Latin, Gothic, Slavonic, or Anglo-Saxon. The principal of them number more than twenty; and, of course, the design of making them was to present the Divine Record in the living languages of the people for common use. They were all vulgates.

It is enough, however, for my purpose to add the remark, that the world has been searched by Jews, Romanists, and Protestants, and that, as the result of the search so far, copies of the most important of all classes of sacred manuscripts, both originals and versions, have been largely collected and diligently collated, and are now known, located, numbered, described, and, in common with multitudes of inferior value, distributed in public and private libraries and among the synagogues and monasteries of all lands, are generally free to scholastic investigation.

It is in relation to *modern* versions, however, that the fact

I wish to illustrate becomes most impressive, and especially as connected with operations of the art of printing.

The first printed book was the Latin Bible, the Mazarin Bible, as it is called, from the discovery of a copy of it in the last century in the library of the cardinal of that name. The date assigned to it is 1455. "We may see in imagination," says Mr. Hallam, "this venerable and splendid volume leading up the crowded myriads of its followers, and imploring as it were, a blessing on the new art, by dedicating its first fruits to the service of heaven." Since then four hundred years have gone by, and, to a considerable extent, they have all been employed in printing Bibles; within the last half century, however, an altogether incomparable work has been accomplished in this connection by means of Bible Societies. Since 1804 more than fifty-four millions of Bibles and Testaments have been thus distributed. The list of "languages into which translations of the Scriptures have either been made or attempted" included, six years ago, some two hundred and thirty. Doubtless the number has since increased. The versions of course are much more numerous, as in many instances a single language like our own has quite a large variety of them. In "The Bible of Every Land" may be found about two hundred and seventy "typographical specimens" of different translations. Of these, nearly two hundred have been published by the Bible Societies, and more than a hundred and twenty of this number were "never before printed." According to official statements, they have been circulated wherever practicable, in adaptation to national and provincial peculiarities, in every district of Western, Northern, Central, and Southern Europe; in Russia; in the Caucasian and other border countries; in Persia; in India—Northern, Central, and

Southern—in Ceylon; in the Indo-Chinese countries; in the Chinese Empire; in Hither Polynesia, Further Polynesia, Africa, and America.

Meantime, as one effect of this universal charity, the Bible trade, as it may be distinctively called, instead of being checked, has been wonderfully quickened, strengthened, and enlarged. Notwithstanding the copies given away, and the readiness with which they may be almost anywhere obtained, no book in the world sells like the Bible. Within the period already alluded to, therefore, thousands of private publishers—some with state patronage, others with church patronage, but most of them without either, and all far more at liberty than the Bible Societies—have issued, it is reported, upwards of fifty millions more, *seemingly* in every possible diversity of style, and accommodated to every age and condition of life, every desire of taste, and every degree of ability to buy. In reality, however, it is believed that the diversity has just begun, and that hereafter it will be greatly extended and incomparably improved.

And now, tell me—Is not the Bible fairly and fully abroad, and beyond all possibility of reconcealment? who can follow its flight? every effort to do so is discouraging. Whatever centre I occupy, I see the Bible passing away—in a thousand forms, by a thousand lines—to the utmost circumference. If I follow it in one line the others are left unexplored.

A sort of bird's-eye-view—or rather angel's view—is all that is allowed me. To gain this, for a moment, I soar into the sky and poise myself there.

And what now? I ask for the nations and tribes who read the languages and dialects in which the Bible has been so far printed. I wish to see them in all their localities and other associations.

"Fold your pinions," says the angel in the sun, "and stand by my side. Instead of descending in a moment, you must wait twenty-four hours, and watch the revolution of the whole globe; for there is not a spot on its surface where some one of these languages does not reach."

And so I wait and watch, and find it is even so. I see these readers—self-taught, mission-taught, home-taught, or school-taught—in all natural conditions, from the equator to the poles—enduring every climate, traversing every sea, covering every continent, and filling every island—scaling the mountains, cultivating the plains, girding and crossing the deserts. I see them in all civil conditions—savage, barbarians, semi-civilized, and wholly civilized: among the latter, monarchists, aristocrats, and republicans, abolutists, constitutionalists, and revolutionists. I see them in all religious conditions—Fetichists, Foheists, Boodhists, Brahminists, Parseeists, Mohammedans, Jews, and Christians: among the latter, Romanists and Jansenists, Orthodox Greeks and Heterodox Greeks, established Protestants and Dissenting Protestants. I see them, moreover, in all social conditions—sovereigns, nobles, and magistrates; priests and pastors; scholars and philosophers; professors of literature, science, and art; merchants and manufacturers; mechanics and operators; farmers and planters; herdsmen and shepherds; hunters and fishermen; soldiers and sailors; paupers and slaves; dwelling in caves and thickets, in tents and huts, in cabins and mansions, in castles and palaces, in colleges and convents, in hamlets, towns, cities, and mighty capitals—or, again, off-shore, in canoes, in ships, on vast rafts, or in fixed fleets—great water capitals rivalling those on land; and, moreover, with all varieties of dress and address, ceremonies, manners, customs, and usages, at births, weddings, and funerals, in private and in public, in all the stages and relations of life—in connections quite innumerable and indescribable.

Wherever I look, I see the same visitant—the Bible. Everywhere it bears the same message—the same to old nations and new, to the people of yesterday, and the people with a history of two or three thousand years. Moreover, in substance it is a message equally needed by all and equally adapted to all.

I ask for the motives and objects of the various parties employed in this cause of Bible distribution at home and abroad. Why is there so much zeal in regard to this one book? It is not so with the sacred books of other religions. Even the kings and priests having them in charge do nothing to promote their circulation. Rather, they are careful to keep them secluded. How is this? Why does not some one of the many Mohammedan nations form Koran Societies, to fill the world with Korans? Why are there no Zend Avesta Societies among the Parsees? Why no Veda Societies among the Hindoos? Why no King's Societies among the Chinese? Why no Edda Societies among the antiquarian Scandinavians? Is it not strange that there are no such societies? And yet stranger facts are found nearer home. Why have the Jews no Bible Societies? Why the Roman Catholics none? Why the Greek Catholics none? Why the Oriental Churches none? Nay, why are Unevangelical Protestants without them? Nay, still further, why are some of our Evangelical Churches beginning to draw off and stand aloof from the Bible Societies? As to Pagans, they make no pretension to the means of a common salvation. As to Mohammedans, if they ever had such pretensions, they have lost confidence in them. Besides, their trust was always in the sword rather than the book. As to the Jews, they know that the Old Testament alone is an imperfect revelation, and are waiting themselves for the consummating development. As to the Catholics, they all substitute the Church for the Bible. As to Unevangelical Protestants, they are chilled by doubt and checked by error, and can make no progress in good. And as to the withdrawing Evangelicals, they are becoming less Christian and more sectarian every day. Only the Bible Societies, and their supporters of all parties, seem to be influenced by the highest motives and devoted to the noblest objects. In contrast to Pagans, they do claim the means of a common salvation. In contrast to Mohammedans, their confidence increases rather than declines. In contrast to Jews, they possess the perfected revelation. In contrast to Catholics, they acknowledge the Bible as infallible instead of the Church. In contrast to the Unevangelicals, they are all aglow with faith and impelled by truth. And in contrast to their offended brethren among the Evangelicals, they daily become less and less sectarian and more and more Christian. In a word, with certain exceptions which it may be hoped will disappear, their motives and objects are worthy of all commendation—immediately and exclusively connected with the one all-sufficient and incomparable work of glorifying God in the salvation of mankind. It is the just appreciation of their work in these two relations that sustains their zeal. Private publishers, in most instances, find their reward in pecuniary profits. Sectarian publishers blend personal and partisan interests in deceitful semblance of Christian sublimity. But the true sublime is with those who have nothing to do but to fill the world with the highest truth for the glory of God, and the entire and eternal redemption of man. They "rejoice with joy unspeakable" that the Bible is at last abroad in all the world, and that it can never again be concealed. They are not like those who fear for its fate. "Do not send it forth without Tradition," say some. "Do not let it loose without the Apocrypha," say others. "Do not trust it without the Prayer-book," say others. "Do not expose it without the Creed, or Confession, or Constitution, or Platform, or Discipline," say others. "We have no fear," reply the faithful ones. We would as soon charge God with folly for issuing the sun without the pendant of a lamp to illustrate it, as for issuing the Bible without the attachment of some human authority to make it plain. No, no, let it go, even as the sun itself goes, asking no patronage of men or angels, but demonstrating its Divinity by the silent, serene, and blissful vitality of its supreme, universal, and perpetual glory.—*T. H. Stockton.*

MORAL POWER OF THE BIBLE.

DOES this Bible change the character and the lives of those who embrace it? I would I could take you to a little village near my station, where they had embraced Christianity in a body but eight months before, and where the high priest of the temple near by came secretly to me in my tent, and asked me: "Sir, will you please impart to me the secret: what is it that makes that Bible of yours have such power over the lives of those that embrace it? Now, it is but eight months since these people joined you. Before that they were quarrelsome, they were riotous, they were lazy, they were shiftless; and now see what a difference there is in them. Now they are active, they are energetic, they are laborious, they never drink, they never quarrel. Why, sir, I joined in the persecution when they became Christians, and tried to stamp out Christianity before it gained a foothold here, but they stood firm, and now in all the region around here the people all respect and honor them. What is it that makes the Bible have such a power over the lives of those that embrace it? Our Vedas have no such power. Please, sir, give me the secret?"

Does it sustain its recipients? Our first convert in the new region, in the Telugu Country, where I went in 1863, was a young Brahmin. We knew that there was danger of his being murdered, and tried to guard him. But after a while he was decoyed away and taken over one hundred miles to a town where his relatives lived. He was immured in a close room. Nothing was left him but a cloth around his loins. In the room there was naught but a grass-mat for him to lie on, with another to cover him. Day by day just a little rice and salt were placed there for him to eat, just enough to keep body and soul together; and he was told that he should never come out alive unless he abjured his new fangled doctrines and came back to Orthodox Hinduism. His grandfather, a wealthy man, offered half his fortune to the Brahmins if they would reconvert him. They brought the logicians, the rhetoricians, and the priests of all the region to argue with him. They had taken away his Bible. They argued with him, and they kept him for months. I have not time to tell you the thrilling story of his escape, but at last he got back to us, all skin and bones; he had lost all his flesh, but had not lost his faith and his trust in Jesus, nor his love for the Bible. He had never

PETER PREACHING ON PENTECOST.

Repent, and be baptized every one of you in the name of Jesus Christ for the remission of sins, and ye shall receive the gift of the Holy Ghost. ACTS 2: 38.

denied him. A year after that we met his uncles who had imprisoned him. They said to us: "Sirs, what is it in that Bible of yours that gives such strength and courage to those that embrace it? Now, we had that nephew of ours right in our power; we told him that he should never get away alive unless he renounced Christianity, and there was no probability that he would. He expected to die from starvation there; but, sirs, every day, no matter who were there, he would kneel in his cell and he would pray to that *Yesu Kristu*, the Divine Redeemer, that he called God, and when he arose there was no doing anything with him; you never saw such a stubborn fellow. What is it that makes this Bible give such nerve and such courage to those that embrace it?"

Does this Bible quell opposition? Is it quick and powerful? I would take you to a scene in that same city of Hyderabad that I witnessed fourteen years ago; there in a city, a walled town of 18,000 inhabitants, the people had arisen in a mob to drive us out because we tried to speak of another God than theirs. We had gone to the market-place, and I had endeavored to preach to them of Christ and his salvation, but they would not hear. They ordered us to leave the city at once, but I had declined to leave until I had delivered to them my message. The throng was filling the streets; they told me if I tried to utter another word I should be killed; there was no rescue; they would have the city gates closed, and there should never any news go forth of what was done; I must leave at once or I should not leave alive. I had seen them tear up the paving-stones and fill their arms with them to be ready, and one was saying to another: you throw the first stone and I will throw the next. By an artifice, I need not stop to detail, I succeeded in getting permission to tell them a story before they stoned me, and then they might stone me if they wished. They were standing around me ready to throw the stones when I succeeded in getting them to let me tell the story first. I told them the story of all stories; of the love of the Divine Father that had made us of one blood, who "so loved the world that he gave his only begotten Son, that whosoever believeth in him might not perish, but have everlasting life." I told them the story of that birth in the manger at Bethlehem; of that wonderful childhood, of that marvellous life, of those miraculous deeds, of the gracious words that he spake.

I told them the story of the cross, and pictured in the graphic words that the Master gave me that day the story of our Saviour nailed upon the cross, for them, for me, for all the world; when he cried in agony, "My God, my God, why hast thou forsaken me?" When I told them that, I saw the men go and throw their stones in the gutter and come back, and down the cheeks of the very men that had been clamoring the loudest for blood I saw the tears running and dropping off upon the pavement that they had torn up; and then I finished the story and told them how he had been laid in the grave, and after three days he had come forth triumphant, and had ascended again to heaven, and that there he ever lives to make intercession for them, for us, for all the world, and that through his merits every one of them there assembled could obtain remission of sin and eternal life.

I told them that I had finished my story and that they might stone me now. But no: they didn't want to stone me now; they didn't know what a wonderful story I had come there to tell them. They came forward and bought eighty copies of the Scriptures and gospels and tracts, and paid the money for them, for they wanted to know more of that wonderful Saviour of whom I had told them.

—Dr. Jacob Chamberlain.

INSPIRATION OF THE BIBLE.

WHENCE, but from Heaven, could men unskill'd in arts,
  In several ages born, in several parts,
  Weave such agreeing truths? or how, or why,
  Should all conspire to cheat us with a lie?
Unask'd their pains, ungrateful their advice,
Starving their gain, and martyrdom their price.
If on the book itself we cast our view,
Concurrent heathens prove the story true;
The doctrine, miracles; which must convince,
For Heaven in them appeals to human sense:
And though they prove not they confirm the cause,
When what is taught agrees with nature's laws.
Therefore the style, majestic and divine,
It speaks no less than God in every line:
Commanding words; whose force is still the same
As the first fiat that produced our frame,
All faiths beside, or did by arms ascend;
Or sense indulg'd has made mankind their friend:
This only doctrine does our lusts oppose;
Unfed by nature's soil, in which it grows;
Cross to our interests, curbing sense and sin;
Oppressed without, and undermined within,
It thrives through pain; its own tormentors tires,
And with a stubborn patience still aspires.

—John Dryden.

PROOF OF SPIRITUAL INSPIRATION.

HOW sublime are their doctrinal developments! The nature, character, and government of God; the spiritual universe; the material universe; the history, condition, and destiny of both: in all these connections, what an infinite loftiness and sweep of severe and simple thought there is! What an assurance of truth there is! What mind can even imagine the dissolution of this circle of accepted reality, and the substitution of something now unknown, as essential and eternal truth? Certainly, the God of the Bible, the man of the Bible, the creation, providence, and redemption of the Bible—these are the facts that occupy immensity, and have no need to be superseded, and cannot be superseded.

How holy, also, are the precepts of the Scriptures! They are all embodiments of love, pure love, and nothing but love. They are full of love—love from God to every man, and to all men; and love from every man to God, and from all men to each other. They are solemn with love—so solemn that they allow nothing ludicrous from the beginning of the Bible to the end of it. They are tender with love—so tender that they allow not the slightest disrespect toward God, or the least ill to mankind. They are happy with love—so happy that they intimate the source of God's own bliss, and make the obedient among men, under all circumstances, wishful of no other joy. They sanction the obligations and prescribe the duties, flowing from all relations, and leave nothing to be desired, by individuals, by members of families, by neighbors, or by nations, but the due practical observance of their directions. The beauty of holiness is here—the dignity of holiness—the divinity of holiness.

How remarkable, also, is the harmony of the Scriptures! So many of them, so different in their special subjects and objects, and so variously produced—really, it is wonderful that they should be so consistent, so thoroughly pervaded by one supreme design, and so co-operatively intent on the same gracious and saving result. As in the sky over Bethlehem, when one angel sang "Glory to God in the highest, and on earth peace, goodwill toward men," there was a multitude of other angels, at first unseen and unheard, to make the melody a sudden and mighty harmony: so, in the heaven of revelation, when even the least of the inspired ones lifts up a similar song, as though only to arouse the sleeping echoes around, the very leaders of the band, though before unnoticed, instantly acknowledge the ever charming challenge, and the whole company join the chorus without one lagging or jarring tone.

How strangely, also, have the Scriptures been preserved! Thousands of other books, more admired and prized by the great men of the world, have been utterly lost, or are known only by a few fragments—while these have been kept entire and comparatively uncorrupted. The effort has been to save other books, and yet they have perished. The effort has been to destroy the Scriptures, and yet they survive. Tyrants have assumed their utmost terrors, and threatened the holders of these books with death, and given to the flames all the copies extorted from the fears of the faithless, but other copies still escaped. Ten whole tribes of the very people among whom they originated have failed from the nations, and the remaining two are no longer separately distinguishable, but every one of their sacred books retains its place, and exercises, at this moment, a far more decided, extended, and impressive sovereignty, than in the days of old. The breath of God, on a bit of parchment, is infinitely mightier than the most magnificent empire on the globe. Not only tribes and kingdoms, but "heaven and earth" may pass away, and yet "one jot or one tittle shall in no wise pass from the law till all be fulfilled."

But once more—how blessed, also, have been the effects of the Scriptures! To a great extent, and in the noblest sense, they have already revolutionized the world. They have changed the principles, sentiments, and habits of mankind; enlightening, purifying, and elevating all. In many cases they have reformed constitutions, equalized laws, and given a peaceable and liberal character to the administration of government. They imparted a new impulse to the progress of art and science, of literature and philosophy, and are, at this moment, carrying the elements of the highest civilization to the ends of the earth. Compare the vilest horde of savages with the purest society of Christians, and the advantages of the latter are only a partial demonstration of the power of the Scriptures. Nay, compare the most degraded and disgusting individual savage with the most exalted and enchanting example of Christian wisdom and saintliness, and still the illustration remains imperfect. That is, the Scriptures are capable of greater good than they have ever yet accomplished, even in the best specimen of their influence. It is in personal relations, however, rather than social, that their actual effects are most admirable. They take the man as he is—whether high or low, rich or poor, bond or free, intelligent or ignorant, moral or immoral, sick or well, living or dying, and make him and keep him, in fact or by promise, all he ought to be.

Oh, what grandeurs of thought, what raptures of feeling, what glories of relation and destiny, they silently but surely excite and sustain! How many myriads, like angels from heaven in disguise, are now living, in the midst of all the sins and sorrows of earth, holy and happy, through the sanctifying virtue of the Bible! How many other myriads, like angels laying aside their disguise and returning to heaven, are now dying, in the paleness of perfect peace, or with the transfiguring splendor of triumphant joy—assured of a blissful immortality by the undoubted authority of the same cherished word!

And what now? Can it be supposed that these Scriptures—so sublime in doctrine, so holy in precept, so harmonious in structure, so imperishable in texture, and so inestimably productive of spiritual and practical blessings—are of merely human origin? Surely not. Read them, realize their influence, observe their influence, reflect upon the history of their influence, and innumerable most affecting proofs will confirm the conclusion that they were given by inspiration of God.—*T. H. Stockton.*

This Divine Book, the only one which is indispensable to the Christian, need only be read with reflection to inspire love for its author, and the most ardent desire to obey its precepts. Never did virtue speak so sweet a language, never was the most profound wisdom expressed with so much energy and simplicity. No one can arise from its perusal without feeling better than he was before.—*Rousseau.*

THE BIBLE PROVES ITSELF.

SUPPOSE I had never seen or heard of a sewing-machine. I have no idea of its parts, of its construction, or of its use; but after a time—no matter how—I come into possession of one; it is not set up, however, or even put together. I have the wheels, and bands, and arms, and the cloth-plate, and the shuttle, and the needles, and the treadle; but not being a machinist, I do not know how to put the parts together so I put them away.

By and by there comes to me through the mail a pamphlet; the post-mark is dim, and I cannot make it out; it has no name on it, either of author or sender. I look it curiously through, and find it full of cuts and explanatory letterpress, and as I turn over the leaves I am struck by the resemblance of some of the plates to some parts of the almost forgotten and useless machine.

I look more closely and find that it is a guide for the setting up and running of what it calls a sewing-machine. I compare the pieces and the book, and following its instructions I find it all goes accurately together. I thread the needle, and taking a piece of cloth I find it works precisely as the book said it would.

Now I care not where the machine came from or where the book came from. I may not know who wrote the book, or even so much as that the inventor of the machine ever heard of him or his writing; but I know the idea of him who made the machine and the idea of him who made the book are identical. In that wherein it pretends to be a guide—that is, in putting together and running the machine—it is an accurate guide-book, and being true for the ends for which it was made, it is for such ends an absolute authority. No conceivable thing could add to this authority. If it could be proved that the inventor of the machine wrote the book with his own hands, and that it was free from mistakes throughout, even to the grammar and punctuation, it could not add to its authority one iota.

It works, it stands trial, it does what it claims to do. Now, suppose somebody should go to picking flaws in its grammar, or spelling, or chronological calculations, or obscurities of style, or because a stray leaf from an old almanac had got bound up in it; suppose, for such reasons, he should counsel throwing it away, and trusting to luck to get the machine together, would you not call him a fool?

Come back, now, to the book and the world, and see if you have not for Christianity an argument equally simple. Here is a disordered humanity; we have only the separate and unjointed parts; they do not work together. Here is also a book: it pictures the present condition of humanity, it tells how to put the parts together and make it complete. Try it by this test, on its principle—the principle of love—you can build up a perfect man, a perfect family, a perfect society.

This one fact proves conclusively that the essential idea which is embodied in humanity and the essential idea of the book are the same, in that wherein it pretends to be a guide; that is, putting together and building up humanity, it is an accurate guide-book, and being thus true to the ends for which it was made, it is for such ends an absolute authority.—*Minot F. Savage.*

THE PRESERVATION OF THE SCRIPTURES.

AS the wonderful harmony and connection of all the parts of the Scriptures cannot rationally be ascribed to any other cause than their being all dictated by the same spirit of wisdom and foreknowledge; so also is their astonishing and (we may say) miraculous preservation a strong instance of God's providential care, a constant sanction and confirmation of the truth contained in them, continued by him without intermission in all ages of the Church.

Whence comes it, that while the histories of mighty empires are lost in the waste of time, the very names of their founders, conquerors, and legislators are consigned with their bodies to the silence and oblivion of the grave? Whence comes it that the history of mean, insignificant people, and the settlement of God's Church, should from its very beginning, which is coeval with the world itself, to this day remain full and complete? Whence comes it that nothing is left of innumerable volumes of philosophy and polite literature, in the preservation of which the admiration and care of all mankind seemed to conspire, and the Scriptures have in spite of all opposition come down to our time, entire and genuine?

During the captivity, the Urim and Thummim, the ark itself, and every glory of the Jewish worship, were lost; during the profanation of Antiochus, whoever was found with the book of the Law was put to death, and every copy that could be found burned with fire; the same impious artifice was put in practice by several Roman Emperors during their persecutions of the Christians, especially by Dioclesian, who triumphed in his supposed success against them. After the most barbarous havoc of them, he issued an edict, commanding them, on pain of death under the most cruel forms, to deliver up their Bibles. Though many complied with this sanguinary edict, the greater part disregarded it; and notwithstanding these and numberless other calamities, the sacred volumes have survived, pure and uncorrupted, to the present time. It is not necessary to mention that more than Egyptian darkness which overwhelmed religion for several centuries; during which any falsification was secure, especially in the Old Testament, the Hebrew language being entirely unknown to all but the Jews; and yet they have, in spite of their prejudices, preserved with scrupulous care even those passages which most confirm the Christian religion; the providence of God having been graciously pleased to make their blindness a standing evidence of the truth of the Scriptures, and their obstinacy an instrument to maintain and promote his doctrine and his kingdom.

To this may be added the present low state of many churches, and the total annihilation of others, of which nothing now remains but the Scriptures translated for their use; happy in this respect, that their particular misfortune is of service to the general cause, insomuch as so many copies, in so many different languages, preserved under so many untoward circumstances, and differing from each other in no essential point, are a wonderful proof of their authenticity, authority and divinity. All the designs of the enemies of the Scriptures, whether ancient or modern, have been defeated. The Bible still exists, and is triumphant, and doubtless will exist as long as there is a church in the world; that is, until the end of time, and the consummation of all things.—*Thomas Hartwell Horne.*

THE PRESERVATION OF THE BIBLE A STANDING MIRACLE.

WHEN Europe arose from her watery grave, bearing on her bosom, like some re-born isle, treasures long buried in the deep; though many a palimpsest sea-worm had long worn its way through the most precious remains of literature and science; though philosophy and the arts reappeared with features defaced and with many a mutilated limb; though of Livy, the historian, the more instructive half is irrevocably lost; of Polybius, almost the whole; though of Varro, the contemporary of Virgil—considered, by those who heard him, a bard able to strike the lyre to bolder measures, if not to more persuasive strains—not one lingering note has strayed behind him; of Menander's humor, not a shred remains; of Socrates, nought but the name, the example, and a few memorable drops of wisdom from his lips; though of numbers of authors, mentioned in terms of veneration by their contemporaries, all we can gather now consists barely of their names; though thoughts, tens of thousands of thoughts, high and glorious thoughts, noble aspirations, bright and deep conceptions have been lost forever with the names of their owners, as unknown as the skulls from whence they were once evolved, now parcel of this earth—yet, blessed be God! by a disposal of events, as marked by miraculous evidence as the preservation of the dead body of Lazarus, pure and sweet in the tomb, the sacred records of redeeming love have been preserved for men.

Varro and the rest of them are gone forever; but still is Moses extant, though upwards of three thousand years of age. Still are sketched out for us the first beginnings of what is now; still come down to us the annals of those men whose plough first furrowed this earth, "soft from the deluge." Still, "for our learning," the dealings of God with his people remain written. Still, have we recorded for our admonition, the rise and progress, the decline and fall, the favors and the warnings, the struggles and the triumphs, the virtue and the corruption, the apostasy and the punishment of the ancient people of God. Still, through those long ages has come down to us that strange mysterious book of Job—allegory or biography, a poet's dream or a woeful reality—which celebrates the contest between piety and pietism, and the victory of the plain, home-spun, God-reliant heart, over the trite maxims of the Orthodox conventional expert; a book written for the nineteenth century of grace, as well as for the simple age when the shepherd watched the flocks of Jethro. Still can the royal psalmist tune his harp, and lead a myriad worshippers through the golden-gates of praise and prayer; still the wisdom of Solomon is here; still he can pipe the *epithalamium* of Christ and his Church; and "the man-about-town," in our modern Babylon, "stuffing his hollowness" with "mouldy hay," can still find the "vanity and vexation" in his "vision of sin," depicted in the experiences of the ancient preacher, and from him learn that the judgment to which God shall bring every work, with every secret thing, is begun already, even in this life. Still are the mighty prophets full in teachers in the education of the world, the reliable pioneers in the progress of mankind, as halting on the successive heights of fulfilled prophecy: they point to far-off and greater glories yet to be revealed. Still can Matthew tell his plain, unvarnished tale, Mark corroborate the story, and the skilful Luke collect and record the testimony of his age; still can John, the beloved, in humble gratitude, illustrate the wonder of incarnate Deity; still are preserved for us the deep philosophy, the trenchant argument, the simple, sweeping eloquence of Paul; still can James stimulate to deeds worthy of our calling; still, with holy zeal, and undying fervor—his brows almost crowned in martyrdom—the venerable Peter can watch and warn the Church; Jude exhort; and John, again, shed forth those drops of love, sweet and bright—the love of him who loved him, and, in sublime and mystic language—sublime since he speaks of heavenly things; mystic, since with inspired wisdom he beclouds the sunlit vision, and tempers it to suit our weak and trembling human gaze—describe the line and issue in and to which Eternal Providence doth shape events. These all—all these have been preserved for men—though Varro and the rest of them are gone forever.

In its preservation, this book—the Bible—is a standing miracle of the providence of the *now* of God, the ever-present, the ever-active, the ever-overruling, the ever-interposing influence of the divine energy—the Divine Energetic One. I hold in my hand the proof of the energy of my Creator. I ask the Atheist to *account for this book?* When came it, and how? Why it be preserved intact, and how? And in accounting for its being here with us now, to explain, if he can, on any mere human grounds, how it is that a book written by illiterate shepherds and herdsmen, fishermen and taxgatherers, when the world was young, contains truths and suggests aspirations which find their echo and answer in the most advanced periods and amongst the most cultivated people? Why is this book, and this book only, the book for all peoples and all times? Why has this book, and almost this book only, been so fully, so wonderfully preserved through the long ages? Is not that wonder a sign, a miracle?—*J. Stewart Gumley.*

THE SURVIVAL OF THE FITTEST.

THERE is not one book out of a thousand that lives five years; any publisher will tell you that there will not be more than one book out of fifty thousand that will live a century. Yet here is a book, much of it 1,600 years old; much of it 4,000 years old, with more rebound and strength in it than when the book was first put upon parchment or papyrus. This book saw the cradle of all other books, and it will see their grave. Would you not think that an old book like this, some of it forty centuries old, would come along hobbling with age and crutches? Instead of that, more potent than any other book of the time, more copies of it printed in the last ten years than of any other book—Walter Scott's "Waverley" novels, Macaulay's "History of England," Disraeli's "Endymion," and all other popular books of the day having no such sales in the last ten years as this old book.

Do you know what a struggle a book has to get through one century or two centuries? A lot of books during a fire in a seraglio of Constantinople were thrown into the street; a man without any education picked up one of those books, read it, and did not see the value of it; a scholar looked over his shoulder and saw it was the first and second decades of Livy, and he offered the man a large reward if he would bring the books to his study; but in the excitement of the fire the two parted, and the first and second decades of Livy were forever lost. Pliny wrote twenty books of history, all lost. The most of Meander's writings lost. Of 130 comedies of Plautus, all gone but twenty. Euripides wrote a hundred dramas, all gone but nineteen. Eschylus wrote a hundred dramas, all gone but seven. Varro wrote the laborious biographies of 700 Romans, not a fragment left. Quintilian wrote his favorite book on the Corruption of Eloquence, all lost. Thirty books of Tacitus lost. Dion Cassius wrote eighty books, only twenty remain. Berosius' history all lost. Nearly all the old books are mummified and lying in the tombs of old libraries, and perhaps once in twenty years some man comes along and picks up one of them and blows the dust off, and opens it and finds it the book he does not want; but this old book, much of it forty centuries old, stands to-day more discussed than any other book, and it challenges the admiration of all the good, and the spite, and the venom, and the animosity, and the hypercriticism of earth and hell.

I appeal to your common sense if a book so divinely guarded and protected in its present shape must not be in just the way that God wants it to come to us, and if it pleases God, ought it not to please us? Not only have all the attempts to detract from the book failed, but all the attempts to add to it; many attempts were made to add the apocryphal books to the Old Testament. The Council of Trent, the Synod of Jerusalem, the Bishops of Hippo, all decided that the apocryphal books must be added to the Old Testament. "They must stay in," said those learned men;

but they stayed out. There is not an intelligent Christian man that to-day will put the Book of Maccabeus or the Book of Judith beside the Book of Isaiah or Romans. Then a great many said we must have books added to the New Testament, and there were epistles and gospels and apocalypses written and added to the New Testament; but they have all fallen out. You cannot add anything, you cannot subtract anything. Divinely protected book in the present shape: let no man dare to lay his hands on it with the intention of detracting from the book, or casting out any of these holy pages.—*T. Dewitt Talmage.*

THE BIBLE SURVIVES FRIENDS AND FOES.

THE volume itself survives both friends and foes. Without being able to speak one word on its own behalf, but what it has already said; without any power of explanation or rejoinder in depreciation of the attacks made upon it, or to assist those who defend it; it passes along the ages in majestic silence. Impassive amidst all this tumult of controversy, in which it takes no part, it might be likened to some great ship floating down a mighty river, like the Amazon or the Orinoco, the shores of which are inhabited by various savage tribes. From every little creek or inlet, from every petty port or bay, sally flotillas of canoes, some seemingly friendly and some seemingly hostile, filled with warriors in all the terror of war-paint, and their artillery of bows and arrows. They are hostile tribes, and soon turning their weapons against one another, assail each other with great fury and mutual loss. Meantime the noble vessel silently moves on through the scene of confusion, without deigning to alter its course or to fire a shot; perhaps here and there a seaman casts a compassionate glance from the lofty bulwarks, and wonders at the hardihood of those who come to assail his leviathan.—*Henry Rogers.*

THE PYRAMID AMONG BOOKS.

WHAT has become of those millions of once famous books which were written in past ages? They have nearly all perished, but amid this wreck of ancient literature the Bible stands almost a solitary monument, like the Pyramids of Egypt amid the surrounding wastes.—*Archbishop Gibbons.*

THE BIBLE THE MARVEL OF THE AGES.

ASIDE from the factor of divine agency in its authorship, the Bible is the insoluble enigma of the literary world. It well may be. It must be. Think of it! It is the oldest book upon the earth, still read among men; going back beyond the Roman or the Greek literature; going back farther than any other in parts of it, toward the time when the waters of the deluge subsided from the hills of Western Asia, farther than any other toward the very morning of creation, when the sons of God shouted for joy, yet its vitality continues, and its power over the human mind remains unwasting.

It is a large book; it sets its stately front for two millenniums along the lines of chronology, history, biography, philosophy, and human science. It challenges assault at ten thousand points. It says to science, "Search the strata beneath and the stars above, and find a God more equal to the problems of the universe than whom I reveal!" It says to philosophy, "Find anything in human nature, any power, or, any passion, any mean inclination or sublime possibility, of which I do not give the manifestation and the explanation:" thus challenging assault, and opening its line along the whole extent of it to any endeavor to overthrow it, it remains the most remarkable of books.

It presents to us the literature of a people, in whom, aside from it and their relation to it, we have comparatively but insignificant interest. We read the Grecian poetry or philosophy, and it is luminous to us with the light of the Attic heavens, it is musical to us with the lofty echoes of the Attic life and history, all that is tragic, and all that is splendid in that history, commands the poetry or the philosophy to us. We read it partly for our love of the people which originated the most exquisite and perfect instrument of thought which the world has ever seen in the Greek language; we read the pages of Roman law, Roman eloquence, Roman history, and they to our minds are reverberating with the tread of that mighty and imperial people, whose place in history is so eminent and large, and to which we ourselves are under such constant and immense obligation. But we read the literature of the Jewish People, and that people, except as connected with the literature which is thus presented to us, has for us no attraction, and but small importance.

Then it is a book full of mysterious utterances, of thought and of fact. And the human mind does not love mystery. It desires plain statements of the truth, which it may receive, apprehending and understanding them at a glance. It presents these utterances in a tone of authority, by which men are repelled; for the human mind enjoys receiving suggestions from others, enlightening instructions, delicately and persuasively communicated, but it re-acts, and sometimes with violence, when it is told that it must accept, under tremendous pains and penalties, that which is declared to be as true.

It requires from us also, such forms of character, such forms of action, as are in themselves distasteful to us; against the requisition of which we fight, with a native and an instant impulse; and while this is the astonishing character of the book it is seemingly most irregular in construction, shaped by no formula of art, conformed to no critical canon of taste or judgment, such as are now current in the world.

It seems incredible, therefore, that such a book should hold its place, while the civilizations advance and change. We have, instead of the slender bark of the ancients, pursuing its slow course through the waters of the narrow seas, and looking out anxiously for the Pharaohs at Alexandria, the mighty steamship, steering by the stars, conquering the oceans, treading its unobstructed way through storm and tempest toward distant coasts; instead of the camel, we have the rail-train; instead of the pen of the scribe, the type, multiplying copies of human thought a million-fold, as against the pen. Instead of the goat's-hair tent of the desert, we have the splendid and sumptuous palaces and cities of modern civilization; instead of the javelin and the bow, we have the modern artillery, with its thunderous and fatal power, almost rivalling the artillery of the heavens.

How is it, then, that this book survives all changes in human civilization, and is as apt and powerful in its appeal to us as to those of any earlier time? The wonder grows, when we remember that it widens always in its appeal with the expansion of civilization, and is already in more than two hundred languages. It grows still further, when we remember that the best and noblest of the race are those who love it most, and search most fondly and profoundly; who stand as humble scholars before this book of the centuries and of the earth, and the wonder comes to its very climax when we remember that this oldest, largest, roughest, and most unworldly of books, is the source and spring of civilization everywhere; before it, inventions multiply at its touch, commerce extends beneath its influence, churches rise, and spires ascend as songs toward the heavens; it prints its story on blazoned windows, it carves its record in the delicate and enduring marbles; art, invention, enterprise, liberal governments, human legislations, all come from this book. This is simply incredible, if it be a book of merely human authorship. Skepticism says that such a Bible has no business to be in the world, but here it is! and we pause marvelling before its mysterious and astonishing wonders, until we recognize the fact that God is in it; it is the Lord's doing; and so it is marvellous in our eyes.—*R. S. Storrs.*

No true bard will ever contravene the Bible. Coming steadily down from the past, like a ship, through all perturbations, all ebbs and flows, all time, it is to-day his art's chief reason for being.—*Walt Whitman.*

THE CITADEL OF CHRISTIAN FAITH.

THE fortress at Gibraltar is reputed to be the world's strongest military fortification. Every available point bristles with artillery, the mountain is honey-combed with galleries and bomb-proofs. Batteries hewn in the rock frown in every direction. For twelve hundred years this cannon-crowned rock has been the object of international envy. Around it from the days of the Saracens, the thunder of battle has roared. Africans, Arabs, Castilians, Moors and Englishmen have in turn been its masters. But around the Bible—the Citadel of Christian faith—the noise of conflict has rung more loudly and for a longer period. Yet it stands to-day in the possession of its Christian defenders. Celcus, Porphyry and Hierocles opened the long campaign with their mortars of Platonic learning. Behind them came on long ranks of pagan monarchs, heathen philosophers and military commanders; and the friends of the God-protected stronghold trembled as it seemed for centuries to stand like the bush of Horeb invested with flame. Then the most extensive ecclesiastical hierarchy the world has known began sapping and mining around this asylum within which were sheltered the hopes of humanity. Invested by foes wearing every uniform of hate and badge of opposition, the little garrison held at bay century by century the great army of besiegers. Behind these and their civil allies came lines of atheists, deists, pantheists, materialists, rationalists and varied infidels, led by men like Holbach and Comte, Herbert and Bolingbroke, Hume and Gibbon, Hobbes and Blount,

Spinoza and Hegel, Cousin and Schelling, Rousseau and Condorcet, Voltaire and Paine, Renan and Strauss, Emerson and Parker; and these forgetting their quarrels in a common contest against the Sacred Oracles, were defeated in individual assaults and in combined onsets. Occasionally some misguided son of science has gone to the stars and into the bowels of earth for effective ammunition, and like proud Goliath challenged the hosts of Israel only to be utterly discomfited. Even ranks of traitors clad in Christian dress and carrying the flag of the cross have levelled their heaviest artillery at this divinely protected Malakoff. All arsenals of learning, political power and ecclesiastical hate have been emptied for this bombardment, lasting nearly two thousand years, while shot and shell, battering ram and lance, arrow and javelin, rock and firebrand have been hurled against the Bible. The map of the world has been repeatedly changed; kingdoms and republics have flourished and fallen, and great arts and armies have been born and perished. Walk round this citadel to-day and examine its condition after the protracted siege. Its foundations were never so strong, not one of its sixty-six bulwarks has been impaired. Its blocks stand to-day as they were laid by Moses, the prophets, the evangelists and the apostles. From its base, laid in Genesis at God's command by the greatest architect of Hebrew history, high up to the cornice of Revelation placed on the impregnable structure under Divine direction by John, as from its lofty watch tower he looked over the river and saw the New Jerusalem, this old Redan stands to-day as fresh as the everlasting hills. The long cannonade of lingual criticism, philosophical review, educational prejudice, political position and carping ridicule have left this fortress as fair as some structure of Parian marble.

Over it waves to-day the same blood-stained flag that floated when the Roman emperors rallied their armies for the early assaults. Surely it promises to withstand the attack as Mr. Ingersoll flings against its walls his torpedoes of ridicule. This Bible! It has stood as impregnable amidst hostility and surrounding disaster as the fabled pillars of Seth. Crucial tests have not impaired a chapter or invalidated a verse. The tears of silver-haired patriarchs continue to bedew its pages. The widow amid her poverty still reads its precious promises to her fatherless children. The troubled heart and sorrow-bowed head find its divine covenants softer than the pillows of down on which wearied kings have rested their aching foreheads. The sick yet touch their spirit lips to the crystal current of this "river of the water of life." Its pledges of a coming resurrection keep the graves of loved ones green, and have made the cemetery magnetic to surviving friends. The dying turn their closing eyes to it as their only lamp through the "valley of the shadow of death," and clasp it as their last treasure while their fingers stiffen in the final ordeal. Old Sun! twin brother of Time! thou wilt cease to shine. Empress of the evening! thy form will disappear from the night-draped sky. Lamps of Ether! ye will drop into the emptiness of destined darkness. Old Bible! thou wilt survive infidelity, outlive criticism, and stand immortal, indestructible, imperishable.—*S. V. Leech, D. D.*

WITHOUT the Scriptures men can never attain a high state of intelligence, virtue, security, liberty or happiness. The whole hope of human progress is suspended on the ever-growing influence of the Bible.—*W. H. Seward.*

TEACHINGS OF THE BIBLE.

HAST thou ever heard
Of such a book? the author, God himself;
The subject, God and man; salvation, life
And death—eternal life, eternal death—
Dread words; whose meaning has no end, no bounds—
Most wondrous book! bright candle of the Lord!
Star of eternity! the only star
By which the bark of man could navigate
The sea of life, and gain the coast of bliss
Securely; only star which rose on time,
And, on its dark and troubled billows, still
As generation, drifting swiftly by,
Succeeded generation, threw a ray
Of heaven's own light, and to the hills of God!
The everlasting hills, pointed the sinner's eye,
By prophets, seers, and priests and sacred bards
Evangelist, apostles men inspired,
And by the Holy Ghost anointed, set
Apart and consecrated to declare
To earth the counsels of the Eternal One.
This book, this holiest, this sublimest book,
Was sent—Heaven's will, Heaven's code of laws
To man, this book contained; defined the bounds entire
Of vice and virtue, and of life and death;
And what was shadow, what was substance taught.
Much it revealed; important all; the least
With more than what else seemed of highest worth;
But this of plainest, most essential truth—
That God is one, eternal, holy, just,
Omnipotent, omniscient, infinite,
Most wise, most good, most merciful and true.
In all perfection most unchangeable:

That man—that every man of every clime
And hue, of every age, and every rank,
Was bad—by nature and by practice bad;
In understanding blind, in will perverse,
In heart corrupt; in every thought and word,
Imagination, passion, and desire,
Most utterly depraved throughout, and ill,
In sight of Heaven, though less in sight of man;
At enmity with God his Maker born,
And by his very life an heir of death;
That man—that every man was, farther, most
Unable to redeem himself, or pay
One mite of his vast debt to God—nay, more,
Was most reluctant and averse to be
Redeemed, and sin's most voluntary slave;
That Jesus, Son of God, of Mary born
In Bethlehem, and by Pilate crucified
On Calvary for man thus fallen and lost,
Died; and by death, life and salvation bought,
And perfect righteousness, for all who should
In this great name believe; that He, the third
In the eternal essence, to the prayer
Sincere should come, should come as soon as asked,
Proceeding from the Father and the Son,
To give faith and repentance, such as God
Accepts—to open the intellectual eyes,
Blinded by sin; to bend the stubborn will,
Perversely to the side of wrong inclined,
To God and his commandments, just and good;
The wild rebellious passions to subdue,
And bring them back to harmony with heaven;
To purify the conscience, and to lead
The mind into all truth, and to adorn
With every holy ornament of grace,
And sanctify the whole renewed soul,
Which henceforth might no more fall totally

But persevere, though erring oft, amidst
The mists of time, in piety to God,
And sacred works of charity to men ;
That he, who thus believed, and practised thus,
Should have his sins forgiven, however vile;
Should be sustained at midday, morn and even,
By God's omnipotent, eternal grace,
And in the evil hour of sore disease,
Temptation, persecution, war, and death—
For temporal death, although unstinged,
Beneath the shadow of the Almighty's wings remained—
Should sit unhurt, and at the judgment day
Should share the resurrection of the just,
And reign with Christ in bliss forever more ;
That all, however named, however great,
Who would not thus believe, nor practise thus :
But in their sins impenitent remained,
Should in perpetual fear and terror live ;
Should die unpardoned, unredeemed, unsaved,
And at the hour of doom should be cast out
To utter darkness in the night of hell,
By mercy and by God abandoned, there
To reap the harvest of eternal woe :
This did that book declare in obvious phrase,
In most sincere and honest words by God
Himself selected and arranged ; so clear,
So plain, so perfectly distinct, that none
Who read with humble wish to understand,
And asked the Spirit, given to all who asked,
Could miss their meaning, blazed in heavenly light.
This book—this holy book, on every line
Marked with the seal of high divinity,
On every leaf bedewed with drops of love
Divine, and with the eternal heraldry
And signature of God almighty stamped
From first to last—this ray of sacred light,

This lamp, from off the everlasting throne,
Mercy took down and in the night of time
Stood, casting on the dark her gracious love;
And ever more beseeching men, with tears
And earnest sighs, to read, believe, and live,
And many to her voice gave ear, and read,
Believed, obeyed; and now as the Amen,
True, Faithful Witness swore, with snowy robes
And branchy palms surround the fount of life,
And drink the streams of immortality,
Forever happy, and forever young.—*Robert Pollok.*

WISDOM OF BELIEVING THE BIBLE.

ARE you an unlearned man? There is more information contained in the first three chapters of Genesis, concerning the creation of all things—the original condition of man—his shameful fall—and the origin of all evil, than you will find in so short a compass, in any other book in the world.

There is more solid information in the Bible than in any other book. There is that which you will find in no other book whatever, that which will "make you wise unto salvation, through faith in Christ Jesus." All learning is not knowledge; there are those that are "ever learning, yet never able to come to the knowledge of the truth."

When you take up such a work as Homer's Iliad, and particularly Pope's Homer, beautiful as it is, you do not know that the author speaks truth; you read of the siege of Troy, but you do not know that these things were so; but when you take up the Saviour's prediction of the siege of Jerusalem, and compare it with Josephus' history of that event, you can come at the knowledge of the truth in the case. When you read "Milton's Paradise Lost," sublime and beautiful as it may be in poetry, you do not know but it may be false in fact; but when you read the sacred narrative of our Saviour's discourses and miracles, you may know that these things were so. All knowledge is not wisdom; we may be very knowing, and at the same time very unwise; but whoever will follow the maxims of the Old Testament, and the precepts of the new, cannot be unwise; therefore there is wisdom in believing.

Are you a learned man? a linguist, an antiquarian, a historian, a philosopher, a poet, a statesman, a grammarian, a logician, a rhetorician, a traveller? Here you may gratify your taste as a linguist, in comparing manuscripts, in noticing the structure, genius, and idiom of many languages, for the Bible exists in many. Here you may notice paraphrases, versions, and various readings, ad libitum, if not ad infinitum. Here you may indulge your speculations on the origin of nations, and of languages, and with the antiquarian travel through Rome and Greece into Egypt, and learn the origin of almost all the mythological fables of the ancients. Here, if you love to trace history to its fountains, you may go farther back than the days of Hesiod or of Homer, and obtain certain information of cities and of nations that have long since gone to decay.

Here, if you are a philosopher, you may find entertainment in some parts, at least, of the writings of Moses, or of Job, or of David. What think you of that expression of Job's, " He hangeth the earth upon nothing," philosophically considered, and of that of the Psalmist, " He gathereth the waters of the sea together as a heap," in view of the convexity of the sea, and the modern theory of tides? Or of those expressions of Solomon: "Or ever the silver cord be loosed, or the golden bowl be broken, or the pitcher be broken at the fountain, or the wheel be broken at the cistern." Most interpreters agree that Solomon in this beautiful allegory is speaking of the human system. How can the blood in the human body "ascend without reluctance and descend with precipitancy," as one observes, "contrary to the common laws of nature," and how could Solomon describe these things as he has done without some knowledge of the principles of modern science?

Here, if you are a poet, you may gather flowers as rich as ever grew on Mount Parnassus; to be convinced of this, you need only read Bishop South on Isaiah, Dr. A. Clark's notes on the Psalms, and his sketch of the life and character of David; or "The Song of Moses Explained According to the Rules of Rhetoric," by Rollin, in his second book of his method of studying the belles-lettres. "Every one," says the elegant writer, "knows the energy with which the Scriptures make the impious man to vanish, who a moment before seemed like the cedar, to raise his proud head to the skies." Thus for example, "I have seen the wicked in great power, spreading himself like a green bay tree, yet he passed away, and lo, he was not; yea, I sought him, but he could not be found." He is so completely annihilated that the very place where he stood was destroyed. Racine gives a different translation which is thus Englished:

> "We saw the impious wretch adored on earth,
> And, like the cedar, hide his daring front,
> High in the heavens: he seemed to rule at will
> The forked thunder, and to crush his captive.
> I only passed, and lo! he was no more."

Are you a statesman? Look again at the laws of Moses, and the character of Joseph, Joshua, Samuel, and Daniel. We often hear of corruption in ministers of state; here are instances of unsullied integrity. "Behold here I am," says Samuel: "witness against me before the Lord, and before this anointed, whose ox have I taken, or whose ass have I taken, or whom have I defrauded, whom have I oppressed, or of whose hand have I received any bribe to blind mine eyes therewith, and I will restore it unto you."

Are you a grammarian, a logician, a rhetorician? have you a passion for the recondite in philology? then with Gerand's Elements of Biblical Criticism in one hand, and a Polyglott Bible in the other, you may find entertainment "till life's" sun shall set. "The simplicity and grandeur of Scripture style is above all praise. Notice the simplicity of the following passages: "He made the stars, also." Here the sacred historian speaks with indifference of the most astonishing display of omnipotence imaginable. Think of the creation of millions of suns, systems, worlds. The act was God's, the manner of relating it worthy of himself. "Those who study the Scriptures attentively," says Rollin, "find that the beauty consists in the strength and greatness of the thoughts." Almost all writers on the sublime have noticed that passage in Genesis where Moses speaks of the creation of light. God said: "Let light be, and light was." Where was it a moment before? How could it spring from darkness, from nothing? The world that had hitherto been plunged in darkness seemed to issue a second time from nothing, and everything by being enlightened was beautified in an instant. All the colors that sprang from light embellished all nature.

How magnificent is that description of the Psalmist:

"Oh Lord, my God, thou art become exceeding glorious; thou art clothed with majesty and honor, thou deckest thyself with light as it were with a garment." One would almost think that the God of ages had clothed himself with magnificence, and that, issuing from the secret of his pavilion, he displayed himself in light. But all this is but his outward clothing and as a mantle which hides him: "Thy majesty, oh God, is infinitely above the light that surrounds it. I fix my eyes on thy garments, not being able to fix them on thyself."

Are you a traveller or fond of reading books of travel? Here, then, you may visit Egypt in the time of the Pharaohs, when the art of embalming was in its glory; when the pyramids probably were raised; certainly, when the firstborn was slain by the angel of the Lord. From thence you may visit Palestine, Syria, Greece, Chaldea, Italy and Spain, and as you travel through these countries in the book of God you may notice the constant allusions to places and things and manners and customs peculiar to these countries which will convince you, perhaps, that the Bible is no forgery; here you will read of "threshing-floors," but never of threshing-machines; of "women grinding at the mill," but never of wind-mills, water-mills, or saw-mills; here frequent mention is made of the "sword," the "bow," the "spear," the "helmet," the "girdle," the "sandal" and the "shield," but no mention is made of the pistol, the rifle, the cannon, the epaulette, or the boot; here you will read of the "vine," the "fig-tree," the "pomegranate," the "olive" and the "cedar," but never of the plum, the peach, the pear, the maple and the walnut, and the reason is obvious—those things are peculiar to that country, these are peculiar to this.

If the authors of the Bible, to say nothing of its inspiration, had lived in this country or in the north of Europe they would have made use of a language conformable to the climate and the customs of the country. Had the book of Isaiah been the "offspring of the genius of some gloomy monk," as Mr. Paine wickedly insinuates, then how shall we account for the beautiful imagery employed by that prophet in his most magnificent yet truly evangelical poems? Notice particularly the thirty-fifth chapter, where you can almost see

"Old Jordan roll his yellow waves along
With joy, like Lebanon in ancient day;"

where you can almost hear

"Carmel and Sharon join the heavenly song,
While joyous shepherds chant the solemn lay."

If a "gloomy monk" of St. Bernard, for instance, had "conjured up" the book of the prophet Isaiah he would by a slip of the pen, probably, have written instead of Lebanon Mt. Blanc.

"Whose head in wintry grandeur towers,
And whitens with eternal sleep;
While summer, in a vale of flowers,
Is sleeping rosy at his feet."

And then the whole forgery would have been detected; but now you may take Maundrell, Pocock, Shaw, Clarke, Bruce and Chateaubriand, or even Volney, in your hand and you shall find, so far as they have visited the holy land and the adjacent countries, that their descriptions substantially confirm the Scripture account of those places.

Had the writers of the New Testament been ignorant and as wild as some of their accusers, St. Paul, in sailing from

Cesarea to Rome, would have been wrecked at Eziongeber instead of Miletus or Malta. A little attention to these things will help to correct sundry mistakes into which the enemies of Divine Revelation sometimes fall, and he that is wise will understand these things and make proper use of them.—*George Coles.*

THE BIBLE OF INTEREST TO ALL.

THE BIBLE interests the world; is of real, great, matchless, interest to all mankind.

It interests all historically; the origin of our race is here; the primitive and proper condition of our race is here; the cause of its present and improper condition is here; the brotherhood of our race is here with its early unity; its subsequent division of tongues and tribes, and the progress of territorial discoveries, and of national migrations and settlements—in a word, the beginnings of all history are here; and without the Bible there is nothing worthy the name of history.

It interests all legally: the first principles of all law are here—those principles which are essential, universal, everlasting, and from which, therefore, there is and can be no appeal or escape. The master truth is here evident, that the constitution of the universe is a moral constitution; and, of course, that all material elements and combinations, causes and consequences, are subordinate to spiritual agencies and destinies. The moral law, therefore, comes first; claiming voluntary obedience to God. The natural law comes next, securing involuntary, mechanical, and disciplinary obedience to God, according to the moral exigencies of his higher administration. Then come civil law, and ecclesiastical law, as representative modifications and adaptations of the divine common law; both of them being bound by this common law to the due observance of all personal, domestic, and social rights—leaving all men free, first of all, to fulfil their duties to their God and to their families, and then protecting and assisting them in all proper efforts to promote their social and public elevation and improvement. In a word, the beginnings of all law are likewise here; and without the Bible there is nothing worthy the name of law.

It interests all evangelically; the consciousness of sin is universal, whether the law of God be in the heart alone, as among the heathen, or in the heart and book both, as among ourselves; it is not more plain that the law exists, than it is that it has been broken, but, here is the atonement for sin; an atonement made by the blood of the Son of God, acting as Mediator between God and men; an atonement designed to make God and man one again; an atonement meeting the utmost claims of the law, and proffering its benefits without exception of nation or respect of person to the whole world of transgressors. Here, moreover, is provision for the regeneration of our nature—that being renewed by the agency of the Holy Ghost we may recover ability in spirit at least to keep the law; awakening to a life of holy love toward God and all our race; here, in a word, the consciousness of sin may be exchanged for the consciousness of deliverance from sin; all remorse for the past and fear for the future being succeeded by perfect peace, and the gladness and glory of heavenly expectation in all the world. Without the Bible there is nothing which it would not be an utter disgrace to call salvation.

It interests all prophetically. A better time to come has been the presentiment of every age, the delusion or the warranted assurance of all generations. With the Bible before us we have no doubt of the happier theory. God has declared the restitution of all things by the mouth of all his holy prophets since the world began. When the promise of a Saviour was first announced in the Garden of Eden the angel of hope stood by the side of the Almighty, and, as soon as she heard the joyful news, began to sing the song that ever since has charmed the waiting heavens and earth. Paradise withered, indeed, and the outer world soon smoked with the curse; but when the last leaf fell from the tree of life, and the first fire flashed from the volcanic peak, Hope, unalarmed, prolonged her certain chant as sweetly and serenely as ever. Then the deluge swept from pole to pole, but over the sea and over the storm the seraph sunned herself in the smile of the highest and now looks down through the clouds at the ark, and anon, looking up through the glory at the throne, she floated through the changeless sky with heart as calm and plumes as smooth as ever, singing as soft a strain and as sure a triumph as in any moment of beauty and bliss before. True, when Jesus died, she did, indeed, stand shuddering by the cross, hiding her face with her wings, and when he was buried she sat in the shadow of his sepulchre, weeping with sympathy if not with fear, and watching, wondering for the breaking of that strange repose. But, when he rose, instantly the morning star was startled and thrilled in its sphere with the electric rapture of her song renewed, and still she sings, though many now, alas, mistake her strain. The good times coming are all her own, and infinitely better than myriads of the friends of progress have ever imagined. But the angel never forgets that Christ alone can bring them. The resurrection of Christ was the pledge of our own resurrection; the ascension of Christ was the symbol of our own ascension; the return of Christ will be the signal of the new creation and the consummate enthronement of immortal joy. Such is the prophecy of the Bible. But without the Bible there is nothing worthy the name of prophecy.

So much for the point that the Bible deserves to be out before the world. It interests the world historically, legally, evangelically and prophetically. I would like to add philosophically, for the soul of philosophy is here; I would like to add poetically, for the bloom of all poetry is here; I would like to add divinely, for the unveiled splendor of the majesty and government of the Eternal Jehovah is here. Here, and here only, is an absolutely inexhaustible universe of reliable intelligence. Personally and socially, temporally and eternally interesting to every faculty and to every destiny of our race, these hints must suffice where the longest and richest discourse would still fall short of the fullness of the theme.—*T. H. Stockton.*

THE BIBLE A MANY-SIDED BOOK.

BECAUSE of the constant variety in the literary structure of the Bible it becomes a universal book; since there is no tribe or nation that does not enjoy story, song, parable, eloquence; that does not, therefore, welcome the Bible, as opening to it new realms of thought, presenting that thought in the most engaging and fascinating forms and giving the mind intellectual gratification while tending all the time to irradicate and renew the moral nature. There is almost no other Oriental book which is valued and sought in the Western world. But this is just as familiar to the Western mind, as congenial to it, as if it had been prepared in Europe. There is no other book read studiously in Europe, which is read with equal interest and gladness in the Society Islands, in India, China and among the barbarians of South Africa just emerging from their dense darkness. But the Bible goes to the African as to the European; goes to the Islander of the Sea, to the Chinaman and the Hindoo, to the Indian and the Arab, as well as to the citizen trained by schools, expert in business, in the most civilized nations. There is, of course, a certain local color in it which makes the missionary who reads it in the East and who interprets it into the Arabic; which makes the traveller reading it in the East, among the localities where its writings first found their life and form, appreciate the beauty and the wonder of it the more. But it is, beyond all others, a universal book, and largely by reason of this amazing many-sidedness of its literary constitution.

Then it is, also, a comprehensive and commanding book, as addressed to any individual student, because it appeals to each faculty of the mind, interests all and leaves none unchallenged. It appeals to men in all moods of their feeling. It appeals to them in all stages of this life, from childhood onward through maturity, until the extreme limit of age. It appeals to them thus not merely by reason of the substance of the truth which it communicates, but also of this variety of means by which it conveys it—in song and story, in law and proverb, in parable, argument and nightly vision. Every faculty of mind is therefore addressed by it and is gratified by it. We are sometimes in trouble because certain parts or passages of the Bible are less interesting to us, at least in certain moods of feeling, than they have been before; are not so interesting to us now as they were when we were children, or have lost the celestial glow which was upon them when we read them with tears and with triumph in our grief. But the Bible is intended to furnish something for every mood, the most sorrowful and the most cheerful; when the soul is sunken in grief and when it is rising in new-born ecstacy of strength and hope. It has parts for the little child and parts for the aged. It is the only universal book in the world, because it is the only one which has this marvellous completeness of constitution which the little child and the venerable grandparent will gladly sit down and read together; which is at home in the Sunday-school and equally at home in the highest university; which the most disciplined mind can never exhaust, yet which the youngest and most immature can find full of attraction, instruction, inspiration. This, by reason of the marvellous manifoldness of its literary structure, as well as by reason of the grandeur and the glory of that system of truth which is evermore contained within it.

Observe, too, what an educating book it becomes, by reason of this astonishing variety in its constitution. It requires a man to match one part against another; to read the poem in the light of the narrative; to interpret the argument by the light of that revelation of the Son of God which is given in the four matchless, divine biographies of him; to interpret the primitive precept, even under the radiance of that final vision of judgment which flashes its startling splendor on us from the great white throne; to interpret Christ's declaration of forgiveness by the miracles which he works, and the doctrine of sanctification by the

Spirit by the crystaline sheen of the golden streets of the New Jerusalem. We are to analyze, and combine, and reconcile parts, to bring one into a close comparison with another, so that out of all we may derive the ultimate truth which God would give us in the Scripture. The flower, the oak, the forest and the stream, the continent and the ocean, are alike parts in this manifold whole; and we cannot fully comprehend one without considering all. So it comes to be a book which educates the mind as no other can; which tasks every faculty in it; which requires in its student a moral state sympathetic with his from whom it comes, and which requires our careful perusal, from end to end, in order that we may wholly understand it.—*Dr. R. S. Storrs.*

THE BIBLE ADAPTED TO ALL CLASSES.

F books, the oldest, truest and best, this book, for the rules it supplies for this life and the hopes it presents of a better one, is adapted to all classes of society, and should be equally valued by all. This was well expressed by two very different, but both impressive scenes.

There, in yonder palace where a royal lady, about to leave our shores and rise in time to the position of a queen, receives a deputation. They have come to offer her in the name of the women of our country a parting marriage gift. It is no costly ornament, fashioned of gold and flashing with precious gems—diamonds from Indian mines, or pearls from the deep, such as the wealth and willingness of the donors could have purchased. A healthy sign of the age and a noble testimony to its religious character, the gift is a copy of the Holy Scriptures. This, as in long centuries hence it will be told, was the marriage gift it was thought worthy of a Christian nation to bestow, and worthy of a royal princess to receive.

And there also, on yon stormy shore where, amid the wreck the night had wrought and the waves, still thundering as they sullenly retire, had left on the beach, lies the naked form of a drowned sailor boy. He had stripped for one last, brave fight for life, and wears naught but a handkerchief bound round his cold breast. Insensible to pity, and unawed by the presence of death, those who sought the wreck, as vultures swoop down on their prey, rushed on the body and tore away the handkerchief; tore it open, certain that it held within its folds gold; his little fortune; something very valuable for a man to say, I'll sink or swim with it. They were right, but it was not gold: it was the poor lad's Bible—also a parting gift, and the more precious that it was a mother's.—*Thomas Guthrie.*

A MOTHER'S GIFT—THE BIBLE.

REMEMBER, love, who gave thee this,
  When other days shall come;
  When she who had thine earliest kiss
  Sleeps in her narrow home.
Remember, 'twas a mother gave
The gift to one she'd die to save.

That mother sought a pledge of love,
  The holiest for her son,

And from the gifts of God above
   She chose a goodly one;
She chose for her beloved boy
   The source of light, and life, and joy.

She bade him keep the gift, that when
   The parting hour should come,
They might have hope to meet again,
   In an eternal home.
She said his faith in this would be
Sweet incense to her memory.

And should the scoffer, in his pride,
   Laugh that fond faith to scorn,
And bid him cast the pledge aside,
   That he from youth had borne,
She bade him pause, and ask his breast
If she or he had loved him best.

A parent's blessing on her son
   Goes with this holy thing:
The love that would retain the one
   Must to the other cling,
Remember! 'tis no idle toy:
A mother's gift! remember, boy.
                             —*Anonymous.*

THERE is not a boy on all the hills of New England, not a girl born in the filthiest cellar which disgraces a capital in Europe, and cries to God against the barbarism of modern civilization; not a boy or girl in all Christendom through; but their lot is made better by that great book.
                             —*Theodore Parker.*

THREE BIBLES.

THERE are three Bibles that are great powers in the formation of character. First and foremost comes the *Family Bible*. It transforms many a humble dwelling-place, many a cotter's abode, into a home. A castle may be a lodging-house, without being a home. A mansion may be an eating-house, a resting place, and not a home. A home is God's idea, an earthly approach to the heavenly reality—the Father's house. And to us it is incomplete without the Family Bible. I have known many a servant lass with her first earnings purchase this first piece of furniture for her new home to come. Others, more fortunate, have inherited the old Bible of their family. This is their heirloom; no family jewels, but the old book with their humble pedigree, names well known in their religious circle—a good stock, honest, true and pious. And the first day in that new home it is placed on the table after the morning meal by the young wife. A chapter is read, and then the knee is bent; and if a prayer is not forthcoming, as is often the case at first, under the burden of the responsibility of starting a new home, the young husband breaks down possibly, and sends aloft one of those unspoken prayers on the wings of a sigh, and they understand all of that up yonder. And so a new spot of this earth, a new home, is won for him whose right it is. And are not these the happiest homes in the land? Would it not be well to multiply such homes, full of trust, cleanliness, purity, contentment, industry and sobriety in our land? Are not these homes an improvement upon the dens of brutality, drunkenness and wife-kicking that we often read of—so often that it makes us all sad? Are not our efforts to multiply happy homes, such as I have described, in other lands worthy of all support? Why, the most cheerful people I have ever met live in these sneered at, pious homes! And the parents, who love their children so dearly, covet for them no higher blessing than that they, too, may one day dwell in peace in a similar home. And is not this a divine stamp upon our religion—that it makes cheerful, happy homes? Is it not a fact that all the religious systems of man's making render it necessary for him to mortify, to pain and injure himself physically, to make himself miserable? As if he thought God envied man his happiness! But this one exceptional religion goes forth everywhere with its glad tidings, inviting all, not to a prison, but to a feast; proclaiming not the laws of a tyrant, but a Father's way to happiness—a safe, sure way to fill the homes of the earth with cheerfulness, with happiness, by filling them with holiness.

Then comes another Bible that plays a most important part in the formation of the character of a Christian people—the *Sunday-school Teacher's Bible*—presented to him, as a rule, by his class, as a recognition of his faithfulness; and it is wonderful how every class will find out and recognize true faithfulness. There are hundreds of them throughout the world. Try to think of the influence of one Teacher's Bible. He has been in that class for forty years. Hundreds of young men have passed under the influence of his teaching; many have gone early, cheered by its light in tne dark valley. Others are now fighting a noble, brave, faithful battle, scattered everywhere throughout the earth, but all under the spell of the faithful words spoken to them by their old teacher, who had nothing to gain but their good. Think of his work in one short life; how he has moulded other lives, expecting no renown, no reward, not a penny, but the "well done," of the Master, and the heavenly welcome home of the faithful servant. He leaves, however, a name remembered by hundreds, and when buried in that silent God's Acre, one of his old disciples, returning from a distant land, inquires for his grave, and stands over it, weeping as naturally as April showers fall. "And it is here he is laid." He bedews his resting place with the tears of thankfulness. "When that illness came, how I remember his words; how they came back in the silence of my sick chamber, how they scattered my fears, and ever since how they have changed me! I owe this humble teacher literally my salvation, and I bless God for his life."

Next comes the *Mother's Bible:* it is placed in the box of every young man and maiden when they leave home, by a loving mother, who seems to say: "I cannot go with him— I cannot go with my boy, but may the God of this book— the God that went with Joseph to Egypt and Daniel to Babylon—may he watch over him?" And there it is hid, to be found when the box is opened away from home. I have it now on my study table. I have often felt that I should like a larger Bible in my study; but this one, with a reminder on the first page that it was a mother's wish that I should read it and believe it, has a charm about it, and, when opened, has its sweet and sad recollections that can never be regained by another Bible. Is it not a wonderful fact that the very first instructress of every one of us—a mother—every uncorrupted woman, is, by nature, susceptible of deep religious impressions? Hardly a young lad or a young lass leaves home in Wales but carries a Mother's Bible, with a few words written in a trembling hand on its white page. It is hardly readable, but to the eye of a child the trembling of the hand speaks of the anxiety of the heart, when he left home that morning. The book may be neglected for years occasionally, and thrown aside, and hid in the bottom of the box, but wait a few years, until the mother is gone, and her voice comes back to him now like a cry from another world: "Read it for your mother's sake," and the handwriting seems to bring up that old home with its tender memories, to subdue, to melt the prodigal.

—*E. Herbert Evans.*

THE OLD FAMILY BIBLE.

WHOEVER has travelled among the Scottish hills and dales cannot have failed to observe the scrupulous fidelity of the inhabitants to the old family Bible. A more honorable trait of character than this cannot be found; for all men, whether Christians or infidels, are prone to put reliance in those who make the Bible their companion, the well-thumbed pages of which show the confidence their owners repose in it.

A few years ago there dwelt in Ayrshire an ancient couple possessed of this world's gear sufficient to keep them independent from want or woe, and a canny daughter to bless their gray hair and tottering steps. A gallant of a farmer became enamored of the daughter, and she, nothing loth, consented to be his.

The match being every way worthy of her, the old folks gave their approval, and as they were desirous to see their child comfortably settled, the two were made one. In a few short years, the scythe of time cut down the old people, and they gave their bodies to the dust and their souls to the Creator.

·The young farmer, having heard much of the promised land beyond the sea, gathered together his property, and, selling such as was useless, packed up what was calculated to be of service to him at his new home. Some neighbors, having the same desire for adventure, sold off their homes and homesteads, -and, with the young couple, set sail for America.

Possessed of considerable property in the shape of money this company were not like the generality of emigrants, poor and friendless, but happy and full of hope of the future. The first thing done after the landing was the taking out of the old family heirloom, the Bible, and returning thanks and praise to Him who had guided the vessel to a safe haven.

The farmer's object in coming to this country was to purchase a farm and follow his occupation: he therefore spent but little time in the city at which he arrived; and as his fellow-passengers had previously determined on their destination, he bid them farewell, and, with a light heart, turned his face toward the setting sun. Indiana, at this time, was fast becoming settled, and, having heard of its cheap and fertile lands, he determined on settling within its borders.

He fixed on a farm on the banks of the Wabash, and having paid cash for one-half, gave a mortgage for the balance, payable in one year. Having stocked his farm, and rested from his labor, he patiently awaited the time when he might go forth to reap the harvest; but, alas! no ears of grain gladdened his heart or rewarded his toil. The fever of the country attacked him, and at the time when the fields are white with the fulness of the laborer's skill, death called him home, and left his disconsolate wife a widow, and his only child an orphan.

We leave this first sorrow and pass on to witness the struggles of the afflicted widow a year afterward. The time having arrived when the mortgage was to be paid, she borrowed the money off a neighbor who had been very attentive to her husband and herself. Hard and patiently did she toil to repay the sum at the promised time; but all would not do; fortune frowned, and she gave way to her accumulated troubles. Disheartened and distracted, she relinquished her farm and stock for less than she owed her neighbor, who, not satisfied with that, put an execution on her furniture.

On the Sabbath previous to the sale, she took courage and strengthening herself with the knowledge of having wronged no one, went to the temple of her heavenly Father, and with a heart filled with humanity and love, poured out her soul to him, "who turneth not away;" and having communed side by side with her neighbor, returned to her desolate home. Here her fortitude had liked to have forsaken her, but seeing the old "family Bible," she reverently put it to her lips, and sought for consolation in its pages. Slowly she perused its holy and inspiring verses, and gathered hope from its never-failing promises.

The day of sale having arrived, her few goods and chattles were, in due course, knocked off to the highest bidder. Unmoved she saw pass from her possession article after article, without a murmur, till the constable held up the old family Bible. This was too much. Tears flowed and gave silent utterance to a breaking heart. She begged the constable to spare her this memento of her revered and departed parents; and the humane man of the law would

THE BIBLE. 101

willingly have given it to her, but her inexorable creditor declared everything should be sold, as he was determined to have all that was due to him.

The book was, therefore, put up, and about being disposed of for a few shillings, when she suddenly snatched it, and declaring she would have some relic of those she loved, cut the slender thread that held the brown linen cover with the intention of retaining that. The cover fell into her hands, and with it two flat pieces of thin dirty paper.

Surprised at the circumstance, she examined them, and what was her joy and delight to find each to be a banknote, good for five hundred pounds, on the bank of England! On the back of one, in her mother's handwriting, were the following words: "*When sorrow overtakes you seek your Bible.*" And on the other, in her father's hand, "*Your Father's ears are never deaf.*"

The sale was immediately stopped, and the family Bible given to its faithful owner. The furniture sold was readily offered to her by those who had purchased it, and she gladly took it back. Having paid off her relentless creditor to the uttermost farthing, and rented a small house, she placed the balance of her money in such a way as to receive interest enough to keep her comfortable, and is now able to enjoy the precepts of the old family Bible without fear or molestation.—*Anonymous.*

STUDY the Holy Scriptures, especially the New Testament; therein are contained the words of eternal life. It has God for its author, salvation for its end, and truth without any mixture of error for its matter.

—*John Locke.*

THE PICTURE BIBLE.

THOU folio dusk and olden,
   My friend in early days,
When loving hands oft opened
   Thy secrets to my gaze.
Oft o'er thy pictures bending,
   Delighted I would stand,
My sports forgot while dreaming
   About the Orient land.

Thou openest the portals
   Of distant zones to me;
In thee, as in a mirror,
   Their glittering stores I see.
Thanks, for through thee are glimpses
   Of strange, far regions sent,
Of camels, palms and deserts,
   The shepherd and his tent.

More near to view thou bringest
   The hero and the sage,
By gifted seers depicted
   Upon thy priceless page;
The fair and bride-like maidens,
   As well their words portray.
Of each a living semblance
   Thy figured leaves display.

The patriarchal ages,
   What simple times were they!
When men on every journey
   Met angels by the way.

THE BIBLE.

Their wells and herds of cattle,
  How often have I seen,
While on thy pages gazing,
  With quiet thoughtful mien.

Again thou seemest, as lying
  Upon the stool of yore,
While I, intently musing,
  Upon thy pages pore,
As if the old impressions,
  So oft with rapture viewed,
In fresh and brilliant colors
  Before me stood renewed.

As if, more bright than ever,
  Again before me placed,
I saw the quaint devices
  Around thy borders traced;
Branches and fruit combining,
  Round every picture wrought,
Each to some picture suited,
  And all with meaning fraught.

As if in days departed,
  My eager steps I bent,
To ask my gentle mother
  What every picture meant;
As if some song or story,
  I learned of each to tell,
While beaming mildly on us,
  My father's glances fell.

Oh, time now fled forever!
  Thou seemest a tale gone by;
The picture Bible's treasures,
  The bright believing eye,

The glad delighted parents,
The calm contented mien,
The joy and mirth of boyhood,
All, all, alas! have been.
—*Ferdinand Freiligrath.*

THE LEADERSHIP OF THE BIBLE.

THE word of God has exhibited the power of continuous leadership. This is perhaps the severest, most exacting test to which it can be exposed; none of the ethnic religions have sustained it with success. China has been stagnant for ages. India was essentially what it is to-day 2,500 years ago; the power of its religious literature is expended. Books are mortal; the best of them live their briefer or longer day and then perish. Galen was an authority in medicine for 1,300 years, but his works are now antiquarian rubbish. Our school-children have more knowledge of physics than can be found in Opus Majus of the great Roger Bacon. Lavoisier destroyed the chemistry of Bagdad, and Lavoisier himself has perished by the hand of his successors. The speculations of Plato and Aristotle, with all their wealth of intellect, are comparatively worthless. The immortal books, as we call them, seize upon and expound the *unprogressive* side of humanity. There are unprogressive elements in our life, elements the same yesterday, to-day, and forever. Love, fear, hate, revenge—the whole group and array of the passions—are not different in the earliest and in the latest man. Homeric wrath before the walls of Troy was quite what wrath is in the streets of our own city. The literature portraying with a touch of genius qualities that all races possess in common—qualities that have the perpetuity of the spring, of the sunset, remaining the same year by year without progression or decay—will live; but the book which aspires to lead the *growth* of mankind from first to last, to pilot its indefinite expansion, to fling off its outworn old and welcome its dawning new, has attempted the most intractable enterprises known on earth. Even here we maintain the word has succeeded, and is succeeding.

No one will claim that anything less than power of the amplest magnitude and of the happiest adaptation could prosper in this field. The tremendous mental force in the book seems to be fully attested by the vast intellectual energy, friendly and hostile, it has roused. Mind stimulates mind, thought provokes thought. There is in the cause a vitality equal to all the developments in the effect. A catalogue of the books called into existence by the Scriptures, in the line of direct defence or direct attack, would probably fill 5,000 quarto pages.

This power of the word has left its mark in all the great departments of civilization. It has inspired the grandest creations of the brush—Raphael's Madonna in the Dresden Gallery, and the frescoes of Michael Angelo in the Sistine Chapel. It has inspired the noblest musical compositions, like Handel's Messiah, or Hayden's Creation, or Mendelssohn's Elijah. It was the pioneer in giving form to our English prose literature. A pathetic interest clings to the story.

On the last day of Baeda's life he gathered his pupils about him that his translation of John's Gospel might proceed. As the old man continued to dictate, his increasing weakness became noticeable. "There is still a chapter wanting," said Wilberch, the amanuensis, "and it is hard for thee to question thyself." "It is easily done," replied Baeda, "take thy pen and write quickly." They wrote on until nightfall. "There is one sentence unwritten, dear master." "Write it quickly," answered the dying scholar. "It is now finished." "Thou sayest true; all is finished now." They carried him to his accustomed place of prayer; he sang the "Glory of God," and died.

"It is to that scene," says Stopford Brooke, "that English prose looks back as its sacred source." The power, the creative impulse of the word in our literature, from Baeda to the present hour, can scarcely be overestimated. The late Henry Rogers critically examined the writings of some of its acknowledged masters to determine, if possible, their obligations to the Bible for felicities of thought and expression. He remarks the fact that not less than three works have been written to trace its presence in Shakespeare. In Bacon's Essays "one is perpetually struck," he writes, "with the felicity with which passages of Scripture are introduced." He found a single contribution from this source "in the matchless energy of Milton's diction." Of Carlyle's French Revolution he says, "In describing the scenes of his tremendous 'Triology of Tragedies,' fragments of Scripture language come unbidden to his pen as the best and most forcible he can employ."

However an energy working on this gigantic scale, reaching forth into literature and the fine arts, of which we have given only hasty hints, may astonish us, yet that energy which descends into the abyss of moral life, at home among the degradations of the past and among the higher civilizations of the present, swaying, tutoring, purifying, Christianizing all alike, seems to me something still more wonderful. This is so familiar—this work of conversion in all the years and in all the races—that we miss its infinite significance. The Bible has existed, at least in fragments, for thirty centuries. It adjusted itself to the early period, brought out the possible good in that life, revealed what of God and of truth, of duty and of purity, could be grasped in that era. It has prosecuted the same work during all the lapse of the widening years. For the citizens of the three millenniums it has been light and hope, peace and salvation. And when to-day, with all our experience and progress, we raise inquiries after the ideal life, even Renan is quick to answer: "Whatever may be the surprises of the future, Jesus will never be surpassed!"

It should not be forgotten that this amazing accumulation of power in the Word, with its unparalleled variety, flexibility and continuity, was secured under seemingly impossible conditions. It was sixteen hundred years in composition. Forty different authors were engaged upon it, representing every variety of condition and culture—writing without concert, without design of composing a sacred book —flinging off *occasional* narratives, biographies, poems, or letters, that were designed only for local purposes. But when these fugitive, and in part anonymous, works are gathered into a volume they are found to be the world book. It was as if snatches of song, sung in every part of the globe, when brought together should weave themselves into the harmonies of some grand oratorio. We seem to be driven for an explanation of the power of the Word, by the sheer necessities of the case, to the theory of a divine inspiration.—*L. W. Spring.*

INFLUENCE OF THE BIBLE ON MODERN AUTHORS.

DANTE, we have seen, has snatched fire from the Hebrew Sun, to light up his own deep sunk Cyclopean hearth. Tasso's great poem is "Jerusalem Delivered," and the style, as well as the subject, shows the influence of Scripture upon a feebler and more artificial spirit than Dante's. Spencer has been called by Southey a "high priest;" and his "Faery Queen," in its pure moral tone, nothing lessened by its childlike *naivete* and plain spoken descriptions, as well as in its gorgeous allegory, betrays the diligent student of the "Song," the Parables and the Prophets. Giles and Phineas Fletcher—the one in his "Temptation and Victory of Christ," and the other in his "Purple Island"—are more deeply indebted to the Scriptures; their subjects are more distinctly sacred, and their piety more fervid than Spencer's; their master, George Herbert, was called by excellence " holy," and his " Temple " proclaims him a poet "after God's own heart;" it is cool, chaste and still, as the Temple of Jerusalem on the evening after the buyers and sellers were expelled. The genius, rugged and grand, of Dr. Donne, and that of Quarles, so quaint and whimsical, and that of Couley, so subtile and cultured, were all sanctified. Of Milton, what need we say? His poems deserve, much more than Wisdom or Ecclesiasticus, to be bound up between the two Testaments. Nor let us omit a sacred poem to which he was somewhat indebted, "The Weeks and Works of Du Bartas," a marvellous medley of childish weakness and manly strength, with more seed-poetry in it than any poem except "Festus"—the chaos of a hundred poetic worlds. Bunyan seems to have read scarcely a book but the Bible; when he quotes it, it is by chapters at a time, and he has nearly quoted it all. He seems to think and dream, as well as speak and write, in Scripture language. Scripture imagery serves him for fancy —for, with the most vivid of imaginations, fancy he has none—and Scripture words for eloquence, for though his invention be Shakespearian, his language is bare and bald. He alone could have counterfeited a continuation of the Bible. He was not the modern Isaiah nor Jeremiah, for he had no lofty eloquence; and his pathos was wild and terrible rather than soft or womanly—the "man in the cage" is his saddest picture; but he was the modern Ezekiel in his vehement simplicity, his burning zeal, and the almost diseased objectiveness of his genius. Macaulay says there were in that age but two men of original genius—the one wrote the "Paradise Lost," and the other the "Pilgrim's Progress;" and he might have added that both seemed incarnations of the spirit of Hebrew poetry, and that the tinker had more of it than the elaborate poet. The age of Elisha and Amos seemed to have rolled round, when from among the basest of the people sprung up suddenly this brave man, like the figure of his own Pilgrim, and cried out to the Recorder of immortal names, "Set mine down," and the song was straightway raised over him—

"Come in, come in,
Eternal glory thou shalt win."

Macaulay, however, here is wrong, and has sacrificed, as not infrequently is his manner, the truth on the sharp prong of an antithesis. There were in that age men of original genius besides Milton and Bunyan, and almost all of them had baptized it at "Siloa's brook, which flowed hard by the oracle of God." Cromwell's sword was a "right Jerusalem blade." Hobbes himself had studied Scripture, and borrowed from it the names of his books "Behemoth" and "Leviathan." If a Goliath of Gath, he came at least from the borders of the land of promise. Jeremy Taylor soared and sang like Isaiah. John Scott copied the severe sententiousness and unshrinking moral anatomy of James, and had besides touches of sublimity, reminding you of the loftier of the minor prophets. Barrow reasoned as if he had sat, a younger disciple, at the feet of Paul's master, Gamaliel. John Howe rose to calm Platonic heights, less through the force of Plato's attraction than that of the beloved disciple. And Richard Baxter caught, carried into his pulpit, and sustained even at his solitary desk, the old fury of pure and passionate zeal for God, hatred at sin, and love to mankind, which shook the body of Jeremiah, and flamed around the head and beard, and shaggy raiment of the Baptist.

In the century that succeeded—even in the "godless eighteenth century"—we find numerous traces of the power of the Bible poetry. The allegories, and all the other serious papers of Addison, are tinged with its spirit. He loves not so much its wilder and higher strains; he gets giddy on the top of Lebanon, the valley of dry bones he treads with timid steps, and his look cast up toward the "terrible crystal," is rather of fright than of admiration. Well able to appreciate the "pleasures," he shrinks from those tingling "pains" of imagination. Nor has he much sympathy with that all absorbing earnestness which surrounded the prophets. But the lovelier, softer, simpler and more pensive parts of the Bible are very dear to the gentle

"Spectator." The "Song" throws him into a dim and languishing ecstasy. The stories of Joseph and of Ruth are the models of his exquisite simplicity, and the 8th and 104th Psalms of his quiet and timorous grandeur. We hear of Addison "hinting a fault, and hesitating dislike;" but, more truly, he hints a beauty, and stammers out love. He says himself the finest thing, and then blushes, as if detected in a crime. Or he praises an obvious and colossal merit in another, and if he has done it above his breath, he "starts at the sound himself has made." His encomiums are the evening whispers of lovers—low, sweet, and trembling. Thus timidly has he panegyrized the beauties of the Bible; but his graceful imitations, and particularly his vision of Mirza (was he ashamed of it, too, and therefore left it a fragment?), so Scriptural in its spirit, style, and nameless, unconscious charm, show how deeply they had engraved themselves upon his heart.

Even Pope, the most artificial of true poets, has found "his own" in Scripture poetry. Isaiah's dark, billowy forests have little beauty in his eye; but he has collected the flowers which grow beneath, and woven them into that lovely garland, the "Messiah." In his hand, Homer the sublime becomes Homer the brilliant, and Isaiah the majestic becomes Isaiah the soft and elegant. But, as Warton remarks, Pope's "Messiah" owes its superiority to Virgil's "Pollis" entirely to the Hebrew poets. Young has borrowed little from them, or from any one else; he is the most English original poet of the eighteenth century; his poetry comes from a fierce fissure in his own heart; still, the torch by which he lights himself through the "Night" of his "Thoughts" has been kindled at the New Testament; and his "Last Day," and his "Paraphrase on Job," are additional proofs of the ascendency of the Hebrew genius over his own. Thomson's Hymn is avowedly in imitation of the later Psalms; and his mind, in its sluggish magnificence and lavish ornaments, is distinctly Oriental. Every page of the "Seasons" shows an imagination early influenced by the breadth, fervor, and magniloquence of prophetic song. Johnson, too, in his "Rasselas," "Rambler" and "Idler," is often highly Oriental, and has caught, if not the inmost spirit, at least the outer roll and volume of the style of the prophets. Burke, in his "Regicide Peace," approaches them far more closely, and exhibits their spirit as well as style, their fiery earnestness, their abruptness, their impatience, their profusion of metaphor, their "doing well to be angry, even unto death," and the contortions by which they were delivered of their message, as of a demon. How he snatches up their words, like the fallen thunderbolts of the Titan war, to heave them at his and their foes! No marvel that the cold-blooded eighteenth century thought him mad. Burns admired his Bible better than he ever cared to acknowledge, and during his last illness, at the Brow, was often seen with it in his hands. Some of the finest passages in both his prose and verse are colored by Scripture, and leave on us the impression that, had he looked at it more through his own naked eagle-eye, and less through the false media of systems and commentaries and critics, he had felt it to be the most humane, the most liberal, the least aristocratic, the most loving, as well as the sublimest and the one divine book in the world. As it was, that dislike to it natural to all who disobey its moral precepts, was aggravated in him by the wretchedly cold critical circles among whom he fell, who in their hearts preferred Racine's "Athalie" to the Lamentations, and "Douglas" to Job. Hence he praises Scripture with something like misgiving, and speaks of the *pompous* language of the Hebrew bards, an epithet which he means partly in praise, but partly also in blame, and applies to the expression, as simple as it is sublime, "Who walketh on the wings of the wind."

Cowper, the most timid of men, was, so far as *moral* courage went, the most daring of poets. He was an oracle, hid not in an oak, but in an aspen. His courage, indeed, sometimes seems the courage of despair. Hopeless of heaven, he fears nothing on earth. "How can I fear," says Prometheus, "who am never to die?" How can I fear, says poor, unhappy Cowper, who shall never be saved? And in nothing do we see this boldness more exemplified than in his "Bibliolatry." Grant that Bibliolatry it was; it was the extreme of an infinitely worse extreme. In an age when religion was derided, when to quote the Bible was counted eccentric folly, when Lowth was writing books to prove the prophets "elegants," a nervous hypochondriac ventured to prefer them by infinitude to all other writers, defended their every letter, drank into their sternest spirit, and poured out strains which, if not in loftiness or richness, yet in truth, energy, earnestness and solemn pathos, seem omitted or mislaid "burdens of the Lord." Blessings on this noble "Castaway," rising momentarily o'er the moonlit surge, which he dreamed ready to be his grave, and shouting at once words of praise to that luminary which was never to rescue him, and words of warning to those approaching the same fearful waters.

In the nineteenth century all our great British authors have more or less imbibed the fire from the Hebrew fountains. There had been, in the meantime, a reaction in the favor of them, as well as of other things "old." For fifty years the

Bible, like its author, had been exposed on a cross to public ignominy; gigantic apes, like Voltaire, chattering at it; men of genius turned, by some Circean spell, into swine, like Mirabeau and Paine, casting filth against it; demoniacs, whom it had half rescued and half inspired, like Rousseau, making mouths in its face till, as darkness blotted out the heaven above and an earthquake shook Europe around, and all things seemed rushing into ruin, men began to feel, as they did on Calvary, that this was all for *Christ's sake;* and they trembled; and what their brethren there could not or did not—they stopped ere it was too late. The hierophants of the sacrilege, indeed, were dead or hopelessly hardened, but their followers paused in time, and the mind of the civilized world was shaken back into an attitude of respect, if not of belief in the Book of Jesus.

This reaction was for a season complete. No poetry, no fiction, no belles-lettres, no philosophy was borne with unless it professed homage to Christianity. And even after, through the influence of the "Edinburgh Review" and other causes, there was a partial revival of skeptical spirit, it never ventured on such daring excesses again. It bowed before the Bible, although it was sometimes with the bow of a polite assassin, who had studied murder and manner both in the south.

Nay, more, Scripture poetry began to be used as a model more extensively than ever heretofore, alike by those who believed and those who disbelieved its Supreme authority. Wordsworth, Coleridge and Southey we name first, because they never lost faith in it as a word, or admiration of it as a poem, and hence its language and its element seem more natural to them than to others. Campbell was attracted to it originally by his exquisite poetical taste. He came forth to see the "Rainbow," like some of the world's "gray fathers," because it was beautiful; but ultimately, we rejoice to know, he felt it to be the "rainbow of the covenant." He grew up to the measure and the stature of his own poetry. Moore, like Pope, has been fascinated by its flowers; and we find him now imitating the airy gorgeousness of the "Song of Songs," and now the diamond-pointed keenness of the Book of Ecclesiastes. Scott, as a writer, knew the force of Scripture diction; as a man, the hold of Scripture truth upon the Scottish heart; as a poet, the unique inspiration which flowed from the Rock of Ages; and has, in his works, made a masterly use of all this varied knowledge. Rebecca might have been the sister of Solomon's spouse. Her prose speeches rise as the sound of cymbals, and her "Hymn" is immortal as a psalm of David. David Deans is only a little lower than the patriarchs, and time would fail us to enumerate the passages in his better tales which, approaching near the line of high excellence, are carried beyond it by the dexterous and sudden use of "thoughts that breathe," or "words that burn," from the Book of God. Byron, Godwin, Shelley, and Hazlitt, even, are deeply indebted to the Bible. Byron, in painting "dark bosoms," has often availed himself of the language of that book, which is a discerner of the thoughts and intents of the heart. Many of his finest poems are just expansions of that strong line he has borrowed from it—

"The worm that cannot sleep, and never dies."

His "Hebrew Melodies" have sucked out their sweetness from the Psalms; and "Cain," his noblest production, employs against God the power it has derived from his Book. Godwin was originally a preacher, and his high didactic tone, his measured and solemn march, as well as many images and many quotations, especially in "St. Leon" and "Mandeville," show that the influence of his early studies was permanent. When Shelley was drowned, it was rumored that he had a copy of the Bible next his heart; "and," says Byron," it would have been no wonder, for he was a great admirer of it as a composition." The rumor was not literally correct, but was so mythically. It is clear to us that Shelley was far advanced on his way to Christianity ere he died, and was learning not only to love the Bible as a composition, but to appreciate its unearthly principles—that disinterested heroism especially which characterizes Christ and his Apostles. Indeed he was constituted rather to sympathize with certain parts of its morale, than with the simple and terse style of its writing. It was the more mysterious and imaginative portion of it which he seems principally to have admired, and which excited the rash emulation of his genius, when he projected a variation of "Job." Hazlitt's allusions to Scripture are incessant, and are to us the most interesting passages in his works. He was a clergyman's son, and in youth the Bible had planted stings in his bosom which none of his after errors, in thought or life, were able to pluck out. "Heaven lay about him in his infancy," and his comparison of the Bible with Homer, and his picture of the effects of its translation into English, show that the earnest though erring man *never* altogether saw its glory.

"Die away,
And fade into the light of common day."

This is one of the features in Hazlitt's writings which exalt them above Lord Jeffrey's. Scotchman though he was, we do not recollect one eloquent or sincere-seeming sentence from his pen about the beauties of the Bible.

Such writers as Sheridan, Rogers, Alison, Dugal Stewart, Lord Erskine, William Tennant, Mrs. Hemans, and a hundred others are suffocated in flowers; but not a word, during all his long career, from the autocrat of criticism about Moses, Isaiah, Job, or John. To have praised their poetry might have seemed to sanction their higher pretensions, and might; too, have reflected indirect credit upon that school of fervid poets who were sittting at the feet of Jewish men, as well as of Cumberland Mountains. Need we name, finally, Chalmers and Irving—those combinations of the prophet of the old and the preacher of the new economy?

Our living writers have, in general, shown a sympathy with the Hebrew genius. We speak not merely of clergymen, whose verdict might by some be called interested, and whose enthusiasm might unjustly be thought put on with their cloaks. And yet we must refer to Millman's "Fall of Jerusalem," and to Croley's magnificent "Salathiel." Keble, too, and French, Kingsley, William Anderson, are a few out of many names of men who, while preaching the Bible doctrine, have not forgotten its literary glories, as subjects of earnest imitation and praise. But the Levites outnumber and outshine the priests in their service to the bards of the Bible. Isaac Taylor's gorgeous figures are elaborately copied from those of Scripture, although they sometimes, in comparison with them, remind you of that root of which Milton speaks—

> "The leaf was darkish, and had prickles in it,
> But in another country, as he said,
> Bore a bright golden flower, but *not in this soil.*"

The eastern spirit is in them; they want only the eastern day. Sir James Stephen has less both of the spirit and the genuine color, ardent as his love of the Hebrew is. Macaulay quotes Scripture, as Burdett, in Parliament, was wont to quote Shakspeare—always with triumphant rhetorical effect, and seems once, at least, to have really loved its literature. Professor Wilson approaches more closely than any modern since Burke, to that wild prophetic movement of style and manner which the bards of Israel exhibit—nay, more nearly than even Burke, since, with Wilson, it is a perpetual afflatus: he is like the he-goat in Daniel, who came from the West, and touched not the ground; his "Tale of Expiation," for instance, is a current of fire. Thomas Carlyle concentrates a fury, enhanced by the same literary influences, into deeper, straiter, more molten and terrible torrents. Thomas Aird has caught the graver, calmer, and more epic character of the Historical Books, especially in his "Nebuchadnezzar," which none but one deep in Daniel could have written. From another poem of his, entitled "Herodion and Azala," we quote two etchings of prophets:

"Winged with prophetic ecstacies, behold
The Son of Amos, beautifully bold,
Borne like the scythed wing of the eagle proud,
That shears the winds, and climbs the storied cloud
Aloft sublime! And through the crystalline,
Glories upon his lighted head doth shine.
. . . .
Behold! behold, uplifted through the air,
The swift Ezekiel, by his lock of hair!
Near burned the Appearance, undefinedly dread,
Whose hand put forth, upraised him by the head.
Within its fierce reflection, cast abroad,
The Prophet's forehead like a furnace glowed.
From terror half, half from his vehement mind,
His lurid hair impetuous streamed behind."

From a hint or two in Scripture, he has built up his vision of hell, in the "Devil's Dream upon Mount Acksbeck," a vision mysterious, fiery, and yet distinct, definite and fixed, as a frosted minster shining in the moonlight. But in his "Demoniac," he absolutely pierces into the past world of Palestine, and brings it up with all its throbbing life and thaumaturgic energies, its earth quaking below the footsteps, and its sky darkening above the death of the Son of God.

Of the rising poets of the day "two will we mention dearer than the rest;" dearer, too, in part, because they have sought their inspiration at its deepest source—Bailey, of " Festus," and Yendys, of " The Roman." This is not the place to dilate on their poetical merits. We point to them now, because, in an age when so many young men and young poets are forsaking belief in the oracular and divine inspiration of the Bible, they have rallied around the old shrine, have expressed their trust in that old and blessed hope of the Gospel, and may be hailed as morning stars, prognosticating the rising of a new "day of the Lord." May their light, already brilliant and far seen, shine "more and more" not only unto its own, but into the world's "perfect day."

—*George Gilfillan.*

TEST THE INFLUENCE OF SCRIPTURE.

IN order to try to form some conception of the influence of the Scriptures upon the minds of the millions who have read them, let our readers ask each himself the question, What have I gained from their perusal? and if he has read them for himself, and with an ordinary degree of intelligence, there must arise before his memory a "great multitude which no man can number," of lofty conceptions of God—

of glimpses into human nature—of thoughts "lying too deep for tears;" of pictures, still or stormy, passing from that age to the canvas of imagination to remain forever; of emotions, causing the heart to vibrate with a strange joy, "which one may recognize in more exalted stages of his being;" of inspiration, raising for a season the reader to the level of his author—and of perpetual whispered impressions, "this is the highest thought and language I ever encountered: I am standing on the pinnacle of literature." And then, besides, he will remember how often he returned to this volume, and found the charm remaining, and the fire still burning, and the fountain of thought and feeling (thought suggestive, feeling creative) still flowing—how every sentence was found a text, and how many texts resembled deep and deepening eyes: "orb within orb, deeper than sleep or death"—how each new perusal showed firmaments, rising in the book, as in the night sky, till at last he fell on his knees, and forgetting to read, began to wonder and adore; how, after this trance was over, he took up the book again, and found that it was not only a telescope to show him things above, but also a microscope to show him things below and a mirror to reflect his own heart, and a magic grace to bring the future near, and how he was compelled to exclaim: "How dreadful is this book; it is none other than the Book of God; it is the gate of heaven;" multiply this, the experience of one, by an unknown number of millions, and you have the answer to the question as to the direct intellectual influence of the Scriptures upon those who have really read them.—*George Gilfillan.*

I KNOW the Bible is inspired, because it finds me at greater depth of my being than any other book.—*Coleridge.*

OUT OF DARKNESS INTO LIGHT.

The wages of sin is death; but the gift of God is eternal life through Jesus Christ our Lord. ROM. 6 : 23.

THE BIBLE IN THE SCHOOL AND COLLEGE.

FROM all that has been said in favor of the Bible, as a classic, and as a book adapted to childhood and youth, it follows as a legitimate inference of great practical importance that it ought, invariably, to form a part of the regular course of instruction in all our schools and colleges. In every system of classical, collegiate education it ought to be studied in its original tongues, just as our youth study the Greek and Latin authors. We see no reason why, as models of beauty, or as exercises of mental culture, the language and literature of Rome or of Athens should be preferred to that of Jerusalem. On the single ground of taste and genius, we believe that Moses and the Prophets, in their venerable Hebrew, are fully equal to Homer and Virgil, Herodotus and Livy. And, accordingly, an acquaintance with them in the original, ought to be regarded as an essential part of a liberal, accomplished, collegiate education.

But the Bible has much wider claims than these. Few, comparatively, can ever study it in its original tongues. Every man, every child at school may study it in English. And it is chiefly as an English classic, the best and most important in our language, that we advocate its claims. No school ought to be found without the Bible. No course of education ought to be considered complete without it. No individual ought to be regarded as adequately educated without a knowledge of it. If there is any one book which deserves to be held as indispensable in every school, and in every course of education, it is the Bible. As an English classic, and a text-book of daily instruction, it ought to hold the same foremost place in all our schools which we know a part of it did hold as a Hebrew classic, and that by Divine commandment, in all the schools of the Jews for thousands of years; and which, indeed, it does still hold amongst the remnants of the chosen people throughout the world.

It is in no spirit of dogmatism that we set up this claim for the Bible as a book of education at school. Argument could be given, if any argument were needed except the bare statement of the case. Does it require any argument to show that the book which has caused all our learning, as well as our religion, to differ from that of the Mohammedans, the ancient Pagans, and the modern heathen nations, ought to be read in our schools? that the book which tells us all we know with certainty about God and a future state, and gives us the highest sanctions we have for our morality, our laws, our institutions of marriage, the family and the state, ought to be read and studied at school? Surely, if argument is to be brought, it would requite much argument to show that such a book ought not to be studied there. If ancient history ought to be studied at school, then ought the Bible to be studied, as containing the most ancient, most important, and most interesting history in the world. If the lives of illustrious men ought to be read, then ought this book to be read, with its biography of illustrious names extending from Adam to Jesus Christ. If our youth may read at school the great masters of eloquence and poesy, then may they read the Bible there, as containing the sublimest strains of the one and the most finished specimens of the other which our race has ever produced. If the elements of all moral and mental science, the principles of virtue and political wisdom may be taught at school, then may the

Bible be taught, for it is the fountain whence all these have flowed. If religion itself ought to be taught at school as a legitimate part, and by far the most important part of all education, then ought the Bible to be taught, as being the book of our common Christianity, the only true and Divine revelation in the world.

But, independently of this last consideration, our plea for the Bible as a school-book still stands good. You tell us you do not receive the Bible as the book of your religion; or, you do not wish your child to learn Christianity at school; or, that this is a part of instruction which you reserve for yourself. Well, be it so. And what then? Our claim for the Bible as a school-book is still untouched. If you deny the inspiration of God, you cannot deny the inspiration of genius which breathes forth on every page. If you choose to ignore all its evidences as a Divine revelation, you cannot ignore its history, and biography, and morality, and learning, its eloquence and poetry, without at the same time forfeiting your own claim to be a man of taste, capable of appreciating the sublime and beautiful. If unwilling to have the religion of the Bible taught at school, what objection can you have to its learning and morality? You cannot wish to exclude from our schools the most effective and beneficial history, biography, literature and philosophy which the world has ever produced.

If it could be proved, by an absolute demonstration, that the religion of the Bible is a cunningly devised fable, so that Christianity should henceforth take its place with the mythology of Greece and Rome as an exploded system, still it would remain true as a historical fact, and, indeed, the most remarkable fact on that assumption in the world's history, that this book has been more widely known and received by the nations of the earth, has exerted a more beneficial and enduring influence upon them than any other book, whether of facts or of mythologies. And, therefore, both for what it contains itself and for what it has done in the world, even as a book of mythology, it would be entitled to take rank, in our schools and colleges, above Homer or Hesiod, Virgil or Ovid. True or false, then, inspired or uninspired, Divine or human, the Bible deserves to be studied at school, so long as anything is studied; so long as men have any interest in knowing, and in causing their children to know, what has been said and done in this world of ours in past ages. And we must be permitted here to say, that the child in this Christian land who is permitted to go through all the elegant, fashionable schools of learning and complete his education without even a reading of the Bible, is chargeable with a degree of ignorance which, if the book were only human, would be a disgrace to him, and which, if it be Divine, is both a disgrace and an incalculable injury.

—*Le Roy J. Halsey, D. D.*

THE BIBLE THE BEST CLASSIC.

TO the parent I would say, your offspring are the children of God; on you they depend for education; God has commanded you to train them betimes to know and serve, to love and enjoy him; the paths of business are equally the paths of temptation and duty; religion belongs to every thought, and word, and deed; as, then, the Bible is the only standard of duty, why do you not interweave it with the whole scheme of secular education?

To the instructor, I would say, you stand in the place of parent and guardian; their duties are unquestionably yours; to you is transferred not only the obligation to teach, but more especially the selection of appropriate books and the regulation of the order and proportion of studies. What parent or guardian has ever interfered with your plans? how entirely, and with what a cordial confidence, have they appointed you to think, to consult, to decide, to act for them? why, then, have you excluded the Bible of those very parents and guardians from the whole scheme for the education of their children and wards?

To the patriot, I would say, can you doubt that to the Bible your country owes not only her religious liberty and her entire moral condition, but to a great extent her civil and political rights, her science, literature and arts? The Bible is emphatically the book of truth and knowledge, of freedom and happiness to your country. Children you regard as public property; and you know that they will honor and serve their country best, the more they are instructed in the Scriptures, and imbued with their spirit. Why, then, do you withhold the full benefit of those sacred oracles, by thus proscribing them in every scheme of education?

To the Christian, I would say, you admit the Divinity of the Scriptures, their absolute authority, and inestimable worth; you concede that they are the common property of all; that even children may profit by them, since they are so simple and plain; that the wayfaring man, though a fool, shall not err therein; why, then, do you not give them this lamp of life, as well as the lamp of knowledge to guide them daily, with harmonious beams, in their preparation for the inseparable duties and business of life?

To the scholar, I would say, we offer you a more ancient,

venerable, noble classic than is to be found in the whole compass of Grecian and Roman literature.—*Grimke.*

UNDERSTANDING THE BIBLE.

A LADY came to me in the inquiry room and said: "There are so many things in the Bible I cannot understand." No doubt about that; God says the carnal man cannot understand spiritual things, and the Bible is a spiritual book. How *can* the unregenerate heart understand the Bible? Well, you say, if it is a sealed book, how am I going to be saved? well, when God put salvation before the world, he put *that* very plain.

The Word of God may be darkened to the natural man, but the way of salvation is written so plain that the little child of six years old can understand it if she will. Take this passage, and see if you do not understand it: "The Spirit and the Bride say, Come; And let him that heareth say, Come; And let him that is athirst, Come." Are not many of you thirsty? God says, Come. "And whosoever will, let him take the water of life freely."

Then you know what it is to take a gift? God puts salvation before you as a gift: "He came unto his own and his own received him not; but as many as received him, to them gave he power to become the sons of God." You can understand that? "Believe on the Lord Jesus Christ, and thou shalt be saved." You know what it is to believe? At any rate you know what it is to trust, to commit your soul to the Lord Jesus Christ—that is all. There are dark and mysterious things in the Bible now, but when you begin to trust Christ, your eyes will be opened, and the Bible will be a new Book to you. Many things that are dark and mysterious to-day, to-morrow will have a new beauty. It will become the Book of books to you. To-day Christ may be a root out of a dry ground, without form or comeliness; but he will become to you the chiefest among ten thousand, the altogether lovely, the bright and the morning star; if you take him as your Saviour, then you will understand the Bible.

No book in the world has been so misjudged as the Bible. Men judge it without reading it. Or perhaps they read a bit here and a bit there, and then close it, saying: "It is so dark and mysterious!" You take a book now-a-days and read it: "Well," you say, "I have only read it through once, not very carefully, and I should not like to give an opinion;" yet people take up God's book, read a few pages, and condemn the whole of it. Of all the skeptics and infidels I have ever met speaking against the Bible, I have never met one who read it through. There may be such men, but I have never met them. It is simply an excuse. There is no man living who will stand up before God and say that the Bible kept him out of the kingdom.

It is the devil's work, trying to make us believe it is not true, and that it is dark and mysterious. The only way to overcome the enemy of souls is by the written Word of God. He knows that, and so tries to make men disbelieve it. As soon as a man is a true believer in the Word of God, he is a conqueror over Satan. Young man! the Bible is true; what have these infidels to give you in its place? What has made England, but the open Bible?

Every nation that exalteth the Word of God is exalted, and every nation that casteth it down is cast down. Oh! let us cling close to the Bible. Of course we shall not understand it all at once. But men are not to condemn it on that account. Suppose I should send my little boy, five years old, to school to-morrow morning, and when he came home in the afternoon I say to him, "Willie, can you read? can you write? can you spell? do you understand all about Algebra, Geometry, Hebrew, Latin and Greek?" "Why, papa," the little fellow would say, "how funny you talk! I have been all day trying to learn the A, B, C." Well, suppose I should reply, "If you have not finished your education, you need not go any more." What would you say? Why, you would say I had gone mad.

There would be just about as much reason in that, as in the way that people talk about the Bible. My friends, the men who have studied the Bible for fifty years; the wise men and the scholars, the great theologians, have never got down to the depths of it. There are truths there that the Church of God has been searching out for the last eighteen hundred years; but no man has fathomed the depths of that ever living stream.—*D. L. Moody.*

A KNOWLEDGE OF THE BIBLE A REMEDY FOR DOUBTS.

H! my brethren, if any of us have any doubts about any part of the Bible, or if any of us be eager to answer any doubts in others, first and before all things learn the mind and spirit of Christ, as set forth in the four Gospels.

In that mind and spirit lies the true solution of all our disputes about the nature of the Infinite. In that mind and spirit lies the true key to all the mysteries of his life and death; the meaning of his miracles, the salt of his words, the virtue of his sacrifice, the power of his resurrection.

It was a true feeling which gave to our religion the name of that one single pre-eminent portion of the Sacred volume—the Gospel. It was a true feeling which led the Fathers to take as the subject of the creeds the one doctrine which, above all others, belongs to the Gospels, namely: the Incarnation.—*Arthur Penrhyn Stanley.*

VALUE OF THE BIBLE.

O LADY fair, these silks of mine are beautiful and rare—
The richest web of the Indian loom, which beauty's queen might wear;
And my pearls are pure as thy own fair neck, with whose radiant light they vie;
I have brought them with me a weary way—will my gentle lady buy?

And my lady smiled on the worn old man, through the dark and clustering curls
Which veiled her brow as she bent to view his silks and glittering pearls;
And she placed their price in the old man's hand, and lightly turned away;
But she paused at the wanderer's earnest call—My gentle lady, stay!

O lady fair, I have yet a gem which a purer lustre flings
Than the diamond flash of the jewelled crown on the lofty brow of kings—

A wonderful pearl of exceeding price, whose virtue shall not decay,
Whose light shall be as a spell to thee, and a blessing on thy way.

The lady glanced at the mirroring steel where her form of grace was seen,
Where her eyes shone clear and her dark locks waved, their clasping pearls between;
Bring forth the pearl of exceeding worth, thou traveller gray and old,
And name the price of thy precious gem, and my page shall count thy gold.

The cloud went off from the pilgrim's brow, as a small and meagre book,
Unchased with gold or gem of cost, from his folding robe he took.
Here, lady fair, is the pearl of price, may it prove as such to thee!
Nay, keep thy gold; I ask it not, for the Word of God is free.

The hoary traveller went his way, but the gift he left behind
Hath had its pure and perfect work on that high-born maiden's mind,
And she hath turned from the pride of sin to the loveliness of truth,
And given her human heart to God in its beautiful hour of youth.
—*J. G. Whittier.*

THE BIBLE AND CIVILIZATION.

TO outline what the Bible has done for the promotion of civilization would be like attempting to teach all known science. Civilizing agencies are to be tested by their fruits. The Gospel entered Europe when Paul preached at Philippi. For more than a thousand years antecedent to the discovery of the art of printing it was practically claimed by the civil and ecclesiastical powers. Yet it early shut up the vast Roman Coliseum, where forty thousand applauding spectators watched the doomed slaves as they fought with wild beasts and more desperate men. It soon chiselled off the licentious carvings from the vases, lamps, and tables of Roman homes. It quickly closed the pagan temples of the "eternal city." It promptly threw from their pedestals the countless gods of Greece. Gradually it has planted Western Europe with almost numberless institutions, both beneficent and educational; it has organized in its cities and villages associations for the relief of every phase of distress.

Volumes could be written descriptive of its work in England alone since the days of Wickliffe. Perchance Edward VI., the boy king, saw with prophetic eye its relation to his country's greatness when he demanded that the Scriptures should be laid on the three swords in the ceremony of his coronation. What the Bible has done for Scotland, the most moral and Bible-loving state on the map of the world; for Prussia since the days of Luther; for the heroic Waldenses, amid the fastness of their mountain homes; for the Indian tribes, when taught by such men as Eliot and Brainerd; for the moral transformation of the West India islands; for Madagascar since the accession of Radama II.; and even recently for the three great heathen empires, the doors of whose sealed cities were opened by Morrison, Judson, and Goble with the Golden Key of the Gospel, and for other lands has won the praise of impartial historians.

It has entered no wilderness that under its magic wand has not blossomed as the rose, appealing to eternal relationships for its motives; overshadowing temporal convenience with the fact that "the wages of sin is death, but the gift of God is eternal life;" with its pages glittering with admonitions against every form of personal, social, and national wrong, and with encouragements to the pursuit of all that tends toward the universal reign of peace, purity, justice, and love; the Bible has marched on, winning a long series of conquests, before which the victories of renowned generals fade into nothingness. An infinite mind only can comprehend what it has accomplished for the educational, social, and moral uplifting of the nations.—*S. V. Leech.*

WOMAN AND THE BIBLE.

NOT only is it the tendency of the Bible and its teachings to elevate woman, and to give her, in every relation of life, influence and respect, but the sacred pages abound in illustrations of the fact that, through the divine teachings, woman has been raised to a position of dignity and social importance which heathenism in its palmiest days never knew. Throughout all heathen nations woman has ever been the drudge and slave of man, either the debased and degraded instrument of his grossest passions and pleasures, or the oppressed and toiling servant to do his most menial work—a stranger to everything like love, or even respect, and cared for only as one might care for his beasts of burden or the dog at his feet.

The Chinese regard the birth of a female child as both a misfortune and a shame. One of the standard works of the Hindoos says: "The four qualities of woman are ignorance, impurity, shame, and fear." One of our missionaries tells us that in Africa he has often seen the husband and sons walking leisurely along to their hut at sundown, while the heavy load was placed on the shoulders of the wife and mother, of whom no notice whatever was taken, except in the sharp order, and even the brutal blow, to make her quicken her pace. And the correspondent of one of our widely circulated papers, who has been making a tour around the world, says: "I have not seen anywhere, even in Turkey, Egypt, or India, or among the Mohammedan or Hindoo women, one single happy or hopeful face." There is nothing in these religions to make them happy or hopeful, and the whole history of women, except where the principles of the Bible have had sway, has been but the record of oppression, and debasement, and toil, and suffering, and shame. It is only where the Bible comes, or where the power of its teachings is felt, that woman is elevated to her true position as the companion and socially the equal of man, his sympathizing helpmate and friend, his wise and trusted counsellor, and the object of his respect and love.

Look at the Bible record, and see how, in every age, it has exalted and honored woman: There is Sarah, a princess in character as well as name; Rebekah, the honored wife of Isaac; Rachel, the loved helpmeet of Jacob; Miriam, leading the daughters of Israel in response to the sublime song of triumph in which Moses, six hundred years before Homer, and in even loftier strains than his, sounded the praises of Jehovah, who had delivered them; Deborah, who rose to be the judge and deliverer of her people; Ruth, whose loving and lovely character has been the admiration of every age; Esther, whose self-denying courage and wisdom was the salvation of her nation; Elizabeth, the honored mother of John; the Virgin Mary, declared by the angel blessed among women, as she has been and forever will be honored among men; Martha and Mary, the companions and friends of Jesus hims.'; and Dorcas, whose name and good works will be a memorial and an example while the world itself shall stand; and then there are such names as Naomi, and Hannah, and Lydia, and Eunice, and Lois, and Phebe, and the widow of Nain, and the Shunammite widow, and the woman of Canaan, and the long list of the faithful women saluted by Paul in his various epistles, the mention of each of whom is a standing rebuke of the libel that woman is ignored or lightly esteemed in the sacred records of inspiration.

The Bible disparaging or depressing woman! It is a base and most slanderous assertion—the offspring of gross ignorance or malicious falsehood. It is from the Bible, and only from the Bible and its teachings, that woman has been saved from the oppression and cruelty, and raised from the degradation, that have ever been her lot among uncivilized and savage nations, and elevated to her true position as the daughter, the wife, the mother, and as the honored and loved associate and helpmeet and friend of man, the source of his true happiness and of his highest earthly enjoyments, if she herself is but faithful to the Saviour.—*Tryon Edwards.*

ONE OF THE SWEET OLD CHAPTERS.

NE of the sweet old chapters,
   After a day like this;
The day brought tears and trouble,
   The evening brings no kiss.

No rest in the arms I long for—
   Rest, and refuge, and home;
Grieved, and lonely, and weary,
   Unto the Book I come.

One of the sweet old chapters—
The love that blossoms through
His care of the birds and lilies
Out in the meadow dew.

His evening lies soft around them;
Their faith is simply to be.
O, hushed by the tender lesson,
My God, let me rest in thee.
—*Christian Advocate.*

THE BLESSINGS OF THE BIBLE.

ONE of the great blessings which the Bible takes with it everywhere is—a day once a week when the hard worker can rest and forget that he is a beast of burden, and remember that he is a man. Addison wrote of the Sabbath, that it was "a good institution, because it made poor people wash and dress themselves respectably once a week." The Sabbath was made for man—for man, not as shop-keeper, ploughman, statesman, but as a rational, moral, religious creature. A great authoress in one of our London dailies not long since pointed out the contrast between the Christian and the Moslem in this respect. He attends the mosque on his Sabbath Friday, devout, perhaps, as the Christian, but always in his work-a-day dress; there is no change of attire, no general rest from labor. No; the poor Arab, toiling in his one sordid garment, is never able to say to himself: "I am a man, and not a beast of burden;" but wherever this Book goes, it seems to hush the machineries of every day life into silence. Man everywhere throws aside the tools and the soiled garments, by means of which he earns his daily bread; he goes forth after his weekly ablutions and change, refreshed in soul and body; and often in this hushed silence—like John in the spirit—on the Lord's Day, he thinks of the white robes of the eternal Sabbath. He remembers that he is more than a mere animal, to be fed and sheltered—more than a mere creature of intellect capable of education; that his highest interests are spiritual, and that the noblest relations which he sustains are to God and eternity.

This Book takes with it, again, a heart ready to sympathize, and a hand ready to help the suffering of every class and in every clime throughout the earth. Look through the "History of Great Suffering!" Who were the most ready to help them? were they not the people called Christians? To help people they had never seen—to help with no selfish motive? Was not that over half a million sent over to India a grand fact in favor of the religion of this land? And now the reply comes back. I am told that 16,000 have come to Bishop Caldwell in India, ready to lay aside their heathenism —whole villages. Why, all other religious systems are religions of "self-help." But this one exceptional system leavens people everywhere with a religion of "helping others." It introduces them into a new joy. It reveals to us the grand secret that by helping others we enter into the joy of our Lord. The rose is not sweeter for the fragrance with which it perfumes the morning; the well is no brighter for its cup of cold water to the passer-by; but you cannot give a shilling to that poor widow in her desolate home without feeling that your own home is brighter for the Christian act. You cannot send a bunch of flowers from your garden to that poor invalid in the garret, without adding a new bloom to every flower. The very garden smiles upon you with a new beauty, and exhilarates you with a sweeter fragrance. Canon Mozley has, with a master hand, shown that this principle of compassion that converts into a pleasure that which was of incalculable advantage to society —the alleviation of pain and misery—was a discovery of Christianity—a discovery like that of a new scientific principle. The Spartans did not believe in this compassion when they cut off at birth their sickly and maimed children, but they did believe in "the survival of the fittest." Hindooism, when it places the old and the infirm on the banks of the Ganges to be carried away by the next rising of the waters, does not believe in this joy of Christian compassion, but in "the survival of the fittest." The religion of this Book, however, brings God down to the side of men, not as an everlasting condemner, but as a present help in time of trouble—brings down a Divine Consoler, who was crowned to be the King of suffering humanity; not when he was crowned above with the royal diadem of heaven, but when he was crowned with thorns here below. It was that lifting up under a crown of thorns to the cross, that marked him forever as the Man of Sorrow—that draws all men to Him. It is he of whom we learnt when children the shortest and sweetest verse in the whole Bible—"Jesus wept." That attracts us to him under our burdens, trials and sorrows. You say that our God is a hard, unsympathetic Being. I answer: "Jesus wept;" and it is this Jesus, with a loving heart in his bosom, and tears in his eyes, that draws human hearts to him for sympathy, and sends them forth full of help and compassion to heal the woes of humanity.

—*E. Herber Evans.*

BUT ONE BOOK.

WHEN Sir Walter Scott lay dying, he was carried at his request into his dining-room, that his dying eyes might once more rest upon the Tweed, which he so much loved. Some of you have been in that room; you now remember the view from its front window. He asked his son-in-law, Mr. Lockhart, to read for him. "What book?" said Mr. Lockhart. "What book?" asked Sir Walter; "there is but one book— the Bible—read that." Mr. Lockhart read those blessed words which have been balm to thousands of hearts; words which came from the grace-anointed lips of Jesus: "Let not your heart be troubled; ye believe in God, believe also in me. In my Father's house are many mansions; if it were not so, I would have told you. I go to prepare a place for you." "That is comfort," said the dying man. "I am myself again."

What has infidelity to offer compared with these blessed words? It gives gloom, not glory; darkness, not brightness; death, not life. The dying Scotchman, who read so widely, and contributed so many immortal pages to literature, gives this testimony to the value of the Bible. Mr. Dickens was in the habit of writing a letter to each of his sons as he left the parental roof. In one he urged his son to read the Bible, whatever other books he neglected, as it contained the purest morality and the best rules of life known in the world. When Milton would become "a poet, soaring in the high reason of his fancies, with his garland and singing robes about him," he must go to the Bible for his high theme. When Raphael would perpetuate his name to unborn generations he must ascend "the holy mount," stand in the supernal glory, and gaze on the transfigured Christ. As the "Transfiguration" was his greatest, so it was his last work. He died in early manhood, with the "Transfiguration" on his heart and brain. That picture was carried before him through the streets of Rome to his place of burial in the Pantheon. When Handel was discouraged by attempting opera in a foreign language, he accepted an invitation from several notables of Ireland to visit Dublin. From a friend he received a text from the Bible, and on that text he composed his immortal work, known at first as the "Sacred Oratorio," now known as the "Messiah." In Dublin and in London this work crowned him with triumphant success and unfading glory. It has since made his name famous throughout the world. The Bible gave all these men—working in different departments of genius—their inspiration. Shall we be so inconsistent as to rejoice in the streams while we despise the fountain whence they flowed? No literature has in it the elements of immortality except that which draws its inspiration from God's Word. This gave Tasso his strength in song, and Michael Angelo his glory in art. The music of this world dies with the breath which gives it utterance. Only as literature, music, poetry, sculpture and painting are linked with him whose name is above every name can they possess something of the enduringness of him who is the King Immortal. They must at least embody the best religious thought of their time. This is true both of the Greek poems and plays.

The office which has been honored by the gifts of Paul and the graces of John, by the immortal names of heroes and martyrs in the past, and is filled now by some of the ablest and best men living, needs no further vindication from me. To a blind man only is it necessary to prove that the sun at noonday in midsummer gives light. Because of its intellectual advantages, then, we should to-day say, "We will not forsake the house of God."—*Dr. R. S. MacArthur.*

ONE BIBLE ENOUGH.

IT is enough, one sun in heaven, one Bible on earth; one the light of the natural world, the other the light of the spiritual world. Where is natural day? wherever the sun shines! and where is spiritual day? wherever the Bible shines! in either case, day is nowhere else! true, the moon gives light when the sun has set; and so the church may give light when the Bible is withdrawn, but in both cases it is night light, not day light; besides, the sun is not set to the moon, but only to the earth; the moon sees it still, though the earth does not, and the moon shines because she sees it.

And so the Bible is not withdrawn from the church, but only from the world; in all such instances the church sees it though the world does not; and the church shines only because she sees it. If all the moon be dark except half its edge line, even that is proof that the sun is still in sight; and so if all the church be dark save some small segment, even that, however small, is proof that the Bible has not quite passed away. Still, the moon rejoices most when the sun returns and she is allowed to hide herself in his glory; and so the church triumphs most when the Bible returns and she is permitted to fade in its excelling splendor.

—*T. H. Stockton.*

JESUS THE GLORY OF THE BIBLE.

YOU have often admired the line of shimmering light which shines on the ruffled waters when the moon is in the heavens. Look in any other direction, and the waters are dark and troubled. Look toward the orb of night, and you see the glory all over the way, right from your feet to the heavens above.

Another standing beside you, looking at another angle, will see another line of light and glory; and another, and so on endlessly; the moon is really shining over all the water, but each one sees only a portion of its radiance, and that portion only by looking in one direction.

So it is in the Bible the glory is shining all over it; you may see nothing of heaven in it so long as you will not look in the right direction, but look at the point of sight, look to Jesus, and you will see the glory of the Bible; you cannot see it all. Another will see something else that you do not; and another, standing at another point, will see something that you and he have missed; but every one who looks earnestly in the right direction will see something—a path of light and glory leading from his own feet across the troubled waters of this life up to the heaven above.

—*Christian World.*

I HAVE many books that I cannot sit down to read; they are indeed good and sound, but, like half-pence, there goes a great quantity to a small amount. There are silver books and a few golden books; but I have a book worth them all called the Bible.—*John Newton.*

CHRIST IN THE BIBLE.

TO ramble over the pages of Scripture without finding Christ is like the tourist strolling through the aisles and corridors of Westminster Abbey without finding the famous Chapel of Henry VII. It is there, somewhere within those ancient walls—a thing of beauty, perhaps the finest piece of Gothic architecture in the world, the tomb of England's kings, and the thing which the traveller desires to see more than anything else in the Abbey, but there are many other objects of interest to draw him aside. He may linger in the cloisters over the gray tombs of abbots and bishops; he may tarry long over the mouldering ashes of warlike knights and barons, or he may muse in the poets' corner among the sleeping bards until the shades of evening gather, and never penetrate to the highest beauty and glory of the Abbey, this wonderful chapel.

And there are in the Bible poetry and eloquence, and history, and philosophy, beauty and sublimity, which may engross our attention and delay our researches until the shades of death gather, and we fail to find the highest glory of the Bible, the royal chapel where a crucified Christ was buried, and the Christian's King and Redeemer laid down his life for the world.

Our time will be but poorly spent in searching the Scriptures unless we find our way to Christ. Better visit the royal chapel first, and make sure we behold its glories, and then we can give what time remains to the shady aisles and poets' corner; better find Christ in the Bible first, and then it will be time to consider the poetry and eloquence and beauty of Scripture. Christ is there somewhere—there as a redeeming Saviour, there as our exalted Intercessor, there in every respect as the Captain of our salvation.

And when we enter the tangled aisles of this wonderful Abbey we must have a divine guide, or we shall never discover the royal chapel. When we enter this labyrinth of sacred truth, we must have a heavenly torch, borne by a divine hand, to precede us, or we shall lose our way, and find no Christ and no salvation in the Bible.—*H. Graham.*

THE BIBLE GOD'S LIGHT.

WAS once lost for an hour in a subterranean cavern; the oozing moisture from the rocks had extinguished our candles, and in creeping through the low passes, from chamber to chamber, all our matches had become damp. Between us and the outer air stretched a mile of perilous, and sometimes almost impassable labyrinths, and the chill, black air around us was full of weird, hideous reverberations. Oh, how carefully we strove to kindle the old light, and when at last it slowly caught and kindled, flinging its blessed lustre along those grim rocks and miry ways, then did not that old cavern ring again with a great shout of gladness!

And such a light the blessed Bible pours through the gloomy ways and dark night of life; and this is the light infidelity is trying to extinguish. Thank God, they cannot. This they may do, with their hideous and revolting blasphemy—they may persuade a few poor, deluded creatures to put out their own eyes, that, unable to see the light, the blind may lead the blind into the ditch of defilement, and over the precipice of destruction. But glory unto God! they cannot put out God's great light in the heavens. It will shine along our paths; it will shine on our death-bed; it will shine on our grave—every hour, every day, it is flinging a broader, brighter effulgence into all the dark places of this redeemed world.

But meantime, not so much in indignation as in pitying sorrow, the Christian heart moves over the ineffable madness of men who, with their love of darkness, will war with the light. They showed me a grand light-house on the shore of yonder sea, fitted up at great cost with metallic mirrors and crystal lenses, whose ever-burning lamps pour forth a flood of light over leagues of weltering waters, and when the midnight deepens, hundreds of weather-beaten mariners catch afar off the friendly lustre, and warned of rocks and breakers, lift up joyous eyes heavenward and thank God for the flame. But meanwhile, alas! flocks of swift-winged birds, rushing through night and storm, dash themselves against the crystal lenses, not, indeed, extinguishing the lustre, but falling back into the roaring waters, bleeding—*self-destroyed, dead.* Oh! be warned, ye that set yourselves against God, and take counsel against the Almighty. Alas! alas! that the very light of heaven should only guide your mad feet along the broad road of destruction, down the awful precipice of despair, into the terrible abyss of death.—*Charles Wadsworth.*

No man ever did or ever can become truly eloquent without being a constant reader of the Bible, and an admirer of its purity and sublimity.—*Fisher Ames.*

BLESSED BIBLE.

LESSED Bible! how I love it!
How it doth my bosom cheer!
What hath earth like this to covet?
O, what stores of wealth are here!
Man was lost and doomed to sorrow;
Not one ray of light or bliss
Could he from earth's treasures borrow,
Till his way was cheered by this.

Yes, I'll to my bosom press thee,
Precious Word, I'll hide thee here;
Sure my very heart will bless thee,
For thou ever sayest "Good cheer;"
Speak, my heart, and tell thy ponderings,
Tell how far thy rovings led,
When this book brought back thy wanderings,
Speaking life as from the dead.

Yes, sweet Bible! I will hide thee
Deep, yes, deeper in this heart;
Thou, through all my life will guide me,
And in death we will not part.
Part in death? No, never! never!
Through deaths vale I'll lean on thee;
Then, in worlds above, forever,
Sweeter still thy truths shall be.
—*Phœbe Palmer.*

THE basis and rock on which I, and we all, are bound to fix our foothold is the unadulterated faith as taught us by the Bible.—*William, Emperor of Germany.*

THE BIBLE AND SCIENCE.

THE Bible is not a scientific, but a religious book, intended not to inform the scientific and philosophic understanding, but to instruct the religious intelligence of man in those things that make for the life that now is, and that which is to come.

What a blessed fact it is that we thirsty mortals can drink a glass of pure water, and quench our burning thirst without having to know the chemical analysis of water, or how it was originally created; we are thirsty beings, and if our thirst is not slaked we shall die. Meantime, we find water is provided; it is offered to us, and we are told it will slake our thirst; that it was provided in nature for that very purpose, and, without stopping to have it analyzed, we drink it, and live; we then experimentally prove it to be water, and that all that was claimed for it is true.

We likewise are religious beings, and if we do not find truth, and love, and happiness, and regeneration, and eternal life, and resurrection, we shall die and perish. God's Word is brought to us; it contains truths, or at least statements and promises that stand over against these spiritual hungerings and thirstings just as food and drink stand over against the hunger and thirst of the body. We take hold by faith of these promises, and the hunger and thirst of our souls is satisfied. We know the truth of the Bible, therefore, not by metaphysical or intellectual demonstrations, but by experimental proof—as real in the sphere of our religious nature as scientific demonstration is real in the realm of matter.

Two and two make four—that is mathematics; hydrogen and oxygen in certain proportions make water—that is science; Christ and Him crucified is the power and wisdom of God for salvation—that is revelation. But how do you know? Put two and two together, and you have four; count, and see. Put hydrogen and oxygen, and you have water; taste, and prove. Believe on the Lord Jesus Christ, and thou shalt be saved; believe, and thou shalt know. The last is as clear a demonstration as the others.—*George F. Pentecost.*

SCIENCE AND THE BIBLE.

THE thing to be lamented is, that the moment men of science get hold of a fact they instantly begin to set it in opposition to God's Word. But the vaunted "fact" of Tuesday often takes another shape on Wednesday, and by Thursday is found to be no fact at all. The truth is, that geology, as a science, consists mainly of probable guesses. "That field of peat," says Sir Charles Lyell, "has probably been 7,000 years in course of formation." "No," replies a friend of his own, in a published criticism, "I think it quite possible that it has only been 700 years in growing." A piece of pottery is found in the Valley of the Nile, and a geologist immediately argues that it must have lain there more than 20,000 years; but an antiquary soon points out marks upon it which show it to be less than 2,000 years old. Yet it is upon guesses of this kind, which do not amount to a tenth part of a proof, that the Lyells and Owens and Colensos venture boldly to assert that it is clear that Moses knew nothing whatever of the subject on which he was writing. Just in the same spirit do

Bunsen and his followers unhesitatingly assert that the growth of languages proves that the world must be more than 20,000 years old. We refer them to the confusion of tongues described by Moses, which at once dissipates their dream. "Oh! but that was a miracle," they reply; "and we have made up our minds never to believe a miracle." Very well, gentlemen, there we must leave you; for men who make up their minds before inquiring are not acting like reasonable beings. A dozen other little Juntos are now at work in the same laudable fashion. One set is not quite certain that man was "developed" out of an ape. Well, and what was the ape "developed" out of? They do not know. Our comfort in all this is, that this influenza will wear itself out like tractarianism or like the infidel fashion of the days of Bolingbroke. Men have been striving to get rid of the Bible and its inconvenient morality for nearly these 2,000 years, but they were never further off from this end than they are at present.—*Earl of Shaftesbury.*

STRIKING THE BIBLE.

THE religious world has been recently agitated by a determination on the part of theologians to square off and fight the religion of their fathers. Some think it argues great pluck for a man to assail the Bible and the Church, and set up a new religion. The fact is, it requires no courage at all to do so, for he is always sure of the favor and applause of a multitude who hate the Bible, and would be glad to see it struck on any side, and to have Christianity crippled.

The Bible antagonists do not realize they are attempting

to stop an express-train by putting their foot on the track, or arrest an Alpine avalanche by bracing themselves against one of the ice-cakes. The Bible goes right on, and the Church of God goes right on, and Christianity goes right on, and the chief damage is done to the critics.

There have never been so many live churches in the United States as to-day, more people believe the Gospel than ever before, and vaster multitudes are attempting to practise its precepts. The attempt to shatter the Bible for the last 300 years has not rent asunder or dislodged a single doctrine or sentiment. After its present assailants are all dead their funeral sermons will be preached from King James' translation, not one verse omitted from the first page of Genesis to the last page of Revelation.

One would think the world would get tired of a bombardment of the Bible castle when, with all their concentrated fire of 300 years, they have not been able to knock out of its walls a splinter large enough to make the most sensitive eyeball quiver. O! I am so glad we are in the army which will finally win the day. Here and there a repulse may come through the perfidy of some officer, or the backing out of some traitor in the camp, but there are enough of the mounted cavalry of the King to ride down all opposition and to dismount the guns of the enemy. I have no nervousness as to the result. I am only anxious to be on the right side in the contest, and to do my share of the hard marching and hard fighting.—*T. DeWitt Talmage.*

THAT book, sir, is the rock upon which our republic rests.—*Andrew Jackson.*

RESISTANCE TO THE BIBLE.

WE have heard that the resistance of ages to this blessed book is not yet over—resistance to a book that alights everywhere with healing in its wings. Is not this a crowning proof that it comes from the same high world that Christ came from, and that the book, like the Saviour, is too good for the race it has come to bless? It comes to heal, like the angel to the pool of Bethesda; but it troubles too many waters in its work to please all, and they cry, "Away with it!" It comes like the ark to the house of Dagon; but it smites the idols and breaks in pieces the objects of trust in which men have vested interest, and the Philistines cry, "Away with it!" It comes like the sun; but all who have their own private schemes to enlighten the age—just as members of gas companies would like to put out the sun that they may hasten to be rich—unite in the cry, "Away with it." It comes like the Christ, casting out the demons of iniquity from the souls of men; but there are yet Gadarenes in the world, ready to part with the Christ in order to save their swine.

"Away with it!" But can you replace it? Will you drag down my old home without building me another? This old home may not be built exactly to answer your modern, newly-discovered ideas, but this old faith has been our dwelling-place for generations. It has sheltered our fathers from many a storm. It has been to us as the shadow of the Almighty. We have prayed and sung with joy under its protection; we have thought it faced another home over there, and that when our dead ones went out here, we knew where to find them again. The eternal sun seemed to us to shine on that old home, and will you drag it all down and turn us out as homeless vagabonds to the unsheltered wilderness, without hope and without a God in the world? Shall we be foolish enough to act like the sloth spoken of by Bulwer, which, having eaten up the last green leaf upon the tree upon which it has established itself, ends by tumbling down from the top, and dying by inanition.

We know it is boldly asserted in popular reviews in these days that all this is already accomplished; that the old book is demolished once more. Yes, once more. How many times has it been demolished before? Bishop Butler, in the advertisement to his great work, says: "It has come, I know not how, to be taken for granted by many people, that Christianity is not so much a subject of inquiry, but that it is now at length discovered to be fictitious." That was just one hundred and forty-two years ago. Discovered to be fictitious? Then, is it not strange that so much ink has been wasted, so many books written to destroy it since, and all passed up, one after the other, to the cobwebs of the higher shelf in the library? and the Bible, still remaining on the study table as an unsolved problem, with a self-conscious sense of power, seems to address all the other volumes in the library, "Books may come, and books may go, but I go on forever."
—*E. Herber Evans.*

HE who believes the Scriptures to have proceeded from Him who is the Author of nature, may well expect to find the same sort of difficulties in it as are found in the constitution of nature.—*Origen.*

WHY MEN HATE THE BIBLE.

NO thoughtful and well-informed person can deny that many persons of skeptical tendencies are persons of good behavior, correct morals, and apparently blameless lives, while at the same time there are men who profess Christianity who seem far beneath them in the average excellence of their character and conduct. But it is nevertheless undeniable that while these persons treat religion with some respect, the vicious, the dissolute, the depraved, and the criminal as a class, *dislike the Bible*. How many Bibles will you find in the pockets of the roughs arrested in a street fight? Among the weapons, curiosities and possessions taken from the pockets of criminals and laid up in police stations, who ever saw a New Testament? Was it a *Bible* with which that drunken wretch knocked his wife down? Oh, no; it was a *bottle!*

Now what is the reason that drunkards over their cups, gamblers at their dice, rogues dividing their plunder, and assassins plotting against men's lives, all hate the Bible, curse Christianity, and blaspheme Christ? Do these men dislike any other religion as much? Do they find fault with the Koran? Do they curse the "Age of Reason?" Do they damn infidels for a pack of fools and hypocrites? What, then, is the cause of this malignant hate against the Bible—a book which, if some infidels may be believed, justifies, approves, and fosters every wrong, and which hence ought to be as often found in the pockets of rogues as a pack of cards, a revolver, a slung-shot, or a bottle of whiskey?

The fact is well known that bad men hate the Bible, and good men love it. Why? Simply because the Bible condemns sin and approves righteousness. The instinct of self-preservation causes evil men to object to a book which condemns their course, and warns them of perdition at the end of it. But what would the laws be worth if villains and thieves were suited with them? Where would be the propriety of appointing a committee of murderers and cut-throats to revise the statutes of a nation? Rogues are not partial to good laws; thieves hate officers of justice; liars dislike men who will tell the truth; licentious men sneer at purity and piety, and infidels find fault with the Bible and Christianity. One of the Western States, it is said, was settled largely by absconding debtors. The result was seen in the laws of the new commonwealth, by which the collection of an honest debt was rendered almost an impossibility.

There has been published by skeptics a New Testament "revised by the spirits"—that is, the spirits of devils that swarm the earth on every hand. Of course every passage relating to adultery or immorality is expunged or explained away; loving your enemies is not required; laying up treasures in heaven is not enjoined, and, as a whole, the book is toned down to the moral plane of those lying devils and their followers, and affords an unmistakable index of the character of those who did the work. They are suited with a Bible that allows adultery and uncleanness, and are angry at one which forbids it. They are suited with a God who allows them to do as they like, and angry if their sins are forbidden, their iniquities condemned, or their lusts restrained. The blasphemer wants no Bible which forbids cursing; the drunken deist wants no book which warns him that he cannot enter the kingdom of God; the rum-selling infidel wants no prophet to thunder in his ears, "Woe unto him that giveth his neighbor drink, that puttest thy bottle to him, and maketh him drunken" (Hab. xi. 15), and the licentious scoffer has no relish for a book which pronounces blessings on the pure in heart, and which points to the lake of fire as the destiny of the votaries of wickedness and lust.

Of course all skeptics are not bad men, nor are all who pretend to honor the Bible good men. There are infidels who live above their principles, while there are professors of Christianity who live contrary to Christ's words. There are skeptics who may be Christian in sentiment and life, while there are church members who are infidel all through, and ought to be drummed out of the camp where they are traitors, and sent through the enemy's lines, where they belong. There are skeptics who have not forgotten, and can never forget, the lessons which Christian parents taught them long ago; and there are also Christians who retain in their nature and manifest in their lives the hereditary faults which vicious, godless, and unbelieving ancestors have conferred upon them. But still the general rule holds good: a book which bad men hate must be a good one, and a book which good men love can hardly be a bad one. Let us, then, be wary, lest while we condemn the Bible we find in the end that the Bible will condemn us; for if we believe the Bible to be wrong in theory, we are quite likely to be ourselves wrong in practice.—*H. L. Hastings.*

HE who, after a patient and laborious investigation of the Christian evidences, is in doubt as to the authenticity of the sacred Scriptures, is very near to a total rejection of them. —*James Hamilton Davies.*

THE EFFECTS OF DESTROYING THE BIBLE.

LET me be permitted to suppose somewhat, at least, of an approach toward the utter destruction of the Book. First, copies of the volume itself, in all shapes and sizes, in all tongues and versions, shall have been collected, heaved in pyramidal piles, and fired until but dust and ashes remain; no Bible anywhere! This is but a very little thing, however, compared with that to be accomplished. Then all literature —prose, poetry, tome and folio, essay and sermon, drama and lyric, hymn and idyll—must be subjected to a process either of utter destruction or of perfect, absolutely perfect, expurgation, so that no grace of style, nor elegance of allusion, or aptness of quotation, nor felicity of metaphor, suggestive of or derived from the Book, shall remain in such volumes.

Then visit the galleries, private and public, devoted to the exhibition of art. Here are halls frescoed with the products of old masters and new; here are pedestals and niches crowned and crowded with the triumphs of the chisel and the sculptor. Blot from the canvas the "Last Supper," the "Transfiguration," the "Ascension," the "Light of the World;" pluck from the pedestal and from yonder niches the "Moses" and the "David" of Angelo, or such forms and expressions of majesty, tenderness, purity, and grace as their creators learned and caught from study of the teachings, or fellowship with the heroes of the Book.

Then haste to the baptismal registries of the Church, and

instead of Mary, write Cleopatra; of Rachel, Messalina; of John, Nero; and of Peter, Caligula—erase whatever there reminds one of the Bible. Then on to the libraries of law, and let all codes, statutes, enactments, constitutions, in which shall be found reverence for God, respect for liberty, protection for reputation and person, defence of woman and of feebleness, and guarantee of equal and impartial justice, for meanest plebeian as for meanest plutocrat; let all such as owe their humanity, their justice, their impartiality to the genius and the teachings of the Book vanish and be forgotten.

Then, away to the cemeteries, urban and suburban, civic and rustic; to the crypts and vaults; to the stately minister and to the humble chapel where sleep the dead, and on whose tombs Hope, Faith, and Love have carved the blessed texts in which the widow found a calm and the despairing consolation. See! see! 'Tis a November midnight; nor star nor moon rides the cloud-draped heavens. No light, save the fitful flash from yonder moving form. That is one of the myriad conspirators against the human race, who on this grim night simultaneously visit the graveyards of the Christian world, that from the slab and obelisk they may blot out the Bible. See! he bends, and with light of lantern reads: "I am the resurrection and the life;" "Blessed are the dead;" "In my Father's house are many mansions." Now, he seizes chisel and mallet, and begins—chip! chip! chip! The lone night winds as they travel o'er the spot take up upon their dusky wings a burden sadder than they ever bore—the sob, the sigh, the low-toned throb of heartchords snapping; for henceforth the chamber of the dying shall be one of horrors, death's rule a reign of terror, and the graveyard "the abomination of desolation."

I need not imagine more, though the half is not yet pictured; for the fruits of Christianity in manners, in civilization, in treatment of criminals and of the insane, in homes for aged, for orphans, for widows, for idiots, for outcast women; in popular education, and in kindred generous and gracious institutions; these all must also suffer destruction before we shall have by any means attained unto the extermination of either the Book or the Faith.—*Rev. Thomas Guard.*

OUR ANSWER TO THE SKEPTIC.

WE will say, then, to all who hate the Bible, and would tear it from us, if they could:

> "We won't give up the Bible,
> God's holy book of truth;
> The staff of hoary age,
> And guide of early youth."
> —*Andrew Manship.*

THE BIBLE OUR ONLY SOLACE IN DEATH.

TO real mourners there is left only a single comfort that will prove satisfactory. We may reason and argue, but all in vain. No assurance about its being better for the friends we have lost to be where they are; no chilly philosophy as to manly fortitude or womanly endurance; no professions of sincere sympathy counselling courage—nothing is sufficient for our terrible bereavements except the calm declaration: "Thy brother shall rise again." We insist upon the certainty that some time we must be reunited to the hearts we regret and remember with our tears.

Just here the Scripture meets us positively: "For if we believe that Jesus died and rose again, even so them also which sleep in Jesus will God bring with him." We cannot take away death; but we can take the sting out of death. We must enter the conflict with the last enemy. "But thanks be to God, which giveth us the victory, through our Lord Jesus Christ." At last there comes something authoritative; the moment we read a verse of inspiration like these we are studying, we feel as we do when we see a great meteoric stone—we say, " This is a piece of another planet." —*Charles S. Robinson.*

A BOOK FOR A DYING PILLOW.

D*O you know a Book that you are willing to put under your head for a pillow when you lie dying? Very well; that is the Book you want to study while you are living.* There is but one such Book in the world. For one, I have not made up my mind to put under my head when I lie dying anything written by Voltaire, or Strause, or Parker. We are to be scientifically careful when we choose a book for a dying pillow. If you can tell me what you want for a dying pillow, I will tell you what you want for a pillow of fire in life—that is the Bible; spiritually and scientifically understood by being transmuted into deeds; sentiment is worth nothing until it becomes principle, and principle is worth nothing until it becomes action.—*Joseph Cook.*

THE BIBLE PRECIOUS.

HOW precious is the book divine,
    By inspiration given;
Bright as a lamp its doctrines shine,
    To guide our souls to heaven.

It sweetly cheers our drooping hearts,
    In this dark vale of tears;
Life, light, and joy it still imparts,
    And quells our rising fears.

This lamp, through all the tedious night
    Of life, shall guide our way;
Till we behold the clearer light
    Of an eternal day.
                      —John Fawcett.

THE BIBLE A PARADISE OF DELIGHTS.

THE reading of the sacred Scriptures is a spiritual meadow, and a Paradise of delights; moreover, far superior to that Paradise where Adam dwelt. For God has planted this Paradise, not upon earth but in the souls of believers. He has not placed this Paradise in Eden, confining it to one place; but He has expanded it everywhere upon the earth.

And that you may see that He has diffused the Scriptures everywhere throughout the habitable world, hear the prophet saying: "Their line is gone forth into all the earth, and their words to the ends of the world." Whether you transport yourself to the Indies, which the rising sun first regards; whether you go to the ocean, whether you navigate the Black Sea, or depart to the Southern regions, you hear all, everywhere, reasoning upon these things that are in the Scriptures with a different voice, but with the same faith; with a different tongue, but with the same understanding, for the sound of the tongue differs, but the practice of religion does not differ; and they speak in a boisterous tongue, but they are wise in understanding; they commit errors in the sound, but they cultivate piety in their manners. Do you see the magnitude of the Paradise which extends to the ends of the earth?—*Chrysostom.*

HOLD fast to the Bible as the sheet-anchor of your liberties; write its precepts on your hearts, and practice them in your lives.—*U. S. Grant.*

    WITHIN this awful volume lies
    The mystery of mysteries.
    Oh! happiest they of human race,
    To whom our God has given grace
    To hear, to read, to fear, to pray,
    To lift the latch, and force the way;
    But better had they ne'er been born,
    Who read to doubt, or read to scorn.
                    —*Sir Walter Scott.*

OUR CHURCH.

"I LOVE thy Church, O God;
Her walls before thee stand,
Dear as the apple of thine eye,
And graven on thy hand."

"The Church of the living God, the pillar and ground of the truth."—1 Tim. iii. 15.

OUR CHURCH.

BEHOLD! the daughter of the King, the bride
All glorious within, the bride adorned
Comely in broidery of gold! behold,
She comes apparelled royally, in robes
Of perfect righteousness, fair as the sun,—
With all her virgins, her companions fair,—
Into the Palace of the King she comes.
She comes to dwell forevermore! Awake.
Eternal harps, awake, awake, and sing!—
The Lord, the Lord, our God Almighty reigns!
—*Robert Pollock.*

OUR CHURCH.

[WRITTEN EXPRESSLY FOR THIS WORK BY AMANDA ELIZABETH DENNIS.]

WE leave our sandals at the door,
    And walk, with noiseless, rev'rent feet,
Within the walls, where, evermore,
    Resounds in measures soft and sweet
        The boundless praise of Christ.

We leave outside all pain and care,
    And every vexing thought of ill,
And wait, with hearts athrob with prayer,
    The troubling of the waters still
        Of His all-healing love.

Dear Church of Christ, our souls are glad
    To wait within thy walls of peace;
Whatever woes our hearts have had
    Shall find in Thee a glad surcease,
        A satisfying balm!

No outside hurt shall weave its thrall,
    To mar the peace of thy dear fame;
One Church, one love, one Christ o'er all,
    Sweet peace and unity maintain
        Forever and for aye!

THE CHARACTER OF THE CHURCH.

WHAT, then, is the true notion of the Church? What is the ideal of its constitution? I answer: The Church is a religious society, governed by divine revelation alone. This statement, in my judgment, embodies all that is essential to the constitution of the Church. I will not say that there cannot be a church without certain articles, officers, or ordinances. Neither will I say that any association must be a church which has certain articles, officers, or ordinances. But this I do say: that no society can be a church unless it be a religious society, governed by divine revelation, and by this alone; and further, that every such society must be a church. There never was, is not now, and never can be, any other true Church than one of this description. Nor can I hesitate a moment to add that, when I speak of its being governed by divine revelation alone, I mean by *its own understanding* of that revelation; only requiring that it exercise its understanding with due reverence toward God and due respect for the whole Christian brotherhood, in ardent, patient, studious, prayerful, practical desire to be led into all truth by the spirit of truth. All this, indeed, is logically and philosophically involved in the proposition itself.

To me it is clear that the original intention was that the whole human race should constitute the one undivided membership of the Church. Church and state, if designed to be separately and differently organized, were always to exist in close union and perfect harmony. Their separation, however expedient now, could not have been demanded by the primitive condition of things. This expediency is an effect of the introduction of evil. Revelation, in whatever form furnished and to whatever organs restricted, would have qualified these organs for the exercise of infallible authority. The multiplying generations, with no tendency to error in themselves, with nothing to suggest it in creation or providence, and with nothing to occasion it among their social instructors, would have continued forever to enlarge their acquaintance with truth, and to enrich their character and estate with the blessings of obedience; every birth into the world would have been a birth into the Church. The prattle of the child of a year or two old would have been readily inspired with the worshipful spirit of the patriarch of a thousand years, and the softest lisping of its all-believing love might have been more touching to the heart of God than the sublimest anthem of angels ever sung before His throne.—*Thomas H. Stockton.*

SPIRITUALITY OF THE CHURCH.

WHEN the main business of life has become involved in subtleties and questions of critical scholarship and philosophy, so that the people are bewildered by cries of Lo here! and Lo there! we all need to be brought back to common sense by some plain-speaking Micah, who demands: "To what purpose is the multitude of your speculations? What does the Lord your God require but to do justly, to love mercy, and to walk humbly with your God?"

We must compel scholarship to bear a part in this work of implifying religion, instead of multiplying conundrums. The literature of recent inquiry is already immense; and, for its proper purpose, much of it is both necessary and invaluable. But, except to a limited constituency of students, it has become quite unmanageable. We may all find it worth while to follow its drift and weigh its results, but whoever attempts to find in it a guide of life must be thrown into despair by finding that ten new questions are raised for every one that is settled. Much of this sort of trouble comes from looking to external authorities and ancient records, not for the confirmation and support of faith, but for its origin and essence.

Never mind the old obscurities; the sun shines to-day! Alas for him who must go hunting up and down the centuries for documentary evidence of his title to a spiritual inheritance, or who cannot be certain that he is "a man with a mind" till the chemist and antiquarian have brought in their final report! Alas for him who thinks it necessary to settle the authorship of the fourth Gospel, or the primacy of Peter, or the possibility of miracles, or the genesis of life, before he can begin to live like a glad-hearted child of God! And alas for the Church if, in her conscious ignorance of spiritual mysteries, or her weariness of scholastic noises, she should yield to the temptation to put religious work on low grounds, by ignoring man's inmost need, to become a caterer to his intellectual curiosity, or to minister chiefly to his physical and social welfare! Nothing which concerns humanity is wholly foreign to our work. But if we fall in with the plausible philanthropy which seeks only to make the human animal more comfortable and more intelligent, we shall soon lose the power for these lower services; and the reproving voice will say, "These ought ye to have done, and not to leave the other undone." Dr. Johnson speaks to the point: "As no man is good but he who wishes the good of others, so no man has the highest goodness but he who wishes the highest good of others."

All religion assumes that man is spirit as God is spirit, and that thus they are related. Some religions make little of this relation. Christianity makes everything of it. The Church that fails to affirm and emphasize the fact of man's spiritual nature has lost its reason for existence. And what is meant by man's spiritual nature? At least this: the super-material quality of mind, its potency and promise of divinity; that man is not all body; that he is capable of converting his animal nature and sense surroundings into stepping-stones to a higher life—a life of wisdom and goodness; that, as his body is built up from the material world, so his spirit derives its nourishment from a realm of its own kind. Hence, by failing to give the spiritual nature its just supremacy, man arrests his own development, misses his birthright, condemns himself to a lower range of existence and an inferior sort of happiness. To admit this fact of man's spiritual nature is, therefore, to admit that his position is one of solemn moral exposure; that whatever defiles or degrades the spirit shuts out heaven; that the supremacy of spiritual interests is more important than all the wealth, pleasures, and honors of the world, or than life itself; that for the promotion of spiritual interests the higher resources of the universe can be depended upon and drawn upon; and that the truths which relate to these matters are the very highest order of truths.

The Church, whose mission is to testify to man's spiritual nature, needs and resources, falls into apostasy whenever she allows anything else to take the first place. A weak faith in spiritual facts and powers makes a weak ministry and a lean-souled laity. The vision of heavenly things fades out; zeal for diffusing spiritual good declines; the Church drops toward the lower levels, merges itself in the world, and becomes a power for evil rather than good.

The measure of a true Church appears, therefore, in its power to promote spirituality; that is, the higher life of wisdom and goodness, the love of truth and of duty, which are all one with the love of God and man. Ever since faith in the ascending Jesus gladdened the hearts of believers with the vision of humanity immortalized by divinity, the missionary zeal of the Church has been kept alive by the persuasion that every human being is capable of rising into God's likeness and blessedness through obedience to spiritual truth, or of sinking into infernalism of character and condition through rejection and disobedience. I suppose this persuasion, or something like it, reflects the serious wisdom and experience of mankind, and still constitutes the reason for the existence of the Church, and a large part of its working capital.

M. Guizot speaks of the idea of a spiritual society as "perhaps the highest idea that ever drew men together." But if there is to be a spiritual society, a kingdom of God on earth, it must be composed of spiritual persons; that is, of persons devoted to truth and good. Hence, every herald of the true life must summon men to prepare the way of the Lord by putting away evil and putting on the new man. The Divine order must be set up in the private soul; spiritual life, which is easily choked by foul weeds, must be cultivated; and those who love it must be drawn together in a fellowship of faith and labor. From each congregation, as from a luminous centre, the life must spread, claiming and winning for itself the possession and sovereignty of the world. All the kingdoms of trade, industry, literature, science, art, politics, must merge in this kingdom of the Spirit and in the service of a purified humanity. Thus alone shall we secure freedom, peace and progress. Thus alone will the desire of nations be realized in the ideal society and the solidarity of interests, classes and races. Only in this supremacy of spiritual laws and this sunshine of spiritual love will be found a field for deploying all human powers and a climate for the generous growths of a civilization whose fruits shall not be poisonous. Beautiful upon the mountains are the feet of him that cometh in the name of the Lord with these tidings of good! Beautiful and glorious the Church which can thus make itself felt as a power for bringing in everlasting righteousness.—*Rev. C. G. Ames.*

THE REVIVAL THE CHURCH NEEDS.

NOT all revivals are a blessing to the Church. Some are exclusively human as to agencies and results, and do little to raise the moral tone of society. They are mere outbreaks of spasmodic excitement, kindled by artificial methods. The interest passes away with the excitement, and in a short time there remain no evidences either in the Church or out of it that there has been a revival. And so there have been in the history of the Church what are called "man-made" and "spurious" revivals. It is not the fact that these were attended with great excitement that condemns them as spurious. In all genuine revivals there is intense excitement. Peter and John made no small stir in Jerusalem, and every man who is eminently successful in the awakening and conversion of souls does the same. But the excitement is an incident and not an end. When it passes away the blessings of the spiritual shower remain. The nature of the work will be seen by an application of the Divine test: "By their fruits ye shall know them." When there are no visible fruits, in continued zeal and devotion of the Church, and in the thorough reform of those who profess to have been converted, we may be sure that the work was not of God.

The revival we need is not a temporary excitement, but a revival of true Christian living. We do not need a revival of that religion which consists simply of devout fervors of the prayer-meeting and camp-ground, which sings sweet hymns and applauds sweet sermons, and then goes straight off to engage in worldly and sinful self-indulgence and in doubtful business transactions. The Church needs such a revival of righteousness that the closest scrutiny will not reveal any business "crookedness" in any of its members. The religion which keeps God's commandments, which tells the truth and sticks to its promises; which pays a hundred cents to the dollar; which cares more for a righteous character than for a fine coat; which denies ungodly lusts, and can be trusted in every stress of temptation; which leads men to do justly, love mercy, and act charitably in all their relation to their fellow-men, is what the world needs. A conversion that means anything less than this is not worth much to the Church or to the subjects of it.

This revival of practical religion must begin in the Church. Judgment must begin at the house of God. Do all those who have sworn allegiance to Christ give evidence that they are following him? Do they show by their meekness, humility, and Christian conversation that they are the Lord's? Can we go on "Change," and, by the way in which they deal, select from business men of the world those who have vowed to follow the Saviour? Are there not some in the Church whose business morality is far below the Gospel standard? If there are, then the first step toward a revival is to insist on their reformation as the only alternative to excision. If such a reform is needed, it must be made as the indispensable condition of the Divine blessing. God will not bless a church that winks at immorality in any of its members. Such hindrances must be removed to prepare the way for the Lord to work.

We need also a revival of spiritual religion. Many in the Church whose character for integrity is above suspicion, who are true and upright in all the relations of life, are yet cold and formal in religion. They have no enthusiasm, no joy in their own religious experience, and no zeal for the salvation of souls. They need to be "quickened" into "newness of life," to have that fresh influx of vitality and power which equips for the work, and fills the soul with joy in doing it. A religion of forms and ceremonies, however scrupulously observed, is unsatisfying to the possessors, and has no attractions for the unconverted. Without the presence and work of the Spirit religion has no value, and a genuine revival of religion is impossible.

We need a continuous revival. We have had enough "high tides" and "tidal waves," enough of ebb and flow. The element of periodicity in revival effort works injury to the Church by making the impression on the memberships that there are only special times and seasons when they are expected to do personal work for souls, or can do it successfully. It is fraught with unspeakable peril to the unconverted by encouraging the habit of deferring repentance to "a more convenient season." They wait for a revival; and many die waiting. What we need, therefore, is a revival that shall last all the year and years. Nor is this impossible nor impracticable. There can be no doubt that God would have the Church in a state of revival all the time; and what God wants the Church to do, it certainly can do. A genuine revival is the normal condition of the Church. There is something abnormal and unhealthful in a revival that so exhausts the energies of the Church that it has to be discontinued. All that is essential to do for a revival may be done at any and all seasons of the year. Personal work for souls is indispensable, and that can be done at any time, and should be done all the time. The Divine power needed is available all the time; souls are in peril all the time; why, then, should not the Church be incessantly active? Some one has said, "The Church should always be up to the conversion point." That this is possible is proved by the fact that in some churches there are conversions every week in the year. O that this might be true of every church!—*Central Christian Advocate.*

WORLDLINESS A FOE TO THE CHURCH.

THE Christian is assailed by no temptations more subtle, more constant, or harder to resist, than the temptation to worldliness. He is in the world and has to attend to worldly business, and constantly breathes a worldly atmosphere, and is therefore subject to the strongest inducements to lower his life and conduct to the standards prevailing about him. It is the influence of the multitude, the example of the wealthy, and many in high positions, that he has to withstand. How few there are who resist these influences! It has come to be a proverb that Christians cannot be distinguished from worldlings. The greatest curse and danger to the Christian Church of to-day is its worldliness. Worldly maxims, and customs, and habits prevail to an alarming extent in Christian households, in ecclesiastical affairs, and even in the worship of the sanctuary. It requires more than the ordinary moral stamina and religious integrity not to yield to the tide of worldliness which threatens to engulf the Church and extinguish all vital godliness among the people. Only the strongest resolution, fortified by the grace of God, can enable us to resist the contagious example of wicked men in high places, and stand firmly in the truth and unsullied purity of a genuine Christian character. How much we need, in these latter days, the spirit of such strong, heroic souls as Daniel and the three Hebrew children who could resist all the seductions of the Babylonish court, and maintain their fidelity to God in spite of the den of lions and the fiery furnace! The history of the Church is filled with examples of heroic fidelity to duty against the voice of the world, and in face of the greatest perils. "Nothing on earth surpasses the moral grandeur of those scenes in which one man alone, for the sake of truth, stands opposed to many." Such was Stephen before the Jewish Sanhedrin, and Luther at the Diet of Worms, and Knox. Such were thousands of martyrs who have died rather than conform to the world. Such, also, was Milton's Abdiel, who when a third part of the host of heaven had revolted, was still faithful.

> "Among the faithless, faithful only he;
> Among innumerable false, unmoved;
> Unshaken, unseduced, unterrified,

His loyalty he kept, his love, his zeal ;
Nor number, nor example with him wrought
To swerve from truth, or change his constant mind,
Though he stood single and alone."

—*Western Christian Advocate.*

THE CHURCH IN THE WORLD.

THE Church in the world is like a ship in the ocean. The ship is safe enough in the ocean so long as the ocean is not in the ship. The Church is safe enough in the world so long as the world is not in the Church.

THE WORLD FEARS THE CHURCH.

WE may have learnt, both from sacred history, and times of reformation, that the kings of this world have both ever hated and instinctively feared the Church of God, whether it be for that their doctrine seems much to favor two things to them so dreadful—liberty and equality; or because they are the children of that kingdom, which, as ancient prophecies have foretold, shall in the end break to pieces and dissolve all their great power and dominion. And those kings and potentates who have strove most to rid themselves of this fear by cutting off or suppressing the true Church, have drawn upon themselves the occasion of their own ruin, while they thought with most policy to prevent it. Thus Pharaoh, when once he began to fear and wax jealous of the Israelites, lest they should multiply and fight against him, and that his fear stirred him up to afflict and keep them under, as the only remedy of what he feared, soon found that the evil which before slept came suddenly upon him, by the preposterous way he took to prevent it.—*John Milton.*

THE CHURCH A BRIDE.

CLAD in a robe of pure and spotless white,
  The youthful bride, with timid steps, comes forth,
  To greet the hand to which she plights her troth,
  Her soft eyes radiant with a strange delight.
  The snowy veil which circles her around
  Shades the sweet face from every gazer's eye,
  And thus enwrapt, she passes calmly by,
Nor casts a look, but on the unconscious ground
So should the Church, the Bride elect from Heaven,
Remembering whom she goeth forth to meet,
And with a truth that cannot brook deceit,
Holding the faith which unto her is given,
Pass through this world, which claims her for a while,
Nor cast about her longing look nor smile.
                             —*Alice B. Neal.*

THE CHURCH CHRIST'S BRIDE.

CHURCH of God! believe thyself invincible, and thou art invincible; but stay to tremble and fear, and thou art undone. Lift up thy head and say, "I am God's daughter; I am Christ's bride." Do not stop to prove it, but affirm it; march through the land, and kings and princes shall bow down before thee, because thou hast taken thine ancient glory.—*Charles Spurgeon.*

PURITY OF THE CHURCH.

IN the purity of the Church lies its strength. Its spirituality is its health, its vitality, its power. In proportion as it is free from worldliness will be its power for good and its purifying influence on human society; and, on the other hand, the more the spirit of the world pervades the Church, the less fitted for its divine mission of disciplining all nations the Church will be, because of the consequent diminution of its strength. The Church preserved in its pristine purity, "looketh forth as the morning, fair as the moon, clear as the sun, and terrible as an army with banners," but its alliance with the world, or its subjection to prevalent worldly influences, corrupts its purity, mars its beauty, destroys its lustre, and impairs its strength. Samson paid dearly for his incontinent intercourse with Delilah, by the loss of his power: "The Lord departed from him, and he did grieve in the prison house." We must guard with a jealous eye the spirituality and purity of the Church of Christ—" the bride, the Lamb's wife.' Some attempts have been made to abolish the distinction between the Church and the congregation, and it has been maintained that the mere desire to join the Church is sufficient without the ordinary tests of spiritual life. But "we have no such custom." The spiritual distinction between believers and unbelievers must be maintained; and to the utmost of our ability we must guard the Church against corruption and constant feebleness, by requiring in those who seek admission to its fellowship evidence of their being "new creatures in Christ Jesus." We have our faults—not a few—and we are often told that one is an undue glorification of ourselves. For all of them we implore divine forgiveness; but we trust we shall never be able to lay it to our charge that we have done aught to lower the standard of Christian life, or to erase any of the distinctive marks which must ever define the Church in its separation from the world.—*Rev. J. Baxandale.*

THE SHINING CHURCH.

THE Church illuminates the world by a manifestation of its piety. Its power to fulfil this, its most peculiar and essential function, may be measured by the faith, zeal, and holiness of its members.

A church may be what the world calls strong in point of members and influence. A church may be made up of men of wealth, men of intellect, men of power, high-born men, and men of rank and fashion, and being so composed, may be in a worldly sense a very strong church. There are many things that such a church can do. It can launch ships and endow seminaries. It can diffuse intelligence, can uphold the cause of benevolence, can maintain an imposing array of forms and religious activities. It can build splendid temples, can rear a magnificent pile and adorn its front with sculptures, and lay stone upon stone, and heap ornament upon ornament, till the costliness of the ministrations at the altar shall keep any poor man from ever entering the portal. But I will tell you one thing that it cannot do—it cannot *shine*. It may glitter and blaze like an iceberg in the sun, but without inward holiness it cannot shine.

Of all that is formal and material in Christianity it may make a splendid manifestation, but it cannot shine.

It may turn almost everything into gold at its touch, but it cannot touch the heart. It may lift up its marble front, and pile tower upon tower, and mountain upon mountain, but it cannot touch the mountain, and they shall smoke; it cannot conquer souls for Christ; it cannot awaken the sympathies of faith and love; it cannot do Christ's work in man's conversion. It is dark in itself, and cannot diffuse light. It is cold at heart, and has no overflowing and subduing influences to pour out upon the lost. And with all its strength, that church is weak, and for Christ's peculiar work, worthless. And with all its glitter of gorgeous array, it is a dark church—it cannot shine.

On the contrary, show me a church poor, illiterate, obscure, unknown, but composed of praying people; they may be men of neither power, nor wealth, nor influence; they may be families that do not know one week where they are to get their bread for the next; but with them is the kindling of God's power, and their influence is felt for eternity, and their light shines, and is watched, and wherever they go there is a fountain of light, and Christ in them is glorified, and his cause advanced.—*Stephen Olin.*

God's house is not the place to make aching heads, it is the place to heal aching hearts. The most outrageous nonsense that is current in theological seminaries is that which deludes young men into the folly of aiming at profound and philosophic treatises for the pulpit.

—T. L. Cuyler.

A GLORIOUS CHURCH.

CHRIST gave himself for the Church, "that he might sanctify and cleanse it with the washing of water by the word, that he might present it to himself a glorious church, not having spot, or wrinkle, or any such thing: but that it should be holy and without blemish." The Church is Christ's personal possession. He has bought it, and built it, and inhabits it. He has given himself for it, and he has designated the Church as his own special heritage. It is not to be the possession of any man or any class of men; it is not to be controlled by ecclesiastics or ruled by magistrates; there are no lords over God's heritage; one Lord alone claims the allegiance of the Church; and it is the purpose of Christ to "present it *to himself*, a glorious church," as his eternal heritage.

Christ's Church will be glorious at the end. There is one glory of the sun, another glory of the moon; but there are moral glories which eclipse all material splendors. Christ's Church will be glorious in its moral excellence, and glorious in its visible and physical manifestations. But it must first be purged from every spot and stain. He gave himself for the Church that he might wash it and cleanse it. His people are washed from their sins in his own blood; and by his Spirit and his Word they are sanctified, purged—fitted for his service and his presence.

The redeemed Church will be without spot. How different from those bodies which call themselves churches in the world. How many of them are spotted by worldliness and stained by vice! Evil habits insinuate themselves among them; wicked men creep in unawares, who are spots in their feasts of charity, feeding themselves without fear; dishonesty, fraud, craft, and worldly guile, ambition, self-seeking, frivolity, vanity, and pride, luxury, idleness, contempt of the poor, love of human praise and worldly pomp and show— all these things are spots and stains upon the Church. There are spots which are visible to the outside world, and which make the Church the scoff and scorn of the ungodly; there are spots which the Church herself beholds with tearful eyes; but what must be the aspect of the Church in the sight of Him whose eyes are as a flame of fire, who reads every thought, and who searches the hearts and tries the reins?

A Church that is glorious in her own eyes may be vile in the eyes of the all-seeing Lord. Such was the Church of Laodicea: rich, prosperous, and contented, but in the sight of the Lord loathesome and defiled. But Christ is to present unto himself a glorious Church. He will at last be satisfied with his redeemed people. The last spot removed, the last stain purged, the Church redeemed, purified, glorified, to stand faultless in the presence of her King, robed in his own righteousness, crowned with his own glory, without fault, before the throne of God.

Are we included in that spotless Church? or are we spotted and defiled, that we should be rejected and cast out from that glorious fellowship? Let us lay our hearts bare before the Lord, and so seek to know his mind and to do his will concerning us, that we shall stand at last accepted in the presence of his glory, faultless, and with exceeding joy.—*The Christian.*

HISTORY OF THE PRIMITIVE CHRISTIANS; THE PURITY OF THEIR LIVES.

CHRISTIANITY offered itself to the world armed with the strength of the Mosaic law and delivered from the weight of its fetters. An exclusive zeal for the truth of religion and the unity of God was as carefully inculcated in the new as in the ancient system, and whatever was now revealed to mankind concerning the nature and designs of the Supreme Being was fitted to increase their reverence for that mysterious doctrine. The divine authority of Moses and the prophets was admitted and even established as the firmest basis of Christianity. The ceremonial law, which consisted only of types and figures, was succeeded by a pure and spiritual worship, equally adapted to all climates as well as to every condition of mankind; and for the initiation of blood was substituted a more harmless initiation of water. The promise of divine favor, instead of being partially confined to the posterity of Abraham, was universally proposed to the free man and the slave, to the Greek and to the barbarian, to the Jew and to the Gentile. Every privilege that could raise the proselyte from earth to heaven, that could exalt his devotion, secure his happiness, or even gratify that secret pride which, under the semblance of devotion, insinuates itself into the human heart, was still reserved for the members of the Christian Church, but at the same time all mankind was permitted and even solicited to accept the glorious distinction which was not only proffered as a favor but imposed as an obligation. It became the most sacred duty of a new convert to diffuse among his friends and relations the inestimable blessing which he had received, and to warn them against a refusal, that would be severely punished as a criminal disobedience to the will of a benevolent but all-powerful Deity.

Whatever difference of opinion might subsist between the orthodox, the Ebionites and the Gnostics concerning the divinity or the obligation of the Mosaic law, they were all equally animated by the same exclusive zeal and by the same abhorrence for idolatry which had distinguished the Jews from the other nations of the ancient world. The philosopher who considered the system of polytheism as a composition of human fraud and error could disguise a smile of contempt under the mask of devotion without apprehending that either the mockery or the compliance would expose him to the resentment of any invisible, or, as he conceived them, imaginary powers. But the established religions of paganism were seen by the primitive Christians in a much more odious and formidable light. It was the universal sentiment both of the Church and of heretics that the demons were the authors, the patrons and the objects of idolatry. Those rebellious spirits who had been degraded from the ranks of angels and cast down into the infernal pit were still permitted to roam upon earth to torment the bodies and to seduce the minds of sinful men. The demons soon discovered and abused the natural propensity of the human heart toward devotion, and, artfully withdrawing the adoration of mankind from their Creator, they usurped the place and honors of the Supreme Deity. By the success of their malicious contrivances they at once gratified their own vanity and revenge and obtained the only comfort of which they were yet susceptible—the hope involving the human species in the participation of their guilt and misery. It was confessed, or, at least, it was imagined, that they had distributed among themselves the important characters of polytheism, one demon assuming the name and attributes of Jupiter, another of the Æsculapius, a third of Venus and a fourth, perhaps, of Apollo, and that by the advantage of their long experience and aerial nature they were enabled to execute with sufficient skill and dignity the parts which they had undertaken. They lurked in the temples, instituted festivals and sacrifices, invented fables, pronounced oracles and were frequently allowed to perform miracles. The Christians who by interposition of evil spirits could so readily explain every preternatural appearance, were disposed and even desirous to admit the most extravagant fictions of the pagan mythology. But the belief of the Christian was accompanied with horror. The most trifling mark of respect to the national worship he considered as a direct homage yielded to the demon and as an act of rebellion against the majesty of God. In consequence of this opinion it was the first duty of a Christian to preserve himself pure and undefiled from the practice of idolatry. The religion of the nations was not merely a speculative doctrine professed in the schools or preached in the temples. The innumerable deities and rites of polytheism were closely interwoven with every circumstance of business or pleasure, of public or of private life, and it seemed impossible to escape the observance of them without at the same time renouncing the commerce of mankind and all the offices and amusements of society. The important transactions of peace and war were prepared or concluded by solemn sacrifices, in which the magistrate, the senator and the soldier were obliged to preside or to participate. The public spectacles were an essential part of the cheerful devotion of the pagans, and the gods were supposed to accept as the most grateful offering the games that the prince and people celebrated in honor of their peculiar festivals. The Christian who with pious horror avoided the abomination of the circus or the theatre found himself encompassed with infernal snares in every convivial entertainment; as often as his friends, invoking the hospitable deities, poured out libations to each other's happiness; when the bride, struggling with well-affected reluctance, was forced in hymeneal pomp over the threshold of her new habitation, or when the sad procession of the dead slowly moved towards the funeral pile. The Christian on these interesting occasions was compelled to desert the persons who were the dearest to him rather than contract the guilt inherent to those impious ceremonies. Every art and every trade that was in the least concerned in the framing or adorning of idols was polluted by the stain of idolatry. A severe sentence, since it devoted to eternal misery the far greater part of the community which is employed in the exercise of liberal or mechanic professions. If we cast our eyes over the numerous remains of antiquity we shall perceive that besides the immediate representations of the gods and the holy instruments of their worship, the elegant forms and agreeable fictions consecrated by the imagination of the Greeks were introduced as the richest ornaments of the houses, the dress and the furniture of the pagan. Even the arts of music and painting, of eloquence and poetry, flowed from the same impure origin. In the style of the fathers, Apollo and the muses were the organs of the infernal spirit. Homer and Virgil were the most eminent of his servants, and the beautiful mythology which pervades and animates the composition of their genius is destined to celebrate the glory of the demons. Even the common language of Greece and Rome abounded with familiar but impious expressions which the imprudent Christian might too carelessly utter or too patiently hear. The dangerous temptations which on every side lurked in ambush to surprise the unguarded believer assailed him with redoubled violence on the days of solemn festivals. So artfully were they framed and disposed throughout the year that superstition always wore the appearance of pleasure and often of virtue. Some of the most sacred festivals in the Roman ritual were destined to salute the new calends of January with vows of public and private felicity, to indulge the pious remembrance of the dead and living, to ascertain the inviolable bounds of property, to hail on the return of spring the genial powers of fecundity, to perpetuate the two memorable eras of Rome, the foundation of the city and that of the republic, and to restore during the human license of the Saturnalia the primitive equality of mankind.

Some idea may be conceived of the abhorrence of the Christian for such impious ceremonies by the scrupulous delicacy which they displayed on a much less alarming occasion. On days of general festivity it was the custom of the ancients to adorn their doors with lamps and with branches of laurel, and to crown their heads with a garland of flowers. This innocent and elegant practice might perhaps have been tolerated as a mere civil institution, but it most unluckily happened that the doors were under the protection of the household gods; that the laurel was sacred to the lover of Daphne, and that garlands of flowers, though frequently worn as a symbol of joy or mourning, had been dedicated in their first origin to the service of superstition. The trembling Christians who were persuaded in this instance to comply with the fashion of their country and the commands of the magistrate, labored under the most gloomy apprehensions from the reproaches of their own conscience, the censures of the Church, and denunciations of divine vengeance. Such was the anxious diligence which was required to guard the chastity of the Gospel from the infectious breath of idolatry. The superstitious observances of public or private rites were carelessly practised from education and habit by the followers of the established religion, but as often as they occurred they afforded the Christians an opportunity of declaring and confirming their zealous opposition. By these frequent protestations their attachment to the faith was continually fortified, and in proportion to the increase of zeal they combated with the more ardor and success in the holy war, which they had undertaken against the empire of the demons. The writings of Cicero represent in the most lively colors the ignorance, the errors and the uncertainty of the ancient philosophers with regard to the immortality of the soul. When they are desirous of arming their disciples against the fear of death, they inculcate as an obvious, though melancholy position, that the fatal stroke of our dissolution releases us from the calamities of life, and that those can no longer exist. Yet there were a few sages of Greece and Rome who had conceived a more exalted, and, in some respects, a juster idea of human nature, though it must be confessed that in the sublime inquiry their reason had been often guided by their imagination; had been prompted by their vanity. When they viewed with complacency the extent of their own mental powers; when they exercised the various faculties of memory, of fancy and of judgment in the most profound speculation or the most important labors, and when they reflected on the desire of fame which transported them into future ages, far beyond the bounds of death and of the grave, they were unwilling to confound themselves with the beast of the field, or to suppose that a being for whose dignity they entertained the most sincere admiration could be limited to a spot of earth, and to a few years of duration. With this favorable prepossession they summoned to their aid the science, or, rather, the language of Metaphysics. They soon discovered that as none of the properties of matter will apply to the operations of the mind, the human soul must consequently be a substance distinct from the body, pure, simple and spiritual, incapable of dissolution, and susceptible of a much higher degree of virtue and happiness after the release from its corporeal prison. From these specious and noble principles the philosophers, who had trod in the footsteps of Plato, deduced a very unjustifiable conclusion, since they asserted, not only the future immortality, but the past eternity of the human soul, which they were too apt to consider as a portion of the infinite and self-existing spirit which pervades and sustains the universe. A doctrine thus removed beyond the senses and the experience of mankind might serve to amuse the leisure of a philosophic mind, or in the silence of solitude it might sometimes impart a ray of comfort to desponding virtue, but the faint impression which had been received in the schools was soon obliterated by the commerce and business of active life. We are sufficiently acquainted with the eminent persons who flourished in the age of Cicero, and of the first Cæsars, with their actions, their characters and their motives, to be assured that their conduct in this life was never regulated by any serious conviction of the rewards or punishments of a future state. At the bar and in the

Senate of Rome, the ablest orators were not apprehensive of giving offence to their hearers, by exposing that as an idle and extravagant opinion, which was rejected with contempt by every man of a liberal education and understanding.

Since, therefore, the most sublime efforts of philosophy can extend no farther than feebly to point out the desire, the hope, or at most the probability of a future state, there is nothing except a divine revelation that can ascertain the existence and describe the condition of the invisible country which is destined to receive the souls of men after their separation from the body. But we may perceive several defects inherent to the popular religions of Greece and Rome which rendered them very unequal to so arduous a task. The general system of their mythology was unsupported by any solid proofs, and the wisest among the pagans had already disclaimed its usurped authority. The description of the infernal regions had been abandoned to the fancy of painters and of poets, who peopled them with so many phantoms and monsters who dispensed their rewards and punishments with so little equity that solemn truth, the most congenial to the human heart, was opposed and disgraced by the absurd mixture of the wildest fictions. The doctrine of a future state was scarcely considered among the devout polytheists of Greece and Rome as a fundamental article of faith. The providence of the gods, as it related to public communities rather than to private individuals, was principally displayed on the visible theatre of the present world. The petitions which were offered on the altars of Jupiter and Apollo expressed the anxiety of their worshippers for temporal happiness, and their ignorance or indifference concerning a future life. The important truth of the immortality of the soul was inculcated with more diligence as well as success in India, in Assyria, in Egypt, and in Gaul, and since we cannot attribute such a difference to the superior knowledge of the barbarians, we must ascribe it to the influence of an established priesthood which employed the motives of virtue as the instrument of ambition. We might naturally expect that a principle so essential to religion would have been revealed in the clearest terms to the chosen people of Palestine, and that it might safely have been intrusted to the hereditary priesthood of Aaron. It is incumbent on us to adore the mysterious dispensations of Providence when we discover that the doctrine of the immortality of the soul is omitted in the law of Moses. It is darkly insinuated by the prophets, and during the long period which elapsed between the Egyptian and Babylonian servitudes the hopes as well as fears of the Jews appear to have been confined within the narrow compass of the present life. After Cyrus had permitted the exiled nation to return into the Promised Land, and after Ezra had restored the ancient records of their religion, two celebrated sects, the Sadducees and the Pharisees, insensibly arose at Jerusalem. The former, selected from the more opulent and distinguished ranks of society, were strictly attached to the literal sense of the Mosaic law, and they piously rejected the immortality of the soul as an opinion that received no countenance from the divine book which they revered as the only rule of their faith. To the authority of Scripture the Pharisees added that of tradition, and they accepted under the name of traditions several speculative tenets from the philosophy or religion of the Eastern nations. The doctrines of fate or predestination of angels and spirits and of a future state of rewards and punishments were in the number of these new articles of belief, and as the Pharisees, by the austerity of their manners, had drawn into their party the body of the Jewish people, the immortality of the soul became the prevailing sentiment of the synagogue under the reign of the Asmonean princes and pontiffs. The temper of the Jews was incapable of contenting itself with such a cold and languid assent as might satisfy the mind of a polytheist, and as soon as they admitted the idea of a future state they embraced it with the zeal which has always formed the characteristic of the nation. Their zeal, however, added nothing to its evidence, or even probability, and it was still necessary that the doctrine of life and immortality, which had been dictated by nature, approved by reason and received by superstition, should obtain the sanction of divine truth from the authority and example of Christ. When the promise of eternal happiness was proposed to mankind on condition of adopting the faith and of observing the precepts of the Gospel, it is no wonder that so advantageous an offer should have been accepted by great numbers of every religion, of every rank, and of every province in the Roman Empire. The ancient Christians were animated by a contempt for their present existence and by a just confidence of immortality, of which the doubtful and imperfect faith of modern ages cannot give us any adequate notion. In the primitive Church the influence of truth was very powerfully strengthened by an opinion which, however it may deserve respect for its usefulness and antiquity, has not been found agreeable to experience. It was universally believed that the end of the world and the kingdom of heaven were at hand. The near approach of this wonderful event had been predicted by the apostles, the tradition of it was preserved by their earliest disciples, and those who understood in their literal senses the discourse of Christ himself, were obliged to expect the second and glorious coming of the Son of man in the clouds before that generation was totally extinguished which had beheld his humble condition upon earth, and which might still be witness of the calamities of the Jews under Vespasian or Hadrian.

The revolution of seventeen centuries has instructed us not to press too closely the mysterious language of prophecy and revelation, but as long as for wise purposes this error was permitted to subsist in the Church it was productive of the most salutary effects on the faith and practice of Christians, who lived in the awful expectation of that moment when the globe itself and all the various races of mankind should tremble at the appearance of their Judge. The primitive Christian demonstrated his faith by his virtues, and it was very justly supposed that the divine persuasion which enlightened or subdued the understanding must at the same time purify the heart and direct the actions of the believer. The first apologists of Christianity who justify the innocence of their brethren and the writers of a later period who celebrate the sanctity of their ancestors, display in the most lively colors the reformation of manners which was introduced into the world by the preaching of the Gospel. As it is my intention to remark only such human causes as were permitted to second the influence of revelation, I shall slightly mention two motives which might naturally render the lives of the primitive Christians much purer and more austere than those of their pagan contemporaries, or their degenerate successors—repentance for their past sins and the laudable desire of supporting the reputation of the society in which they were engaged. It is a very ancient reproach suggested by the ignorance or the malice of infidelity that the Christians allured into their party the most atrocious criminals who, as soon as they were touched by a sense of remorse, were easily persuaded to wash away in the water of baptism the guilt of their past conduct for which the temples of the gods refused to grant them any expiation. But this reproach, when it is cleared from misrepresentation, contributes as much to the honor as it did to the increase of the Church. The friends of Christianity may acknowledge without a blush that many of the most eminent saints had been before their baptism the most abandoned sinners. Those persons who in the world had followed, though in an imperfect manner, the dictates of benevolence and propriety, derived such a calm satisfaction from the opinion of their own rectitude as rendered them much less susceptible of the sudden emotions of shame or grief and of terror which have given birth to so many wonderful conversions. After the example of their divine Master, the missionaries of the Gospel disdained not the society of men, and especially of women, oppressed by the consciousness and very often by the effects of their vices. As they emerged from sin and superstition to the glorious hope of immortality, they resolved to devote themselves to a life not only of virtue but of penitence. The desire of perfection became the ruling passion of their soul, and it is well known that while reason embraces a cold mediocrity, our passions hurry us with rapid violence over the space which lies between the most opposite extremes. When the new converts had been enrolled in the number of the faithful and were admitted to the sacraments of the Church they found themselves restrained from relapsing into their past disorders by another consideration, of a less spiritual but of a very innocent and respectable nature. Any particular society that has departed from the great body of the nation, or the religion to which it belonged, immediately becomes the object of universal as well as invidious observation. In proportion to the smallness of its numbers, the character of the society may be affected by the virtues and vices of the persons who compose it, and every member is engaged to watch with the most vigilant attention over his own behavior and over that of his brethren, since as he must expect to incur a part of the common disgrace he may hope to enjoy a share of the common reputation. When the Christians of Bittrynia were brought before the tribunal of the younger Pliny, they assured the proconsul that far from being engaged in any unlawful conspiracy they were bound by a solemn obligation to abstain from the commission of those crimes which disturb the private or public peace of society from theft, robbery, adultery, perjury and fraud. Near a century afterward Tertullian with an honest pride could boast that very few Christians had suffered by the hand of the executioner except on account of their religion. Their serious and sequestered life, averse to the gay luxury of the age, inured them to chastity, temperance, economy and all the sober and domestic virtues. As the greater number were of some trade or profession it was incumbent on them by the strictest integrity and the fairest dealing to remove the suspicions which the profane are too apt to conceive against the appearances of sanctity. The contempt of the world exercised them in the habits of humility, meekness and patience. The more they were persecuted the more closely they adhered to each other. Their mutual charity and unsuspecting confidence has been remarked by infidels and was too often abused by perfidious friends. It is a very honorable circumstance for the morals of the primitive Christians that even their faults or rather errors were derived from an excess of virtue. The bishops and doctors of the Church, whose evidence attests and whose authority might influence the professions, the principles and even the practice of their contemporaries, had studied the Scriptures with less skill than devotion, and they often received in the most literal sense those rigid precepts of Christ and the apostles to which the prudence of succeeding commentators has applied a looser and more figurative mode of interpretation. Ambitious to exalt the perfection of the Gospel above the wisdom of philosophy, the zealous fathers have carried the duties of self-mortification, of purity and of patience to a height which it is scarcely possible to attain and much less to preserve in our present state of weakness and corruption. A doctrine so extraordinary and so sublime must inevitably command the veneration of the people, but it was ill calculated to obtain the suffrage of those worldly philosophers who, in the conduct of this transitory life, consult only the feelings of nature and the interest of society.

—*Edward Gibbon.*

THE CHURCH STILL UNFLINCHING.

THE Church of Christ, if called to pass again through the age of martyrdom, would, I believe, be as unflinching in maintaining the truth, or in sealing her testimony in blood, as in the days of Ridley and Latimer, or in the earlier age of Perpetua and Felicita, when rich and poor, bond and free, were one in a common loyalty to the truth and in pouring out their blood in its defence.—*Bishop Hurst.*

THE CHURCH STRENGTHENED BY PERSECUTION.

THERE are other things besides the sturdy oak which the roaring tempest nurses into strength. The storms that strip the tree of some leaves, perhaps of some rotten branches, but moor it deeper in the rifts of everlasting rock. Christ's words cannot fail: On this rock have I built my Church, and the gates of hell shall not prevail against it.—*Rev. Thomas Guthrie.*

LOVE FOR THE CHURCH.

I LOVE thy kingdom, Lord,
   The house of thine abode,
The Church our blest Redeemer saved
   With his own precious blood.

I love thy Church, O God!
   Her walls before thee stand,
Dear as the apple of thine eye,
   And graven on thy hand.

For her my tears shall fall,
   For her my prayers ascend,
To her my cares and toils be given,
   Till toils and cares shall end.

Beyond my highest joy
   I prize her heavenly ways,
Her sweet communion, solemn vows,
   And hymns of love and praise.

Sure as thy truth shall last,
To Zion shall be given
The brightest glories earth can yield,
And brighter bliss of heaven.
—*Timothy Dwight.*

THE CHURCH INDISPENSABLE.

F all the dispositions and habits which lead to political prosperity, religion and morality are indispensable supports. In vain would that man claim the tribute of patriotism, who should labor to subvert these great pillars of human happiness—these foremost props of the duties of men and citizens. The mere politician, equally with the pious man, ought to respect and to cherish them. A volume could not trace all their connection with private and public felicity. Let it be simply asked, where is the security for property, for reputation, for life, if the sense of religious obligation desert the oaths which are the instruments of investigation in courts of justice? And let us with caution indulge the supposition that morality can be maintained without religion. Whatever may be conceded to the influence of refined education on minds of peculiar structure, reason and experience both forbid us to expect that national morality can prevail in exclusion of religious principles.—*George Washington.*

CHRISTIANITY came into the world with a cross in one hand and a crown in the other—the one bending earthward, marked "Present," and the other flashing skyward, marked "Future."—*Rev. W. C. Richards.*

THE CHURCH THE MOTHER OF ALL GOOD.

ST. PAUL carried in his own person across the Ægean Sea to Europe the printing-press, the telescope, the cotton gin, the power loom, the modern plow, the steam engine, the microscope, the magnetic telegraph, railroads, Kepler, Sir Isaac Newton, the Herschels, Christopher Columbus and America.
—*Bishop Marvin.*

THE WORLD WITHOUT THE CHURCH.

REFLECT what kind of a world this was when the disciples of Christ undertook to reform it, and compare it with the condition in which their teachings have put it. In its mighty metropolis, the centre of its intellectual and political power, the best men were addicted to vices so debasing that I could not even allude to them without soiling the paper I write upon. All manner of unprincipled wickedness was practised in the private life of the whole population without concealment or shame, and the magistrates were thoroughly and universally corrupt. Benevolence in any shape was altogether unknown. The helpless and the weak got neither justice nor mercy. There was no relief for the poor, no succor for the sick, no refuge for the unfortunate. In all pagandom there was not a hospital, asylum, alms-house, or organized charity of any sort. The indifference to human life was literally frightful. The order of a successful man to assassinate his opponents was always obeyed by his followers with the utmost alacrity and pleasure. It was a special amusement of the populace to witness the shows at which men were compelled to kill one another, to be torn in pieces by wild beasts, or otherwise "butchered to make a Roman holiday." In every province paganism enacted the same cold-blooded cruelties; oppression and robbery ruled supreme; murder went rampaging and red over all the earth.

The Church came, and her light penetrated this darkness like a new sun. She covered the globe with institutions of mercy, and thousands upon thousands of her disciples devoted themselves exclusively to works of charity at the sacrifice of every earthly interest. Her earliest adherents were killed without remorse—beheaded, crucified, sawn asunder, thrown to the beasts, or covered with pitch, piled up in great heaps, and slowly burned to death. But her faith was made perfect through suffering, and the law of love rose in triumph from the ashes of her martyrs. This religion has come down to us through the ages, attended all the way by righteousness, temperance, mercy, transparent truthfulness, exulting hope and white-winged charity. Never was its influence for good more plainly perceptible than now. It has not converted, purified, and reformed all men, for its first principle is the freedom of the human will, and there are those who choose to reject it. But to the mass of mankind, directly and indirectly, it has brought uncounted benefits and blessings. Abolish it—take away the restraints which it imposes on evil passions; silence the admonitions of its preachers; let all Christians cease their labors of charity; blot out from history the record of its heroic benevolence; repeal the laws it has enacted and the institutions it has built up; let its moral principles be abandoned and all its miracles of light be extinguished—what would we come to? I need not answer; the experiment has been partially tried. The French nation formally renounced Christianity, denied the existence of the Supreme Being, and so satisfied the hunger of the infidel heart for a time. What followed? Universal depravity, garments rolled in blood, fantastic crimes, unimagined before, which startled the earth with their sublime atrocity. People have, and ought to have, no special desire to follow that terrible example of guilt and misery.—*Judge Black.*

OBJECT OF THE CHURCH.

THE Church was built to disturb the peace of man; but often it does not perform its duty, for fear of disturbing the peace of the Church. What kind of artillery-practice would that be which declined to fire for fear of kicking over the gun-carriages, or waking up the sentinels asleep at their post?—*H. W. Beecher.*

BUSINESS OF THE CHURCH.

IT is the business of the Church to echo God. Any church which does this will be heard around the world. Not the man for the times, but the Church for the times, is the proper rallying cry of reform. No one man will ever save the world. A combination of aggressive, omnipresent churches may.—*Joseph Cook.*

WHAT THE CHURCH MUST DO.

THE Church must grope her way into the alleys and courts and purlieus of the city, and up the broken staircases, and into the bare room, and beside the loathsome sufferer; she must go down into the pit with the miner, into the forecastle with the sailor, into the tent with the soldier, into the shop with the mechanic, into the factory with the operative, into the field with the farmer, into the counting-room with the merchant. Like the air, the Church must press equally upon all the surfaces of society; like the sea, flow into every nook of the shore line of humanity; and like the sun, shine on things foul and low as well as fair and high; for she was organized, commissioned and equipped for the moral reformation of the whole world.—*Bishop Simpson.*

THE SPECIFIC WORK OF THE CHURCH.

THE specific work of the Church of God is the work of proclaiming the gospel, saving sinners and building up saints in the most holy faith. When they address themselves to this work God blesses and prospers them in their endeavors. When they turn aside to other pursuits they find themselves involved in difficulties. The Church of God is not a trading corporation, organized for the purpose of holding fairs and bazaars and dealing in knick-knacks and fancy goods, thus entering into a damaging competition with legitimate traders and spending infinite labor for infinitessimal gains. In matters of merchandise no church can long compete with private individuals or commercial companies, and the success they achieve by levying contributions and calling persons from other duties to assist them may be apparent, but it is by no means permanent.

Christians are not called to the business of furnishing amusements. There are places of amusement, and proprietors of theatres, play-houses and concert-rooms can out-do them in this field of endeavor. It is impossible for the Church, with her amateur theatricals and other modes of amusement, to compete with men whose lives and energies are devoted to catering to the public taste. Christians may degrade or disgrace themselves and cultivate an appetite for worldly amusements, which will allure their followers on to other and still more objectionable enjoyments, but they cannot succeed as pleasure-makers in the sharp competition which exists in the present day, when men are lovers of pleasure more than lovers of God.

The Church of Christ is not an institution for the exhibition of imposing architecture. They may waste their Lord's money and involve themselves in debts and embarrassments; they may worship beneath the towering spires of mortgaged meeting-houses and tax themselves for generations to pay the expenses which their pride engenders, but when they have done all the world will distance them. They cannot build temples like those which ancient art dedicated to the basest idolatries, and their performances are mean and paltry compared with the grander structures of heathen antiquity which, conceived in the most artistic taste, were conjoined with the most beastly idolatries.

Whatever enterprises the Church may undertake, whether educational, architectural, social or commercial, she will find herself at a disadvantage and be distanced in the race. But if she will keep to her work as a witness-bearer for the Lord of hosts; if she will testify of the gospel of God's grace and in lowliness and humility pursue the path appointed by the Lord, she will find in his presence her strength and in his smile her joy—a strength that is made perfect in weakness and a joy that no man can take away. Let the energies that are devoted to secular pursuits and worldly devices be poured into the legitimate channels of Christian life and Christian labor, and the results will appear in the winning of sinners from the error of their ways and in the building up of the Church of Christ in their most holy faith. The day of eternity will show how light are all these earthly trifles compared with the glory of those who, having turned many to righteousness, "shall shine as the brightness of the firmament" and "as the stars for ever and ever."—*The Common People.*

THE CHURCH SEEKS THE LOST.

TO-DAY Christianity in her white robes stands upon the threshold of each great idolatry and of each idolatrous nation and tribe and knocks for admission, and, in spite of the devil, she will enter into the sanctuaries of earth's darkest idolatries and preach Christ and him crucified, and before the calm splendor of Christ's gospel heathen gods will fall as Dagon fell before the ancient Shekinah of Jehovah's presence.—*Rev. I. G. Bidwell.*

THE CHURCH AGGRESSIVE.

THE Christian Church is in principle and by divine authority missionary. Its life is one with the spirit of propagation, diffusion, aggression. No one can mistake this or fail to apprehend it as the genius of her founder and his apostles. Lacking this, Christianity proves herself fallen from her high estate. She has that which every nation under the sun needs and which but herself can adequately supply. Her empire, by right, is a universal one, unrestricted by zones, races or governments. And to win to herself that which by right is hers she must be missionary. To all who have not what she has she is compelled to carry and offer her gifts.—*Rev. Thomas Guard.*

WHAT THE CHURCH HAS ACCOMPLISHED.

IT expelled cruelty; it curbed passion; it branded suicide; it punished and repressed an execrable infanticide; it drove the shameless impurities of heathendom into a congenial darkness. There was hardly a class whose wrongs it did not remedy: it rescued the gladiator; it freed the slave; it protected the captive; it nursed the sick; it sheltered the orphan; it elevated woman; it shrouded with a halo of sacred innocence the tender years of the child. In every region of life its ameliorating influence was felt. It changed pity from a vice into a virtue; it elevated poverty from a curse into a beatitude; it ennobled labor from a vulgarity into a dignity and a duty; it sanctified marriage from little more than a burdensome convention into little less than a blessed sacrament. It revealed for the first time the angelic beauty and purity of which men had despaired, of meekness at which they utterly scoffed. It created the very conception of charity, and broadened the limits of its obligations from the narrow circle of a neighborhood to the widest horizons of the race. And while it thus involved the idea of humanity as a common brotherhood, even where its teachings were not believed—all over the world, wherever its tidings were believed, it cleansed the life and elevated the soul of each individual man. And in all lands where it moulded the character of its true believers, it has created hearts so pure, and lives so peaceful, and homes so sweet, that it might seem as though those angels who had heralded its advent had also whispered to every despairing and depressed sufferer among the sons of men: "Though you have lain among the pots, yet shall ye be as the wings of a dove covered with silver, and her feathers with yellow gold."—*Farrar*.

THE CHURCH A LEADER.

THE time chosen for the advance of Israel into the promised land seemed singularly unpropitious. The spring rains had filled the Jordan with a rapid and dangerous flood. At this season of the year it cannot be forded; swimming it is even a dangerous feat. Bridges there were none; the inhabitants on the other side rested for the time in absolute security. But the host was set in motion, wondering, doubtless, to what useful end. The priests led the way, bearing the Ark of the Covenant upon their shoulders; the army followed at a little distance. No sooner had the soles of the priests' feet touched the swelling flood than the waters suddenly opened a way for the host of Israel. "High up the river, far away, in Adam, the city which is beside Zaretan, that is at a distance of thirty miles from the place of the Israelite encampment, the waters there stood which descended from the heights above—stood and rose up as if gathered into a waterskin; as if in a barrier or heap; as if congealed; and those that descended toward the sea of the desert—the salt sea—failed, and were cut off. Thus the scene presented is of the descending stream not parted asunder, as we generally fancy, but, as the Psalm expressed it, turned backwards; the whole bed of the river left dry from north to south, through its long windings; the huge stones lying bare here and there, embedded in the soft bottom, or the shingly pebbles drifted along the course of the bottom. The Ark stood above; the army passed below. The women and children, according to the Jewish traditions, were placed in the centre, from fear lest they should be swept away by the violence of the current. The host, at different points probably, rushed across. The priests remained motionless, their feet sunk in the deep mud of the channel." The rude monument, made of twelve stones taken from the bed of the Jordan, long remained on the bank at this spot to mark the locality, and to keep alive the memory of the passage.

The fact that stands out in notable prominence in this narrative is the position of the Church, represented by the Ark and the priests, as a leader in this memorable passage. The Church was both vanguard and rearguard. The priests were first to enter the river valley; not till their bare feet were washed by the flood did it draw back; and they were the last to leave the centre of the river-bed, after all else had passed over. The fact is typical.

The Church has at some times, nay, often, resisted human progress; but it has been only when she was degenerate and apostate. The true Church has always been the advanced guard; first to lead the way, bold to press forward, patient to wait. In the journeyings in the wilderness the Tabernacle was the leader of the host when in motion, and the centre and heart of the camp when at rest. When Christ was born the Jewish Church was given over wholly to traditionalism and ceremonialism; but the new advance to a Christian civilization was inspired by Christ and led by Paul; the Ark and the Church—the new Christian Church—went before, and humanity followed after. Throughout the Middle Ages the Church, with all its faults, with all its apostate endeavors to resist the irresistible progress of human thought, yet furnished the great thought-leaders. She gave literature its refuge and *literati* their resting-places. She furnished science with her pioneers and agriculture with her first advance from an ignorant drudgery to an intelligent industry. She educated Luther, and Copernicus, and Columbus, and Ridley, and Latimer, and Tyndal, and William of Orange, and Coligny, and Cromwell. It was her energy that founded the first successful colonies in New England. It was her voice in Whitefield and Wesley that first awoke the common people of England to that life whose nineteenth century fruits are household suffrage, a public-school system, and a national temperance movement. Her ships, sent out by a missionary church, have opened the ports where tardier commerce has followed. And the same Church to-day in our own land is planting the school, academy, college, and house of worship alongside the station and the farmhouse in the far West.

It is true that the Church has often resisted progress, sometimes with fire and sword; but it has itself furnished the antidotes to its own deathly content. The victors over its own torpor have been its own children. Paul was a Jewish Rabbi, and Luther a Roman Catholic monk. Infidelity has sometimes broken down obstacles, but it has pioneered no one; it has led nowhere. The leaders in scientific progress have been the men who have taught that nature is the handiwork of God, and therefore to be studied as his book, bestowed upon man, and therefore to be used as his inheritance. Copernicus and Galileo were both faithful children of the Church. Liberty has been nurtured in her lap; religious liberty has preceded civil; belief in the equality of all men before God's judgment throne has prepared the way for belief in the equality of all men before earthly courts and thrones. Alfred the Great was a great king because he was a true believer; he hewed out of the Bible the grand foundations of the British Constitution. The Franciscan friars were the educators of that Simon de Montfort, who was founder of the English Parliament. A Puritan conscience and a Puritan church won for England and for us the supremacy of government of the people, by the people, for the people. In all ages the Church which has dreaded progress and resisted it has been a degenerate and apostate Church; the Church which has led the very vanguard of thought and life has been the Church of the living God. To-day in America the true Church is not the one which rests in cushioned pews, content with fields already occupied and victories already won, but that which is pressing forward to occupy new fields and conquer in new battles. The Church never fulfils its highest and noblest function except when its priests bear the ark of God in advance of humanity, and pioneer the way, that civilization, with all its accompaniments of liberty, education, and personal comfort, may follow. In every good word and work, in everything which tends to ameliorate the condition or improve the character of mankind, in every movement to enlarge the sphere or deepen the current of education, to give industry a large play and a better reward, to promote temperance, cleanliness, health, happiness, good government, in village, county, State or nation, the preacher, the teacher, the Christian, in a word the Church, should be in the front rank, leading the way, inspiring courage, inciting hope, strengthening purpose, elevating and clarifying faith, fearless of obstacles, confident in God, assured of victory.—*Lyman Abbott.*

THE CHURCH TO BE UNIVERSAL

LIKE Sion, the Church is, in one view, very small. Hindoos and Chinese speak of her as a low heresy, creeping about the mountains and marshes of Europe; and contrast her with their ancient and colossal establishments. Jews and Mahometans deride her, as cemented by the blood of him that was crucified. And in one sense they are right in so judging; in another, they are fearfully mistaken. Christianity is nothing, except that it is divine—nothing, except that it comes from heaven—nothing, except that it is to cover the whole earth with its power and its praise. The arm of a prophet was just like any other human arm; it possessed precisely the same number of bones, sinews, muscles, and veins. And yet, when raised to heaven, when electrified from above, it could divide the sea, raise the dead, and bring down fire from the clouds. So the true Church of Christ is just an assemblage of simple, humble, sincere men—that is all; but the Lord is on their side, and there we discern a source of energy, which shall yet shatter thrones, change the destiny of nations, and uplift, with resistless force, the mountain of the Lord's house above the mountains and above the hills.

This despised and struggling Church shall yet become universal. "All nations shall flow unto it." Those who wander on the boundless steppes of Tartary, those who shiver amid the eternal ice of Greenland, those who inhabit Africa, that continent of thirst, those who bask in the lovely regions of the South Sea—all, all are to flow to the mountain of the Lord. They are to "flow," they are to come, not in drops, but with the rush and the thunder of mighty streams. "Nations are to be born in one day." A supernatural impulse is to be given to the Christian cause. Christ is again to be, as before, his own missionary. Blessed are the eyes which shall see this great gathering of the nations, and the ears which shall hear the sound thereof. Blessed above those born of woman, especially the devoted men, who, after laboring in the field of the world, shall be rewarded, and at the same time astonished, by finding its harvest home hastened, and the work which they had been pursuing, with strong crying and tears, done to their hands, done completely, and done from heaven. In *this* belief lies the hope and the help of the world. But for a divine intervention we despair of the success of the good cause. Allow us this, and Christianity is sure of a triumph, as speedily as it shall be universal. On Sabbath, the 16th of May, 1836, we saw the sun seized, on the very apex of his glory, as if by a black hand, and so darkened that only a thin round ring of light remained visible, and the chill of twilight came prematurely on. That mass of darkness within seemed the world lying in wickedness, and that thin round ring of light, the present progress of the Gospel in it. But not more certain were we then, that that thin round ring of light was yet to become the broad and blazing sun, than are we now, that through a divine interposal, but not otherwise, shall the "knowledge of the glory of the Lord cover the earth as the waters the sea."—*George Gilfillan.*

ONENESS OF CHRISTIANITY.

I CANNOT but hope that a fairer vision than ever yet has charmed the eyes of men has been reserved, in the wisdom and goodness of God, to illustrate our beloved Union. Union! That is the watchword! Thank God for its meaning, its music, and its power! Union! Civil and religious; the oneness of humanity, and the oneness of Christianity! A religion worthy of our liberty! A religion that may be as much a light to the churches of the world as our liberty is to the states of the world! If Canadians, Mexicans and South Americans; if Irishmen, Englishmen, Welshmen and Scotchmen; if Swedes, Danes and Norwegians; if Portuguese, Spaniards and Frenchmen; if Belgians, Hollanders and Germans; if Swiss, Italians, Poles, Hungarians, Russians and Greeks; if even Turks and Arabs and Persians and Hindoos and Siamese and Chinese and Australians and Polynesians; if, in a word, all the varieties of humanity—except the poor Africans, and even some of them in some of our States—may be here assembled, and made, to all intents and purposes, civilly one, then, I ask, may not even Greek Catholics, if they should come among us, and Roman Catholics, here at least, if nowhere else, and Protestants from all the State Establishments, and Dissenting Protestants of all classes, and our own Independent Protestants of all parties—in a word, may not all the varieties of Christianity be made ecclesiastically one? If all the obstructions of distance, danger, poverty, language, habit, manners and social customs have been overcome in the civil Union, may not the single obstruction of tradition be overcome for the accomplishment of the ecclesiastical union—a simple Christian union—a Holy Bible Union? Here we are, by the good providence of God, one mighty brotherhood, gathered from all nations. Here we are, with the grandest seas of the globe tossing all their billows between our happy shores and the haughty tyrannies of the Old World. Here we are, as citizens, already one. Why not also be one as Christians? Have we not already thrown off a thousand political traditions? And are we not equally at liberty to throw off all sectarian traditions? Then let us use our liberty. Away with the false authority of all divisive traditions! Away with this ecclesiastical opposition to the Bible! The Bible belongs to all! The Bible is acknowledged by all! Let the Bible be obeyed, and it will unite all! If, however, in this, as in the former case, it shall seem that there must be some exceptions, let us pity and pray for them. But let all who can come make haste to come. Let the union be consummated! The tidings of it will electrify the world! Popery, like Lucifer, having ascended to the highest heaven in all the pride of the Son of the Morning, shall suddenly drop into the deepest depth of mockery and scorn!

Infidelity, like Satan, having covered itself with a cloud and slowly exalted its front against the throne of God, shall fall again like lightning to the marsh from which it rose! Paganism, like Mania, worshipping it knows not what, shall be startled by the quickening voice of truth, and clasping her brow at the thrill of returning reason, shall stand before the Highest, illumined, enraptured, and restored! Judaism, weeping by the temple wall, shall hear strange news from the land where her children have never found cause to weep, and confess that Jesus is the Christ! A second and more sacred national flag shall attend the first in all its flights from pole to pole—a flag flashing with the stars of prophets and apostles, and glowing with the stripes of the Saviour's painful but blessed and beckoning atonement; and the United States of America, and the united churches of America, magnifying the Bible and the God of the Bible, and magnified in turn by the benediction of both, shall become and remain "the joy and the praise of the whole earth."—*T. H. Stockton.*

SPREAD OF THE CHURCH.

THE Banyan of the Indian isle
   Spreads deeply down its massive root,
And spreads its branching life abroad,
   And bends to earth with scarlet fruit;
But when the branches reach the ground,
   They firmly plant themselves again:
They rise and spread and droop and root,
   An ever-green and endless chain.

And so the Church of Jesus Christ,
   The blessed Banyan of our God,

Fast-rooted upon Zion's mount,
  Has sent its sheltering arms abroad;
And every branch that from it springs,
  In sacred beauty spreading wide,
As low it bends to bless the earth,
  Still plants another by its side.

Long as the world itself shall last,
  The sacred Banyan still shall spread,
From clime to clime, from age to age,
  Its sheltering shadow shall be shed.
Nations shall seek its pillar'd shade,
  Its leaves shall for their healing be;
The circling flood that feeds its life,
  The blood that crimsoned Calvary.

NUMERICAL PROGRESS OF THE CHURCH.

LISTEN to a few cold figures. What was the number of the Church on the day of Pentecost? It was 3,000, but some seventy years later, at the end of the first century, the Church had increased to some 500,000 souls, which number had increased by the days of Constantine—glorious days for the Church of Christ—to 10,500,000. Then look on, and I do not fear even to look into the dark middle ages when the Church of the West separated itself from and anathematized the Church of the East. At this time the 10,000,000 Christians of the time of Constantine had become 30,000,000, which again by the time of the glorious Reformation had grown to 100,000,000, and at the present time there are on the face of the globe no less than 450,000,000 of Christians. Now, then, may we dare to look forward? The population of the world, as nearly as we can estimate it, is now 1,400,000,000, and, following the same rate of progress as in the past, the number of Christians will also go on increasing in an equal if not a greater ratio, and the gross number will have become mighty almost beyond computation. The statistics which I have quoted may seem curious, but they will bear the test of inspection, and are such as to fill us with hope.

—*Bishop C. J. Ellicott.*

A NEW LITERATURE.

CHRISTIANITY has originated a new form of literature wholly its own—a literature not known under any ancient form of mythology; not known under any form of modern heathenism; not known to infidelity; not known to philosophy; and it has, at the same time, originated an institution most effective for applying that literature, and for securing its own influence over the young—I allude to the Sabbath-school, and to the literature which has been originated by that institution. This, if there were nothing else, would show that Christianity in its efforts to perpetuate and propagate itself is quite abreast of the world. The literature of the Sabbath-school may not be, in respect to quality, all that could be desired, but it may be doubted whether there is any other department of literature that is exerting as much influence on the destinies of mankind.

Infidelity, Mohammedanism and Buddhism have no peculiar literature for the young, nor have they any peculiar institution where to inculcate their sentiments in the young. Science, with great difficulty, prepares books for the young; but its literature in astronomy, botany, chemistry, designed to guide the young, as compared with the literature of the Sabbath-school, is meagre in the extreme. The Sabbath-school and the Sabbath-school library stand by themselves. Both capable, undoubtedly, of great improvement, they are, nevertheless, exerting a vast power on the coming generation; and it is difficult to see how a religion that has such an agency as the Sabbath-school could be exterminated from the world. One day during each week, of every month in the year, the children of this nation are brought directly under Christian instruction, with all the advantages, in theory at least, of calling into the service the best talent, the highest intelligence, the warmest piety, the most devoted zeal existing in the churches. Through all parts of the country, by agencies of its own, that literature is placed in the hands of the young before other influences are brought to bear on them, to form their hearts pure, to teach them to believe the Bible, and to love and serve God.

—Albert Barnes.

THE FOUNTAIN OF SONG.

TRUE song is the gift of God our Maker. He giveth songs even in the night; and songs have ever celebrated his glory and his grace. The creation of the world was heralded by song. "The morning stars sang together, and all the sons of God shouted for joy." The deliverance of Israel from Pharaoh and the Red Sea was celebrated in a song. The advent of Christ to our world brought all the hosts of heaven to sing a joyous strain above his lowly cradle. The renewing of the soul by the grace of God awakens thanksgiving and the voice of melody. The Psalmist, when brought up from the horrible pit and the miry clay, had a new song put in his mouth, "even praise unto our God." The last act of our Saviour's ministry, before he went out to his agony, was to sing a hymn. What music that must have been! The establishment of the kingdom of God and the overthrow of all his enemies will be hailed and greeted with strains of rapturous melody; and the glad ages of Messiah's reign will be ages of perpetual song. Song is the language of thanksgiving, of devotion, of triumph; hence it is the legitimate expression of the emotions of those who joy in God, having become reconciled to him, and thus prepared to show forth the praises of him who has called them to glory and virtue.

There is, probably, no one point where the difference between believers and infidels, saints and sinners, saved and lost, is more manifest than in the department of sacred song. The pardon of sin brings peace and gladness, and this gladness finds expression in song. Said the Psalmist, "Deliver me from blood-guiltiness, O God, thou God of my salvation; and my tongue shall *sing aloud of thy righteousness.*" The fruit of the spirit is *joy;* and joy perpetually breaks forth in song. But guilt and condemnation, and the dark uncertainties of a hopeless future, wake no songs within rebellious and disbelieving hearts. Backsliding and worldliness vainly strive to sing from the heart their "formal songs." Singing tells the condition of the Church. Worldly professors have very little music in their souls. Dead churches hire sinners to praise God for them. Living Christians would as soon hire sinners to eat their breakfasts for them as to sing their psalms. Nightingales and larks do not go hunting for owls and ravens to "render" their evening songs or morning carols.

Christians are a singing people. From the time when Pliny, the Roman governor of Bithynia, wrote—about A. D. 107—to the Emperor Trajan that the Christians "were wont to meet together on a stated day before it was light, and *sing* among themselves, alternately, a hymn to Christ as a god," down through all the ages of conflict and victory, of storm and sorrow, of persecution and triumph, the voice of rejoicing has been in the tabernacles of the righteous, and sacred song has arisen from the lips of the redeemed. The themes of grace and glory have inspired the Church with never-ceasing songs; and in this respect infidelity has never been able to imitate true Christianity. What hymns and tunes can infidelity show that have sung themselves into the hearts of skeptics of every shore? What infidel hymn can be sung in which a vast assembly of skeptics will join, as Christians in ten thousand churches will unite in singing one of their hymns of joy and hope? Infidelity has few joys; why should it have songs? What has it to sing about? Angels sing, but when did the wildest fancy ever dream of a singing devil?

One of the mightiest forces which God has thrown into this world is sacred song, not the mere artistic and mechanical "rendering" of certain notes and strains of music, but the spontaneous outgush of the emotions of the sanctified heart, telling the sorrows and the joys, the sympathies and the affections of the renewed soul. Such music is not purchasable. Those who think to buy or hire it greatly mistake its character. It has its fountain in the joy of God implanted in the Christian's soul, and meets its response in the hearts of those who know whom they have trusted, and who expect to sing His praises forevermore. Infidels can sneer and swear, but can they sing? What have they to sing about? What had the heathen world to sing? If we leave out a few notable strains which acknowledge and honor the unseen God, what remains but amorous and bacchanalian ditties; odes which celebrated the acts of cut-throat and adulterous deities, most of whom would be hung or sent to prison in any decently civilized land; songs which embodied vile thoughts, celebrated base acts, and awoke base passions?

In the room where these lines are written there are nearly 1,500 volumes of sacred hymns and songs; and the writer has seen two other libraries, each of which contained nearly 3,000 volumes of sacred hymns and poetry. And all there is of poetry, and melody, and harmony, about them all is but the echo of the heavenly harmonies that have sounded down from the upper skies. When we sing of the grandeurs of creation, we but re-echo the anthem of the morning stars; when we sing of the glories of redemption, we but repeat the angel's song above the plains of Bethlehem; when we sing of struggle, of conflict, of victory, and of triumph, we rehearse the hymns of the sweet singer of Israel; and when we sing of joys to come, we only anticipate the music of the "New Song" which shall at last be sung before the throne.

Thus our themes of sacred song are the grandest that earth or heaven affords. And what has infidelity or unbelief to put in the place of them? Where are the poems, the songs, the chorales, the grand anthems that have been born of darkness, doubt, and unbelief? Infidelity has no hymns; it has nothing to sing for—no God, no hope, or Creator, no Preserver, no Christ, no Saviour. Imagine a jubilant infidel, contemplating his glorious origin, breaking out to sing:

"All hail the mighty monkey, all hail the ancient calm,
From which, through evolution, I came to be a man!"

Picture an assembly of festive infidels, singing heartily, to "some familiar tune," of the sublime anticipations which fill their bosoms, thus:

> "Between two vast eternities
> Life lies, a vale of sorrow;
> So eat, and drink, and take your ease,
> For we shall die to-morrow.
>
> "Ascending from our mollusk god,
> A glorious path we travel;
> Our course, commencing in the mud,
> Shall finish in the gravel."

We recollect once, after pointing out the barrenness of infidelity in respect to sacred song, we were assailed by a skeptic, who stoutly disputed our assertion that infidelity had no hymns, and said he had an infidel hymn-book which he would bring to show us. We were thankful for the opportunity of seeing it, and so in the course of the day he brought along a little book largely filled up with Christian hymns, out of which the name of *Christ* had been erased, and "reason," "truth," or some other word had been substituted. And this was the way infidels made a hymn-book; much like the man who promised to show cobblers how to make a pair of shoes in two minutes, and who, after having pocketed the admission fees of the crowd, coolly produced a pair of boots, and made them into shoes *by cutting the tops off!*

We remember the story of that captive prince who

languished in a foreign dungeon, and of whom his friends could hear no tidings, until a faithful servant, eager for his release, travelled from land to land, and sang beside the walls of every dungeon the songs which were his delight in bygone days. At length, as the strain of music rolled upward by an old castle wall, there came a response from a grated window above; the captive was discovered, and the way of deliverance was opened. So, by every dungeon-wall which Satan has erected, and in the hearing of every lost sinner whom Satan has led captive at his will, we would have the songs of joy and gladness sung, in the hope that some imprisoned soul may catch the music of the strain, and know the grace of Him who came to proclaim liberty to the captives, and the opening of the prison doors to them that are bound.—*H. L. Hastings.*

THE ONE CHURCH.

THROUGH the night of doubt and sorrow
    Onward goes the pilgrim band,
Singing songs of expectation,
    Marching to the Promised Land.

Clear before us through the darkness
    Gleams and burns the guiding Light;
Brother clasps the hand of brother,
    Stepping fearless through the night.

One the Light of God's own Presence
    O'er His ransomed people shed,
Chasing far the gloom and terror,
    Brightening all the path we tread.

One the object of our journey,
    One the faith that never tires,
One the earnest looking forward,
    One the hope our God inspires:

One the strain that lips of thousands
    Lift as from the heart of one;
One the conflict, one the peril,
    One the march in God begun:

One the gladness of rejoicing
    On the far eternal shore,
Where the One Almighty Father
    Reigns in love for evermore.

Onward, therefore, pilgrim brothers,
    Onward with the Cross our aid;
Bear its shame, and fight its battle
    Till we rest beneath its shade.

Soon shall come the great awaking,
    Soon the rending of the tomb;
Then the scattering of all shadows,
    And the end of toil and gloom.
            —*Sabine Baring Gould.*

THE CHURCH WILL LIVE.

CHRISTIANITY in spite of the dissensions, the follies, the coldness and the unfaithfulness of its followers, is still living, still spreading, and will grow brighter and purer until there comes to it the light of the perfect day.—*John T. Perry.*

THE TRUE CENTRE OF THE CHURCH.

THE true centre around which the Church of Christ rallies, concentrates and crystallizes, is Christ himself. . . . He is the central shaft, to which the universal Church is attached, and from which all its power is derived. Any effort to belt the machinery on to another shaft, or to connect it with another centre, only ends in calamity and ruin. There is no man who can furnish the power that is needed to energize the Church. There is no man, dead or living, but the man Christ Jesus, whose name is potent to stir the hearts of the disciples of the Lord and rouse their energies to perform the service which he requires. Nor is there any other name which rules the spirit of darkness but that name which is "above every name." Men, like the vagabond Jews of old, may take it upon themselves to pronounce their incantations and exorcisms over the evil spirits of the world, in the name of their sects, their leaders and their founders, but the answer will come: "Jesus I know, and Paul I know, but who are ye?" and they will flee before the onset of the foes whose wrath they have aroused. Christ is the true centre, Christ is the infallible leader, Christ is all and in all. Every attempt at human leadership crowds some poor mortal, living or dead, into a position which he cannot fill, and has no right to occupy. It subjects him to criticism; it displays before the world his weakness and his frailties; it necessitates the defence of that which cannot be defended, and fills the mouths of Christian men with apologies for the faults and follies of sinful men, instead of bold and confident testimonies to the grace and glory of the spotless Son of God. And when all is done nothing is gained, either of authority or power or blessing, for all human exaltation is worse than idle, in the presence of Him who hath purposed to stain the pride of all glory, and to bring into contempt all the honorable of the earth.—*The Christian.*

PERPETUITY OF THE CHURCH.

THE long existence of the Christian Church would be pronounced, upon common principles of reasoning, impossible. She finds in every man a natural and an inveterate enemy. To encounter and overcome the unanimous hostility of the world, she boasts no political stratagem, no disciplined legions, no outward coercion of any kind. Yet, her expectation is that she will live forever.

To mock this hope, and to blot out her memorial from under heaven, the most furious efforts of fanaticism, the most ingenious arts of statesmen, the concentrated strength of empires, have been frequently and perseveringly applied. The blood of her sons and her daughters has streamed like water; the smoke of the scaffold and the stake, where they wore the crown of martyrdom in the cause of Jesus, has ascended in thick volumes to the skies. The tribes of persecution have sported over her woes and erected monuments, as they imagined, of her perpetual ruin. But where are her tyrants, and where their empires? The tyrants have long since gone to their own place; their names have descended upon the roll of infamy; their empires have passed, like shadows, over the rock; they have successively disappeared, and left not a trace behind.

But what became of the Church? She rose from her ashes, fresh in beauty and might; celestial glory beamed around her; she dashed down the monumental marble of her foes, and they who hated her fled before her. She has celebrated the funeral of kings and kingdoms that plotted her destruction, and with the inscriptions of their pride has transmitted to posterity the records of their shame. How shall this phenomenon be explained? We are at the present moment witnesses of the fact; but who can unfold the mystery? The book of truth and life has made our wonder cease. "The Lord her God in the midst of her, is mighty." His presence is a fountain of health, and his protection a "wall of fire." He has betrothed her, in eternal covenant, to himself. Her living head, in whom she lives, is above, and his quickening spirit shall never depart from her. Armed with divine virtue, his Gospel, secret, silent, unobserved, enters the hearts of men and sets up an everlasting kingdom. It eludes all the vigilance and baffles all the power of the adversary.

Bars and bolts and dungeons are no obstacles to its approach: bonds and tortures and death cannot extinguish its influence. Let no man's heart tremble, then, because of fear. Let no man despair (in these days of rebuke and blasphemy) of the Christian cause. The ark is launched, indeed, upon the floods; the tempest sweeps along the deep; the billows break over her on every side; but Jehovah-Jesus has promised to conduct her in safety to the haven of peace. She cannot be lost unless the pilot perish.—*Dr. Mason.*

THE CHURCH IMMOVABLE.

O WHERE are kings and empires now,
    Of old that went and came?
But, Lord, thy Church is praying yet,
    A thousand years the same.

We mark her goodly battlements,
    And her foundations strong;
We hear within the solemn voice
    Of her unending song.

For not like kingdoms of the world,
    Thy holy Church, O God!
Though earthquake shocks are threatening her,
    And tempests are abroad;

Unshaken as eternal hills,
    Immovable she stands,
A mountain that shall fill the earth,
    A house not made by hands.
—A. Cleveland Coxe.

CHRISTIANITY A FINALITY.

THAT Christianity is a finality, that it is the last and only revelation which God may be expected to make, and that it will survive all the changes and revolutions which may take place down to the end of time, is guaranteed by the promise and presence of Christ in the Church, the truth of which has been so strengthened and confirmed during the nineteen centuries of conflict and struggle through which it has passed as to leave no rational doubt of its complete triumph, for if it has gained the strength and influence it has, starting as it did with the combined opposition of both Jews and Gentiles, what power can crush it now since it has made a conquest of more than half the world?

If the gates of hell could not prevail against it in its weakness, what probability is there of a defeat now since it has gained the strength it has?—*Rev. Geo. W. Williard.*

THE CHURCH.

THE gray Church rose on the hill and climbed,
Aloft, stone by stone; and I stood on it,
And saw quite o'er the sea of human life
To that far Port which, like a setting sun,
Swims deep in gold. Then waters vanished,
Vanished east and west, vanished all
But the far zenith, and the rising pile
Beneath, and swift electric speech darting
Between the two. And the climbing temple
Said to God, "I come to thee, O Most High,
Come painfully, but bring with me the thoughts
Of men, their Sabbaths, and their costly selves."
And God said, " Come and bring my little ones,
My gray-haired sires and mothers, all my rich
And poorest, and sheep without a shepherd,
From rough hillside and from vale. Let them climb
By the strong ladder of thy rugged rocks
And graded buttresses and taper tower,
Into these skies which thou dost pierce for them;
Nor let them fear the dizzy thoroughfare.
On every rocky spur and ledge and slope
Shall stand my angels with their helping hands,

And so, Sabbath by Sabbath, age by age,
The stream of souls shall pass securely up
Thy stony steeps into my best Temple."
—*Rev. Dr. Burr.*

THE CHURCH GOD'S HOUSE.

THE term house of God, when used in the Old Testament, we understand as meaning the Church of the Jews. It is said "Moses was faithful in all his house," Heb. iii. 2. That is, he ordered all things in the Jewish church according to the command of God. And in the New Testament the Church of God, or of Christ, is called his house, as in Tim. iii. 15, "That thou mayest know how to behave thyself in the house of God, which is the Church of the living God." And in Heb. iii. 6, "But Christ as the Son over his own house, whose house are we." It is not the walls and pews and adornings of the material building that constitute the Church, but the body of believers in Christ, the institutions connected with religious service and the place where that worship is held and offered, whether it be inside of a building or out in the leafy woods with no covering but the blue bending sky. But there are special places set apart and consecrated to the service of God, and which he has been pleased to own, and bless, and honor as such with his presence and grace. And wherever he reveals himself and this worship is set up, and this communion enjoyed with him, is the house of God. It was so when Noah builded an altar unto the Lord after the flood and offered burnt-offerings thereon. And so when Abraham built an altar on Mount Moriah, on which he intended to present

Isaac as a sacrifice unto the Lord, the name of which place is called Jehovah Jireh; as it is to this day, "In the Mount of the Lord it shall be seen." And so when Isaac went up to Beersheba: "And the Lord appeared unto him the same night and said, 'I am the God of Abraham thy father; fear not, for I am with thee, and will bless thee, and multiply thy seed.' And he builded an altar there and called upon the name of the Lord." And so when Jacob journeyed towards Haran, and in his vision saw a ladder upon which were ascending and descending the angels of God, and at the top of which stood the Lord himself, and spoke to him, "And when he awoke out of his sleep, he said, 'surely the Lord is in this place! This is none other but the house of God, and this is the gate of heaven.'"

Thus all through the Patriarchal Dispensation the house of God was set up, established, and resorted to by his people. They had no settled place of worship, but wherever God met with them and blest them, and covenanted with them, his Church was established, and they set up a memorial.

Then under the Mosaic Dispensation we have a more formal introduction and visible manifestation and representation of the house of God. Its form, and principle, and life were embodied in the Ten Commandments given from Sinai, and the institution of the ceremonial law regulating its worship. And all through this dispensation they had the house of God—the Tabernacle in which the Shekinah dwelt. Thus they worshipped all through the wilderness until the building of the magnificent Temple by Solomon, the types and ceremonies of which prefigured and foreshadowed the glory of the later house, which would be greater than the former, ushered in and established forever by the Lord Jesus Christ. Thus in all ages of the world, from the call of Abraham down to the present time, God has had a house—a Church. Amidst the changes and ravages of time it has stood, an everlasting memorial of the wisdom, and goodness, and power of God. Empires have fallen, and the proudest monuments of art have decayed, but this has stood a living testimony of the promise and faithfulness of Jehovah.

True, she has had her dark seasons, her outward temples have been demolished, her ordinances have been perverted, her worshippers have been scattered, "red-garbed persecution" has assailed her, storms loud and terrible have thundered around her, clouds dark and portentous have enveloped her; but her foundation, deep laid in the Rock of Ages, has never moved. She has come up out of the fire, the storm, and the tempest, purified and still more glorious. And she stands to-day the living Oracle of God, with her spires pointing heavenward, adorned with the beautiful garments of Salvation, and her solemn voices of song and praise calling together the worshippers.—*Rev. J. A. McFaden.*

THE HOUSE OF GOD A REFUGE.

HERE is a refuge of peace from the tempests that beat,
  From the dark clouds that threaten, from the wild wind
    that blows;
A holy, a sweet, and a lovely retreat,
  A spring of refreshment, a place of repose.

'Tis the house of my God—'tis the dwelling of prayer—
  'Tis the temple all hallowed by blessing and praise;
If sorrow and faithlessness conquer me there,
  My heart to the throne of his grace I can raise.

For a refuge like this, ah! what praises are due?
For a rest so serene, for a covert so fair;
Ah, why are the seasons of worship so few?
Ah, why are so seldom the meetings of prayer?
—*James Edmeston.*

THE CHURCH IN THE HOUSE.

WE are making far too little of the Church in the house. We are waiting for our children to be converted by outside influences, when, if we were to look at the matter rightly, it should be our ambition to be ourselves the leaders of our sons and daughters to the Lord. Some years ago I read an account of the manner in which a cold church was stirred into warmth and vitality; and, as it bears directly on the point to which I am now referring, I will take the liberty of introducing it here. At one of the conference meetings a simple man, not remarkable for fluency or correctness of speech, made an appeal something to the following effect: "I feel, brethren, real bad about the people who don't love the Lord Jesus Christ, here in our own neighborhood. We're not as we ought to be, that's very certain, but it's hard work rowing against the stream. We find that out when we talk to men about religion on Sunday who haven't any religion all the week. They don't mind us. And just so with the young folks. Their minds all seem running one way. Now, what's to be done? Not much with the grown folks, for they aren't controlled by us, and we can only drop a word now and then, and pray for them. But here's our own children. I have four boys, and only one of them comes to the communion with his mother and me. And I don't think I have done my duty to those younger boys. They love me, and God knows I love them; but I kind o' hate to speak to them about religion. But rather than see them go farther without my Jesus for their Jesus, I'm going to ask them to join him. I'm going to pray with them; and if I can't tell them all they want to know, why, our minister can. Brethren, I'm going to try to turn the stream for my boys. Home is the head of the river. I mean to begin to-night. Won't some father do like me with his boys, and give me his word out?" Scarcely had he seated himself when, one after another, some thirty people pledged themselves, saying: " I'll do the same at my house;" and the pledge was kept. In a short time the minister's labors began to tell as they had never done before. The influence spread, but there was no excitement. On the occasion of the communion-service, from family after family one and another came to enroll themselves among the followers of Jesus, and nearly every one that came was under twenty-five years of age. So, through revived home effort, the work of God was stimulated both in the church and in the neighborhood. My friends, this witness is true. " Home is the head of the river." Is there no one here to-night who will join in the resolution made by that earnest man, and say, " By the grace of God, I'll do the same at my house?"

—Anonymous.

GIVE Christianity a common law trial; submit the evidence, pro and con, to an impartial jury, under the direction of a competent court, and the verdict will assuredly be in its favor.

—Chief-Justice Gibson.

PICTURE OF FAMILY WORSHIP.

THE cheerful supper done, wi' serious face,
   They, round the ingle, form a circle wide;
The sire turns o'er, wi' patriarchal grace,
   The big ha'-Bible, ance his father's pride;
His bonnet is reverently laid aside,
   His lyart haffets wearing thin an' bare;
Those strains that once did sweet in Zion glide,
   He wales a portion with judicious care;
And "Let us worship God!" he says with solemn air.

They chant their artless notes in simple guise;
   They tune their hearts, by far the noblest aim:
Perhaps "Dundee's" wild-warbling measures rise,
   Or plaintive "Martyrs" worthy of the name;
Or noble "Elgin" beats the heavenward flame,
   The sweetest far of Scotia's holy lays;
Compared with these, Italian trills are tame;
   The tickled ears no heartfelt raptures raise;
Nae unison hac they with our Creator's praise.

The priestlike father reads the sacred page—
   How Abram was the friend of God on high;
Or Moses bade eternal warfare wage
   With Amalek's ungracious progeny.
Or how the royal bard did groaning lie
   Beneath the stroke of Heaven's avenging ire;
Or Job's pathetic plaint, and wailing cry;
   Or rapt Isaiah's wild, seraphic fire;
Or other holy seers that tune the sacred lyre.

Perhaps the Christian volume is the theme—
   How guiltless blood for guilty man was shed;

How He, who bore in Heaven the second name,
  Had not on earth whereon to lay His head;
How His first followers and servants sped;
  The precepts sage they wrote to many a land;
How He, who lone in Patmos banished,
  Saw in the sun a mighty angel stand,
And heard great Bab'lon's doom pronounced by Heaven's command.

Then, kneeling down, to Heaven's eternal King,
  The saint, the father, and the husband prays;
Hope "springs exulting on triumphant wings,"
  That thus they all shall meet in future days;
There ever bask in uncreated rays,
  No more to sigh, or shed the bitter tear,
Together hymning their Creator's praise,
  In such society, yet still more dear;
While circling Time moves round in an eternal sphere.

Compared with this, how poor Religion's pride,
  In all the pomp of method and of art,
When men display to congregations wide,
  Devotion's every grace, except the heart!
The Power, incensed, the pageant will desert,
  The pompous strain, the sacerdotal stole;
But haply, in some cottage far apart,
  May hear, well pleased, the language of the soul;
And in His Book of Life the inmates poor enroll.
—*Robert Burns.*

It is the mission of the Church to preach to all nations, to convert the world, and not confine its efforts to its own vicinage or community. Such is the command of Christ; such the duty of his followers.—*Dr. John Hall.*

THE CHURCH AND THE CHILDREN.

STEEPLES and infants suggest two important elements in our civilization—the Church and the children. The mission of this Church, identical with the mission of the Master, is "to seek and to save that which was lost." The children—divinely appointed to be saved—will be lost, unless, by strong, persistent, wise and loving labors, the Church, divinely appointed to "seek the lost," make sturdy efforts to save them. To do this the Church and the children must be brought together. That gulf lying between the Church and the child must be bridged or filled. The Church does not exist as an adult prerogative. It must recognize, in substantial attention, the boy and the girl. We rejoice that a change for the better is now fairly inaugurated. The multiplication of children's classes, Oxford Leagues, and young people's societies are narrowing the long-existing chasm and giving congratulatory evidence of better days. And yet much remains to be done, by the Church, the Sunday-school, and the home, for the little children.

We insist that the Church shall look after that child. Educationally we are doing something. Socially we need to improve. Company and amusements of some sort the child will have. If the Church fail to provide it the world will surely not neglect to do so. Interesting and wholesome reading matter, Sunday-school concerts, magic lantern or polyopticon exhibitions at our homes on week nights, an occasional tea, with games or chemical and mechanical experiments, summer excursions—these are a few of many suggestive expedients. Only give the world the social training of our children, and soon, instead of a joyful, pure-minded, religious child-life among us, we shall have a silly, depraved and godless life developing into a youth-time either alienated from the Church or interested in it only for what in a social or business way it can extract from it.

Then, too, the children must be trained for heaven. Children's classes should be formed, and led, say, by some woman of tact, expedients and consecration, who *loves* children. The Sunday-school must be *used* to *make Christians* of the boys and girls. The Bible is to be taught and expounded, but above all things the soul is to be saved. Transcendental philosophy, theory and humbug, the "mistakes of Moses," "higher (or lower) criticism," may be lightly passed by the average child. Is the Sunday-school to teach negations or doubt? Is the exposition of Scripture the only work of the Sunday-school? We doubt. It must exalt the divine Christ as a personal Saviour, show the sinfulness of the heart and our tendency to evil, impress moral responsibility and the necessity of regeneration and purification. It must teach Christ, the Word, and whatsoever truth may relate to the life temporal or the life immortal.

To make the Sunday-school thus efficient we must exercise care in the elevation of Christians to the dignity of teachers and officers. The superintendent must not be a man of wood or putty or mud. He ought not to be dull, weak, or unsavory, in habit or speech. If possible, he ought to have a strong mind, but he must have a warm heart, good judgment, tact, common sense, vivacity, and complete consecration to the salvation of his school. Teachers should have good minds, warm Christian experiences, and love for souls. Inefficient or disinterested teachers ought to be pupils.

The pastor can "lend a hand" in filling this gulf between the Church and the children by taking a lively interest in the boys and girls. But he must really care for them. It will not do to smooth Mary's curls in public and then forget her in the study. He must preach to the children. He must preach intelligently, and get never above their mental grasp. He must have a care *what* he preaches and *how*. Children are neither fools nor half-witted. Frequently they are very bright and critical. It is easy to secure and hold the child's respect, but when the preacher lets himself down to weak stories, silly talk and patronizing airs because he is speaking to children, it will be strange if they do not despise both him and his platitudes. Be men, and preach a manly gospel to them in easy language. Then, out of the pulpit, have their confidence, love them, notice them, call them by name, give them a good word, and in every right manner aim at capturing their souls for the Master.

The membership of the Church also ought to be interested in the child. As far as practicable adult members should remain in the Sunday-school to give it the benefit of their influence, and to show the child that he is never "too big" or "too old" for that place. Parents who are members must live bright, godly lives at home, and never neglect the paramount duty of a family altar. We owe the children this. We promised God when we united with the Church that we would "promote the advancement of the Redeemer's kingdom." This we cannot do if we ignore the "little ones." If our children are baptized, then we must remember that at the fount we solemnly pledged ourselves to teach the child "to give reverent attendance upon the appointed means of grace, to read the Scriptures, learn the Lord's Prayer, the Ten Commandments, the Apostle's Creed and the Catechism." Have we done these things? In this connection let me urge the importance of attention to the quality of the reading matter upon our tables. Exclude the weak, immoral and skeptical; but do not fail to provide a better feast in some of the wholesome literature of the day. A story need not be silly, empty, untruthful, or immoral, to be fascinating. Put *Our Youth* or some other periodical of kindred merit upon the table. Have, by all means, a religious weekly. Buy occasionally a good book. It is to me a dreadful thought that a lost soul may be the price paid for neglecting to subtract the bad and to add the good. Let me here refer to that evil habit of idle gossip in our homes, where, in presence of our children, the preacher and members are criticised or held up to ridicule. If we must do this horrible thing let us spare the children from hearing our unkind and perhaps untrue remarks. The child will catch up our word, adopt the sentiment and doubtless lose confidence in the men and religion we denounce. Leave that Christian alone. Though not perfect, he, like ourselves, is probably doing the best he can. Speak a good word for him, and it may be he will lead even your children into the kingdom. Having now alluded to some possibilities and duties before the Church I may close by considering several motives that ought to actuate us in our labors for the children. And, first, the motive of *obedience to God*. The God-imposed obligation on the Church is to bring the children to Christ. "Suffer them to come," said Jesus, " for of such is the kingdom of heaven." "Take heed that ye despise not one of these little ones." "Let him that heareth say, Come." A second motive is found in the increase of righteousness and decrease of sin. The children of to-day will be helpful or harmful to the world and the Church just in proportion as they accept or reject Christ. Do we stop to think that these children, many of them with no training for righteousness, coming up in ignorance, immortality and spiritual darkness, are to be masters of men and the moulders of thought, the law-makers and the law-breakers of to-morrow?

Soul interest is a third motive. Remembering the mission of the Church, the motive for her to win the children is sublimely urgent when you consider the efforts put forth by the world for their destruction. An analogy will sufficiently illustrate this. In the Middle Ages, among the many crusades for the recovery of the Holy City, was a movement on the part of the children, and called the "children's crusade." Coming together in great numbers and receiving recruits along the route they started for Jerusalem. Unorganized, inexperienced, inured to no hardships, they soon found themselves dropping in the way. By fatigue, by hunger, by treachery, by hostile forces, their numbers suffered constant diminution until the bones of hundreds of the innocents lay bleaching under the sun. To-day, as in all time, children are born for heaven—the New Jerusalem. By thousands they travel on, beset by passion within and temptations without. The world, the flesh and the devil are after them. By the cigar, the rum-shop, the dance, the theater, the impure novel, the sensational newspaper, by the brilliant light, the enchanting music, the magnificent display, the evil companion, they are lured to ruin. The world is doing its utmost, O father, O mother, to ruin your boy and girl. What will you do for them? Brothers, the motives of obedience, of righteous expediency, of soul interest are urgent. They counsel care and dispatch. Shall we be led by these motives, and labor as churches, as ministers, and as members, to save the child? God help us to be true to the children, loyal to conviction and true to God in order that the child-soul may find refuge in the many-mansioned house.—*Rev. W. P. Stoddard.*

EVERY FAMILY A CHURCH.

EVERY family should be a little church, and every church should be a large family.—*Dr. Arnot.*

THE FAMILY A NURSERY.

CHRISTIAN families are the nurseries of the Church on earth as she is the nursery of the Church in heaven.
—*J. M. Mason.*

THE YOUNG FOR CHRIST.

AS the wise men of the East brought their choicest offerings to the infant Jesus, so, in the unfolding ages, the wisdom of the Church turned toward infant humanity. True philosophy, as well as true Christianity, calls for increasing attention to childhood. The children of to-day will, in twenty years, wield the social and civil power of the globe. Whoever wins the youth will govern the world. The motto of Sunday-school workers everywhere should be: "All the youth for Christ."—*Bishop Simpson.*

COMING INTO THE CHURCH.

THE greatest forces that ever have been exerted in this world have been those against which all the chances ran. If, from any point of view, eighteen hundred years ago or more, you had been asked to select the man that was destined to have the most power in the world, you would have gone over all creation before you would have selected that poor peasant, in a district of a province in Galilee, the child of a carpenter, and a child, as the world must then have seen it, having a putative father only. He had no commission during his three ministerial years. He did not go out as one sent; he was as one rejected by all the authorities of his own people. He was arrested by the most eminent of his kind. He was condemned by his government. He suffered a death that was not only extremely cruel, but that always carried with it an odious element. The cross at that time was what the gallows is nowadays— and even worse; the ignominy of it cannot be overstated; and if you could in imagination hover over that scene and time, you would say that there never was a more unfortunate creature living than Christ. Can you conceive of any one humbler than he was—born of poverty; rejected by his own family; at first for a little time followed, from curiosity, by the common people; repudiated, cast out of the synagogue and temple, and given over to death? And yet the name of Christ is the name that to-day stands above every other name for power and for influence. Think of what that name has done in modifying manners, changing institutions, overthrowing laws, and raising the thought of humanity in the minds not only of Christians, but even of those who reject religion as a revelation of God! There has been that gain.

Then take the gathering of the Church. Christ was the leader of a small band of men. He was taken from them, crucified and buried. There were a dozen folks or more that came together, as it were, to keep their sorrow warm. Their every single aspiration had come to nothing. They cherished the expectation that one day he would restore Israel. They thought that he was really a divine creature, and that he had the power of God, inasmuch as he raised the dead, cured the sick, healed the blind, and made the deaf to hear; but in so far as his kingdom was concerned, was there ever anything that seemed more utterly hopeless to them?

And when, with fear and trembling, they were finally brought to believe that he had risen from the dead, and gone up again on high, what sort of a body was the cluster of disciples that composed the primitive Church? If anybody, looking in upon that handful of squalid people, without wealth or literature, assembled secretly for fear of the Jews, and holding their little prayer-meetings, had been told by them that they expected to shake the kingdoms of the world, he would have said to them, "You ought to be put in a lunatic asylum."

Paul foresaw that Christ's Church was to become a great power; he had some conception of that power; but his mind could not compass it; and he was obliged to say, "We cannot calculate the effects of what we are attempting to do; we live by faith, and not by sight." What is faith? Imagination. We are living in the realm of the imagination, in the ideal world, in the sphere of emotion; but we know that we shall produce great results in time to come.

When, now, young people are gathered into the Christian Church, one might stand outside and say, "It is all well enough, but what does it amount to? they are not going to be very much changed. They are examined, they join the Church, they perhaps behave themselves a little better at home, and that is about all there is of it;" but Christ himself tells us that the kingdom of God is like leaven, which a woman took and hid in three measures of meal. It is invisible; but nevertheless it is the most powerful of influences.

When you go on board one of those enormous steamers that are now flying across the deep, and performing in a week a journey that used to require five or six weeks, and look at its massive engines, it seems to you that they illustrate the perfection of forces, and that the power which they exert is without a parallel; and yet, if you were to go and look at the trees in yonder meadow or in some forest, and could measure their force, you would find that they beat those engines. A single tree, in drawing up sap to augment its trunk and develop its branches and unfold its leaves, exerts more physical power, silent and imperceptible though it be, than any one engine that ever was built was capable of.

Now, the work of God in the human heart is just as silent and just as imperceptible, and it is powerful beyond all comparison; and though entering the Church of Christ does not seem to be very much now, call to mind the congratulations of the Apostle Paul to those who had come out of royal ceremonials into fellowship with the Saviour:

"For ye are not come unto the mount that might be

touched, and that burned with fire, nor unto blackness, and darkness, and tempest, and the sound of a trumpet, and the voice of words; which voice they that heard entreated that the word should not be spoken to them any more. But ye are come into Mount Sion, and unto the city of the living God, the heavenly Jerusalem, and to an innumerable company of angels, to the general assembly and church of the firstborn, which are written in heaven, and to God the Judge of all, and to the spirits of just men made perfect, and to Jesus the mediator of the new covenant, and to the blood of sprinkling, that speaketh better things than that of Abel."

When a young person unites himself with the Church of Jesus Christ no banners are lifted, no trumpets are sounded, no dramatic ceremonies are gone through with; but he takes the first step along that airy highway which leads to the communion of all the dead that die in Christ Jesus. It is the portal of heaven to him. It is the beginning of a career that shall last in glory and blessedness as long as the gevernment of God himself shall last. Although there is no outward show, this inward beginning is destined to go on producing results through eternity.

THE CHURCH AND TEMPERANCE.

THE Church has intelligence, so also has she wealth. The thrift of the nation is within the Church. The competency that waits on honest industry, and that renders domestic and social life happy—that competency is in the Church, as it is not outside the Church. As the valuation of Church property in this country is estimated at about three hundred and sixty millions, that is a fact which indicates that the thrift of the nation is within the Zion of our God. Here, then, is the material power wherewith to employ agents, to publish books, to erect temples, if necessary, to employ all the machinery for the advancement of the cause of total abstinence. And then the Church has the numerical strength. Sixty thousand ordained ministers of the Lord Jesus Christ are on the walls of Zion, each one of whom should be a temperance lecturer—not merely once a year. I have no objection to have a temperance Sabbath designated for Chicago, New York, and Washington, but I say that every Sabbath in the year should be a temperance Sabbath. I do not believe in the segregation of the secular from the sacred. All things should be sacred to the man of God, and all things should be total abstinence to the friends of the temperance cause. Then, in addition to the sixty thousand ministers, whose Master said, "No drunkard shall inherit the kingdom of God," and who also commanded them to do unto others as they would have others do unto them—in addition to these ministerial forces there are in this country seven millions of communicants in the Protestant churches, and I say that every man, woman and child of these seven millions should be solemnly pledged before God and his holy angels and before all the people to total abstinence. Yet this is not the case. Social drinking prevails. I rejoice that so many distinguished clergymen in all parts of the country are recognized leaders in the cause of total abstinence. I rejoice that so many Christian men and women in all parts of the country are known as the earnest advocates of abstinence from all intoxicating liquors. Yet it is not too much to say that the custom of social drinking prevails in the Church of Christ. We must cast out this devil. We must cast him out, so that the temple of the Lord shall be beautified with his presence. And then the Church, with so many ministers and so many members, exerts an influence over at least eighteen millions of the population of this country.

The Church has another element or another reformatory force, and that is the ballot. But this has not been used to the maximum. Take it for granted that what the infidels say is true, that two-thirds of the membership of the Church are women. Very well. If we have seven millions, and two-thirds are women, then we have somewhere in the neighborhood of about two millions of men; and it is fair to suppose that we have about a million and a half of voters in the Christian Church. But it is a sad fact that many who are enrolled in the Christian Church take but little interest in the political welfare of the country. Supposing the voting population of this country is nine millions, and that in any general election the number of votes cast amounts to five millions and a half, say in round numbers six millions; then there are three millions who do not vote. Take, for example, the last general election, one of the most popular of the general elections in the history of the Republic, and three millions of the citizens of this country did not *vote*. Well, now, ladies and gentlemen, who were those that did not vote? Were they the thieves, the gamblers, and the drunkards of New York, Buffalo, and Chicago? No; for the thieves, drunkards and gamblers always vote. You can always count on their vote in this city, but those who do not vote are those who are called respectable citizens. I hold that God has given the Church the political power to say who shall be those to administer the laws, and who shall make the laws; and if we have not a prohibitory law for the

State, the responsibility comes upon the Church of the living God.

And the Church of God needs one more thing. She needs an addition to her creed: "I believe in the Holy Ghost, the holy catholic Church, the communion of saints, the forgiveness of sins, total abstinence from all intoxicating liquor, the resurrection of the dead, and the life everlasting." And there wont be any resurrection of the dead in a moral sense until we get that into the creed. I would have not only an addition to the creed, but I would have such a Church discipline that would reach the citizen who rents his property for the manufacture or sale, retail or wholesale, of intoxicating liquor—I would have a Church discipline that would reach every tippler in the Church, and I would make total abstinence an absolute condition of Church membership. The truth is, we must grapple with this monster, and grapple with it with all the sanctities of law, and surround ourselves at the same time with all the muniments of ecclesiastical law. The Church, then, needs first to assume this high ground of total abstinence, and, secondly, she needs an enthusiasm in the cause of sobriety—an enthusiasm that will inspire activity every day in the year; an enthusiasm that will touch the lips of sixty thousand ministers in our country with a temperance eloquence that will enable them to raise rhetoric in logic and metaphor into argument, and thrill the hearts of the people in favor of total abstinence. We want an enthusiasm that will sanctify the family altar and the sacramental altar; an enthusiasm that will send out the men, women and children from our Churches to follow in the footsteps of the Divine Master and go about doing good. O, were I an artist, I would paint a picture of this grand army of Christian ministers in this country, sixty thousand strong, and then this army of Christian men and women of seven millions, and then the greater army of eighteen millions of our citizens under the ministry of our Churches. Nay, were it in my power, I would have a living panorama and have them pass in review; and it seems to me that we would lift our hands in holy clapping, for we would feel that they were all consecrated to the cause of total abstinence, then the rum interest would go down, and go down forever. I am in favor of laws; I believe in the limitations of law. I believe that the law of limitation is as universal as law itself. I believe that the law of limitation binds the Pleiades and guides Arcturus. I believe that the law of limitation binds the waves of the deep, touches vegetation, and touches man; and so long as I read in the Cosmos the limitation of law, and in the order and constitution of nature that God has everywhere said, "Thus far shalt thou go, and no farther," so I must believe in the right, and believe in civil legislation as a means for the suppression of vice and for the development of virtue.

I believe in organization outside of the Church—in Rechabites, Jonadabs, Wideawakes, Red Ribbons, Blue Ribbons, White Ribbons, and all the ribbons in the rainbow—I believe in them all. I believe in Francis Murphy, in Drew, and in Reynolds—let them all come; but, I tell you, you will never suppress this giant evil until you get the Church right on the question. The elements of power are within the Church.—*Bishop J. P. Newman.*

THE mark is on the *sheep*, not on the field.
—*Dr. Thompson.*

THE CHURCH TO SAVE AMERICA.

SHOW me the Church that is willing to wash the feet of the degraded; that goes about from house to house doing good; the Church organized for permanent, aggressive, audacious moral effect; the Church that has not lost its master's whip of small cords, and I will show you the Church, and the only Church, that can save America when it has two hundred inhabitants to the square mile.

—*Joseph Cook.*

OUR CHURCH OUR COUNTRY'S SAFEGUARD.

IF we and our posterity shall be true to the Christian religion—if we and they shall live always in the fear of God, and shall respect his commandments—if we and they shall maintain just moral sentiments, and such conscientious convictions of duty as shall control the heart and life, we may have the highest hopes of the future fortunes of our country; and if we maintain those institutions of government and that political union, exceeding all praise, as much as it exceeds all former examples of political associations, we may be sure of one thing; that, while our country furnishes materials for a thousand masters of the historic art, it will afford no topic for a Gibbon. It will have no decline and fall. It will go on prospering and to prosper.

—*Daniel Webster.*

KEEP THE CHURCH AND STATE FOREVER SEPARATED.

LET us labor to add all needful guarantees for the most perfect security of free thought, free speech and free press, pure morals, unfettered religious sentiments, and of equal rights and privileges to all men, irrespective of nationality, color or religion. Encourage free schools and resolve that not one dollar of money, appropriated for their support, be used for any sectarian school; resolve that neither the State nor nation, or both combined, shall support institutions of learning other than those sufficient to afford every child growing up in the land the opportunity of a good common school education, unmixed with sectarian, pagan or atheistic tenets. Leave the matter of religion to the family altar, the Church and the private school, supported entirely by private contribution. Keep the Church and State forever separated.

—*Ulysses S. Grant.*

THE TRUE TEST OF A CHURCH.

THERE are tests many. When we look back upon the long history of the Church we often find the great body of believers thrust into many a new situation, and made to undergo unexpected ordeals. Sometimes the Church has come out of the fire with undisturbed life. Then, again, it has writhed in torture because of the superstitions and unworthy accretions which have come to it. On the other hand, for long periods it has advanced with steady step, conquered its foes on every hand, gained new territory, and gathered to itself a vast array of political and social forces. In the time of Gregory VII. it dominated over the so-called Holy Roman Empire, and made emperors do obeisance to its mandates. During the Reformation in central and northern Europe the Papacy burned martyrs in its struggle for a new lease of power, and resorted to many other forms of wickedness to conquer the new spiritual uprising.

But, after all, was it really the Church which enacted all this wickedness? No; a thousand times no. Outwardly, it was the Church. It bore the name, assumed the functions, professed to teach the truth. But the real Church was in the background. It looked on, suffered with the sufferer, had boundless sympathies, and waited patiently for the dawn. Who protested? Who nailed the Ninety-five Theses to the door of the castle church in Wittenberg? The vital and praying Church. That was the real Church, though reduced to a few individuals, and the men who wore papal robes and sold indulgences and persecuted the protesters were only the skeleton, in purple robes, gyrating its Dance of Death.

When, therefore, the skeptic of these days proclaims the misdoings of the Church, its opposition to scientific advance, its persecutions of brave souls, its abuse of justice, its proclamation of false doctrines, he makes a great mistake. It was the Church gone astray, drifting off from its ancient and firm moorings, and floating madly over quicksands. One might as well say that the ravings of mediæval seekers of the philosopher's stone and their visions of indescribable wealth and the prophecies of Dr. Faustus were the schemes of an exact science, as to affirm that the ignorance of priests and the protests of the persecutors of Galileo were truly representative of the intelligence and the charity of the one true Church of God. The vital body of Christ's believing servants, the pure but indivisible Church, is no more to be held accountable for the wrongs of false guides, than is the course of a noble merchantman which has been captured by pirates, steered by a bloody helmsman, and stored with stolen silks and gold.

Away, then, with all this maligning of the Church of Christ because of flagrant historical deviations. The Church never deviated from its proper course, and was never anything but pure and progressive, except when in corsair hands. The time came, and sometimes long delayed, but still it came, when the thieves were tossed into the sea, and God's servants walked the deck of the good vessel, and put her in the right direction for the sure and safe haven.

History proves, therefore, that the appearance of power, the stores of wealth, and the vast array of numbers, are never the real test of either the purity or inner life of the Church of Christ. All these may exist, yet the apparent Church may be sinning openly against God and man.

The best way to arrive at a safe criterion of the active and living Church is to find out what kind of members it builds up. Sometimes a jewel is found in the mud. A child of genius comes now and then from the sheep-fold or the miner's hut. But come from whatever quarter, what does the Church do with such a child? Does it let him care for himself and find his own way? By no means. There has always been some one to whom God reveals the duty of opening the way for a poor child of great Christian destiny. In some instances it is the mother who has the best prophetic vision of all human beings. Susannah Wesley knew much of the real future of her boys, John and Charles, when they were lads. Nothing else can explain the depth of her correspondence when they were at Oxford, and the seer-like training which she gave them even before they left the little Epworth rectory. In some instances this motherly care is denied the chosen little ones of God. But the helping-hand of a stranger then comes in to do the sublime service of prophecy. Frau Cotta, of Eisenach, was the elect one to help the little singing, cheerful Martin Luther to his destiny. The Sunday-school teacher who searched the grimy throng of urchins in the Seven Dials of London for scholars for his class was the one to help China to the greatest of all her missionaries, the immortal Morrison.

Such discoveries, resulting from patient work for God, have been the law of Christian life from the beginning. When the Church can produce such spirits, who seek the helpless and bring them within the benign influence of Christian teaching and training, and then develops those helpless ones into majestic characters, who preach the word with new power, and plant the truth on farther shores, and produce Christian hymns for future generations, and work out such great reforms as give a new face to the very globe, we find a test of the quality of the Church concerning which there can be no mistake. The hand which can achieve this victory has the strength of God to make it forceful.

The proper and safe training of children we regard as the fundamental test of a Church. It might acquire wealth, establish missions, print a vast literature, rear educational institutions by the score, and lay magnificent humane foundations; but if the Church could not train children for God's kingdom, watch over them with careful eyes, and build them up into stately temples for the divine indwelling, it would

not be worthy of the holy and historic name which it bears. The work which it is doing in this line to-day far exceeds all former achievements. There is more discovery of minds in obscurity and extreme youth, more Christian care and culture of them when discovered, and a prompt recognition of them when ready to work upon the wide, needy world, than ever before. Let every one know that the building up of a soul into the divine image, and the guiding it to a mastery in building others into the same harmony and majesty, is the greatest work performed by a human being. Compared to such immortal architecture, the rearing of the Strasburg Minster or the Cologne Cathedral is mere child's play. This is the true test of a Church—its power to create great lives.
—*The Christian Advocate.*

A CHRISTIAN.

A CHRISTIAN man is more than a sectarian. Paul, unrenewed, could be a Jew, but grace only could enlarge his fellowship to the whole race of men. A zealous member of this or that Church is not necessarily a Christian; he may fall far short in dignity of character, breadth of fellowship, purity of heart, nobleness of purpose, excellence of life. Zeal for a sect is often mistaken for Christian earnestness, and devotion to Christ. There is a worldly, selfish power in it, which wins a certain kind of success, but it is not Christian success, does not make childlike men and women, does not save. There is more danger of being caught in this snare than is generally supposed; more souls are deceived by mistaking love for a party and sect for love to Christ, than by any other snare. Thousands " who have done many wonderful works" in a partisan way, will stand at the left hand in the Day of Judgment. They think they do them in the name of Christ, but Christ on their lips has a narrow, carnal meaning; is degraded to be the leader of a sect, rather than the head of all saints. We must be Christians above all things else; more Christian than anything else; so thoroughly Christian as to be nothing else; then, wherever our lot may be cast, the power of Christ will rest upon us, and souls will be saved.—*Baptist Union.*

FOUR THINGS CONSTITUTE A CHRISTIAN.

FOUR things are necessary to constitute a Christian. Faith makes a Christian; life proves a Christian: trials confirm a Christian, and death crowns a Christian.

—Hopfner.

THE CHRISTIAN IS THE WORLD'S BIBLE.

THE Christian is the world's Bible, and the only one that it reads. If we take care that in this book be plainly shown the loving spirit, the grandeur, and the winning friendliness of Christ, then we shall see many hearts open to receive this actual testimony of Christian life and suffering. For many of our opponents in secret envy us our Christian comfort in misfortune and under heavy losses. Their hearts are often stirred by a deep yearning after the support which bears us up; and this superiority of Christian life can often drive the hardest heart to seek help of the Lord. In fine, only life can beget life. Where we wish to defend the Word of Life, our life cannot be separated from it, for the truth of Christianity is the true Christian—the man filled with the spirit of Christ. The best means of bringing the world to a belief in miracles is to exhibit the miracle of regeneration, and its power in our own life. The best proof of Christ's resurrection is a living Church, which is itself walking in new life, and drawing life from him who has overcome death. Before such arguments ancient Rome herself, the mightiest Empire of the world, and the most hostile to Christianity, could not stand. Let us live in like manner, and then, though hell should have a shortlived triumph, eventually must be fulfilled what St. Augustine says: "Love is the fulfilling of the truth."

Already the world is beginning to be divided into great camps of the unbelieving and the faithful. In many unbelief has probably become incurable. Before such we can only confess the truth for a testimony against them. The anti-Christ, who denies Father and Son, can be destroyed, not by men, but only by the Lord in the brightness of his coming. But the holy task that falls to the lot of every Christian is to continue to do battle for the truth after the measure of his strength, in the power of that victory which Christ has already gained for us, and which he has promised one day to complete. May not only individuals, but may every Protestant people recognize that it ought to contribute its special gift toward the great world-apology for Christianity; Germany, her deep and earnest science; England, her trustful meditation on Scriptures, her faithfulness in pastoral work, her open-handed charity; America, her energetic activity, her fearlessness in public testimony for the truth, her indelible love of freedom; and all others, great or small, the talent intrusted to them. If all others unite in holy zeal for God, the victory cannot wanting. Forward, then, my brethren, and let us not weary of the strife. Our field of battle is the wide world, our aim the honor of God, our support amid strife and suffering the certainty that our faith already is the victory which hath overcome the world.—*Prof. Theo. Christleib.*

THE CHRISTIAN SYSTEM OF CHRONOLOGY SUPREME.

JESUS CHRIST IS THE KING AND BASIS OF HUMAN CHRONOLOGY. I mean by this, that Jesus Christ has gotten himself into the warp and woof of earthly history; has become so vitally identified with all human dates, and reckonings, and registers, and laws, and commerce, and business, that he is now essential to human civilization and history. So long as the world stands and the seasons continue; so long as nations and society retain their present order and constitution, Jesus Christ will hold the sceptre and wear the crown of universal Lordship to the joy of his Church and the dismay of his enemies. Aside from the actual, personal witness of the Holy Ghost to the human spirit, I find one of the completest and most irrefragable demonstrations of the Lordship of Jesus Christ in the two letters "A. D.," which we use in all our business, and literature, and civilization; and it is the privilege of the humblest Christian to show these men who reject the Bible and laugh at Christian experience, that they have to bow the knee to Jesus of Nazareth, and confess his Lordship every day, and in each business act of life. This fact can be quickly shown, so that the dullest intellect, or the most unwilling skepticism must confess it. The chronological terms "A." and "D." are abbreviations of the Latin words "Anno" and "Domini" —year and Lord. "Anno Domini" means Year of Our Lord. "A. D., 1878," means Year of Our Lord, 1878.

Let me now assert, that the accepted Christian chronology is the only one that will bear the test of reason, or meet and support the wants and facts of civilization and history. All the systems of chronology which have ever been used before, since, or in opposition to the Christian, have failed and been cast aside, while the Christian system has become impregnably incorporated into the customs, calculations, commerce and civilization of the race, in such a way that it can never be superseded or materially modified. Astronomers, geologists and ethnologists construct speculative chronologies occasionally. No one enjoys them better than I do; they are often very ingenious, amusing, stimulating and profitable. I saw a scientific lecturer once (in the Boston Lowell Institute course) demonstrate on the black-board, from the character of the Niagara river gorge, that the cataract had been thundering down those rocks for 448,000 or 448,000,000 years; I have forgotten whether it was thousands or millions. I do not care which it was; it makes no difference to the Bible student. If he had needed 448,000,000 of times 448,000,000 of years, centuries or millenniums, to cut the Niagara gorge out properly, we could have furnished them from the Bible record, and then have had substantial forms to spare for any other essential or ornamental work of that kind.

We read in books of astronomy, of stars which have just reported themselves to us by star beams, which, travelling at the rate of 192,000 miles per second, have just got in after a journey of 5,000,000 years through the depth of space. These amazing longevities do not trouble the Bible student at all. They bring him a little nearer the tremendous thought of the lifetime of the Almighty. He cannot comprehend them now, but by and by he will master geological and astronomical dates and periods as easily as he can minutes and days by his watch or hour-glass now. We have no dispute with true science, none whatever. Its chronologies are purely speculative; they have nothing to do with us in our human and moral relations; we do not date letters, or trade or travel by them. Jesus Christ has no dispute with geology, or astronomy, ethnology, or any of the sciences.

Let out the links of the scientific chain until the wildest hypothesis is satisfied. These bewildering periods are as pulse-beats in comparison with the lifetime of Jesus Christ, who is the Alpha and the Omega of geology, and astronomy, and all the rest of the sciences. We are in perfect sympathy with science so long as it is scientific and reverent; but when it asks us to slip our chronological cable from the throne of Christ, and cast it out for a scientific hypothesis, we decline with good-natured contempt; for we prefer a safe anchorage ground to the shifting sands of scientific hypothesis.

There are a number of heathen, mythological and classical chronologies, also, which have had a faint showing in history. Babylonian fable imagines 432,000 years of Babylonian antiquity and splendor. Chinese books claim 64,000 years before the birth of their first emperor. Phœnician tradition boasted 30,000 years for itself. Hindu chronologies, under

Brahminical cypherings, give extravagant antiquities. They talk of their four primitive ages, or Yugas: the first, 1,728,000 years; the second, 1,296,000; the third, 864,000; the fourth and present, 432,000, of which 5,000 or 6,000 are already past. These four give a sum total of 4,320,000 years. They have still longer periods, Kalpas, 4,320,000 years each. But these are all fabulous periods. We do not date letters or do business with them; nobody does.

Then we have several historical epochs and eras, which were once in use.

The old Greeks, beginning with July 1, B. C. 776, reckoned time by Olympiads—periods of four years. Once in four years they celebrated the Olympic games, and for three or four hundred years they made this their reckoning date. But the Olympiad system broke down when the Greek nationality was destroyed, and the Greeks had no suitable epoch for their history any longer. The ancient Romans used the year of the founding of Rome—A. U. C., "Anno Urbis Conditæ." They reckoned from that epoch for several centuries, but after a while that broke down. Mohammedans reckoned time by "hegiras," making the flight of Mahomet their chronological epoch.

French infidelity in the great revolution wiped out the Christian era by an edict of the national convention, and opened a new world epoch dating from itself. It pompously dated its decrees as of the year 1. That atheistic farce lasted only a few months. But all of these epochs have gone out of date. Somehow, humanity has outgrown them all. None of them ever fitted the race or met the wants of man. They were local and temporary expedients; none of them had world- and race-organizing power.

One thousand eight hundred and seventy years ago a

young Jewish woman gave birth to a babe in the village of Bethlehem, in Palestine. She called his name Jesus. Some thirty-three years later this Jesus was crucified between two wretched thieves, on Mount Calvary, amid the scoffs and curses of the civilized world. To-day, and for these 1,850 years, the birth date of that Jewish babe has been the epochal date of human chronology, history, and civilization. Mythologies, heathen calendars, Yugas, Kalpas, Olympiads, city foundings, hegiras, all, all have lost their meaning, but the Bethlehem manger and the Virgin-born babe have revised, fixed, and perfected the chronometry of the race and the world! Can any one deny this fact? And who can admit or explain it without yielding Lordship to the Man of Nazareth? Why does not the world reckon time from the birth of Confucius, or Buddha, or Socrates, or Homer, or Julius Cæsar, or Constantine, or Mahomet, or Bonaparte, or Voltaire? Why? Because there is but one name in this universe that is strong enough to balance the ages upon itself without breaking down under the load! Why? Because there is no name but the name of Jesus that can gather all definite data of man, philosophy, and nations, and crystallize them into symmetry and logical significance about itself! Why? Because "God has highly exalted Jesus, and given him a name which is above every name; that at the name of Jesus every knee should bow, of things in heaven, and things on the earth, and things under the earth, and that every tongue should confess that Jesus Christ is Lord, to the glory of God the Father." Surely this divine purpose has had its literal fulfilment in the facts which I have already named. The name of Jesus is above every name. Its memorial is set in the sun and in the stars and in the seasons. It has become the reckoning date of laws, and trade, and literature, and science, and history, so that it can never be pulled down, or blotted out, or obscured. Things have gone on so far that no change is possible. The name of Jesus is the motto of human society and of time so long as the world stands. Strauss, and Renan, and Parker, Emerson, and Frothingham must keep step, living or dying, to the time and tune of the Lordship of Jesus Christ—they cannot help themselves.

Suppose that you wished to locate Confucius in history, you must say born B. C. 551, died B. C. 479; or Buddha, you must say born about the sixth century before Christ; Socrates, Homer, Alexander, born B. C. —; or Voltaire, born A. D. —, died A. D. —. Gibbon's "History of Rome," in which he thrusts so spitefully at the divinity of Jesus and Christianity, is woven upon chronology which centres upon Christ. The date of the Creation is wholly problematical; so is the date of the flood. These dates have no intelligible relations to human history except through the Bethlehem babe and manger. The first reliable epoch is the Christian. You could not get any reliable trace of any good or bad man of antiquity except as they borrow light from Jesus Christ in which to show themselves. Voltaire, Strauss, Paine, and Ingersoll are each dependent upon him for a foothold in history.

Not one of these fighters against Jesus could find his own birthday if it was not linked in with the name that they hate and deny so bitterly. The "Radical" writes: "The Christs belong to a dead epoch; this age has no further use for them," and refutes its own spiteful falsehood by stamping upon its title-page a confession of Christ's divinity—"A. D. 1870." It could not get upon a bookstand but through the influence of Jesus Christ, and it is not strange that its blasphemy sent it into speedy beggary and death.

Mr. Frothingham writes a book to say that "Jesus, the Incarnate, is an old myth;" and in order to get that book copyrighted, or into the world of trade, he has to get down upon his knees before the divinity of Jesus, and write upon its title-page: "Entered according to Act of Congress, A. D. 1872." "The Year of *Our Lord* 1872!"

Warrington wrote: "Jesus as the Son of God, in any peculiar sense, is on the defensive in the Boston Radical Club," superscribed his letter with A. D., "The Year of *Our Lord.*" Why, the members of that club could not appoint a supper without confessing the Lordship of Jesus.

Dr. O. W. Holmes writes, squarely charging that Jesus is a hopeless bankrupt, and refutes the thoughtless babble by dating his letter February, 1873—"Year of Our Lord!" This poor raving blasphemer, Ingersoll, could not print a tract, or publish a lecture, or make an appointment of any kind without confessing the Lordship of Jesus. Do these men ever think of this fact? But they cannot help themselves. The Jews came to Pilate, and said, Take down that superscription; don't say he is King of the Jews, but say, he says he is King of the Jews. You are too late, too late, said Pilate. What I have written, I have written; and Christ's Lordship was published by his own murderers, on his own cross.

"Jesus is not the Lord, Jesus is not the Lord," these poor self-worshipping men say, but each time they say it they have to go down upon their knees before his Lordship as published in that indestructible "Anno Domini," by which God has highly exalted him, and "given him a name which is above every name in heaven or in earth."

What a jubilee atheists and unbelievers would have if they could but reconstruct chronology and get a new epoch for civilization. Oh, if they could only get rid of that hated "Anno Domini;" but they cannot do it. As soon might a bat, covering the figure twelve on the face of a town clock, say, "I have blotted out the sun, and annihilated noon and time," as for these men to try to cover up the Lordship of Jesus with their vapors and fogs of unbelief.

How it must gall their self-conceit to keep saying "Our Lord! Our Lord!" But they must do it, there is no help for them; that thing is settled for this world at least. We cannot write a letter, or print a paper, or publish a book, or a notice without confessing the Lordship of Jesus. We cannot give or collect a note, we cannot sell a yoke of oxen, or buy a house, or mortgage a farm; we cannot be born, or marry, or be buried without bowing the knee to the Lord Jesus Christ. No law of town, State, or nation is valid which does not bow to Jesus. Governors' messages, emancipation proclamations, and Presidential inaugurals all salute Jesus Christ as King of chronology—"Given in this year of Our Lord 1878." All civilized nations have adopted the birthday of Jesus as their epoch, and all heathen nations are doing the same. The Sandwich and Fiji Islands, Madagascar, Japan, China, India, Africa, are wheeling into line in the trail of the Star of Bethlehem, and saluting the Lordship of Jesus Christ, "the Alpha and the Omega." And in this single fact of earth's chronologies all centring upon the birthday of Jesus of Nazareth I find a very remarkable illustration of the truth of the text and of the Lordship of Jesus.

I have never yet heard an infidel solution of this fact. We are not called upon to defend Jesus Christ from their wild assaults until they have invented a new epoch for the world.

Some of the old gods of fable and mythology have given their names to the months and days of the week, but these are in no sense epoch-marks. They are simply trophies chained to the chariot-wheels of the victorious Nazarene. Let our frantic and noisy revilers of Christ invent a new chronological epoch, or stop boasting of their tremendous consequence.—*Rev. J. G. Bidwell.*

THE HAND OF GOD IN MODERN MISSIONS.

I WOULD like to direct your minds to the wonderful ways in which the pillar of Providence has gone before the missionary bands, and opened doors great and effectual with the most startling rapidity; and how obstacles insurmountable to mere human power have vanished before the onward march of the Church in the honest attempt to evangelize the world. Take, for instance, a single fact in regard to the condition of woman. In olden times she was never placed upon equality with man. Look at her, bending under the burden imposed by a ruthless taskmaster in an uncivilized age; see her the slave of her lord, shut up in the seraglios and harems of the East, unapproachable by Christian influences. Look at the daughters of India, unwelcome at birth, untaught in childhood, enslaved when married, accursed as widows, and unlamented when they die, and think at this present day that there are 1,200 seraglios open to the ministrations of the Christian women of one single organization,

anxious to save their sisters in foreign lands. One hundred years ago what was the condition of the world? Japan had closed her ports for three hundred years. China was literally walled in. The islands of Polynesia were sunk in idolatry and degradation, and you would not have been able to put your foot on them without danger of being devoured by these cannibal savages. Look at Africa fifty years ago, the whole interior unexplored, as much removed from us as if on another planet; now see to what an extent her population have been brought to Christianity and civilization. The banner of the Cross has been carried into the very heart of the continent by the bands of missionaries of the Cross. Look at the persecution of the Christians in Madagascar for twenty-five years; yet, wonderful to relate, the Church of Christ has grown stronger in Madagascar than it was before the persecution began; and at last, the modern Christian Church is able to find shelter under the hospitality of a Christian government. That seems to me to be one of the grandest triumphs of the Gospel. We can only hint at a few of the marvels that have been accomplished; but in these there is just as plainly a supernatural interposition as there was in the moving of the pillar of cloud before Israel, or in the prostration of the walls of Jericho. It is all in harmony with the Scripture promise, and shows the power of faith in the divine interposition of a great and all-wise and all-powerful God.—*Rev. Arthur T. Pierson.*

HEAD-QUARTERS OF THE CHURCH.

THE head-quarters of Christ's Church is at the right hand of God, where Christ, the Head over all things to the Church, sitteth. His Church is a body with but *one head;* those many-headed creatures of which the Scriptures speak are emblems of earthly confusion rather than of divine order and ordination. Our Saviour bids us come boldly to his presence; and when there we are at head-quarters; and in submitting ourselves to him we are yielding to an authority higher than that of priest or prelate, the authority of One into whose hands all power in heaven and in earth is committed.—*The Christian.*

A CALL FOR WORKERS.

OUR country's voice is pleading,
    Ye men of God, arise!
His providence is leading,
    The land before you lies;
Day-gleams are o'er it brightening,
    And promise clothes the soil;
Wide fields for harvest whitening
    Invite the reaper's toil.

Go where the waves are breaking
    On California's shore,
Christ's precious gospel taking,
    More rich than golden ore;
On Allegheny's mountains,
    Through all the western vale,
Beside Missouri's fountains
    Rehearse the wondrous tale.

The love of Christ unfolding,
    Spread on from east to west,
Till all, his cross beholding,
    In him are fully blest.

Great Author of salvation,
Haste, haste the glorious day,
When we a ransomed nation
Thy sceptre shall obey.

—*Mrs. Anderson.*

CHRIST'S CHURCH SHOULD LOOK UP.

CHURCH of the living God! the Master says: "Look up." Do you ask me why? The soul-inspiring answer is, "because your redemption draweth nigh." Yes; eternal redemption at the putting on of immortality at Christ's glorious appearing.

Now the bowed head is the symbol of sorrow, but the up-lifted head betokens joy: "Look up and lift up your heads," he commands. Or, as one renders it, "Raise yourselves and lift up your heads." Or, as Wickliffe phrases it, "Behold ye and raise ye your heads." Looking down begets weakness and savors of "the earth, earthy." Looking up inspires courage, hope, and might, indicates the watchful spirit, and tells the world that the heart is in heaven, from whence you expect the Deliverer. You cannot fail to do this without proving disobedient to the Lord. "Raise yourselves, droop no longer, arise and be strong, have certain knowledge of the approach of the great day!" he cries. Will you do it? For centuries the bride of the Lamb has been a prey to death. Her foes have been countless, sleepless, and unrelenting; she walking her bloody, lonely path with bowed head and eyes cast down in sorrow. The grave has ever been before her, yawning to devour. But as if in expectation of a strong deliverer from the skies she has buried her dead with their faces turned upward, and the eyes in the right direction—up. These on opening at his bidding shall catch speedily the sight of the descending King. For the trumpet shall sound, and the good, translated skyward to meet him, shall then be like him forever. Now he is soon to arrive. We have witnessed the predicted signs. We know the proper and plainly revealed final position,—let us take it. It is the posture of expectant joy. It is the glorious privilege as well as the sacred duty of the last generation of Christians, to go about with their heads lifted up. It will be their happy privilege to stand at the bar of judgment with their heads lifted up, for the shame of sin will be exchanged for the boldness of holiness. It will be theirs to march through the golden gates with their heads up. "Thou, O Lord, art a shield for me, my glory, and the lifter up of my head." O Christians, can we afford to become guilty by disregarding the express orders of our King in refusing at the proper time to look toward the door of the heavenly tabernacle, about to swing back on its hinges and let forth the Bridegroom? The time has assuredly come. In the broad clear light of the breaking day there is no excuse for the recreant, the indifferent, the cold-hearted.

What an unfailing well of joy in trial; what a source of strength against the forces of sin and evil, what a weapon of warfare against Satan, this belief would everywhere prove to the dear Church of God, if she would but open her eyes and perceive and embrace it. What an all-absorbing joy, what an unfailing hope as the conflict deepens, and the fierce, evil powers enhance its intensity. The great heart of Christendom would be stirred with a mighty gladness; an exultant shout would ring out through all the camp of the weary hosts; the enemy would hear the plan of victory sounded in advance, while the multitudes of believers, united in the "one hope," would be engirded as with invincible strength from the everlasting arm of the Almighty. Then lift the head, O weary watcher. Turn the eyes to perceive the angel couriers of the returning Redeemer. With ears intent, wait to catch the first signal of the mighty trumpet's blast. Look up, behold it soundeth speedily, and the bell that marks the incoming of eternity is about to strike, One! To the last minute do as the Lord bids, and look up. Keep the head erect, and with it the heart clean, if at the end you would be " caught up to join the Lord in the air." Waiters, watchers, workers, Heads up!

—*D. T. Taylor.*

SOUL-HUNGER OF THE CHURCH.

SOUL-HUNGER is everywhere leading the churches to remarkable activity in the different departments of religious labor. Under the stimulus of this hunger the flocks are ready to follow their shepherds to any work and to any sacrifice. Let the pastors suggest that what is needed is a fine church edifice, and the members generally are ready to give all they can, and bear the more annoying burden of hopeless indebtedness to secure the needed object. Pride may underlie the action of a few, but soul-hunger moves the mass of the membership in the enterprise.

Let the Church leaders intimate that fine music and fine preaching are the wants of the Church, and all possible efforts and sacrifices are at once made to secure them. And these address the æsthetic in human nature, excite intellectual pleasure, and afford a kind of gratification, which many mistake for religious experience, and from what they see and hear, they conclude that these are the highest pleasures which the gospel offers; knowing of nothing better for their souls, they continue from year to year to bear these heavy burdens for the privilege of feeding upon these things, proper in their place, but dry and worthless husks to souls famishing for the bread of life. The same may be said of all the other enterprises of the Church, which should have their proper place, but which have been unfortunately, in too many cases, substituted for spiritual religion.

When some one, "full of faith and the Holy Ghost," enters these congregations and preaches the Gospel, not with enticing words of man's wisdom, but in demonstration of the Spirit and power, the people immediately discern their true wants, and the nature of the hunger which has stimulated their religious labors. As soon as they get a taste of the pure word of life they crowd the churches, not to be entertained by the beautiful in composition, or the eloquent in diction, or the cultured in music, but "to behold the beauty of the Lord, and to inquire in his temple." And if their leaders will go before, or even get out of the way, the body of the churches will march up out of the wilderness and pass over into the land of promise. God's people all over the land, and in all the churches, are ready for a forward movement; the wants of the hour are Joshuas, to give orders and lead the way.

If these remarks are just—and all acquainted with the facts know they are—it is fearful to contemplate the account which the clergy of to-day will have to confront in the final judgment. Oh, that all the spiritual guides of the people understood the situation, felt their responsibility, would take advantage of this hunger, and lead the people on to life and victory.—*Sheridan Baker.*

THE CHURCH WATCHING.

LORD, her watch thy Church is keeping;
  When shall earth thy rule obey?
When shall end the night of weeping?
  When shall break the promised day?
See the whitening harvest languish,
  Waiting still the laborer's toil;
Was it vain, thy Son's deep anguish?
  Shall the strong retain the spoil?

Tidings sent to every creature,
  Millions yet have never heard;
Can they hear without a preacher!
  Lord Almighty, give the Word:
Give the Word; in every nation
  Let the Gospel-trumpet sound,
Witnessing a world's salvation
  To the earth's remotest bound.

Then the end: Thy Church completed,
  All the chosen gathered in.
With their King in glory seated,
  Satan bound, and banished sin;
Gone forever, parting, weeping,
  Hunger, sorrow, death, and pain;
Lo! her watch thy Church is keeping;
  Come, Lord Jesus, come to reign.
            —*Henry Downton.*

THE CHURCH WAITING.

THE Church has waited long,
  Her absent Lord to see;
And still in loneliness she waits,
  A friendless stranger she.
Age after age has gone,
  Sun after sun has set,
And still, in weeds of widowhood,
  She weeps, a mourner yet.
Come, then, Lord Jesus, come!

Saint after saint on earth
  Has lived and loved and died;
And as they left us one by one,
  We laid them side by side,
We laid them down to sleep,
  But not in hope forlorn;
We laid them but to ripen there,
  Till the last glorious morn.
Come, then, Lord Jesus, come.

The serpent's brood increase,
  The powers of hell grow bold,
The conflict thickens, faith is low,
  And love is waxing cold.
How long, O Lord, our God!
  Holy and true and good,
Wilt Thou not judge Thy suffering Church,
  Her sighs and tears and blood?
Come, then, Lord Jesus, come.

We long to hear Thy voice,
  To see Thee face to face,

To share Thy crown and glory then,
    As now we share Thy grace.
    Should not the loving bride
    Her absent bridegroom mourn?
Should she not wear the signs of grief
    Until her Lord return?
    Come, then, Lord Jesus, come.

    The whole creation groans,
    And waits to hear that voice,
That shall restore her comeliness,
    And make her wastes rejoice.
    Come, Lord, and wipe away
    The curse, the sin, the stain,
And make this blighted world of ours
    Thine own fair world again.
    Come, then, Lord Jesus, come.
                  —*Horatinus Bonar.*

THE CHURCH'S LAST TESTIMONY.

THE Church from the first has been God's witness upon earth, and when her testimony shall have been fully delivered the end will come, and the dispensation will be closed. The ripeness of the Church will be when it shall have witnessed for all the truths which are to be opposed by the heretical and the infidel. Already has the protest been uttered on behalf of those doctrines, referring both to man and the Mediator, which are nothing less than the life's blood of Christianity. If you trace heresy downward, from the Apostles' days to our own, you find it fastening itself successively on the several truths of our faith, so that there is scarce a fraction which has not been assaulted, and in defence of which, the Church has not shown itself a witness. What then remains to the rendering the Church fully ripe? We find from the Scriptures that one great feature of the last times shall be disbelief or denial of the second Advent of Christ. As in other days of the dispensation, so, in the concluding, there shall be abroad the covetous, the blasphemers, the traitors, the high-minded, and all those manifestations of evil which have ever called forth the protest of the Church. But, over and above these forms of wickedness, scorners shall be walking the earth, arguing, from the apparent fixedness of things, of the improbability of Christ's interference, and tauntingly asking: "Where is the promise of his coming?" Here, it may be, will be the last and most energetic demand on the witness. The Church must oppose itself to this new and desperate infidelity. She must protest for the Advent of the Lord against the denial and reviling of a profligate generation. And when the Church shall have done this, witnessed that Christ is about to reappear, and invoked a scoffing world to prepare for his approach, then, it may be, will her perfect ripeness be reached, and then, in accordance with the parable, the fruit being brought forth, Christ shall "immediately put in the sickle," gather in the corn, and house his elect, ere vengeance be let loose on the impenitent and unbelieving.

—*Henry Melvill.*

The Church below is often in a suffering state. Christ himself was a man of sorrows; nor should his bride be a wife of pleasure.

—*Dr. Arrowsmith.*

WATCHWORD OF THE CHURCH.

AH, brethren, the times are very evil, the days are very perilous unto us all. I would it were not so; but we have well deserved the evil at the Lord's hand. The Lord is righteous; yea, the Lord is merciful and gracious, who hath not utterly extinguished us, and put us out from being a nation.

But, holy brethren, partakers of the heavenly calling, God never leaveth himself without a witness; his Church will not be prevailed against by all the gates of hell. Though the spirits from the mouth of the dragon, and from the mouth of the beast, and from the mouth of the false prophet be all flown abroad, there is a word, a word of power, which can preserve the Church.

And what is that word of mighty power? It is not that with which Christ withstood Satan's first assault: "Man liveth not by bread alone, but by every word of God." That word might be proper to the Church in her *first* ages, when she was driven from house and home by the persecutions of paganism. Nor is it that word which withstood and defeated Satan's *second* temptation when he tempted the Lord with the kingdoms of the world and the glories of them. "Thou shalt worship the Lord thy God, and him only shalt thou serve;" which might be proper, as some have thought, to the *second* period of the Church, when she was tempted with the co-fraternity and co-habitation of that power of the kings of the earth, with which they had heretofore afflicted her. Nor is it the word with which he defeated the third temptation of Satan, beguiling him to take liberties with the word of God, and to wrest it unto his own convenient uses—" Thou shalt not tempt the Lord thy God"—and which may well be thought proper to the *third*, or Protestant age of the Church, during which and amongst whom the word of God hath been made the tool of the human intellect, to answer the expedient interests and temporal ends of men. No; these three words which were powerful to meet each its proper and several temptations of Satan are not able to meet and overcome the combined and confederate attempts of the three spirits which have gone forth together from the mouth of the dragon, and of the beast, and of the false prophet.

And what, then, is that word of mightiest power, which is to prove the bulwark of the Church against the gates of hell? The Lord himself hath told it in its place where the procession of these evil spirits is declared, for no sooner had the seer seen them go forth than there was lifted up this voice in his hearing: *"Behold, I come as a thief;* blessed is he that watcheth and keepeth his garments, lest he walk naked and they see his shame."

I believe this spirit of the last times, which is the combined mixture and expressed strength of all the others—violence, seduction, and delusion—can be resisted by that mighty word, *"Behold I come!"* The faith of this word will prevail to establish the foundations in these perilous times against the gates of hell. This I believe; and I believe, moreover, that no other word will prevail to do it. And the thing which stirs my hope is, that the truth is not preached unto this nation; and the thing that stirs my fears is, that it findeth welcome with so few. Nevertheless, if you be appointed unto salvation, the Lord's will be done. I would *rather* that it had been many, but the Lord's will be done.—*Edward Irving.*

THE CHURCH TRIUMPHANT.

I SAW, and lo! a countless throng,
  Th' elect of every nation, name, and tongue,
  Assembled round the everlasting Throne;
    With robes of white endued,
    The Righteousness of God;
    And each a palm sustain'd
    In his victorious hand;
When thus the bright melodious choir begun·
    "Salvation to Thy Name,
Eternal God, and co-eternal Lamb!
In power, in glory, and in essence, One!"

    So sung the Saints. Th' Angelic train
Second the anthem with a loud Amen
    (These in the outer circle stood,
    The saints were nearest God);
And prostrate fall, with glory overpower'd,
    And hide their faces with their wings,
    And thus address the King of kings:
"All hail! by Thy Triumphant Church adored!
    Blessing and thanks and honor too,
Are Thy supreme, Thy everlasting due,
Our Triune Sovereign, our propitious Lord!"

    While I beheld th' amazing sight,
A Seraph pointed to the Saints in white,
And told me who they were, and whence they came:
    "These are they, whose lot below
    Was persecution, pain, and woe;
    These are the chosen, purchased Flock,
    Who ne'er their Lord forsook;

Through His imputed merit free from blame;
    Redeemed from every sin;
And, as thou seest, whose garments were made clean,
Wash'd in the Blood of yon exalted Lamb.

    Saved by His Righteousness alone,
    Spotless they stand before the Throne,
And in the etheral Temple chant His praise:
    Himself among them deigns to dwell,
    And face to face His Light reveal:
    Hunger and thirst, as heretofore,
And pain, and heat, they know no more,
Nor need, as once, the sun's prolific rays.
    Immanuel here His people feeds,
    To streams of joy perennial leads,
And wipes, forever wipes, the tears from every face.

    Happy the souls released from fear,
    And safely landed there!
    Some of the shining number once I knew,
    And travell'd with them here:
Nay, some, my elder brethren now,
Set later out for Heaven, my junior saints below;
Long after me, they heard the call of Grace,
Which walked them unto Righteousness;
    How have they got beyond?
Converted last, yet first with glory crown'd;
    Little, once, I thought that these
    Would first the summit gain,
And leave me far behind, slow journeying through the plain.

Loved while on earth! nor less belov'd, tho' gone!
    Think not I envy you your crown:
No! if I could, I would not call you down!
    Though slower is my pace,
    To you I'll follow on,

Leaning on Jesus all the way;
Who, now and then, lets fall a ray
　　Of comfort from His Throne:
　　The shinings of His grace
Soften my passage through the wilderness;
And vines, nectareous, spring where briers grew.
　　The sweet unveilings of His face
Make me, at times, near half as blest as you!
O! might His beauty feast my ravish'd eyes,
　　His gladdening presence ever stay,
　　And cheer me all my journey through!
But soon the clouds return: my triumph dies;
　　Damp vapors from the valleys rise,
And hide the hill of Zion from my view.

　　Spirit of Light! thrice Holy Dove!
Brighten my sense of interest in that love,
Which knew no birth, and never shall expire!
Electing Goodness, firm and free,
My whole salvation hangs on Thee.
Eldest and fairest daughter of Eternity!
Redemption, grace, and glory too,
　　Our bliss above, and hopes below,
　　From her, their parent fountain, flow.
Ah, tell me, Lord, that Thou hast chosen me!
Thou, who hast kindled my intense desire,
Fulfil the wish Thy influence did inspire,
　　And let me my election know!
Then, when Thy summons bids me come up higher,
　　Well pleased I shall from life retire,
And join the burning hosts, beheld at distance now.
　　　　　　—*Augustus Montague Toplady.*

WHERE Christ is there is the Church.—*Pressense.*

GOD IN THE CHURCH.

THERE is no truth which men find so difficult to accept as God revealed in themselves. Christ asked no question which has received so many different answers as, "Whom say ye that I am?" Every possible theory of his personality and life has been advanced and finally discarded. The mythical theory of Strauss falls to pieces by its own weight of improbability, and is abandoned; Renan's exquisite fancy and charming literary skill cannot conceal the hopeless inadequacy of his treatment of this marvelous character. The men who looked upon the face of Christ and listened to those words in which, even to their untrained spiritual sense, eternal truths uttered themselves, were not less skeptical than the doubters of our time. A revelation of God in the flesh seemed incredible to them even under the supernal glow of that transcendent life and the spell of a teaching, which, even while they rejected, they declared was such as never man spoke before.

The same difficulty meets the Christian Church in every age; men will not see God in human tabernacles. They will recognize him shrined in the temple of nature: they will not bow to him throned in humanity; and yet this thought of God is not utterly foreign to human thought; on the contrary, it is found in almost every great religion. "There is but one temple in the world, and that is the body of man; nothing is holier than this high form," says Novalis; and, measuring the gifts, the powers and possibilities of humanity against all its environment of earth, and sky, and mighty flow of unseen force, what is so august and worthy the indwelling of the divine Spirit as the soul of man, as the great company of faithful people in all the generations! Paul had his faults and his limitations; but, setting the incalculable results of his strenuous life beside the stainless beauty of the Parthenon, the noblest of all temples built with hands, does not fluted column, and carved architrave, and faultless statue shrink into insignificance?

The Church has made its mistakes and committed its sins, and the Christian should be the last to understate or extenuate them; but where else has the fruit of the Spirit ripened so steadily? Webster said that he found one evidence of the divine origin of the Christian religion in the fact that it had outlived written sermons; more deeply and seriously it may be said that a crowning evidence of the divine commission and the work of the Church is found in the fact that it has moved steadily on in spite of the sluggishness and blindness of men; that it has survived continual mistakes and shortcomings, and that out of the ashes of repented sins it has blossomed in ever-recurring seasons of fruitfulness. The God of human thought would reveal himself in some miraculous appearance outside human experience and above human limitations; a revelation distinct and apart from all human life, and touching it only with a sense of wonder and awe. The God higher than all human conceptions appears in the very dawn of history, discovering himself to undeveloped men in a language which they could understand, and continuing that disclosure to this very hour in a speech that has steadily deepened in meaning and risen in spiritual expression. He is not apart from men, but in and with them; he shines not more clearly in his sublime heavens than in the troubled life of his children; he works not more divinely in the hidden depths of the universe than in human history and with human co-operation. To the reverent mind, open to the highest revelation, God is nowhere so unspeakably beautiful, so wholly divine, as in his fellowship with men; and this is what gives the Church its sanctity. In all its history the human weakness and the divine Spirit have wrought together; follies and failures have been over-ruled by that omnipotent power which can harness even the wrath of men to the chariot of praise.

Very few intelligent and honest men are satisfied with the manner in which our government is administered; their indignation at corrupt methods and corrupt men, and their disgust with ignorant and inefficient measures are expressed in continual condemnation and criticism; but if they are good citizens they do not stay away from the polling place. They know that all human organizations, however high their aims and exalted their functions, are but imperfect machinery, likely to get out of order in spite of the most careful watching. The Church, on its practical, working, organizing and governing side, is a piece of human machinery; full, therefore, and necessarily, of flaws and imperfections; likely at all times to get out of order, and often undoing, by the carelessness or ignorance of those who direct it, the very work it was framed to perform. That such elements of disorder and failure lurk in it, and that in spite of them it continues to serve the highest interests of the world as no other instrumentality has ever served them, ought to deepen the reverence of all thoughtful men rather than shake their faith in the divine mission and work of the Christian Church.—*Christian Union.*

JOYS OF THE CHURCH TRIUMPHANT.

REST! how sweet the sound! It is melody to my ears. It lies as a reviving cordial at my heart, and thence sends forth lively spirits, which beat through all the pulses of my soul. Rest—not as the stone that rests on the earth, nor as this flesh shall rest in the grave, nor such a rest as the carnal world desires. Oh, blessed rest! when we rest not day and night, saying, " Holy, holy, holy, Lord God Almighty;" when we shall rest from sin, but not from worship; from suffering and sorrow, but not from joy. Oh, blessed day! when I shall rest with God! when I shall rest in the bosom of my Lord! when my perfect soul and body shall together perfectly enjoy the most perfect God.

This is that joy which was procured by sorrow; that crown which was procured by the cross. My Lord wept, that now my tears might be wiped away; he bled, that I might now rejoice; he was forsaken, that I might *not* be; he died, that I might live. Oh, free mercy, that can exalt so vile a wretch! Free to me, though dear to Christ; free grace, that hath chosen me when thousands were forsaken!

Oh, sweet reconciliation! happy union! Now the Gospel shall no more be dishonored through our folly. No more, my soul, shalt thou lament the suffering saints, or the Church's ruins, or mourn thy suffering friends, nor weep over their dying beds or their graves. Thou shalt never suffer thy old temptations from Satan, the world, or thy flesh. Thy pains and sickness are all cured; thy body shall no more burden thee with weakness and weariness; thy aching head and heart, thy hunger and thirst, thy sleep and labor, are all gone.

Oh, what a mighty change is this! From persecuting sinners, to praising saints; from a vile body, to this which shines as the brightness of the firmament; from a sense of God's displeasure, to the perfect enjoyment of him in love; from all my fearful thoughts of death, to this joyful life. Blessed change! Farewell sin and sorrow forever; farewell my rocky, proud, unbelieving heart; my worldly, sensual, carnal heart; and welcome my most holy, heavenly nature. Farewell repentance, faith, and hope; and welcome love, joy, and praise.

I shall now have my harvest without ploughing or sowing; my joy without a preacher or a promise; even all from the face of God himself. Whatever mixture is in the streams, there is nothing but pure joy in the fountain. Here I shall be encircled with eternity, and ever live, and ever, ever praise the Lord. My face will not wrinkle, nor my hair be gray; for this corruptible shall have put on incorruption, and this mortal immortality; death shall be swallowed up in victory.

"O death! where is now thy sting?
O grave! where is thy victory?

The date of my lease will no more expire, nor shall I trouble myself with thoughts of death, nor lose my joys through *fear* of losing them. When millions of ages are past, it is no nearer ending. Every day is all noon, every month is harvest, every year is a jubilee, every age is a full manhood, and all this is one eternity! the glory of my glory! the perfection of my perfection.—*Richard Baxter.*

THE SPIRITUAL TEMPLE.

AND the house, when it was in building, was built of stone made ready before it was brought thither: so that there was neither hammer nor axe nor any tool of iron heard in the house, while it was in building" (1 Kings iv. 7).

And whence, then, came these goodly stones 'twas Israel's pride to raise,
The glory of the former house, the joy of ancient days;
In purity and strength erect, in radiant splendor bright,
Sparkling with golden beams of noon, or silver smiles of night?

From coasts the stately cedar crowns, each noble slab was brought,
In Lebanon's deep quarries hewn, and on its mountains wrought;
There rung the hammer's heavy stroke among the echoing rocks,
There chased the chisel's keen, sharp edge, the rude, unshapen blocks.

Thence polished, perfected, complete, each fitted to its place,
For lofty coping, massive wall, or deep imbedded base,
They bore them o'er the waves that rolled their billowy swell between
The shores of Tyre's imperial pride and Judah's hills of green.

With gradual toil the work went on, through days and months and years,
Beneath the summer's laughing sun, and winter's frozen tears;
And thus in majesty sublime and noiseless pomp it rose,—
Fit dwelling for the God of Peace,—a temple of repose!

Brethren in Christ! to holier things the simple type apply;
Our God himself a temple builds, eternal and on high,

Of souls elect; their Zion there—that world of light and bliss;
Their Lebanon—the place of toil—of previous moulding—this.

From nature's quarries, deep and dark, with gracious aim he hews
The stones, the spiritual stones, it pleaseth him to choose:
Hard, rugged, shapeless at the first, yet destined each to shine,
Moulded beneath his patient hand, in purity divine.

Oh! glorious process! see the proud grow lowly, gentle, meek;
See floods of unaccustomed tears gush down the hardened cheek:
Perchance the hammer's heavy stroke o'erthrew some idol fond;
Perchance the chisel rent in twain some precious, tender bond.

Behold, he prays whose lips were sealed in silent scorn before,—
Sighs for the closet's holy calm, and hails the welcome door:
Behold, he works for Jesus now, whose days went idly past;
Oh, for more mouldings of the hand that works a change so vast!

Ye looked on one, a well-wrought stone, a saint of God matured,—
What chisellings that heart had felt, what chastening strokes endured!
But marked ye not that last soft touch, what perfect grace it gave,
Ere Jesus bore his servant home across the darksome wave?—

Home to the place his grace designed that chosen soul to fill,
In the bright temple of the saved, "upon his holy hill;"
Home to the noiselessness,—the peace of those sweet shrines above,
Whose stones shall never be displaced—set in redeeming love.

Lord! chisel, chasten, polish us, each blemish work away,
Cleanse us with purifying blood, in spotless robes array;
And thus, thine image on us stamped, transport us to the shore,
Where not a stroke is ever felt, for none is needed more.

THE UNREVEALED CHURCH.

BEHOLD, what manner of love the Father hath bestowed upon us, that we should be called the sons of God: therefore the world knoweth us not, because it knew him not. Beloved, now are we the sons of God, and it doth not yet appear what we shall be: but we know that, when he shall appear, we shall be like him; for we shall see him as he is."

The Church of God is only manifested in this present world, by the excellencies of its character. Owing to human imperfection and weakness, the positive validity of any one's claim to the relationship of son and daughter of the Lord Almighty may not be perfectly obvious to the world, or even to fellow-heirs of the like precious faith. The salvation that God impresses on the heart, a living tracery, graven by the Holy Spirit, is discernible only by the Omniscient eye. Where mortal eyes, looking at the outward appearance, contemplate only the frail child of earth, the divine vision may distinguish an heir of eternal glory, a son of God yet unrevealed. The closed bud in a wintry day may seem small and even contemptible, wrapped in its scaly integuments, while the plant is rooted in this desert soil: but that bud may enwrap a blossom which when unfolded in the sunshine of paradise will display tinting incomparable, and everlasting loveliness. The rich in faith and heirs of the kingdom are among the poor in this present world. Royal halls and imperial palaces, rich with carving, gilding, and tapestry, are not the abodes of the most excellent of the earth. God's own dear Son was houseless and homeless while in this world, and though the birds had nests and the foxes had holes, divine Royalty had not where to lay its head. Dens, caves, huts and hovels have sheltered; sheepskins, goatskins, rags and sackcloth have clothed, and lowliness and obscurity have hidden, the heirs of the heavenly kingdom from the gaze of a careless world. And if they have been lost among the humble and abject classes of humanity while living, how utterly forgotten while sleeping the sleep of death, are those who shall yet be held in everlasting remembrance. No garnished sepulchres are built for the dust of many of the heirs of immortality: no monumental marble or lettered granite tells where many sleep who in coming ages shall be equal with the angels of light. While the carved and graven pillar marks the place where wealth and honor are reposing, the wild rose and the tangled sweetbriar grow untended over forms destined to wear a crown of glory through endless futurity. Some who shall walk the golden streets in the New Jerusalem sleep beneath their mantle of snow in Arctic graves, where unsetting stars look down through the long nights on the unmarked resting-places of the dead. Some who shall yet follow the Lamb whithersoever he goeth, amid the spreading groves of the tree of life in the glad garden of God, rest now beneath the green turf once crimsoned with their martyr blood. The hot sands of the torrid deserts drift over dust more precious than gold, which is yet to be reformed in deathless beauty, and sing among the morning stars in the new creation. Others who shall come forth at the Redeemer's call, to sit upon the Saviour's throne, lie deep down upon the ocean's floor, where coral insects build their gorgeous tombs.

To-day the Church, the Redeemer's Bride, is a forlorn and outcast wanderer—a dweller in a wilderness of toils and cares; but she will one day put on her bridal robes and appear in the ages to come as the heavenly Princess, the Bride, the Lamb's Wife. The day of re-genesis and redemption will dawn upon this chaotic world, and break through the shadows of death's silent night. This which is now earthly shall bear the image of the heavenly, weakness shall be changed for power, corruption transformed into imperishability, mortality into deathlessness, and all the imperfections of humanity shall be transfigured, when these vile bodies shall be made like unto Christ's glorious body.

Those who have the first fruits of the Spirit groan within themselves, and struggle for the resurrection of life. For this promised redemption, a sin-paralyzed creation groans, and from the martyrs comes up the cry, "How long, O Lord?" The closing history of the world, that "lieth in the Wicked One," will soon be written. The annals of the future will be the records of the glorified and triumphant Church. May it be ours to share in its unending blessedness.

—*S. A. Chaplin.*

THE BLESSINGS OF ZION.

THE wilderness and the solitary place shall be glad for them; and the desert shall rejoice, and blossom as the rose. It shall blossom abundantly, and rejoice even with joy and singing: the glory of Lebanon shall be given unto it, the excellency of Carmel and Sharon; they shall see the glory of the Lord, and the excellency of our God. Strengthen ye the weak hands, and confirm the feeble knees. Say to them that are of a fearful heart, Be strong, fear not: behold, your God will come with vengeance, even God with a recompense;

he will come and save you. Then the eyes of the blind shall be opened, and the ears of the deaf shall be unstopped. Then shall the lame man leap as an hart, and the tongue of the dumb sing; for in the wilderness shall waters break out, and streams in the desert. And the parched ground shall become a pool, and the thirsty land springs of water; in the habitation of dragons where each lay, shall be grass, with reeds and rushes. And an highway shall be there, and a way, and it shall be called the way of holiness; the unclean shall not pass over it; but it shall be for those: the wayfaring men, though fools, shall not err therein. No lion shall be there, nor any ravenous beast shall go up thereon, it shall not be found there; but the redeemed shall walk there. And the ransomed of the Lord shall return, and come to Zion with songs and everlasting joy upon their heads: they shall obtain joy and gladness, and sorrow and sighing shall flee away.—Isaiah xxxv.

OUR COUNTRY.

LET the noble motto be,
"God, the country, Liberty!"
Planted on Religion's rock,
Thou shalt stand in every shock.

The lines are fallen unto me in pleasant places, yea I have a goodly heritage.—Psa. 16 : 6.

OUR COUNTRY.

GOOD God! we thank thee for this home—
This bounteous birthland of the free;
Where wanderers from afar may come,
And breathe the air of liberty!—
Still may her flowers untrampled spring,
Her harvests wave, her cities rise;
And yet, till time shall fold his wing,
Remain earth's loveliest paradise."

Just the Star Spangled Banner, O! long may it wave o'er the Land of the Free and the Home of the Brave

OUR COUNTRY.

[WRITTEN EXPRESSLY FOR THIS WORK BY AMANDA ELIZABETH DENNIS.]

OH! blest and fairest of the fair!
　Oh! beautiful beyond compare!
　　Oh! lovely sunset land!
　Our hearts, grown tender 'neath the grace
　And witchery of thy dear face,
　　With grateful love expand.

Thou seemest a dear and tender friend,
Upon whose love our souls depend
　For sunshine sweet and bland;
No other land so dear can be;
Our hearts go out in love to thee,
　Oh! beauteous sunset land!

Our country's God, to Thee we raise
Our hearts in hymns of boundless praise
　For this dear, gleaming strand—
This home of ours, by Freedom blest,
This Darling of the glorious West,
　This radiant sunset land!

And in the shelter of thine arms
We'll hush to rest the weak alarms
　We cannot understand,
Content to trust the loving care
That clothes with beauty ever fair
　Our own dear sunset land!

AMERICA.

SEARCH creation round, where can you find a country that presents so sublime a view, so interesting an anticipation? What noble institutions! What a comprehensive policy! What a wise equalization of every political advantage! The oppressed of all countries, the martyrs of every creed, the innocent victim of despotic arrogance or superstitious frenzy, may there find refuge; his industry encouraged, his piety respected, his ambition animated; with no restraint but those laws which are the same to all, and no distinction but that which his merit may originate. Who can deny that the existence of such a country presents a subject for human congratulation! Who can deny that its gigantic advancement offers a field for the most rational conjecture! At the end of the very next century, if she proceeds as she seems to promise, what a wondrous spectacle may she not exhibit! Who shall say for what purpose mysterious Providence may not have designed her! Who shall say that when in its follies or its crimes, the old world may have buried all the pride of its power, and all the pomp of its civilization, human nature may not find its destined renovation in the new! When its temples and its trophies shall have mouldered into dust—when the glories of its name shall be but the legend of tradition, and the light of its achievements live only in song; philosophy will revive again in the sky of her Franklin, and glory rekindle at the urn of Washington.

Is this the vision of romantic fancy? Is it even improba-

ble? Is it half so improbable as the events, which for the last twenty years have rolled like successive tides over the surface of the European world, each erasing the impressions that preceded it? Many I know there are who will consider this supposition as wild and whimsical, but they have dwelt with little reflection upon the records of the past. They have but ill observed the progress of national rise and national ruin. They form their judgment on the deceitful stability of the present hour, never considering the innumerable monarchies and republics, in former days, apparently as permanent, their very existence become now the subject of speculation—I had almost said of skepticism. I appeal to history! Tell me, thou reverend chronicler of the grave, can all the allusions of ambition realized, can all the wealth of a universal commerce, can all the achievements of successful heroism, or all the establishments of this world's wisdom, secure to empire the permanency of its possessions? Alas, Troy thought so once; yet the land of Priam lives only in song! Thebes thought so once; yet her hundred gates have crumbled, and her very tombs are but as the dust they were vainly intended to commemorate! So thought Palmyra—where is she! So thought Persepolis, and now—

> "Yon waste, where roaming lions howl,
> Yon aisle, where moans the gray-eyed owl,
> Shows the proud Persian's great abode,
> Where sceptred once, an earthly god,
> His power-clad arm controlled each happier clime,
> Where sports the warbling muse, and fancy soars sublime."

So thought the countries of Demosthenes and the Spartan; yet Leonidas is trampled by the timid slave, and Athens insulted by the servile, mindless and enervate Ottoman. In his hurried march, Time has but looked at their imagined immortality, and all its vanities, from the palace to the tomb, have, with their ruins, erased the very impression of his footsteps! The days of their glory are as if they had never been; and the island that was then a speck, rude and neglected, in the barren ocean, now rivals the ubiquity of their commerce, the glory of their arms, the fame of their philosophy, the eloquence of their senate, and the inspiration of their bards! Who shall say, then, contemplating the past, that England, proud and potent as she appears, may not one day be what Athens is, and the young America yet soar to be what Athens was! Who shall say, when the European column shall have mouldered, and the night of barbarism obscured its very ruins, that that mighty continent may not emerge from the horizon, to rule, for its time, sovereign of the ascendent.

Such, sir, is the natural progress of human operations, and such the unsubstantial mockery of human pride.—*Charles Phillips.*

AMERICA THE OLD WORLD.

FIRST-BORN among the continents, though so much later in culture and civilization than some of more recent birth, America, so far as her physical history is concerned, has been falsely denominated the *New World*. Hers was the first dry land lifted out of the waters, hers the first shore washed by the ocean that enveloped all the earth beside; and while Europe was represented only by islands rising here and there above the sea, America already stretched an unbroken line of land from Nova Scotia to the Far West.

In the present state of our knowledge, our conclusions respecting the beginning of the earth's history, the way in which it took form and shape as a distinct, separate planet, must, of course, be very vague and hypothetical, yet the progress of science is so rapidly reconstructing the past that we may hope to solve even this problem, and to one who looks upon man's appearance upon the earth as the crowning work in a succession of creative acts, all of which have had relation to his coming in the end, it will not seem strange that he should at last be allowed to understand a history which was but the introduction of his own existence. It is my belief that not only the future, but the past also, is the inheritance of man, and that we shall yet conquer our lost birthright.

Even now our knowledge carries us far enough to warrant the assertion that there was a time when our earth was in a state of igneous fusion, when no ocean bathed it and no atmosphere surrounded it, when no wind blew over it, and no rain fell upon it, but an intense heat held all its materials in solution. In those days the rocks which are now the very bones and sinews of our mother Earth—her granites, her porphyries, her basalts, her sienites—were melted into a liquid mass. As I am writing for the unscientific reader, who may not be familiar with the facts through which these inferences have been reached, I will answer here a question which, were we talking together, he might naturally ask in a somewhat skeptical tone. How do you know that this state of things ever existed, and, supposing that the solid materials of which our earth consists were even in a liquid condition, what right have you to infer that this condition was caused by the action of heat upon them? I answer, because it is acting upon them still; because the earth we tread is but a thin crust floating on a liquid sea of molten materials; because the agencies that were at work then are at work now, and the present is the logical sequence of the past. From artesian wells, from mines, from geysers, from hot springs, a mass of facts have been collected, proving incontestably the heated condition of all substances at a certain depth below the earth's surface; and if we need more positive evidence, we have it in the fiery eruptions that even now bear fearful testimony to the molten ocean seething within the globe and forcing its way out from time to time. The modern progress of geology has led us by successive and perfectly connected steps back to a time when what is now only an occasional and rare phenomenon was the normal condition of our earth, when those internal fires were enclosed in an envelope so thin that it opposed but little resistance to their frequent outbreak, and they constantly forced themselves through this crust, pouring out melted materials that subsequently cooled and consolidated on its surface. So constant were these eruptions and so slight was the resistance they encountered, that some portions of the earlier rock-deposits are perforated with numerous chimneys, narrow tunnels as it were, bored by the liquid masses that poured out through them and greatly modified their first condition.

There is, perhaps, no part of the world, certainly none familiar to science, where the early geological periods can be studied with so much ease and precision as in the United States. Along their northern borders, between Canada and the United States, there runs the low line of hills known as the Laurentian Hills. Insignificant in height, nowhere rising more than fifteen hundred or two thousand feet above the level of the sea, these are nevertheless the first mountains that broke the uniform level of the earth's surface, and lifted themselves above the water. Their low stature, as compared with that of more lofty mountain ranges, is in accordance with an invariable rule, by which the relative age of mountains may be estimated. The oldest mountains are the lowest, while the younger, more recent ones, tower above their elders, and are usually more torn and dislocated also. This is easily understood when we remember that all mountains and mountain chains are the result of upheavals, and that the violence of the outbreak must have been in proportion to the strength of the resistance. When the crust of the earth was so thin that the heated masses within easily broke through it, they were not thrown to so great a height, and formed comparatively low elevations, such as the Canadian hills or the mountains of Bretagne and Wales. But in later times, when young, vigorous giants, such as the Alps, the Himalayas, or, later still, the Rocky Mountains, forced their way out from their fiery prison-house, the crust of the earth was much thicker, and fearful indeed must have been the convulsions which attended their exit.

The Laurentian Hills form, then, a granite range, stretching from Eastern Canada to the Upper Mississippi, and immediately along its base are gathered the Azoic deposits, the first stratified beds, in which the absence of life need not surprise us, since they were formed beneath a heated ocean. As well might we expect to find the remains of fish, or shells, or crabs at the bottom of geysers or of boiling springs, as on those early shores bathed by an ocean of which the heat must have been so intense. Although from the condition in which we find it, this first granite range has evidently never been disturbed by any violent convulsions since its first upheaval, yet there has been a gradual rising of that part of the continent, for the Azoic beds do not lie horizontally along the base of the Laurentian Hills in the position in which they must originally have been deposited, but are lifted and rest against their slopes. They have been more or less dislocated in this process, and are greatly metamorphosed by the intense heat to which they must have been exposed. Indeed, all the oldest stratified rocks have been baked by the prolonged action of heat.

It may be asked how the materials for those first stratified deposits were provided. In later times, when an abundant and various soil covered the earth, when every river brought down to the ocean, not only its yearly tribute of mud or clay or lime, but the *debris* of animals and plants that lived and died in its waters or along its banks, when every lake and pond deposited at its bottom in successive layers the lighter or heavier materials floating in its waters and settling gradually beneath them, the process by which stratified materials are collected and gradually harden into rock is more easily understood. But when the solid surface of the earth was only just beginning to form, it would seem that the floating matter in the sea can hardly have been in sufficient quantity to form any extensive deposits. No doubt there was some abrasion even of the first crust; but the more abundant source of the earliest stratification is to be found in the submarine volcanoes that poured their liquid streams into the first ocean. At what rate these materials would be distributed and precipitated in regular strata it is impossible to determine; but that volcanic materials were so deposited in layers is evident from the relative position of the earliest rocks. I have already spoken of the innumerable chimneys perforating the Azoic beds, narrow outlets of Plutonic rock, protruding through the earliest strata. Not only are such funnels filled with the crystalline mass of granite that flowed through them in a liquid state, but it has often poured over their sides, mingling with the stratified beds around. In the present state of our knowledge, we can explain such appearances only by supposing that the heated materials within the earth's crust poured out frequently, meeting little resistance; that they then scattered and were precipitated in the ocean around, settling in successive strata at its bottom,—that through such strata the heated masses continue to pour again and again, forming for themselves the chimney-like outlets above mentioned.

Such, then, was the earliest American land—a long, narrow island, almost continental in its proportions, since it stretched from the eastern borders of Canada nearly to the point where now the base of the Rocky Mountains meets the plain of the Mississippi Valley. We may still walk along its ridge and know that we tread upon the ancient granite that first divided the waters into a northern and southern ocean; and if our imaginations will carry us so far, we may look down toward its base and fancy how the sea washed against this earliest shore of a lifeless world. This is no romance, but the bald, simple truth; for the fact that this granite band was lifted out of the waters so early in the history of the world, and has not since been submerged, has, of course, prevented any subsequent deposits from forming above. And this is true of all the northern part of the United States. It has been lifted gradually, the beds deposited in one period being subsequently raised, and forming a shore along which those of the succeeding one collected, so that we have their whole sequence before us. In regions where all the geological deposits, Silurian, Devonian, Carboniferous, Permian, Triassic, etc., are piled one upon another, and we can get a glimpse of their internal relations only where some rent has laid them open, or where their ragged edges, worn away by the abrading action of external influences, expose to view their successive layers, it must, of course, be more difficult to follow their connection. For this reason the American Continent offers facilities to the geologist denied to him in the so-called Old World, where the earlier deposits are comparatively hidden, and the broken character of the land, intersected by mountains in every direction, renders his investigation still more difficult. Of course, when I speak of the geological deposits as so completely unveiled to us here, I do not forget the sheet of drift which covers the continent from north to south; but the drift is only a superficial and recent addition to the soil, resting loosely above the other geological deposits, and arising from very different causes.

In this article I have intended to limit myself to a general sketch of the formation of the Laurentian Hills with the Azoic stratified beds resting against them. In the Silurian epoch following the Azoic we have the first beach on which any life stirred; it extended along the base of the Azoic beds, widening by its extensive deposits the narrow strip of land already upheaved.—*Louis Agassiz.*

Moor the anchor of your politics to the rock of righteousness, not to the shifting sands of supposed interest, and it will hold firm amid the rushing tides of popular opinion.

—Canon Farrar.

THE DISCOVERY OF AMERICA BY COLUMBUS.

IT was on Friday morning, the 12th of October, 1492, that Columbus first beheld the New World. As the day dawned he saw before him a level island, several leagues in extent, and covered with trees like a continual orchard. Though apparently uncultivated, it was populous, for the inhabitants were seen issuing from all parts of the woods and running to the shore. They were perfectly naked, and, as they stood gazing at the ships, appeared by their attitudes and gestures to be lost in astonishment.

Columbus made signals for the ships to cast anchor, and the boats to be manned and armed. He entered his own boat richly attired in scarlet, and holding the royal standard, whilst Martin Alonzo Pinzon and Vincent Janes, his brother, put off in company in their boats, each with a banner of the enterprise emblazoned with a green cross, having on either side the letters F and Y, the initials of the Castilian monarchs, Fernando and Ysabel, surmounted by crowns.

As he approached the shore, Columbus, who was disposed for all kinds of agreeable impressions, was delighted with the purity and suavity of the atmosphere, the crystal transparency of the sea, and the extraordinary beauty of the vegetation. He beheld, also, fruits of an unknown kind upon the trees which overhung the shores. On landing, he threw himself on his knees, kissed the earth, and returned thanks to God with tears of joy. His example was followed by the rest, whose hearts indeed overflowed with the same feelings of gratitude.

Columbus, then rising, drew his sword, displayed the royal standard, and assembling round him the two captains, with Rodrigo de Escobedo, notary of the armament, Rodrigo Sanchez, and the rest who had landed, he took solemn possession in the name of the Castilian sovereigns, giving the island the name of San Salvador. Having complied with the requisite forms and ceremonies, he called upon all present to take the oath of obedience to him, as admiral and viceroy representing the persons of the sovereigns.

The feelings of the crew now burst forth in the most extravagant transports. They had recently considered themselves devoted men, hurrying forward to destruction; they now looked upon themselves as favorites of fortune, and gave themselves up to the most unbounded joy. They thronged around the admiral with overflowing zeal, some embracing him, others kissing his hands. Those who had been most mutinous and turbulent during the voyage were now most devoted and enthusiastic, some begged favors of him, as if he had already wealth and honors in his gift. Many abject spirits, who had outraged him by their insolence, now crouched at his feet, begging pardon for all the trouble they had caused him, and promising the blindest obedience for the future.

The natives of the island, when, at the dawn of day, they had beheld the ships hovering on their coast, had supposed them monsters which had issued from the deep during the night. They had crowded to the beach, and watched their movements with awful anxiety. Their veering about, apparently without effort, and the shifting and furling of their sails, resembling huge wings, filled them with astonishment.

When they beheld their boats approach the shore, and a number of strange beings clad in glittering steel, or raiment of various colors, landing upon the beach, they fled in affright to the woods. Finding, however, that there was no attempt to pursue or molest them, they gradually recovered from their terror, and approached the Spaniards with great awe, frequently prostrating themselves on the earth, and making signs of adoration. During the ceremonies of taking possession, they remained gazing in timid admiration at the complexion, the beards, the shining armor, and splendid dress of the Spaniards. The admiral particularly attracted their attention, from his commanding height, his air of authority, his dress of scarlet, and the deference which was paid him by his companions; all which pointed him out to be the commander.

When they had still further recovered from their fears, they approached the Spaniards, touched their beards, and examined their hands and faces, admiring their whiteness. Columbus was pleased with their gentleness and confiding simplicity, and suffered their scrutiny with perfect acquiescence, winning them by his benignity. They now supposed that the ships had sailed out of the crystal firmament which bounded their horizon, or had descended from above on their ample wings, and that these marvellous beings were inhabitants of the skies.

The natives of the island were no less objects of curiosity to the Spaniards, differing as they did from any race of men they had ever seen. Their appearance gave no promise of either wealth or civilization, for they were entirely naked, and painted with a variety of colors. With some it was confined merely to a part of the face, the nose, or around the eyes; with others it extended to the whole body, and gave them a wild and fantastic appearance. Their complexion was of a tawny or copper hue, and they were entirely destitute of beards. Their hair was not crisp, like the recently discovered tribes of the African coast, under the same latitude, but straight and coarse, partly cut short above the ears, but some locks were left long behind and falling upon their shoulders. Their features, though obscured and discolored by paint, were agreeable; they had lofty foreheads, and remarkably fine eyes. They were of moderate stature and well-shaped; most of them appeared to be under thirty years of age; there was but one female with them, quite young, naked like her companions, and beautifully formed.

As Columbus supposed himself to have landed on an island at the extremity of India, he called the natives by the general appellation of Indians, which was universally adopted before the true nature of his discovery was known, and has since been extended to all the aborigines of the New World. The islanders were friendly and gentle. Their only arms were lances, hardened at the end by fire, or pointed with a flint, or the teeth or bone of a fish. There was no iron to be seen, nor did they appear acquainted with its properties; for when a drawn sword was presented to them, they unguardedly took it by the edge.

Columbus distributed among them colored caps, glass beads, hawks' bells, and other trifles, such as the Portuguese were accustomed to trade with among the natives of the gold coast of Africa. They received them eagerly, hung the beads round their necks, and were wonderfully pleased with their finery, and with the sound of the bells. The Spaniards remained all day on shore, refreshing themselves after their anxious voyage amidst the beautiful groves of the island, and returned on board late in the evening, delighted with all they had seen.

On the following morning, at break of day, the shore was thronged with the natives; some swam off to the ships, others came in light barks, which they called canoes, formed of a single tree, hollowed, and capable of holding from one man up to the number of forty or fifty. These they managed dexterously with paddles, and, if overturned, swam about in the water with perfect unconcern, as if in their natural element, righting their canoes with great facility, and baling them with calabashes.

They were eager to procure more toys and trinkets, not, apparently, from any idea of their intrinsic value, but because everything from the hands of the strangers possessed a supernatural virtue in their eyes as having been brought from heaven; they even picked up fragments of glass and earthenware as valuable prizes. They had no objects to offer in return, except parrots, of which great numbers were domesticated among them, and cotton-yarn, of which they had abundance, and would exchange large balls of five and twenty pounds weight for the merest trifle. They brought also cakes of a kind of bread called cassava, which constituted a principal part of their food, and was afterward an important article of provisions with the Spaniards. It was formed from a great root called the yuca, which they cultivated in fields. This they cut into small morsels, which they grated or scraped, and strained in a press, making a broad thin cake, which was afterward dried hard, and would keep for a long time, being steeped in water when eaten. It was insipid, but nourishing, though the water strained from it in the preparation was a deadly poison. There was another kind of yuca destitute of this poisonous quality, which was eaten in the root, either boiled or roasted.

The avarice of the discoverers was quickly excited by the sight of small ornaments of gold, worn by some of the natives in their noses. These the latter gladly exchanged for glass beads and hawks' bells, and both parties exulted in the bargain, no doubt admiring each other's simplicity. As gold, however, was an object of royal monopoly in all enterprises of discovery, Columbus forbade any traffic in it without his express sanction; and he put the same prohibition on the traffic for cotton, reserving to the crown all trade for it, wherever it should be found in any quantity. He inquired of the natives where this gold was procured. They answered him by signs, pointing to the south, where, he understood them, dwelt a king of such wealth that he was served in vessels of wrought gold. He understood, also, that there was land to the south, southwest and the northwest; and that the people from the last-mentioned quarter frequently proceeded to the southwest in quest of gold and precious stones, making in their way descents upon the islands and carrying off the inhabitants. Several of the natives showed him scars of wounds received in battles with these invaders. It is evident that a great part of this fancied intelligence was self-delusion on the part of Columbus, for he was under a spell of imagination which gave its own shapes and colors to every object.

He was persuaded that he had arrived among the islands described by Marco Polo as lying opposite Cathay, in the Chinese Sea, and he construed everything to accord with the account given of those opulent regions. Thus the enemies which the natives spoke of as coming from the northwest he concluded to be the people of the mainland of Asia, the subjects of the great Khan of Tartary, who were represented by the Venetian travellers as accustomed to make war upon the islands and to enslave their inhabitants. The country to the south, abounding in gold, could be no other than the famous island of Cipango; and the king who was served out of vessels of gold must be the monarch whose magnificent city and gorgeous palace, covered with plates of gold, had been extolled in such splendid terms by Marco Polo.

The island where Columbus had thus for the first time set his foot upon the new world was called by the natives Guanahane. It still retains the name of San Salvador, which he gave to it, though called by the English Cat Island. The light which he had seen the evening previous to his making land may have been on Watlings Island, which lies a few leagues to the east. San Salvador is one of the great cluster of the Lucayos or Bahama Islands, which stretch southeast and northwest from the coast of Florida to Hispaniola, covering the northern coast of Cuba.

—*Washington Irving.*

GOD'S HAND IN THE DISCOVERY OF AMERICA.

I WILL pass over and take another period, a period in which we personally, as a people, are more interested—the age of the discovery of America. We shall not have the prophecies that we may see are literally fulfilled, but we can show a wonderful aggregation of agencies that, I think, will convince any reasoning mind that God's hand was in some way in the history. And first, why was this country so long left to be either uninhabited or simply the abode of a few roaming tribes? Who hid it? How was it concealed? Some people had found their way here, possibly from the East. Some ships from Greenland had found their way to the northern coast at about the year 1000, and monuments have been left attesting it. But it was forgotten. It was wholly unknown. Why was it kept? Think of the age of the world; think of the grand events that were occurring. Men had been struggling to get the principles of associated and individual happiness in some way harmonized. The power of government was the Oriental idea, grappling everything, ruling everything by a central power. The idea of the northern element was individual freedom—the man made himself, the government was nothing—came from yon hordes in Asia, finding its way down over toward Spain and over toward the North Sea. And this conflict of peoples, the association of the individual and the governmental, was developing the great laws of human society and human freedom. Colleges were being founded. International law was being studied. The rights of men were being discussed. The art of printing was invented. The mariner's compass was found. Man was being expanded. And just when all this preparation was made and a race, intelligent and strong and developed, was in readiness, then God lifted the curtain. A Genoese navigator was asleep on the banks of his native river, and he dreamed that some one gave to him the keys of empire of a western world. He had had thoughts of a western world before, but his soul was stirred, and he went from rich man to rich man, from prince to prince, from king to king, asking for help to send out vessels to find a western world, or at least a way to Cathay, as they termed it, or China. No one would help him; all thought his visions fanciful dreams. At last, despairing of help elsewhere, he went to Isabella, the pious Queen of Spain. The argument he used was the religious argument. He said to her, If there be a western world, it is probably inhabited; and if it be inhabited, they have never heard of Christ, and they will all perish. Her queenly heart was touched, and she said: "Columbus shall have his ships, if I sell my crown jewels to pay the expense;" and, as used to be the way three hundred years ago, when a woman undertook a thing, she had her own way. The ships were given to Columbus, and Isabella kept her crown jewels. Columbus found America, and found it under the impulse of this religious idea. God opened up America, and opened it up at that age of the world and for a people prepared.—*Bishop Simpson.*

THE COLONIZATION OF AMERICA.

AT this time it is not easy to comprehend the impulse given to Europe by the discovery of America. It was not the gradual acquisition of some border territory, a province or a kingdom, that had been gained, but a new world thrown open to the European. The races of animals, the mineral treasures, the vegetable forms, and the varied aspects of nature, man in the different phases of civilization, filled the mind with entirely new sets of ideas, that changed the habitual current of thought, and stimulated it to indefinite conjecture. The eagerness to explore the wonderful secrets of the new hemisphere became so active that the principal cities in Spain were, in a manner, depopulated, as emigrants thronged one after another to take their chance upon the deep. It was a world of romance that was thrown open, for, whatever might be the luck of the adventurer, his reports on his return were tinged with a coloring of romance that stimulated still higher the sensitive fancies of his countrymen, and nourished the chimerical sentiments of an age of chivalry. They listened with attentive ears to tales of Amazons, which seemed to realize the classic legends of antiquity; to stories of Patagonian giants; to flaming pictures of an *El Dorado* —Golden Land—where the sands sparkled with gems, and golden pebbles as large as birds' eggs were dragged in nets out of the rivers.

Yet that the adventurers were no impostors, but dupes, too easy dupes, of their own credulous fancies, is shown by the extravagant character of their enterprises; by expeditions in search of the magical Fountain of Health, of the Golden Temple of Doboyba, of the Golden Sepulchres of Yenu—for gold was ever floating before their distempered vision, and the name of *Castilla del Ora*—Golden Castle—the most unhealthy and unprofitable region of the Isthmus, held out a bright promise to the unfortunate settler, who too frequently instead of gold found there only his grave.

In this realm of enchantment all the accessories served to maintain the illusion. The simple natives, with their defenceless bodies and rude weapons, were no match for the European warrior, armed to the teeth in mail. The odds were as great as those found in any legend of chivalry, where the lance of the good knight overturned hundreds at a touch. The perils that lay in the discoverer's path, and the sufferings he had to sustain, were scarcely inferior to those that beset the knight-errant. Hunger and thirst and fatigue, the deadly effluvia of the morass, with its swarms of venomous insects, the cold of mountain snows, and the scorching sun of the tropics—these were the lot of every cavalier who came to seek his fortunes in the New World. It was the reality of romance. The life of the Spanish adventurer was one chapter more, and not the least remarkable, in the chronicles of knight-errantry.

The character of the warrior took somewhat of the exaggerated coloring shed over his exploits. Proud and vainglorious, swelled with lofty anticipations of his destiny, and an invincible confidence in his own resources, no danger could appall and no toil could tire him. The greater the danger, indeed, the higher the charm; for his soul reveled in excitement, and the enterprise without peril wanted that spur of romance which was necessary to rouse his energies into action. Yet in the motives to action meaner influences were strangely mingled with the loftier, the temporal with the spiritual. Gold was the incentive and the recompense, and in the pursuit of it his inflexible nature rarely hesitated as to the means. His courage was sullied with cruelty, the cruelty that flowed equally, strange as it may seem, from his avarice and his religion; religion as it was understood in that age—the religion of the Crusader. It was the convenient cloak for a multitude of sins, which covered them even from himself. The Castilian, too proud for hypocrisy, committed more cruelties in the name of religion than were ever practised by the pagan idolater or the fanatical Moslem. The burning of the infidel was a sacrifice acceptable to Heaven, and the conversion of those who survived amply atoned for the foulest offences. It is a melancholy and mortifying consideration that the most uncompromising spirit of intolerance—the spirit of the Inquisitor at home and of the Crusader abroad—should have emanated from a religion which preached "peace upon earth and good-will towards man!"

What a contrast did these children of Southern Europe present to the Anglo-Saxon races, who scattered themselves along the great northern division of the Western Hemisphere! For the principle of action with these latter was not avarice, nor the more specious pretext of proselytism; but independence—independence religious and political. To secure this, they were content to earn a bare subsistence by a life of frugality and toil. They asked nothing from the soil but the reasonable returns of their own labor. No golden visions threw a deceitful halo around their path, and beckoned them onwards through seas of blood to the subversion of an unoffending dynasty. They were content with the slow but steady progress of their social polity. They patiently endured the privations of the wilderness, watering the tree of liberty with their tears and with the sweat of their brow, till it took deep root in the land and sent up its branches high toward the heavens, while the communities of the neighboring continent, shooting up into the sudden splendors of a tropical vegetation, exhibited, even in their prime, the sure symptoms of decay.

It would seem to have been especially ordered by Providence, that the discovery of the two great divisions of the American Hemisphere should fall to the two races best fitted to conquer and colonize them. Thus the northern section was consigned to the Anglo-Saxon race, whose orderly, industrious habits found an ample field for development under its colder skies and on its more rugged soil, while the southern portion, with its rich tropical products and treasures of mineral wealth, held out the most attractive bait to invite the enterprise of the Spaniard. How different might have been the result, if the bark of Columbus had taken a more northerly direction, as he at one time meditated, and landed its band of adventurers on the shores of what is now Free America!—*William Hickling Prescott.*

OUR NATIVE LAND.

GOD bless our native land!
  Firm may she ever stand,
    Through storm and night:
  When the wild tempest wave,
  Ruler of wind and wave,
  Do thou our country save
    By thy great might!

For her our prayer shall rise
  To God, above the skies;
    On him we wait:
  Thou who art ever nigh,
  Guarding with watchful eye,
  To thee aloud we cry,
    God save the State!
        —*John S. Dwight.*

SHALL we regard with indifference the great inheritance which cost our sires their blood, because we find in their gift an admixture of imperfection and evil? Surely there is good enough, in the contemplation of which every patriotic heart may say, "God bless my own, my native land."
—*James A. Garfield.*

FIRST in war, first in peace, and first in the hearts of his fellow-citizens.—*General Henry Lee.*

LOVE OF COUNTRY.

NEXT to the worship of the Father of us all, the deepest and grandest of human emotions is the love of the land that gave us birth. It is an enlargement and exaltation of all the tenderest and strongest sympathies of kindred and of home. In all centuries and climes it has lived, and defied chains and dungeons, and racks to crush it. It has strewed the earth with its monuments, and it has shed undying lustre on a thousand fields on which it has battled. Through the night of ages, Thermopylæ glows like some mountain peak on which the morning sun has risen, because twenty-three hundred years ago this hallowing passion touched its mural precipices and its crowning crags. It is easy, however, to be patriotic in piping times of peace and in the sunny hour of prosperity. It is national sorrow—it is war, with its attendant perils and horrors, that tests this passion and winnows from the masses those who, with all their love of life, still love their country more. We honor commerce with its busy marts, and the workshop with its patient toil and exhaustless ingenuity, but still we would be unfaithful to the truth of history did we not confess that the most heroic champions of human freedom and the most illustrious apostles of its principles have come from the broad fields of agriculture. There seems to be something in the scenes of nature, in her wild and beautiful landscapes, in her cascades, and cataracts, and waving woodlands, and in the pure and exhilarating airs of her hills and mountains, that unbraces the fetters which man would rivet upon the spirit of his fellow-man. It was at the handles of the plough, and amid the breathing odors of its newly-opened furrows, that the character of Cincinnatus was formed, expanded and matured. It was not in the city, but in the deep gorges and upon the snow-clad summits of the Alps, amid the eagles and the thunders, that William Tell laid the foundations of those altars to human liberty, against which the surging tides of European despotism have beaten for centuries, but, thank God, have beaten in vain. It was amid the primeval forests and mountains, the lakes and leaping streams of our own land; amid fields of waving grain; amid the songs of the reaper and the tinkling of the shepherd's bell, that were nurtured those rare virtues which clustered, star-like, in the character of Washington, and lifted him in moral stature a head and shoulders above even the demigods of ancient story.

—*Hon. Joseph Holt.*

OUR NATION A PRODUCT OF CHRISTIANITY.

NO candid observer will deny that whatever of good there may be in our American civilization is the product of Christianity. Still less can he deny that the grand motives which are working for the elevation and purification of our society are strictly Christian. The immense energies of the Christian Church, stimulated by a love that shrinks from no obstacles, are all bent towards this great aim of universal purification. These millions of sermons and exhortations which are a constant power for good; these countless prayers and songs of praise, on which the heavy-laden lift their hearts above the temptations and sorrows of the world, are all the product of faith in Jesus Christ. That which gives us protection by day and by night—the dwellings we live in, the clothes we wear, the institutions of social order, all these are the direct offspring of Christianity. All that distinguishes us from the Pagan world—all that makes us what we are, and all that stimulates us in the task of making ourselves better than we are—is Christianity. A belief in Jesus Christ is the very fountain-head of everything that is desirable and praiseworthy in our civilization, and this civilization is the flower of time. Humanity has reached its noblest thrift, its grandest altitudes of excellence, its highest watermark, through the influence of this faith.

—*Springfield Republican.*

OUR COUNTRY A HOUSEHOLD.

THE great object which the statesmen of the Revolution sought was the defence, protection, and good government of the whole, without injustice to any portion of the people. Experience had taught them that it was impossible for a great republic to grow up where its every act of public policy was liable to be thwarted by the vote of the individual States; therefore they framed an organic law as the foundation of our common government, which gave the men of Carolina and Massachusetts a name dearer than any sectional name—the name of an *American Citizen!* In that conflict of opinions, by a temper of conciliation and brotherly love, by an earnest loyalty to freedom and profoundest reverence for law, they framed that constitution which has been the admiration of the world.

I yield to no man in my admiration for those noble men whose names are our household words; but in this history I see the hand of God, and acknowledge that our nationality was his gift and not the fruits of our fathers' wisdom. Ours is not the only nation which has sought to be free. Strong arms and stout hearts have often failed—the world is filled with the lamentations of the patriots and dirges for the dead. God always gives to a nation its birthright and its name. A nation is not a mere aggregate of households, or villages, or States—national life is something beyond the fact that individual men have banded together for mutual defence. This belonged to the savage tribes who once roamed over this goodly land. They may be strong, daring, freedom-loving men, without national life. There never was a nobler race than the people who dwelt in the fastnesses of Scotland, but their tie was only one of kindred; the family became a clan, separate clans warred with each other in murderous strife, and Scotland was a field of blood. Until the cross was firmly planted in Britain, England had no nationality— it was a land of faction until the law and providence of God became the people's guide, and then the nobler name of Saxon became a Christian name to tell of all that is manly and true. Our national life is the gift of God. No other hand could gather out of other lands millions of people of different tongues and kindred, and mould these into one mighty nation that shall receive into itself the men of every clime, and stamp on them its own mark of individuality; teaching them its language, making them its kin, and binding them as one household under its own constitution and laws.

—*Bishop Whipple.*

WHAT IS OUR COUNTRY?

WHAT is this country? Is it the soil on which we tread? Is it the gathering of familiar faces? Is it our luxury and pomp and pride? Nay, more than these, is it power, and might, and majesty alone? No, our country is more, far more than all these. The country which demands our love, our courage, our devotion, our heart's blood, is more than all these. Our country is the history of our fathers, our country is the tradition of our mothers, our country is past renown, our country is present pride and power, our country is future hope and destiny, our country is greatness, glory, truth, constitutional liberty—above all, freedom forever! These are the watchwords under which we fight; and we will shout them out till the stars appear in the sky, in the stormiest hour of battle.

—*Senator Baker.*

THE OLD THIRTEEN.

THE curtain rises on a hundred years,
A pageant of the olden time appears.
Let the historic muse her aid supply,
To note and name each form that passes by.
Here come the old original Thirteen!
Sir Walter ushers in the Virgin Queen;
Catholic Mary follows her, whose land
Smiles on soft Chesapeake from either strand;
Then Georgia, with the sisters Caroline,—
One the palmetto wears, and one the pine;

Next she who ascertained the rights of men,
Not by the sword but by the word of Penn,—
The friendly language hers, of "thee" and "thou:"
Then, she whose mother was a thrifty frow,
Mother herself of princely children now;
And, sitting at her feet, the sisters twain,
Two smaller links in the Atlantic chain,
They, through those long dark winters drear and dire,
Watched with our Fabius round the bivouac fire;
Comes the free mountain maid in white and green;
One guards the Charter Oak with lofty mien;
And lo! in the plain beauty once she wore,
The pilgrim mother from the Bay State shore;
And last, not least, is little Rhody seen,
With face turned heavenward, steadfast and serene,
She on her anchor, Hope, leans, and will ever lean.
—*Charles Timothy Brooks.*

WASHINGTON.

[This hymn was sung at a celebration on Washington's birthday, in the Old South Church, Boston.]

TO thee, beneath whose eye,
  Each circling century
    Obedient rolls,
  Our nation, in its prime,
  Looked with a faith sublime,
  And trusted in "the time
    That tried men's souls."

  When from this gate of heaven *
  People and priest were driven

---

* The Old South Church was taken possession of by the British while they held Boston, and converted into barracks for the cavalry, the pews being cut up for fuel or used in constructing stalls for the horses.

By fire and sword,
And, where thy saints had pray'd,
The harness'd war-horse neigh'd,
And horseman's trumpet bray'd
    In harsh accord.

Nor was our fathers' trust,
Thou mighty One and Just,
    Then put to shame;
"Up to the hills" for light,
Look'd they in peril's night,
And, from yon guardian height,*
    Deliverance came.

Then, like an angel form,
Sent down to still the storm,
    Stood Washington!
Clouds broke and rolled away;
Foes fled in pale dismay;
Wreath'd were his brows with bay,
    When War was done.

God of our sires and sons,
Let other Washingtons
    Our country bless.
And, like the brave and wise
Of by-gone centuries,
Show that true greatness lies
    In righteousness.

—*Pierpont.*

MILLIONS for defence, but not a cent for tribute.—*Cotesworth Pinckney.*

* From his position on "Dorchester Heights," that overlook the town, Washington succeeded in compelling the British forces to evacuate Boston.

THE BIRTHDAY OF WASHINGTON.

THE birthday of the "Father of his Country!" May it ever be freshly remembered by American hearts! May it ever reawaken in them a filial veneration for his memory; ever rekindle the fires of patriotic regard for the country which he loved so well, to which he gave his youthful vigor and his youthful energy during the perilous period of the early Indian warfare; to which he devoted his life in the maturity of his powers, in the field; to which again he offered the counsels of his wisdom and experience, as president of the convention that framed our Constitution; which he guided and directed while in the chair of state, and for which the last prayer of his earthly supplication was offered up, when it came the moment for him so well, and so grandly, and so calmly to die. He was the first man of the time in which he grew. His memory is first and most sacred in our love, and ever hereafter, till the last drop of blood shall freeze in the last American heart, his name shall be a spell of power and of might.

Yes, gentlemen, there is one personal, one vast felicity, which no man can share with him. It was the daily beauty and towering and matchless glory of his life which enabled him to create his country, and at the same time secure an undying love and regard from the whole American people. "The first in the hearts of his countrymen!" Yes, first! He has our first and most fervent love. Undoubtedly there were brave and wise and good men, before his day, in every colony, but the American nation, as a nation, I do not reckon to have begun before 1774. And the first love of that Young America was Washington. The first word she lisped was his name. Her earliest breath spoke it. It still is her proud ejaculation; and it will be the last gasp of her expiring life! Yes; others of our great men have been appreciated—many admired by all—but him we love. About and around him we call up no dissentient and discordant and dissatisfied elements—no sectional prejudice nor bias— no party, no creed, no dogma of politics. None of these shall assail him. Yes; when the storm of battle blows darkest and rages highest, the memory of Washington shall nerve every American arm, and cheer every American heart. It shall relume that Promethean fire, that sublime flame of patriotism, that devoted love of country which his words have commended, which his example has consecrated:

> "Where may the wearied eye repose,
>   When gazing on the great;
> Where neither guilty glory glows
>   Nor despicable state?
> Yes—one—the first, the last, the best,
> The Cincinnatus of the West,
>   Whom Envy dared not hate,
> Bequeathed the name of Washington,
> To make man blush there was but one."
> —*Rufus Choate.*

AMERICA is a grand place to live in; the inhabitants appreciate the efforts of every man, woman or child who tries to earn an honest living and "go a peg higher."
—*George R. Scott.*

THE CHARACTER OF WASHINGTON.

No matter what may be the birthplace of such a man as Washington, no climate can claim, no country can appropriate him—the boon of Providence to the human race, his fame is eternity, and his residence creation.

Though it was the defeat of our arms and the disgrace of our policy, we almost bless the convulsion in which he had his origin—if the heavens thundered and the earth rocked, yet, when the storm passed, how pure was the climate that it cleared, how bright in the brow of the firmament was the planet it revealed to us!

In the production of Washington it does really appear as if nature was endeavoring to improve upon herself, and that all the virtues of the ancient world were but so many studies preparatory to the patriot of the new.

As a general, he marshaled the peasant into a veteran and supplied by discipline the absence of experience.

As a statesman, he enlarged the policy of the cabinet into the most comprehensive system of general advantage; and such was the wisdom of his views and the philosophy of his counsel that to the soldier and the statesman he almost added the character of the sage.

A conqueror, he was untainted with the crime of blood; a revolutionist, he was free from any stain of treason, for aggression commenced the contest, and a country called him to command. Liberty unsheathed his sword, necessity stained, victory retuned it.

If he had paused here, history might doubt what station

to assign him, whether at the head of her citizens or her soldiers, her heroes or her patriots. But the last glorious act crowned his career, and banished hesitation.

Who like Washington, after having freed a country, resigned her crown, and retired to a cottage rather than remain in a capital?

Immortal man! He took from the battle its crime, and from the conquest its chains; he left the victorious the glory of his self-denial, and turned upon the vanquished only the retribution of his mercy.

Happy, proud America! The lightnings of heaven could not resist your sage; the temptations of earth could not corrupt your soldier.

AN EPITAPH ON WASHINGTON.

[The following epitaph was discovered on the back of a portrait of Washington, sent to the family from England. It was copied from a transcript in the handwriting of Judge Washington.]

THE defender of his Country—the founder of Liberty,
    The friend of man.
History and tradition are explored in vain
    For a parallel to his character.
In the annals of modern greatness
    He stands alone;
And the noblest names of Antiquity
    Lose their lustre in his presence.
Born the benefactor of mankind,
    He united all the greatness necessary
        To an illustrious career.
    Nature made him great,
    He made himself virtuous.
Called by his Country to the defence of her Liberties
He triumphantly vindicated the rights of humanity,

And, on the pillars of National Independence,
Laid the foundation of a Great Republic.
Twice invested with Supreme Magistracy
By the unanimous vote of a free people,
He surpassed, in the Cabinet,
The glories of the field,
And, voluntarily resigning the sceptre and the sword,
Retired to the shades of private life;
A spectacle so new, and so sublime,
Was contemplated with profoundest admiration,
And the name of Washington,
Adding new lustre to humanity,
Resounded to the remotest regions of the earth.
Magnanimous in youth,
Glorious through life,
Great in death.
His highest ambition the happiness of mankind,
His noblest victory the conquest of himself.
Bequeathing to posterity the inheritance of his fame,
And building his monument in the hearts of his countrymen,—
He lived—the ornament of the Eighteenth Century,
He died regretted by a mourning world.

THE LAND OF OUR BIRTH.

THERE is not a spot in the wide peopled earth,
So dear to the heart as the land of our birth;
'Tis the home of our childhood! the beautiful spot
Which mem'ry retains where all else is forgot.
May the blessing of God
Ever hallow the sod,
And its valleys and hills by our children be trod.

Can the language of strangers in accents unknown,
Send a thrill to our bosoms, like that of our own?
The face may be fair, and the smile may be bland,
But it breathes not the tones of our dear native land.
  There is not a spot on earth,
  Like the land of our birth,
Where heroes keep guard o'er the altar hearth.

How sweet is the language which taught us to blend
The dear name of parent, of husband and friend;
Which taught us to lisp on our mother's soft breast,
The ballads she sung, as she rocked us to rest.
  May the blessings of God
  Ever hallow the sod,
And its valleys and hills by our children be trod.

Should the tempest of war overshadow our land,
Its *bolts* could ne'er rend Freedom's temple asunder;
For, unmoved, at its portal would Washington stand,
And repulse, with his breast, the assaults of the thunder,
  His sword from the sleep
  Of its scabbard would leap,
And conduct, with its point, every flash to the deep.

HISTORY OF THE DECLARATION OF INDEPENDENCE.

IT was on the 7th of June, 1776, that Mr. R. H. Lee obeyed the instructions of the Virginia Legislature by moving that Congress should declare independence. Two days' debate revealed that the measure, though still a little premature, was destined to pass, and, therefore, the further discussion of the subject was postponed for twenty days, and a committee of five was appointed to draft a declaration—

Thomas Jefferson, Dr. Franklin, John Adams, Roger Sherman and R. R. Livingston. Mr. Jefferson was naturally urged to prepare the draft. He was chairman of the committee, having received the highest number of votes; he was also its youngest member, and therefore bound to do an ample share of the work; he was noted for his skill with the pen; he was particularly conversant with the points of the controversy; he was a Virginian. The task, indeed, was not very arduous or difficult. Nothing was wanted but a careful and brief recapitulation of wrongs familiar to every patriotic mind, and a clear statement of principles hackneyed from eleven years' iteration. Jefferson made no difficulty about undertaking it, and probably had no anticipation of the vast celebrity that was to follow so slight an exercise of his faculties.

He was ready with his draft in time. His colleagues upon the committee suggested a few verbal changes, none of which were important; but during the three days' discussion of it in the House, it was subjected to a review so critical and severe, that the author sat in his place silently writhing under it, and Dr. Franklin felt called upon to console him with the comic relation of the process by which the sign-board of *John Thompson, hatter, makes and sells hats for ready money*, was reduced to the name of the hatter and the figure of a hat. Congress made eighteen suppressions, six additions and ten alterations, and nearly every one of these changes was an improvement. The noblest utterance of the whole composition is the reason given for making the declaration—"A Decent Respect for the Opinions of Mankind." This touches the heart. Among the best emotions that human nature knows is the veneration of man for man. This recognition of the public opinion of the world—the sum of human sense—as the final arbiter in all such controversies, is the single phrase of the document which Jefferson alone, perhaps, of all the Congress, would have originated; and in point of merit, it was worth all the rest.

During the 2d, 3d and 4th of July, Congress were engaged in reviewing the declaration. Thursday, the fourth, was a hot day; the session lasted many hours; members were tired and impatient. Every one who has watched the sessions of a deliberative body knows how the most important measures are retarded, accelerated, even defeated, by physical cause of the most trifling nature. Mr. Kinglake intimates that Lord Raglan's invasion of the Crimea was due, rather to the after-dinner slumbers of the British Cabinet, than to any well-considered purpose. Mr. Jefferson used to relate, with much merriment, that the final signing of the Declaration of Independence was hastened by an absurdly trivial cause. Near the hall in which the debates were then held was a livery stable, from which swarms of flies came into the open windows and assailed the stockinged legs of honorable members. Handkerchief in hand, they lashed the flies with such vigor as they could command on a July afternoon; but the annoyance became at length so extreme as to render them impatient of delay, and they made haste to bring the momentous business to a conclusion.

After such a long and severe strain upon their minds the members seem to have indulged in many a jocular observation as they stood around the table. Tradition has it, that when John Hancock had affixed his magnificent signature to the paper, he said: "*There*, John Bull may read *my* name without spectacles!"

No composition of man was ever received with more rapture than this. It came at a happy time. Boston was delivered, and New York, as yet, but menaced; and in all New England there was not a British soldier who was not a prisoner, nor a king's ship that was not a prize. Between the expulsion of the British troops from Boston, and their capture of New York, was the period of the Revolutionary War when the people were most confident and most united. From the newspapers and letters of the time, we should infer that the contest was ending rather than beginning, so exultant is their tone; and the Declaration of Independence, therefore, was received more like a song of triumph than a call to battle.

The paper was signed late on Thursday afternoon, July 4th. On the Monday following, at noon, it was publicly read for the first time, in Independence Square, from a platform erected by Rittenhouse for the purpose of observing the transit of Venus. Captain John Hopkins, a young man commanding an armed brig of the navy of the new nation, was the reader; and it required his stentorian voice to carry the words to the distant verge of the multitude who had come to hear it. In the evening, as a journal of the day has it, " our *late* King's coat-of-arms were brought from the hall of the State-house, where the said King's courts were formerly held, and burned amid the acclamations of a crowd of spectators." Similar scenes transpired in every centre of population, and at every camp and post. Usually the militia companies, the committee of safety and other revolutionary bodies, marched in procession to some public place, where they listened decorously to the reading of the Declaration, at the conclusion of which, cheers were given and salutes fired; and, in the evening, there were illuminations and bon-fires. In New York, after the reading, the leaden statue of the *late* King in Bowling Green was " laid prostrate in the dust," and ordered to be run into bullets. The debtors in prison were also set at liberty. Virginia, before the news of the Declaration had reached her, July 5, 1776, had stricken the King's name out of the prayer-book; and now, July 30, Rhode Island made it a misdemeanor to pray for the King *as* King, under penalty of a fine of one hundred thousand pounds!

The news of the Declaration was received with sorrow by all that was best in England. Samuel Rogers used to give American guests, at his breakfasts, an interesting reminiscence of this period. On the morning after the intelligence reached London, his father, at family prayers, added a prayer for the *success* of the colonies, which he repeated every day until the peace.

The deed was done. A people not formed for empire ceased to be imperial; and a people destined to empire began the political education that will one day give them far more and better than imperial sway.—*James Parton.*

INDEPENDENCE BELL.—JULY 4, 1776.

WHEN the Declaration of Independence was announced by ringing the old State House bell, which bore the inscription, "Proclaim liberty throughout the land, to all the inhabitants thereof," the old bellman stationed his little grandson at the door of the hall, to await the instructions of the doorkeeper when to ring. At the word, the young patriot rushed out, and clapping his hands, shouted: "*Ring!* Ring! Ring!"

OUR COUNTRY.

THERE was a tumult in the city,
  In the quaint old Quaker town,
And the streets were rife with people
  Pacing restless up and down—
People gathering at the corners,
  Where they whispered each to each,
And the sweat stood on their temples,
  With the earnestness of speech.

As the bleak Atlantic currents
  Lash the wild Newfoundland shore,
So they beat against the State House,
  So they surged against the door;
And the mingling of their voices
  Made a harmony profound,
Till the quiet street of Chestnut
  Was all turbulent with sound.

"Will they do it?" "Dare they do it?"
  "Who is speaking?" "What's the news?"
"What of Adams?" "What of Sherman?"
  "Oh! God grant they wont refuse!"
"Make some way there!" "Let me nearer!"
  "I am stifling!" "Stifle then!
When a nation's life's at hazard,
  We've no time to think of men!"

So they surged against the State House,
  While all solemnly inside
Sat the "Continental Congress,"
  Truth and reason for their guide,
O'er a simple scroll debating,
  Which, though simple it might be,
Yet should shake the cliffs of England
  With the thunders of the free.

Far aloft in that high steeple
   Sat the bellman, old and gray;
He was weary of the tyrant
   And his iron-sceptered sway,
So he sat, with one hand ready
   On the clapper of the bell,
When his eye could catch the signal,
   The long-expected news, to tell.

See! see! The dense crowd quivers
   Through all its lengthy line,
As the boy beside the portal
   Hastens forth to give the sign!
With his little hands uplifted,
   Breezes dallying with his hair,
Hark! with deep clear intonation,
   Breaks his young voice in the air:

Hushed the people's swelling murmur,
   Whilst the boy cries joyously:
"Ring!" he shouts, "Ring! grandpapa,
   Ring! Oh, ring for Liberty!"
Quickly at the given signal
   The old bellman lifts his hand,
Forth he sends the good news, making
   Iron music through the land.

How they shouted! What rejoicing!
   How the old bell shook the air,
Till the clang of freedom ruffled
   The calmly gliding Delaware!
How the bonfires and the torches
   Lighted up the night's repose,
And from the flames, like fabled **Phœnix**,
   Our glorious liberty arose!

That old State House bell is silent,
   Hushed is now its clamorous tongue;
But the spirit it awaken'd
   Still is living—ever young;
And when we greet the smiling sunlight
   On the fourth of each July,
We will ne'er forget the bellman
   Who, betwixt the earth and sky,
Rung out, loudly, " Independence,"
   Which, please God, shall never die.
                   —*Speaker Garland.*

LIBERTY.

LIBERTY! thou goddess heavenly bright,
Profuse of bliss, and pregnant with delight!
Eternal pleasures in thy presence reign,
And smiling plenty treads thy wanton train.
                   —*Joseph Addison.*

THE FOURTH OF JULY.

DAY of glory! welcome day!
   Freedom's banners greet thy ray;
   See! how cheerfully they play
      With thy morning breeze,
On the rocks where pilgrims kneel'd,
On the heights where squadrons wheel'd,
When a tyrant's thunder peal'd
      O'er the trembling seas.

God of armies! did thy "stars
In their courses" smite his cars,
Blast his arm, and wrest his bars
   From the heaving tide?

On our standard, lo! they burn,
And, when days like this return,
Sparkle o'er the soldiers' urn
  Who for Freedom died.

God of peace!—whose spirit fills
All the echoes of our hills,
All the murmurs of our rills,
  Now the storm is o'er;
O, let freemen be our sons;
And let future Washingtons
Rise, to lead their valiant ones,
  Till there's war no more.

By the patriot's hallowed rest,
By the warrior's gory breast—
Never let our graves be press'd
  By a despot's throne;
By the Pilgrims' toils and cares,
By their battles and their prayers,
By their ashes—let our heirs
  Bow to thee alone.

    —*John Pierpont.*

OUR NATAL DAY.

IT is well that in our year, so busy, so secular, so discordant, there comes one day when the word is, and when the emotion is, "Our country, our whole country, and nothing but our country." It is well that law—our only sovereign on earth—duty, not less the daughter of God, not less within her sphere supreme—custom not old alone, but honored and useful—memories, our hearts, have set a time in which—scythe, loom, and anvil stilled, shops shut, wharves silent, the flag —our flag unrent—the flag of our glory and commemoration waving on masthead, steeple, and highland—we may come together and walk hand in hand, thoughtful, admiring, through these galleries of civil greatness, when we may own together the spell of one hour of our history upon us all; when faults may be forgotten, kindnesses revived, virtues remembered and sketched unblamed; when the arrogance of reform, the excesses of reform, the strifes of parties, the rivalries of regions, shall give place to a wider, warmer, and juster sentiment; when turning from the corners and dark places of offensiveness, if such the candle lighted by malignity, or envy, or censoriousness, or truth has revealed anywhere; when turning from these, we may go up to the serene and secret mountain top, and there pause, and there unite in the reverent exclamation, and in the exultant prayer, "How beautiful at last are thy tabernacles! What people at last is like unto thee? Peace be within thy palaces and joy within thy gates! The high places are thine, and there shalt thou stand proudly, and innocently, and securely."—*Rufus Choate.*

LIBERTY IN AMERICA.

"HERE," might they say, "shall power's divided reign
Evince that patriots have not bled in vain.
Here God-like liberty's herculean youth,
Cradled in peace, and nurtur'd up by truth
To full maturity of nerve and mind,
Shall crush the giants that bestride mankind.
Here shall religion's pure and balmy draught
In form no more from cups of state be quaff'd,

But flow for all through nation, rank, and sect,
Free as that heaven its tranquil waves reflect.
Around the columns of the public shrine
Shall growing arts their gradual wreath intwine,
Nor breathe corruption from the flowering braid,
Nor mine that fabric which they bloom to shade.
No longer here shall Justice bound her view,
Or wrong the many, while she rights the few;
But take her range through all the social frame,
Pure and pervading as that vital flame
Which warms at once our best and meanest part,
And thrills a hair while it expands a heart."

—*Thomas Moore.*

SPIRIT OF LIBERTY.

THE first object of a free people is, the preservation of their liberty, and liberty is only to be preserved by maintaining constitutional restraints and just divisions of political power. Nothing is more deceptive or more dangerous than the pretense of a desire to simplify government. The simplest governments are despotisms; the next simplest, limited monarchies; but all republics, all governments of all law must impose numerous limitations and qualifications of authority, and give many positive and many qualified rights. In other words, they must be subject to rule and regulation. This is the very essence of free political institutions. The spirit of liberty is indeed a bold and fearless spirit, but it is also a sharp-sighted spirit; it is a cautious, sagacious, discriminating, far-seeing intelligence; it is jealous of encroachment, jealous of power, jealous of man. It demands checks, it seeks for guards, it insists on securities; it entrenches itself behind strong defences, and fortifies with all possible care against the assaults of ambition and passion. It does not trust the amiable weaknesses of human nature, and therefore it will not permit power to overstep its prescribed limits, though benevolence, good intent, and patriotic purpose, come along with it. Neither does it satisfy itself with flashy and temporary resistance to illegal authority. Far otherwise, it seeks for duration and permanence. It looks before and after; and, building on the experience of ages which are past, it labors diligently for the benefit of ages to come. This is the nature of constitutional liberty, and this is *our* liberty if we will rightly understand and preserve it. Every free government is necessarily complicated, because all such governments establish restraint, as well on the power of government itself as on that of individuals. If we will abolish the distinction of branches, and have but one branch; if we will abolish jury trials, and leave all to the judge; if we will then ordain that the legislator shall himself be the judge; and if we will place the executive power in the same hands, we may readily simplify government—we may easily bring it to the simplest of all possible forms—a pure despotism. But a separation of departments, so far as practicable, and the preservation of clear lines of division between them, is the fundamental idea in the creation of all our constitutions; and doubtless the continuance of regulated liberty depends on maintaining these boundaries.—*Daniel Webster.*

THE more I studied the political institutions of Europe, the more pleased I am with our own. I bless God I am an American.—*Archbishop Gibbon.*

THE FLOWER OF LIBERTY.

WHAT flower is this that greets the morn,
Its hues from heaven so freshly born?
With burning star and flaming band
It kindles all the sunset land;
O, tell us what its name may be
Is this the Flower of Liberty?
    Is this the banner of the free,
    The starry flower of Liberty?

In savage Nature's far abode
Its tender seed our fathers sowed;
The storm-winds rocked its swelling bud,
Its opening leaves were streaked with blood,
Till lo! earth's tyrants shook to see
The full-blown Flower of Liberty!
    Then hail the banner of the free,
    The starry Flower of Liberty!

Behold its streaming rays unite
One mingling flood of braided light—
The red that fires the southern rose,
With spotless white from northern snows,
And, spangled o'er its azure, see
The sister Stars of Liberty!
    Then hail the banner of the free,
    The starry Flower of Liberty!

The blades of heroes fence it round,
Where'er it springs is holy ground;
From tower and dome its glories spread;
Its waves where lonely sentries tread,

It makes the land, as ocean, free,
And plants an empire in the sea!
  Then hail the banner of the free,
  The starry Flower of Liberty!

Thy sacred leaves, fair Freedom's flower,
Shall ever float in dome and tower,
To all their heavenly colors true, *
In blackening frost or crimson dew—
And God loves us as we love *thee*,
Thrice holy Flower of Liberty!
  Then hail the banner of the free,
  The starry Flower of Liberty!
          —*Oliver Wendell Holmes.*

LIBERTY STILL LIVES.

TO show our influence on the people in the remote corners of the earth, a citizen of the United States, during the trying times of the rebellion, was travelling on the northern coast of Norway; and, landing from a small steamer at a trading town in the early morning, before the inhabitants were astir, found three fishermen from Lapland waiting at the door of a store to do some small business in trade. The fishermen appeared to be a father and two sons. They were dressed in skins of the reindeer, and appeared to be half barbarian, illiterate people. They were introduced to the American, and when the elder of the Laplanders learned that the distinguished stranger was a citizen of this country, his countenance lighted up with an expression of eager intelligence as he asked: "Are you from beyond the great sea?" Upon being answered in the affirmative, he exclaimed: "Tell me, tell me, does liberty still live?" He expressed great satisfaction upon being assured that it did.

If, on the coast of the northern frozen seas, in a land of almost perpetual night, an illiterate fisherman feels such an eager interest in the question of the continued vitality of liberty, what a dangerous messenger will be that ensign of the ship of state flashing "its meteor glories" among the thrones, crowns, and sceptres of the world! The subjects and victims of oppression will catch "inspiration from its glances," and learning that liberty still lives, will pass the inspiring watchword from man to man. And the cry that "Liberty still lives" will be the world's battle-shout of freedom, and the rallying watchword of deliverance.

> "And the dwellers in the rocks and in the vales
> Shall shout it to each other, and the mountain tops
> From distant mountains catch the flying joy.
> Till, nation after nation taught the strain,
> Earth rolls the rapturous hosanna round."

And in the land of liberty's birth the fires of patriotism will be kept aflame by the iteration and reiteration of the answer to the fisherman's question, that "Liberty still lives." And from the hearts of the crowded cities, from the fireside of the farmer, and from the workshop of the mechanic, in the busy hamlets of labor, and in the homes of luxury and ease, the hearts of freemen will be cheered as our noble craft sails on, with the inspiriting assurance that "Liberty still lives." The burden of the cry will float upon the air wherever our banner waves, and its resonant notes will fill the land with a new inspiration as the joyful assurance is heard:

"Coming up from each valley, flung down from each height,
Our Country and Liberty, God for the right."
—*Hon. George Lear.*

LIBERTY AND GREATNESS.

THE name of Republic is inscribed upon the most imperishable monuments of the human race; and it is probable that it will continue to be associated, as it has been in all past ages, with whatever is heroic in character, sublime in genius, and elegant and brilliant in the cultivation of arts and letters. What land has ever been visited with the influences of liberty that did not flourish like the springs? What people has ever worshipped at her altars, without kindling with a loftier spirit, and putting forth nobler energies? Where she has ever acted, her deeds have been heroic. Where she has ever spoken, her eloquence has been triumphant and sublime.

We live under a form of government, and in a state of society, to which the world has never yet exhibited a parallel. Is it then nothing to be FREE? How many nations in the whole annals of human kind have proved themselves worthy of being so? Is it nothing that we are REPUBLICANS? Were all men as enlightened, as brave, as proud as they ought to be, would they suffer themselves to be insulted with any other title? Is it nothing that so many independent sovereignties should be held together in such a confederacy as ours? What does history teach us of the difficulty of instituting and maintaining such a policy, and of the glory that ought to be given to those who enjoy its advantages in so much perfection, and on so grand a scale?

Can anything be more striking and sublime than the idea of an IMPERIAL REPUBLIC, spreading over an extent of territory more immense than the empire of the Cæsars, in the accumulated conquests of a thousand years—without prefects, pro-consuls, or publicans—founded in the maxims of common sense, employing within itself no arms but those of reason, and known to its subjects only by the blessings it bestows and perpetuates, yet capable of directing against a foreign foe all the energies of a military despotism,—a Republic, in which men are completely insignificant, and *principles* and *laws* exercise throughout its vast domains a peaceful and irresistible sway, blending, in one divine harmony, such various habits and conflicting opinions, and mingling, in our institutions, the light of philosophy with all that is dazzling in the associations of heroic achievements, extended dominion, and formidable power.

—*Hugh Swinton Legare.*

INDEPENDENCE.

HAIL! Independence, hail! heaven's next best gift
To that of life and an immortal soul!
The life of life! that to the banquet high
And sober meal gives taste; to the low'd roof
Fair dream'd repose, and to the cottage charms.
Of public freedom, hail, thou secret source!
Whose streams from every quarter confluent flow
My better Nile, that nurses human life,
By rills from thee deduced, irriguous fed,
The private field looks gay, with nature's wealth
Abundant flows, and blooms with each delight
That nature craves.

—*James Thomson.*

THREE BULWARKS OF LIBERTY.

AMERICA has three bulwarks of liberty—a free ballot, a free school, and a free Sunday, and neither domestic treachery nor foreign impudence should be permitted to break them down.—*The Century Magazine.*

UNION LINKED WITH LIBERTY.

WITHOUT Union, our independence and liberty would never have been achieved; without Union, they can never be maintained. Divided into twenty-four, or even a smaller number of separate communities, we shall see our internal trade burdened with numberless restraints and exactions; communication between distant points and sections obstructed or cut off; our sons made soldiers, to deluge with blood the field they now till in peace; the mass of our people borne down and impoverished by taxes to support armies and navies; and military leaders, at the head of their victorious legions, becoming our lawgivers and judges. The loss of liberty, of all good government, of peace, plenty, and happiness, must inevitably follow a dissolution of the Union. In supporting it, therefore, we support all that is dear to the freeman and the philanthropist.

The time at which I stand before you is full of interest. The eyes of all nations are fixed on our republic. The event of the existing crisis will be decision, in the opinion of mankind, of the practicability of our Federal system of government. Great is the stake placed in our hands; great is the responsibility which must rest upon the people of the United States. Let us realize the importance of the attitude in which we stand before the world. Let us exercise forbearance and firmness. Let us extricate our country from the dangers which surround it, and learn wisdom from the lessons they inculcate. Deeply impressed with the truth of these observations and under the obligation of that solemn oath which I am about to take, I shall continue to exert all my faculties to maintain the just powers of the Constitution, and to transmit unimpaired to posterity the blessings of our Federal Union.

At the same time it will be my aim to inculcate, by my official acts, the necessity of exercising, by the General Government, those powers only that are clearly delegated; to encourage simplicity and economy in the expenditures of the Government; to raise no more money from the people than may be requisite for these objects, and in a manner that will best promote the interest of all classes of the community, and of all portions of the Union. Constantly bearing in mind that, in entering into society, "individuals must give up a share of liberty to preserve the rest," it will be my desire so to discharge my duties as to foster with our brethren, in all parts of the country, a spirit of liberal concession and compromise; and, by reconciling our fellow-citizens to those partial sacrifices which they must unavoidably make, for the preservation of a greater good, to recommend our invaluable Government and Union to the confidence and affections of the American people. Finally, it is my most fervent prayer to that Almighty Being before whom I now stand, and who has kept us in his hands from the infancy of our Republic to the present day, that he will so overrule all my intentions and actions, and inspire the hearts of my fellow-citizens, that we may be preserved from dangers of all kinds, and continue forever a united and happy people.—*Andrew Jackson.*

IMPORTANCE OF THE UNION.

IT is to the Union we owe our safety at home, and our consideration and dignity abroad. It is to that Union we are chiefly indebted for whatever makes us most proud of our country. That Union we reached only by the discipline of our virtues in the severe school of adversity. It had its origin in the necessities of disordered finance, prostrate commerce, and ruined credit. Under its benign influences, these great interests immediately awoke, as from the dead, and sprang forth with newness of life. Every year of its duration has teemed with fresh proofs of its utility and its blessings; and although our population spread farther and farther, they have not outrun its protection or its benefits. It has been to us all a copious fountain of national, social, personal happiness.

I have not allowed myself, sir, to look beyond the Union, to see what might lie hidden in the dark recesses behind. I have not coolly weighed the chances of preserving liberty, when the bonds that unite us together shall be broken asunder. I have accustomed myself to hang over the precipice of disunion, to see whether, with my short sight, I can fathom the depth of the abyss below; nor could I regard him as a safe counsellor in the affairs of this Government whose thoughts should be mainly bent on considering, not

how the Union should be best preserved, but how tolerable might be the condition of the people when it shall be broken up and destroyed. While the Union lasts we have high, exciting, gratifying prospects spread out before us and our children. Beyond that I seek not to penetrate the veil. God grant that, in my day at least, that curtain may not rise. God grant that on my vision never may be opened what lies behind. When my eyes shall be turned to behold, for the last time, the sun in the heaven, may I not see him shining on the broken and dishonored fragments of a once-glorious Union; on States dissevered, discordant, belligerent; on a land rent with civil feuds, or drenched, it may be, in fraternal blood! Let the last feeble and lingering glance, rather, behold the gorgeous ensign of the Republic, now known and honored throughout the earth, still full high, advanced, its arms and trophies streaming in their original lustre, not a stripe erased or polluted, nor a single star obscured—bearing for its motto no such miserable interrogatory as, What is all this worth? nor those other words of delusion and folly, Liberty first, and Union afterwards; but everywhere spread all over in characters of living light, blazing on all its ample folds, as they float over the sea and over the land, and in every wind under the whole heavens, that other sentiment, dear to every true American heart,— Liberty *and* Union, now and forever, one and inseparable!
—*Daniel Webster.*

WE ARE ONE PEOPLE.

WE are now one people—we have a common interest in the Union. Let us forget the unhappy past in the brightening prospects of the future.—*Whittier.*

THE UNION AND ITS RESULTS.

MERELY to fill up the wilderness with a population provided with the ordinary institutions and carrying on the customary pursuits of civilized life—though surely no mean achievement—was, by no means, the whole of the work allotted to the United States, and thus far performed with signal activity, intelligence, and success. The founders of America and their descendants have accomplished more and better things. On the basis of a rapid geographical extension and with the force of teeming numbers they have, in the very infancy of their political existence, successfully aimed at higher progress in a generous civilization. The mechanical arts have been cultivated with unusual aptitude. Agriculture, manufactures, commerce, navigation, whether by sails or by steam, and the art of printing in all its forms, have been pursued with surprising skill. Great improvements have been made in all those branches of industry, and in the machinery pertaining to them, which have been eagerly adopted in Europe. A more adequate provision has been made for popular education than in almost any other country. There are more seminaries in the United States where a respectable academical education may be obtained—more, I still mean, in proportion to the population than in any other country, except Germany. The fine arts have reached a high degree of excellence. The taste for music is rapidly spreading in town and country; and every year witnesses productions from the pencil and the chisel of American sculptors and painters which would adorn any gallery in the world. Our astronomers, mathematicians, naturalists, chemists, engineers, jurists, publicists, historians, poets, novelists, and lexicographers have placed themselves on a level with those of the elder world. The best dictionaries of the English language since Johnson are those published in America. Our Constitutions, whether of the United States or of the separate States, exclude all public provision for the maintenance of religion, but in no part of Christendom is it more generously supported; sacred science is pursued as diligently, and the pulpit commands as high a degree of respect in the United States as in those countries where the Church is publicly endowed; while the American missionary operations have won the admiration of the civilized world. Nowhere, I am persuaded, are there more liberal contributions to public-spirited and charitable objects. In a word, there is no branch of the mechanical or fine arts, no department of science, exact or applied, no form of polite literature, no description of social improvement, in which, due allowance being made for the means and resources at command, the progress of the United States has not been satisfactory, and in some respects astonishing.

At this moment the rivers and seas of the globe are navigated with that marvellous application of steam as a propelling power which was first effected by Fulton. The harvests of the civilized world are gathered by American reapers; the newspapers which lead the journalism of Europe are printed on American presses; there are railroads in Europe constructed by American engineers and travelled by American locomotives; troops armed with American weapons, and ships of war built in American dockyards. In the factories of Europe there is machinery of American invention or improvement; in their observatories, telescopes of American construction, and apparatus of American invention for recording the celestial phenomena. America contests with Europe the introduction into actual use of the electric telegraph, and her mode of operating it as adopted through the French empire; American authors in almost every department are found on the shelves of European libraries. It is true no American Homer, Virgil, Dante, Copernicus, Shakespeare, Bacon, Milton, Newton has risen on the world. These mighty geniuses seem to be exceptions in the history of the human mind. Favorable circumstances do not produce them, nor does the absence of favorable circumstances prevent their appearance. Homer rose in the dawn of Grecian culture; Virgil flourished in the court of Augustus; Dante ushered in the birth of the new European civilization; Copernicus was reared in a Polish cloister; Shakespeare was trained in the green-room of the theatre; Milton was formed while the elements of English thought and life were fermenting toward a great political and moral revolution; Newton, under the profligacy of the Restoration. Ages may elapse before any country will produce a man like these, as two centuries have passed since the last mentioned of them was born. But if it is really a matter of reproach to the United States that, in the comparatively short period of their existence as a people, they have not added another name to this illustrious list (which is equally true of all the other nations of the earth), they may proudly boast of one example of life and character, one career of disinterested service, one model of public virtue, one type of human excellence, of which all the countries and all the ages may be searched in vain for the parallel. I need not—on this day I need not—speak the peerless name. It is stamped on your hearts, it glistens in your eyes, it is written on every page of your history, on the battlefields of the Revolution, on the monuments of your fathers, on the portals of your capitols. It is heard in every breeze that whispers over the fields of independent America. And he was all our own. He grew up on the soil of America; he was nurtured at her bosom. She loved and trusted him in his youth; she honored and revered him in his age; and, though she did not wait for death to canonize his name, his precious memory with each succeeding year has sunk more deeply into the hearts of his countrymen.—*Edward Everett.*

WHAT WE OWE TO THE UNION.

THE influence of the government on us is like that of the atmosphere around us. Its benefits are so silent and unseen that they are seldom thought of or appreciated. We seldom think of the single element of oxygen in the air we breathe; and yet, let this simple, unseen and unfelt agent be withdrawn, this life-giving element be taken away from this all-pervading fluid around us, and what instant and appalling changes would take place in all organic creation.

It may be that we are all that we are in "spite of the General Government;" but it may be that without it we should have been far different from what we are now. It is true there is no equal part of the earth with natural resources superior, perhaps, to ours. That portion of this country known as the Southern States, stretching from the Chesapeake to the Rio Grande, is fully equal to the picture drawn by the honorable and eloquent Senator last night, in all natural capacities. But how many ages and centuries passed before these capacities were developed to reach this advanced age of civilization? There these same hills, rich in ore, these same rivers, same valleys and plains, are as they have been since they came from the hand of the Creator; uneducated and uncivilized man roamed over them, for how long no history informs us.

It was only under our institutions that they could be developed. Their development is the result of the enterprise of our people under operations of the government and institutions under which we have lived. Even our people, without these, never would have done it. The organization of society has much to do with the development of the natural resources of any country or any land. The institutions of a people, political and moral, are the matrix in which the germ of their organic structure quickens into life—takes root and develops in form, nature and character. Our institutions constitute the basis, the matrix, from which spring all our characteristics of development and greatness. Look at Greece. There is the same fertile soil, the same blue sky, the same inlets and harbors, the same Ægean, the same Olympus; there is the same land where Homer sung, where Pericles spoke; it is in nature the same old Greece—but it is living Greece no more.

Descendants of the same people inhabit the country; yet what is the reason of this mighty difference? In the midst of present degradation we see the glorious fragments of ancient works of art—temples with ornaments and inscriptions that excite wonder and admiration—the remains of a once high order of civilization which have outlived the language they spoke—upon them all Ichabod is written—their glory has departed. Why is this so? I answer, their institutions have been destroyed. These were but the fruits of their forms of government, the matrix from which their grand development sprung, and when once the institutions of the people have been destroyed, there is no earthly power that can bring back the Promethean spark to kindle them here again, any more than in that ancient land of eloquence, poetry, and song.

The same may be said of Italy. Where is Rome, once the mistress of the world? There are the same seven hills now, the same soil, the same natural resources; nature is the same, but what a ruin of human greatness meets the eye of the traveller throughout the length and breadth of that most down-trodden land! Why have not the people of that heaven-favored clime the spirit that animated their fathers? Why this sad difference?

It is the destruction of her institutions that has caused it, and, my countrymen, if we shall in an evil hour rashly pull down and destroy those institutions which the patriotic band of our fathers labored so long and so hard to build up, and which have done so much for us and the world, who can venture the prediction that similar results will not ensue? Let us avoid it if we can. I trust the spirit is among us that will enable us to do it. Let us not rashly try the experiment, for if it fails, as it did in Greece and Italy, and in the South American republics, and in every other place wherever liberty is once destroyed, it may never be restored to us again.—*Hon. A. H. Stephens.*

BUT ONE UNITED STATES.

I HAVE travelled far, and have seen the best of all the countries of all this world, and there is but one United States of America in the world.—*Father Taylor.*

THE WHOLE UNION.

WE cannot do with less than the whole Union; to us it admits of no division. In the veins of our children flow Northern and Southern blood; how shall it be separated?—who will put asunder the best affections of the heart, the noblest instincts of our nature? We love the land of our adoption: so do we that of our birth. Let us ever be true to both, and always exert ourselves in maintaining the unity of our country, the integrity of the republic.—*S. S. Prentiss.*

THE TRUE GLORY OF AMERICA.

ITALIA'S vales and fountains,
   Though beautiful ye be,
I love my soaring mountains
   And forests more than ye;
And though a dreamy greatness rise
   From out your cloudy years,
Like hills on distant stormy skies,
   Seem dim through Nature's tears,
Still, tell me not of years of old,
   Of ancient heart and clime;
Ours is the land and age of gold,
   And ours the hallow'd time!

The jewell'd crown and sceptre
   Of Greece have pass'd away;
And none, of all who wept her,
   Could bid her splendor stay.
The world has shaken with the tread

Of iron-sandall'd crime—
And, lo! o'ershadowing all the dead,
    The conqueror stalks sublime!
Then ask I not for crown and plume
    To nod above my land;
The victor's footsteps point to doom,
    Graves open round his hand!

Rome! with thy pillar'd palaces,
    And sculptured heroes all,
Snatched, in their warm, triumphal days,
    To Art's high festival;
Rome! with thy giant sons of power,
    Whose pathway was on thrones,
Who built their kingdoms of an hour
    On yet unburied bones—
I would not have my land like thee,
    So lofty—yet so cold!
Be hers a lowlier majesty,
    In yet a nobler mould.

Thy marbles—works of wonder!
    In thy victorious days,
Whose lips did seem to sunder
    Before the astonish'd gaze;
When statue glared on statue there,
    The living on the dead—
And men as silent pilgrims were
    Before some sainted head!
O, not for faultless marbles yet
    Would I the light forego
That beams when other lights have set,
    And Art herself lies low!

O, ours a holier hope shall be
    Than consecrated bust,

Some loftier mean of memory
 To snatch us from the dust;
And ours a sterner art than this
 Shall fix our image here—
The spirit's mould of loveliness—
 A nobler Belvidere!

Then let them bind with bloomless flowers
 The busts and urns of old—
A fairer heritage be ours,
 A sacrifice less cold!
Give honor to the great and good,
 And wreathe the living brow,
Kindling with Virtue's mantling blood,
 And pay the tribute now.

So, when the good and great go down,
 Their statues shall arise,
To crowd those temples of our own,
 Our fadeless memories!
And when the sculptured marble falls,
 And Art goes in to die,
Our forms shall live in holier halls,
 The Pantheon of the sky. .
   —*Greenville Mellen.*

PATRIOTISM.

BREATHES there the man with soul so dead,
Who never to himself hath said,
This is my own, my native land?
Whose heart hath ne'er within him burned,
As home his footsteps he hath turned,
From wandering on a foreign strand?
If such there breathe, go, mark him well;
For him no minstrel raptures swell!

High though his titles, proud his name,
Boundless his wealth as wish can claim:
Despite those titles, power and pelf,
The wretch, concentered all in self,
Living, shall forfeit fair renown,
And doubly dying, shall go down
To the vile dust, from whence he sprung,
Unwept, unhonored and unsung.
—*Sir Walter Scott.*

FREEDOM AND PATRIOTISM.

GOD has stamped upon our very humanity this very impress of freedom. It is the unchartered prerogative of human nature. A soul ceases to be a soul in proportion as it ceases to be free. Strip it of this, and you strip it of one of its essential and characteristic attributes. It is this that draws the footsteps of the wild Indian to his wide and boundless desert paths, and makes him prefer them to the gay saloons and soft carpets of sumptuous palaces. It is this that makes it so difficult to bring him within the pale of artificial civilization. Our roving tribes are perishing—a sad sacrifice upon the altar of their wild freedom. They come among us and look with childish wonder upon the perfection of our arts and the splendor of our habitations; they submit with ennui and weariness, for a few days, to our burdensome forms and restraints and then turn their faces to their forest homes, and resolve to push those homes onward till they sink in the Pacific waves, rather than not be free. It is thus that every people is attached to its country, just in proportion as it is free. No matter if that country be in the rocky fastnesses of Switzerland, amidst the snows of Tartary, or on the most barren and lonely island shore; no matter if that country be so poor as to force away its children to other and richer lands for employment and sustenance; yet when the songs of those free homes chance to fall upon the exile's ear, no soft and ravishing airs that wait upon the timid feastings of Asiatic opulence ever thrilled the heart with such mingled rapture and agony as those simple tones. Sad mementos might they be of poverty and want and toil; yet it was enough that they were mementos of happy freedom. And more than once has it been necessary to forbid by military orders, in the armies of the Swiss mercenaries, the singing of their native songs. And such an attachment, do I believe, is found in our own people, to their native country! It is the country of the free, and that consideration compensates for the want of many advantages which other countries possess over us. And glad am I that it opens wide its hospitable gates to many a noble but persecuted citizen from the dungeons of Austria and Italy, and the imprisoning castles and citadels of Poland. Here may they find rest, as they surely find sympathy, though it is saddened with many bitter remembrances! Yes, let me be free; let me go and come at my own will; let me do business, make journeys without a vexatious police or insolent soldier to watch my steps; let me think, and do, and speak what I please, subject to no limit but that which is set by the common weal; subject to no law but that which conscience binds upon me, and I will bless my country and love its most rugged rocks and its most barren soil.

I have seen my fellow-countrymen and have been with them a fellow-wanderer in other lands; and little did I see or feel to warrant the apprehension sometimes expressed that foreign travel would weaken our patriotic attachments. One sigh for home—home, arose from all hearts. And why, from palaces and courts—why, from galleries of the arts where the marble softens into life, and painting sheds an almost living presence of beauty around it—why, from the mountain's awful brow, and the lovely valleys and lakes touched with the sunset hues of old romance—why, from those venerable and touching ruins to which our very heart grows—why, from all these scenes, were the lookings beyond the swellings of the Atlantic wave to a dearer and holier spot of earth—their own country? Doubtless it was, in part, because they knew that there was no oppression, no pitiful exaction of petty tyranny; because, that there, they knew, was no accredited and irresistible religious denomination; because, that there, they knew, they should not meet the odious soldier at every corner, nor swarms of imploring beggars, the victims of misrule; that there no curse causeless did fall, and no blight worse than plague and pestilence did descend amidst the pure dews of heaven; because, in fine, that there, they knew, was liberty—upon all the green hills and amidst all the peaceful valleys—liberty, the wall of fire around the humblest home—the crown of glory, studded with her ever blazing stars upon the proudest mansion.

My friends, upon our own homes that blessing rests, that guardian care and glorious crown; and when we return to those homes, and so long as we dwell in them—so long as no oppressor's foot invades their thresholds, let us bless them and hallow them as the homes of freedom! Let us make them too the homes of a noble freedom—of freedom from vice, from evil, from passion, from every corrupting bondage of the soul.—*Orville Dewey.*

THE IMMORTALITY OF PATRIOTS.

WHAT parent, as he conducts his son to Mount Auburn or to Bunker Hill, will not, as he pauses before their monumental statues, seek to heighten his reverence for virtue, for patriotism, for science, for learning, for devotion to the public good, as he bids him contemplate the form of that grave and venerable Winthrop, who left his pleasant home in England to come and found a new republic in this untrodden wilderness; of that ardent and intrepid Otis, who first struck out the spark of American independence; of that noble Adams, its most eloquent champion on the floor of Congress; of that martyr Warren, who laid down his life in its defence; of that self-taught Bowditch, who, without a guide, threaded the starry mazes of the heavens; of that Story, honored at home and abroad as one of the brightest luminaries of the law, and by a felicity, of which I believe there is no other example, admirably portrayed in marble by his son? What citizen of Boston, as he accompanies the stranger around its streets, guiding him through its busy thoroughfares, to its wharves crowded with vessels which range every sea and gather the produce of every climate—up to the dome of the Capitol, which commands as lovely a landscape as can delight the eye or gladden the heart, will not, as he calls his attention at last to the statues of Franklin and Webster, exclaim, "Boston takes pride in her natural position, she rejoices in her beautiful environs, she is grateful for her material prosperity; but richer than the merchandise stored in palatial warehouses, greener than the slopes of sea-girt islets, lovelier than this encircling panorama of land and sea, of field and hamlet, of lake and stream, of garden and grove, is the memory of her sons, native and adopted; the character, services and fame of those who have benefited and adorned their day and generation. Our children, and the schools at which they are trained; our citizens, and the services they have rendered; these are our jewels—these our abiding treasures."

Yes, your long rows of quarried granite may crumble to the dust; the corn-fields in yonder villages, ripening to the sickle, may, like the plains of stricken Lombardy, be kneaded into bloody clods by the madding wheels of artillery; this populous city, like the old cities of Etruria and the Campagna Romana, may be desolated by the pestilence which walketh in darkness, may decay with the lapse of time, and the busy mart, which now rings with the joyous din of trade, become as lonely and still as Carthage or Tyre, as Babylon and Nineveh; but the names of the great and good shall survive the desolation and the ruin; the memory of the wise, the brave, the patriotic, shall never perish. Yes, Sparta is a wheat-field; a Bavarian prince holds court at the foot of the Acropolis; the travelling virtuoso digs for marbles in the Roman Forum, and beneath the ruins of the temple of Jupiter Capitolinus; but Lycurgus and Leonidas, and Miltiades and Demosthenes, and Cato and Tully "still live;" and He still lives, and all the great and good shall live in the heart of ages, while marble and bronze shall endure; and when marble and bronze have perished, they shall "still live" in memory, so long as men shall reverence Law, and honor Patriotism, and love Liberty!—*Edward Everett.*

I AM not a Virginian, but an American.—*Patrick Henry.*

SHRINES OF PATRIOTISM.

How sleep the brave, who sink to rest
By all their country's wishes blessed?
When Spring, with dewy fingers cold,
Returns to deck their hallowed mould,
She there shall dress a sweeter sod
Than Fancy's feet have ever trod.
By fairy hands their knell is rung;
By forms unseen their dirge is sung;
There Honor comes, a pilgrim gray,
To bless the turf that wraps their clay;
And Freedom shall a while repair,
To dwell a weeping hermit there.

—William Collins.

THE RESPONSIBILITY OF OUR COUNTRY.

Let it be remembered, that it has ever been the pride and boast of America, that the rights, for which she contended, were the rights of human nature. By the blessing of the Author of these rights on the means exerted for their defence, they have prevailed over all opposition. No instance has heretofore occurred, nor can any instance be expected hereafter to occur, in which the unadulterated forms of republican government can pretend to so fair an opportunity for justifying themselves by their fruits.

In this view, the citizens of the United States are responsible for the greatest trust ever confided to a political society. If justice, good faith, honor, gratitude, and all the other qualities which ennoble the character of a nation, and fulfil the ends of government, be the fruits of our establishments, the cause of Liberty will acquire a dignity and lustre which it has never yet enjoyed; and an example will be set which cannot but have the most favorable influence on the rights of mankind.

If, on the other hand, our government should be unfortunately blotted with the reverse of these cardinal and essential virtues, the great cause which we have engaged to vindicate will be dishonored and betrayed; and the last and fairest experiment in favor of the rights of human nature will be turned against them; and their patrons and friends exposed to be insulted and silenced by the votaries of tyranny and usurpation, storm of battle, and sprinkled with the blood of falling comrades. We honor their sublime devotion, we applaud their heroic deeds. Their bright example of devotion to principle and fidelity to duty should incite us of this age in America to accept joyfully and bravely the responsibilities of our position, and like them be ever ready

"To take
Occasion by the hand, and make
The bounds of freedom wider yet."

—*James Madison.*

GREECE gave freedom birth; Rome fondled the nursling and gave it swaddling clothes; Switzerland rocked its cradle; and America nursed it into the giant of the ages, and all nations are preparing to burn incense to its overshadowing majesty.

—*J. H. Worst.*

SITUATION OF AMERICA.

IT is not to inflate national vanity, nor to swell a light and empty feeling of self-importance, but it is that we may judge justly of our situation, and of our own duties, that I earnestly urge this consideration of our position and our character among the nations of the earth. It cannot be denied, but by those who would dispute against the sun, that with America, and in America, a new era commences in human affairs. This era is distinguished by free representative governments, by entire religious liberty, by improved systems of national intercourse, by a new-awakened and an unconquerable spirit of free inquiry, and by a diffusion of knowledge through the community, such as has been before altogether unknown or unheard of. . . . America, America, our country, fellow-citizens, our own dear and native land, is inseparably connected, fast bound up, in fortune and by fate, with these great interests; if they fall, we fall with them; if they stand, it will be because we have upholden them. Let us contemplate, then, this connection, which binds the prosperity of others to our own; and let us manfully discharge all the duties which it imposes. If we cherish the virtues and the principles of our fathers, Heaven will assist us to carry on the work of human liberty and human happiness. Auspicious omens cheer us. Great examples are before us. Our own firmament now shines brightly upon our path. Washington is in the clear upper sky. Those other stars have now joined the American constellation; they circle round their centre, and the heavens beam with new light. Beneath this illumination let us walk the course of life, and at its close devoutly commend our beloved country, the common parent of us all, to the Divine benignity.—*Daniel Webster.*

OUR COUNTRY'S DEFENCE.

BUT if you ask me, what will save our country from the scourge of war, what will prevent it from becoming the victim of intoxication and licentiousness, what will save it from being exhausted by civil feuds or torn up by the shattering artillery of war? my answer is, Bible education. If you ask me, what will save us from that infidelity that revels in its license without control, and from that superstition that exercises a despotism over soul and body?—if you ask me, what will save us from those wild and sensual opinions that rise like miasma from the fens and marshes of popular ignorance, or what will protect us from those deadly passions that breed like reptiles beneath a scorching sun?—my answer is, Christian education. The good and the pious of past ages have left us noble heritages: we are bound to perpetuate them. We have received from our fathers an open Bible; we have been taught to read, to understand and to rejoice with truth. Let us resolve, that when we lie down, as we must lie down, upon the last bed, and when our children shall gather around us to bid us a last farewell, to be able to tell to them, If we have not increased the blessings of your ancient heritage, we have not impaired them; if we have not added to your religious freedom, we have not crushed it; if we have done nothing to make you nobler, holier, happier, we have done nothing to make you worse.—*Daniel Webster.*

OUR REPUBLIC TRIUMPHANT.

STRETCHING from ocean to ocean, teeming with population, bountiful in resources of all kinds, and thrice happy in universal enfranchisement, it will be more than conqueror—nothing too vast for its power, nothing too minute for its care. Triumphant over the foulest wrong ever inflicted, after the bloodiest war ever waged, it will know the majesty of right and the beauty of peace; prepared always to uphold the one and to cultivate the other. Strong in its own mighty stature, filled with all the fulness of a new life, and covered with a panoply of renown, it will confess that no dominion is of value which does not contribute to human happiness. Born in this latter day, and the child of its own struggles, without ancestral claims, but heir of all the ages, it will stand forth to assert the dignity of man; and, wherever any of the human family is to be succored, there its voice will reach, as the voice of Cromwell reached across France even to the persecuted mountaineers of the Alps. Such will be this Republic—upstart among the nations; ay, as the steam-engine, the telegraph, and chloroform are upstart. Comforter and helper like these, it can know no bounds to its empire over a willing world.—*Charles Sumner.*

WHILE just government protects all in their religious rights, true religion affords to government its surest support.—*George Washington.*

BLESSINGS OF A FREE GOVERNMENT.

WE cannot omit to notice how rapidly the ideas of old times have been liberalized in their practical application in this country, not only in law, politics, government and industry, but in domestic and social life as well as in religion, science and literature. The stiff forms of the old law practice have passed away. Neither interest, race, nor religious belief now disqualifies a witness. Imprisonment for debt, except in cases of fraud, is abolished. Homestead and exemption laws protect the poor. Divorces are obtainable and married women's property rights secured. Equal distribution of property is secured to all heirs alike, and primogeniture and entailments are abolished. Simplicity of deeds and transfers have been introduced, security of possession enforced by liberal statutes of limitation, and many other modifications of the old law adopted tending to equality among all classes and races. So the criminal code has been toned down and prisoners have bail, and counsel and witnesses are allowed at the public charge; and prisoners may even be witnesses for themselves. The stocks and the whipping-post are no more. So everywhere schools are practically free. Charities, asylums, invalid homes, cover the land, so that the young and the imbecile, the erring and the insane, are cared for by private munificence or at the public charge. What the old kings spent on retainers and armies, the young republic devotes to charities. And religious intolerance in our country is quite gone. Excommunication from the fold of the church is a dead letter. Each can worship under his own vine and fig-tree with none to molest or make him afraid, and God alone can call any man to account for his religious belief. The state aids no church, but equally protects all. The cathedral and the synagogue peacefully confront each other, the High Church and the Conventicle are friendly neighbors, and even the Free-thinkers' Hall is under protection of law. And so, too, industry is free. Unlike the old countries, every man here may follow any pursuit without government license or legally prescribed apprenticeship. No property qualification is required for public place, nor even for social standing. Every one may take his place in that rank of life for which he can show himself fitted. Husbands, wives and children are bound together practically by the law of love alone. So freedom of opinion, of speech, of the press, is everywhere recognized and scarcely ever invaded unless it be momentarily in the excitement of political contests, or in the occasional outburst of popular wrath at some flagrant abuse of freedom.—*General Durbin Ward.*

WE MUST TAKE CARE OF OUR GOVERNMENT.

AS we take care of our work, our life and our homes, we must also take care of our government. In a government like ours there is one sure law. It is like that of the water-works in my city, through which the water rises to the exact line of the water-mark in the tower, and not a line above that, no matter if the whole city should pray to have it so; and so in our central and State governments, in everything we have to our name, as citizens of this Republic, we shall find that the public virtue, manliness and honesty in Washington, in Springfield and in Madison are just the marrow of the private nature and good sense of the citizens who elect these men to take care of the machine. We must have honesty, intelligence, courage and manliness in ourselves, or we shall not have it where it can do most good and most harm. So we must not elect our man because he can make a fine speech, but because he is a man to be trusted and is trusted by those who know him best. He may make very fine speeches and do very mean things. Nothing comes cheaper than good talk, and I think we have had about enough of it within the last few years to open our eyes. We are in very much the condition the people were in at a town on one of our South-western rivers. There was an old skipper who ran a steamboat up and down the river, and was by all odds the most profane man in that section. But one day his boat ran into a mud bank, near the little town, and there she stuck, one end in the water and the other in the mud, and would not stir an inch for all his swearing. So, thinking what was best to be done, he called one of the deck hands and said: "You go up into that air town, and find the folks who belong to meetin'; tell 'em I got religion and want 'em to come and hold prayer meet'n on my boat." The news made a vast sensation; the people came in a crowd; they found the old skipper standing ready to receive them. "Go aft, brethren," he said, "go aft, go aft," and aft they went, until the weight at the water end weighed the steamer down, and she began to slip into deep water. This was what he wanted; he saw her clear and then yelled: "Meet'n's out, d—n you, jump ashore, quick!" and jump they did, and that was the end of his conversion.

That is the way of some of the men who want to represent us; they belong to both sides, always did and always will. What they want is to float their venture on false pretences. We must watch them, take care of them, and whether we are Democrat or Republican, elect only the man of a tried honesty, and then when we get hold of such a man we must stand by him and hold up his hands and his heart. Never mind what the other side says in the heat and passion of party strife; the spawn of party strife is the shame and disgrace of our era. It breaks down all the guards of truth and fair speech, looks on every man not on its side with an evil eye, and pursues its antagonists with the relentlessness of the fiend. We can have no part or lot in such mean work. We have to search for and find virtue, honesty and fidelity in Democrat and Republican alike, to maintain those who are well proven in these things at all costs, and no other kind, and then there can be no doubt but that we are to have through the ages to come, a noble, beautiful and strong Republic.—*Rev. Robert Collyer, D. D.*

PUBLIC VIRTUE.

I HOPE that in all that relates to personal firmness; all that concerns a just appreciation of the insignificance of human life—whatever may be attempted to threaten or alarm a soul not easily swayed by opposition, or awed or intimidated by menace—a stout heart and a steady eye, that can survey, unmoved and undaunted, any mere personal perils that assail this poor, transient, perishing frame, I may, without disparagement, compare with other men.

But there is a sort of courage, which, I frankly confess it, I do not possess—a boldness to which I dare not aspire, a valor which I cannot covet: I cannot lay myself down in the way of the welfare and happiness of my country. That I cannot, I have not the courage to do. I cannot interpose the power with which I may be invested—a power conferred, not for my personal benefit, not for my aggrandizement, but for my country's good—to check her onward march to greatness and glory. I have *not* courage enough, I am too cowardly for that.

I would not, I *dare* not, in the exercise of such a trust, lie down and place my body across the path that leads my country to prosperity and happiness. This is a sort of courage widely different from that which a man may display in his private conduct and personal relations. Personal and private courage is totally distinct from that higher and nobler courage which prompts the patriot to offer himself a voluntary sacrifice to his country's good.

Apprehensions of the imputation of the want of firmness sometimes impel us to perform rash and inconsiderate acts. It is the *greatest* courage to be able to bear the imputation of the *want* of courage. But pride, vanity, egotism, so unamiable and offensive in *private,* are vices which partake of the character of crimes, in the conduct of *public* affairs. The unfortunate slave of these passions cannot see beyond the little, petty, contemptible circle of his own personal interests. All his thoughts are withdrawn from his country, and concentrated on his consistency, his firmness—*himself.*

The high, the exalted, the sublime emotions of a patriotism, which, soaring toward heaven, rises far above all mean, low, or selfish things, and is absorbed by one soul-transporting thought of the good and the glory of one's country, are never felt in *his* impenetrable bosom. That patriotism, which, catching its inspirations from the immortal God, and leaving at an immeasurable distance below all lesser, grovelling, personal interests and feelings, animates and prompts to deeds of self-sacrifice, of valor, of devotion, and of *death* itself—*that is public* virtue; that is the *noblest*, the *sublimest* of all public virtues.—*Henry Clay.*

OUR COUNTRY FIRST, LAST, AND ALWAYS.

THE first defence to any people is in the love of country. The nation is one great family, with one common interest, welfare and destiny; a nation dwelling together in love must be a happy people. Kindness begets kindness, and love awakens love; this is that magic touch which makes the world of kin. A confederacy like ours cannot be held together by the strong arm of a central government; if the band of unity is gone, such a union is no whit better than a rope of sand. The danger which besets us is not in individual sins which fasten on the body politic—we may labor with forfearance and firmness for their removal. Our danger lies in that spirit of selfishness and self-will which forgets brotherhood and God. In a nation like ours, with its countless differing interests of rival productions; its conflicts of trade and sectional rivalries of commerce, we must differ on questions of public policy; but it may be the manly difference of manly men. Never did men differ more widely than the fathers of the republic; never did earnest hearts battle with more zeal for their rival interests, nor contend more fiercely inch by inch in political struggles. Never did the rallying cry of parties take a deeper hold on its liege-men, or braver shouts of triumph herald in its victory. But there was a deeper love of country, which made the brotherhood of a nation, and a charity which more respected the opinions of those from whom they differ.

The Christian patriot dare not close his eye to the evils which mar the nation; for their removal he will work and pray, but never with rash hand tear down the sacred edifice of the Constitution, because some stains deface its walls. The query may well arise whether we are not fast reaching the time when the question is not of the right or wrong of this or that legislation, the benefit of this or that public policy, but whether this or that party shall divide the spoils of office among its political camp-followers. We hear of angry words and fierce invectives of rumors of corruption, of bribery in public office; they belong to no one party, they are not ranked under any one leader; these things came because the people have lost sight, in the strifes of men for office, of that great destiny which God offers to Americans. I believe the love of country dwells in the people's hearts. The honest-hearted sons of toil will be true to the country and its Constitution. That love may have slumbered for a time, but the great heart of the country *will* be true to itself. Its love *cannot* be hedged in by the paling of any man's dooryard. It *will* sweep away every barrier of strife, and keep us one united people.—*Bishop Whipple.*

The Republic of the United States is God's creation.— *Justin D. Fulton, D. D.*

NATIONAL GUARDS.

THE perpetuity of our republic is guarded and secured by cherishing the Bible as the word of God. This government was founded upon the Bible. In its customs, in its enactments, in its judicial decisions, by its recognition of the Christian Sabbath, by its oaths in courts of justice, by its prayers in Congress, by its chaplains in the army and navy, by its stamp upon our coin, by its national thanksgiving, and by unnumbered other witnesses, it declares itself to be a religious nation, with the Bible as its sacred book, yet it gives no national church. The open Bible, the grand old Saxon Bible, is our common treasure. The spirit of the government says: "Open it, read it, worship God." A few years ago an African prince, while on a visit to England, asked Queen Victoria the secret of England's greatness. The queen did not send him to the Tower of London to look upon the iron-guarded jewels of the realm, but, presenting him a Bible, said: "Here is the secret of England's greatness." So, when the nations ask for the secret of our prosperity, let us point to the open Bible; let us point to a hundred thousand church spires—fingers of faith pointing heavenward; let us point to our Christian Sabbath, still maintained in its pristine purity, as the most marked and cherished monuments of our national life. True lovers of their country will do it with grateful pride. The salt that preserves this nation and has given it progress and glory, the light that has shined to show it a pathway to exaltation, is from the Bible. It is a rock of diamonds, our nation's wealth. It is a chain of pearls, our nation's ornament. It is our sundial, by which to discern the times. It is our balance, by which to weigh our actions.

Again: *The perpetuity of our nation is guarded by the Church.* There never has been—let there never be here—a union of Church and State. Fifty thousand Protestant ministers proclaim the truths of our holy religion, and over six million members of orthodox churches—the vast majority, we doubt not, loyal to Christ—receive the word, to the ennobling and purifying of them as citizens. God has appointed his Church to preserve, refresh and bless the world —as clouds and mountain springs preserve, refresh and bless mankind. The cloud does not mantle forests and fields, but it sends down its showers to be their life. The springs do not turn wheels and push paddles, but, uniting their waters into rivulets and brooks, they pour down their forces to give us thrift, vitality and power. Such a union of spiritual and temporal things, of Church and State, of religion and politics, is the need and promised redemption of the world. The souls of men are in bondage under sin. Every soul by right is God's. Within his realm, made royal by the blood of Christ, we become kings. The mission of the Church is to free imprisoned kings. Doing this, she offers to the nation loyal subjects, loyal citizens, and so the republic will become safe and enduring.

Again: *The perpetuity of the republic is guarded by free education.* Free from sectarian control, established as they were, and perpetuated, as they have been, to give our children a knowledge of those rudiments that encourage them to industry, virtue, and the practice of duty, let us maintain them still endowed with their original purity and strength. And while we provide instruction in the sciences and in the arts, let us, as in times past, but more earnestly, teach the sciences of God as revealed in the Bible. Let us have no sectarian dogmas; they are born of man and not of God. The Bible is God's book, and therefore cannot be sectarian. No gift of our Father is sectarian. You might as well talk of sectarian rocks and trees, of sectarian soil, of sectarian oceans and stars, of a sectarian sun, as of a sectarian Bible. Will you deny the artisan's apprentice a knowledge of gold and diamonds? They are the gift of God. His laws are within and upon them. The boy must look upon them, handle them, and work upon them, if you would have him skilled in preparing them for use. We give open books in regard to the laws and duties of daily life. So let us give God's revelation, in which are the diamonds of thought and the gold of life. "Hear, ye children, the instruction of a father, and attending to know understanding."

Another guard of our liberties is *a free press:*

> "The press all lands shall sing!
> The press, the press we bring
>   All lands to bless!
> O pallid want! O labor stark!
> Behold we bring the second ark—
>   The press, the press, the press."

Apprehending its high mission, it becomes the nurse of arts; it becomes the strong fence against wrong and oppression. Upon it, as among the mightiest of human means, the arm of progress leans. Those who love right and virtue groan under the burden of an impure press. It has cursed this land. Its day is not yet passed. But, despite all these, the times are auspicious for a purer press:

> "There are, thank heaven!
> A noble troop, to whom this trust is given—
> Who, all unbribed, on Freedom's altar stand
> Faithful and firm, bright warders of the land.
> By them still lifts the press its arm abroad
> To guide all eager men along life's road;
> To cheer young genius—pity's tear to start,
> In truth's bold cause to rouse each fearless heart;
> O'er male and female quacks to shake the rod,
> And scourge the unsex'd thing that scorns her God;
> To hunt corruption from her sacred den,
> And show the monster up, the gaze of wondering men!"

Another guard of our republic is found in the *integrity of its men of business*. A nation can long survive a prostration of its business. It can endure the shocks of war for a generation, if its business men are firm in principle; nay, it will escape many wars, and be free from the depression of hard times if its manufacturers and tradesmen tell the truth when they buy and sell. In times of financial embarrassment, the despondent people are prone to believe that all her manufacturers and tradesmen are dishonest. It is not so; it has never been so in this nation. The cities and villages of our broad land are made thrifty and safe by thousands upon thousands of honorable, upright, true men, whose word is as good as their bond; and they stand against universal ruin, as the shores of the sea against the surging and the tides. Let confidence be established (and there is reason for it), let discretion prevail, and this nation enters upon a growing career of business prosperity.

If you saw a hundred cables stretching from great tossing ships and converging toward one point which was yet unseen: if you saw the ships, under this power, meeting the waves and defeating the tides, you would say there was a strong anchor under the waters. If some of the ships should throw loose their cables and go to ruin, you would not suspect cable or anchor of weakness. So in the business interests of our land, our best men have made their moorings upon the sound basis of integrity. Let us trust them, and they will not only save the nation but increase its strength.

Another guard to our liberties is the *elective franchise*. It is safer to trust the great mass of the people, if they be industrious and virtuous, than to trust a few statesmen. The wants, aspirations, hopes and desires of a great people will be better voiced by the multitude, with their right to speak through the newspaper and the ballot-box, than by a few choice men of the educated class. The elective franchise is not an inalienable right, such as "life, liberty, and the pursuit of happiness," but it is an essential to a democratic government. It is, we believe, an essential to the best government, and, if limited by wise restrictions, it will generally be found that in times of national danger or disaster, when the issues are clearly set forth, the people of such a nation as this will speak with such directness, wisdom and patriotism, as well-nigh to establish the proverb: *Vox populi, Vox Dei.*"

The last guard of our nation's perpetuity I name, is *the home*. No race has a juster conception of home than the Anglo-Saxon. The dangers, sufferings and vicissitudes of two hundred and fifty years have made the typical American home the place of rest and confidence. It is, with us, the miniature republic—where none are slaves, where all are free. The republic by its laws and honored customs guards it, making "every man's house his castle," but no State ever gave to homes what homes gave to the State. Our American homes, when they have reared an altar, upon which piety and patriotism place self as the best offering, have each been like fountains feeding our national life. They have been, like the roots of our forest trees, sources from which the vital current has flowed, to give to the tree of liberty a wider reach and deeper shade.—*Edward P. Ingersoll, D. D.*

OUR COUNTRY.

Y country! 'tis of thee,
Sweet land of liberty,
 Of thee I sing:
Land where my fathers died!
Land of the pilgrims' pride!
From every mountain side
 Let freedom ring!

My native country, thee,
Land of the noble, free,
 Thy name I love;
I love thy rocks and rills;
Thy woods and templed hills;
My heart with rapture thrills
 Like that above.

Let music swell the breeze,
And ring from all the trees
 Sweet freedom's song:
Let mortal tongues awake;
Let all that breathe partake;
Let rocks their silence break,
 The sound prolong.

Our fathers' God! to Thee,
Author of Liberty,
 To Thee we sing.
Long may our land be bright
With Freedom's holy light;
Protect us by thy might,
 Great God, our King!

—*Samuel F. Smith.*

OUR NATIONAL BANNER.

ALL hail to our glorious ensign: courage to the heart, and strength to the hand, to which, in all time, it shall be intrusted! May it ever wave in honor, in unsullied glory and patriotic hope, on the dome of the Capitol, on the country's stronghold, on the entented plain, on the wave-rocked topmast, wherever, on the earth's surface, the eye of the American shall behold it! On whatsoever spot it is planted, there may freedom have a foothold, humanity a brave champion, and religion an altar. Though stained with blood in a righteous cause, may it never in any cause be stained with shame. Alike, when its gorgeous folds shall wanton in lazy holiday triumphs on the summer breeze, and its battered fragments be dimly seen through the clouds of war, may it be the joy and pride of the American heart. First raised in the cause of right and liberty, in that cause alone may it forever spread out its streaming blazonry to the battle and the storm. Having been borne victoriously across the continent, and on every sea, may virtue and freedom and peace forever follow where it leads the way.—*Alexander H. Everett.*

HISTORY OF OUR FLAG.

THE history of our glorious old flag is of exceeding interest, and brings back to us a throng of sacred and thrilling associations. The banner of St. Andrew was blue, charged with a white altier or cross in the form of the letter X, and was used in Scotland as early as the eleventh century. The banner of St. George was white, charged with the red cross, and was used in England as early as the first part of the fourteenth century. By a royal proclamation, dated April 12, 1700, these two crosses were joined together upon the same banner, forming the ancient national flag of England. It was not until Ireland, in 1801, was made a part of Great Britain, that the present national flag of England, so well known as the union jack, was completed. But it was the ancient flag of England that constituted the basis of our American banner. Various other flags had, indeed, been raised at other times by our colonial ancestors. But they were not particularly associated with, or at least, were not incorporated into, and made a part of, the destined "Stars and Stripes." It was after Washington had taken command of the fresh army of the Revolution, at Cambridge, that (January 2, 1776) he unfolded before them the new flag of thirteen stripes of alternate red and white, having upon one of its corners the red and white crosses of St. George and St. Andrew, on a field of blue. And this was the standard which was borne into the city of Boston when it was evacuated by the British troops and was entered by the American army. Uniting, as it did, the flags of England and

America, it showed that the colonists were not yet prepared to sever the tie that bound them to the mother country. By that union of flags they claimed to be a vital and substantial part of the empire of Great Britain, and demanded the rights and privileges which such a relation implied. Yet it was by these thirteen stripes that they made known the union *also* of the thirteen colonies, the stripes of white declaring the purity and innocence of their cause, and the stripes of red giving forth defiance to cruelty and oppression.

On the 14th day of June, 1777, it was resolved by Congress, "That the flag of the thirteen United States be thirteen stripes, alternate red and white, and that the union be thirteen white stars in the blue field." This resolution was made public September 3, 1776, and the flag that was first made and used in pursuance of it was that which led the Americans to victory at Saratoga. Here the thirteen stars were arranged in a circle, as we sometimes see them now, in order better to express the idea of the union of the States. In 1794, there having been two more new States added to the Union, it was voted that the alternate stripes, as well as the circling stars, be fifteen in number, and the flag, as thus altered and enlarged, was the one which was borne through all the contests of the war of 1812. But it was thought that the flag would at length become too large if a new stripe should be added with every freshly admitted State. It was therefore enacted, in 1818, that a permanent return should be made to the original number of thirteen stripes, and that the number of stars should henceforth correspond to the growing number of States. Thus the flag would symbolize the Union as it might be at any given period of its history, and also as it was at the very hour of its birth. It was at the same time suggested that these stars, instead of being arranged in a circle, be formed into a single star—a suggestion which we occasionally see adopted. In fine, no particular order seems now to be observed with respect to the arrangement of the constellation. It is enough if only the whole number be there upon that azure field—the blue to be emblematical of perseverance, vigilance and justice, each star to signify the glory of the State it may represent, and the whole to be eloquent forever of a Union that must be "one and inseparable."—*Rev. Alfred P. Putnam.*

THE AMERICAN FLAG.

WHEN Freedom from her mountain height,
   Unfurl'd her standard to the air,
She tore the azure robe of night,
   And set the stars of glory there.
She mingled with its gorgeous dyes
The milky baldric of the skies,
And striped its pure celestial white
With streakings of the morning light.
Then, from his mansion in the sun,
She called her eagle-bearer down,
And gave into his mighty hand
The symbol of her chosen land!

Majestic monarch of the cloud,
   Who rear'st aloft the regal form,
To hear the tempest trumpings loud,
   And see the lightning lances driven.
When strive the warriors of the storm,
And rolls the thunder drum of heaven,—
Child of the Sun! to thee 'tis given

To guard the banner of the free.
To hover in the sulphur smoke,
To ward away the battle stroke,
And bid its blendings shine afar,
Like rainbows on the cloud of war,
  The harbingers of Victory!

Flag of the brave! thy folds shall fly,
 The sign of hope and triumph high!
When speaks the signal trumpet tone,
 And the long line comes gleaming on,
Ere yet the life-blood, warm and wet,
Has dimm'd the glistening bayonet,
Each soldier's eye shall brightly turn
To where the sky-born glories burn,
And as his springing steps advance,
Catch war and vengeance from the glance.
And when the cannon, mouthing loud,
Heave in wild wreaths the battle shroud,
And gory sabres rise and fall
Like shoots of flame on midnight pall,
Then shall thy meteor glances glow,
And cowering foes shall sink beneath
Each gallant arm that strikes below
  That lovely messenger of death.

Flag of the seas! on ocean wave
Thy stars shall glitter o'er the brave;
When death, careering on the gale,
Sweeps darkly round the bellied sail,
And frightened waves rush wildly back
Before the broadside's reeling rack,
Each dying wanderer of the sea
Shall look at once to heaven and thee,
And smile to see thy splendors fly
In triumph o'er his closing eye.

Flag of the free heart's hope and home,
  By angel hands to valor given;
Thy stars have lit the welkin dome,
  And all thy hues were born in heaven.
Forever float that standard sheet,
  Where breathes the foe that falls before us.
With Freedom's soil beneath our feet,
  And Freedom's banner streaming o'er us.
                        —*Joseph Rodman Drake.*

GOD bless the flag! let it float, and fill
The sky with its beauty—our heart-strings thrill
To the low, sweet chant of its wind-swept bars,
And the chorus of all its clustered stars.
Embrace it, O mothers, and heroes shall grow,
While its colors blush warm on your bosoms of snow.
Defend it, O fathers, there's no sweeter death
Than to float its fair folds with a soldier's last breath;
And love it, O children, be true to the sires
Who wove it in vain by the old camp-fires.
                        —*Samuel L. Simpson.*

OUR FLAG A POWER.

OUR flag is a power everywhere. One has justly said, "It is known, respected, and feared round the entire globe. Wherever it goes, it is the recognized symbol of intelligence, equality, freedom and Christian civilization. Wherever it goes, the immense power of this Republic goes with it, and the hand that touches the honor of the flag touches the honor of the Republic itself. On Spanish soil, a man entitled to the protection of our government was arrested and condemned to die. The American consul interceded for his life, but was told that the man must suffer death. The hour appointed for the execution came, and Spanish guns, gleaming in the sunlight, were ready for the work of death. At that critical moment the American consul took our flag and folded its stars and stripes around the person of the doomed man, and then turning to the soldiers, said, "Men, remember that a single shot through that flag will be avenged by the entire power of the American Republic." **That shot was** never fired, and that man, around whom the shadows of death were gathering, was saved by the stars and the stripes. Dear old flag! Thou art a power at home and abroad. Our fathers loved thee in thine infancy, our heroic dead loved thee, and we love thee, and fondly clasp thee to our hearts to-day. All thy stars gleam like gems of beauty on thy brow, and all thy stripes beam upon the eye like bows of promise to the nation.

Wave on, thou peerless, matchless, banner of the free! Wave on, over the army and the navy, over the land and the sea, over the cottage and the palace, over the school and the church, over the living and the dead; wave *ever more*

"O'er the land of the free and the home of the brave."

—Rev. H. H. Birkins.

People of the United States, humanity expects that your glorious Republic will prove to the world that republics are formed on virtue. It expects to see you the guardians of the law of humanity.—*Louis Kossuth.*

THE STAR-SPANGLED BANNER.

OH! say, can you see, by the dawn's early light,
    What so proudly we hailed at the twilight's last
        gleaming?
    Whose broad stripes and bright stars through the perilous fight
        O'er the ramparts we watched were so gallantly
        streaming;
    And the rockets' red glare, the bombs bursting in air,
    Gave proof through the night that our flag was still there;
Oh! say, does that star-spangled banner yet wave
O'er the land of the free and the home of the brave?

On the shore, dimly seen through the mists of the deep,
    Where the foe's haughty host in dread silence reposes,
What is that which the breeze, o'er the towering steep,
    As it fitfully blows, half conceals, half discloses?
Now it catches the gleam of the morning's first beam,
In full glory reflected now shines on the stream;
    'Tis the star-spangled banner! oh! long may it wave
    O'er the land of the free and the home of the brave!

And where is that band, who so vauntingly swore
    That the havoc of war and the battle's confusion
A home and a country should leave us no more?
    Their blood has washed out their foul footsteps' pollution.
No refuge could save the hireling and slave,
From the terror of death and the gloom of the grave;
    And the star-spangled banner in triumph shall wave
    O'er the land of the free and the home of the brave!

Oh! thus be it ever, when freemen shall stand
    Between their loved homes and the war's desolation;

Blest with victory and peace, may the heaven-rescued land
   Praise the power that has made and preserved us a nation.
Then conquer we must, for our cause it is just,
And this be our motto, "In God is our trust,"
   And the star-spangled banner in triumph shall wave
   O'er the land of the free and the home of the brave!
                              —*Francis Scott Key.*

THE UTOPIA OF CHRISTIANITY.

IT was the fashion fifty years ago to speak of this Constitution as almost a miracle of human wisdom. Of late there seems to be a disposition to regard it a very commonplace affair. The estimate of fifty years ago is much more nearly correct. It was a miracle not only of human wisdom but of Divine teaching. It was the fruit of centuries of the teaching and training of mankind. It was the product of no one mind or class of minds. It was the result of providential circumstances, quite as much as of human thought. It was the work of many centuries and of many men. It was the work of God as well as of men. It was the practical embodiment of the great law of love, in the civil state. It was by far the best translation the world had ever seen, or has seen as yet, the great ideal of democracy—the Utopia of Christianity—into actual institutions and practicable government.—*Rev. John P. Gulliver.*

As once he sat over against the treasury, so now Christ sits over against the ballot box to see what his disciples cast therein."—*Mary Allen West.*

OUR CONSTITUTION WITHOUT PARALLEL.

THE Constitution of the United States, a document of rare, in many respects matchless excellence, prior to its modification by the Thirteenth, Fourteenth and Fifteenth Amendments, is now certainly without parallel in the history of mankind, as an enunciation of organic law; and every American, whatever his political bias or party affiliations, must experience special pleasure in knowing that no other nation of ancient or modern times has been given the genius or the heart to produce such a document, and to establish in accordance therewith a government which in its forms and results realizes so nearly our idea of that perfect government, the subjects of which, while they enjoy the amplest possible freedom, pursue their several occupations, assured of the largest protection to life, liberty and property.—*Prof. John Mercer Langston.*

ORIGIN OF OUR CONSTITUTION.

WHATEVER we may think of it now, the Constitution had its immediate origin in the conviction of the necessity of this uniformity or identity, in commercial regulations.

The whole history of the country, of every year and every month, from the close of the war of the revolution to 1789, proves this. Over whatever other interests it was made to extend, and whatever other blessings it now does or hereafter may confer on the millions of free citizens who do or shall live under its protection; even though, in time to come, it should raise a pyramid of power and grandeur, whose apex should look down on the loftiest political structures of other nations and other ages, it will yet be true that it was itself the child of pressing commercial necessity. Unity and identity of commerce among all the States was its seminal principle. It had been found absolutely impossible to excite or foster enterprise in trade under the influence of discordant and jarring State regulations. The country was losing all the advantages of its position. The revolution itself was beginning to be regarded as a doubtful blessing. The ocean before us was a barren waste. No American canvas whitened its bosom—no keels of ours ploughed its waters. The journals of the Congress of the Confederation show the most constant, unceasing, unwearied, but always unsuccessful appeals to the States and the people to renovate the system, to infuse into that confederation at once a spirit of union and a spirit of activity, by conferring on Congress the power over trade. By nothing but the perception of its indispensable necessity—by nothing but their consciousness of suffering from its want, were the States and the people brought, and brought by slow degrees, to invest this power in a permanent and competent government.

Sir, hearken to the fervent language of the old Congress, in July, 1785, in a letter addressed to the States, prepared by Mr. Monroe, Mr. King, and other great names now transferred from the lists of living men to the records which carry down the fame of the distinguished dead. The proposition before them, the great object to which they so solicitously endeavored to draw the attention of the States, was this, viz.:

that, "the United States, in Congress assembled, should have the sole and exclusive right of regulating the trade of the States, as well with foreign nations as with each other." This, they say, is urged upon the States by every consideration of local as well as of federal policy; and they beseech them to agree to it if they wish to promote the strength of the union, and to connect it by the strongest ties of interest and affection. This was in July, 1785.

In the same spirit, and for the same end, was that most important resolution which was adopted in the House of Delegates of Virginia, on the 21st day of the following January. Sir, I read the resolution entire:

"*Resolved*, That Edmund Randolph and others be appointed commissioners, who, or any five of whom, shall meet such commissioners as may be appointed by the other States in the Union, at a time and place to be agreed on, to take into consideration the trade of the United States; to examine the relative situations and trade of the said States; to consider how far a uniform system in their commercial regulations may be necessary to their common interest and their permanent harmony, and to report to the several States such an act relative to this great object, as, when unanimously ratified by them, will enable the United States, in Congress assembled, effectually to provide for the same; that the said commissioners shall immediately transmit to the several States copies of the preceding resolution, with a circular letter requesting their concurrence therein, and proposing a time and place for the meeting aforesaid."

Here, sir, let us pause. Let us linger at the waters of this original fountain. Let us contemplate this, the first step, in that series of proceedings, so full of great events to us and to the world. Notwithstanding the embarrassment and distress of the country, the recommendation of the old Congress had been complied with. Every attempt to bring the State legislatures into any harmony of action, or any pursuit of a common object, had signally and disastrously failed. The exigency of the case called for a new movement—for a more direct and powerful attempt to bring the good sense and patriotism of the country into action upon the crisis. A solemn assembly was therefore proposed—a general convention of delegates from all the States. And now, sir, what was the exigency? What was this crisis? Look at the resolution itself; there is not an idea in it but trade. Commerce! commerce! is the beginning and end of it. The subject to be considered and examined was "the relative situation of the trade of the States," and the object to be obtained was "the establishment of a uniform system in their commercial regulations, as necessary to the common interest and their permanent harmony." This is all. And, sir, by the adoption of this ever-memorable resolution, the House of Delegates of Virginia, on the 21st day of January, 1786, performed the first act in the train of measures which resulted in that Constitution, under the authority of which you now sit in that chair, and I have now the honor of addressing the members of this body.

Mr. President, I am a Northern man. I am attached to one of the States of the North, by the ties of birth and parentage, education, and the associations of early life, and by sincere gratitude for proofs of public confidence early bestowed. I am bound to another Northern State by adoption, by long residence, by all the cords of social and domestic life, and by an attachment and regard springing from her manifestation of approbation and favor, which grapple me to her with hooks of steel. And yet, sir, with the same sincerity of respect, the same deep gratitude, the same reverence and hearty good-will with which I would pay a similar tribute to either of these States, do I here acknowledge the Commonwealth of Virginia to be entitled to the honor of commencing the work of establishing this Constitution. The honor is hers; let her enjoy it; let her forever wear it proudly; there is not a brighter jewel in the tiara that adorns her brow. Let this resolution stand, illustrating her records, and blazoning her name through all time!

The meeting, sir, proposed by the resolution was holden. It took place, as all know, in Annapolis, in May of the same year; but it was thinly attended, and its members, very wisely, adopted measures to bring about a fuller and more general convention. Their letter to the States on this occasion is full of instruction. It shows their sense of the unfortunate condition of the country. In their meditations on the subject, they saw the extent to which the commercial power must necessarily extend. The sagacity of New Jersey had led her, in agreeing to the original proposition of Virginia, to enlarge the object of the appointment of commissioners, so as to embrace not only commercial regulations *but other important matters*. This suggestion the commissioners adopted because they thought, as they inform us, "that the power of regulating trade is of such comprehensive extent, and will enter so far into the general system of the Federal government, so that to give it efficacy and to obviate questions and doubts concerning its precise nature and limits, might require a correspondent adjustment of other parts of the Federal system." Here you see, sir, that other powers, such as are now in the Constitution, were expected to branch out of the necessary commercial power; and, therefore, the letter of the commissioners concludes with recommending a general convention "to take into consideration the *whole* situation of the *United States*, and to devise further provisions as should appear necessary to render the Constitution of the Federal government adequate to the exigencies of the Union."

The result of that convention was the present Constitution. And yet, in the midst of all this flood of light respecting its original objects and purposes, and with all the adequate powers which it confers, we abandon the commerce of the country, we betray its interests, we turn ourselves away from its most crying necessities. Sirs, it will be a fact, stamped in deep and dark lines upon our annals; it will be a truth, which in all time can never be denied or evaded, that if this Constitution shall not, now and hereafter, be so administered as to maintain a uniform system in all matters of trade; if it shall not protect and regulate the commerce of the country, in all its great interest, in its foreign intercourse, in its domestic intercourse, in its navigation, in its currency, in everything which fairly belongs to the whole idea of commerce, either as an end, an agent, or an instrument, then that Constitution will have failed, utterly failed to accomplish the precise, distinct, original object, in which it had its being.

In matters of trade we were no longer to be Georgians, Virginians, Pennsylvanians, or Massachusetts men. We were to have but one commerce of the United States. There were not to be separate flags, waving over separate commercial systems. There was to be one flag, the *E Pluribus Unum;* and toward that was to be that rally of united interests and affections, which our fathers had so earnestly invoked.

Mr. President, this unity of commercial regulation is, in

in my opinion, indispensable to the safety of the union of the States themselves. In peace, it is its strongest tie. I care not, sir, on what side, or in which of its branches, it may be attacked. Every successful attack upon it, made anywhere, weakens the whole, and renders the next assault easier and more dangerous. Any denial of its just power is an attack upon it. We attack it, most fiercely attack it, whenever we say we will not exercise the powers which it enjoins. If the court had yielded to the pretensions of respectable States upon the subject of steam navigation, and to the retaliatory proceedings of other States; if retreat and excuse, and disavowal of power had been prevailing sentiments then, in what condition at this moment, let me ask, would the steam navigation of the country be found? To us, sir, to us, his countrymen, to us, who feel so much admiration for his genius, and so much gratitude for his services, Fulton would have lived almost in vain. State grants and State exclusions would have covered over all our waters.

Sir, it is in the nature of such things, that the first violation, or the first departure from true principles, draws more important violations or departures after it; and the first surrender of just authority will be followed by others more to be deplored. If commerce be a unit, to break it in any one part is to decree its ultimate dismemberment in all. If there be made a first chasm, though it be small, through that the whole wild ocean will pour in, and we may then throw up embankments in vain.

Sir, the spirit of union is particularly liable to temptation and seduction, in moments of peace and prosperity. In war, this spirit is strengthened by a sense of common danger, and by a thousand recollections of ancient efforts and ancient glory in a common cause. In the calms of a long peace, and in the absence of all apparent causes of alarm, things near gain an ascendency over things remote. Local interests and feelings overshadow national sentiments. Our attention, our regard, and our attachment are every moment solicited to what touches us closest, and we feel less and less the attraction of a distant orb. Such tendencies we are bound by true patriotism, and by our love of union, to resist. This is our duty; and the moment, in my judgment, has arrived when that duty is summoned to action. We hear every day sentiments and arguments which would become a meeting of envoys, employed by separate governments, more than they become the common legislature of a united country. Constant appeals are made to local interests, to geographical distinctions, and to the policy and the pride of particular States. It would sometimes appear that it was, or as if it were, a settled purpose to convince the people that our union is nothing but a jumble of different and discordant interests, which must, ere long, be all returned to their original state of separate existence; as if, therefore, it was of no great value while it should last, and was not likely to last long. The process of disintegration begins by urging the fact of different interests.

· Sir, is not the end obvious, to which all this leads us? Who does not see that, if convictions of this kind take possession of the public mind, our Union can hereafter be nothing, while it remains but a conclusion without harmony; a bond without affection; a theatre for the angry contests of local feelings, local objects, and local jealousies? Even while it continues to exist in name, it may, by these means, become nothing but the mere form of a united government. My children, and the children of those who sit around me, may meet, perhaps, in this chamber in the next generation;

but if tendencies, now but too obvious, be not checked, they will meet as strangers and aliens. They will feel no sense of common interest or common country :. they will cherish no common object of patriotic love. If the same Saxon language shall fall from their lips, it may be the chief proof that they belong to the same nation. Its vital principle exhausted, now productive only of strife and contention, and no longer sustained by a sense of common interest, the Union itself must ultimately fall, dishonored and unlamented.— *Daniel Webster.*

THE CONSTITUTION.

GREAT were the hearts, and strong the minds
    Of those who framed, in high debate,
The immortal league of love, that binds
    Our fair broad Empire, State with State.

And deep the gladness of the hour,
    When, as the auspicious task was done,
In solemn trust, the sword of power,
    Was given to glory's unspoiled son.

That noble race is gone; the suns
    Of sixty years have risen and set;
But the bright links, those chosen ones
    So strongly forged, are brighter yet.

Wide, as our own free race increase—
    Wide shall extend the elastic chain,
And bind in everlasting peace,
    State after State—a mighty train.

                              —*W. C. Bryant.*

THE POSITION OF OUR FLAG.

WE will take our glorious flag—the flag of our country —and nail it just below the cross! This is high enough! There let it wave as it waved of old! Around it let us gather. First Christ, and then our country.
—*Bishop Simpson.*

AMERICAN CITIZENSHIP.

AMERICAN citizenship is of more noble birth than either Greek or Roman, or modern European. It is the offspring of absolute freedom, political and religious, which guarantees to nations the highest development, socially, morally and intellectually. That freedom is founded upon the great truth that "all men are created equal." It is no respecter of persons, sex or condition. It is the outgrowth of a principle of action lying deep in every human breast, formulated by the words —"The right of private judgment."

All through the ages—Pagan, Jew and Christian—this principle had been suppressed by autocrats, by governments, by religions, by persecutions. It was so completely smothered by the Church at the beginning of the sixteenth century, that enlightened reason could no longer endure the thraldom; and at the diet of Spires three hundred and fifty years ago, Luther and his associates publicly protested against the repression, and boldly proclaimed the great principle of free agency, upon which the reformation rests—the right of private judgment in matters of religion.

This proclamation was an electric spark which thrilled the intellect of the Western nations of Europe. Thoughtful men everywhere inquired: "If there shall be freedom in the Church, why not in the state? Has a king at the head of the state a better right to mould my thoughts or control my actions, than a pontiff, at the head of a church?"

> "If I'm yon haughty lordling's slave
> By Nature's law designed,
> Why was an independent wish
> E'er planted in my mind?"

This thought was the seed of republicanism, planted in generous soil. It widely germinated in France, Italy, Germany and England; and it soon blossomed and bore fruit in Holland. In England it assumed the aspect of non-conformity to the discipline of the Church, and for more than half a century the recusants felt the scourge of persecution. Finally, the sufferers fled to the wilds of America, where the grand ideas of religious and political liberty might crystallize into a commonwealth of free men.

Zealous sectarians in theology, the Puritans in America so hedged the idea of personal independence, that for more than a century its expansion seemed almost hopeless. Then the walls of bigotry began to crumble, and soon afterward there was fixed upon American soil, the language, the manners, the ideas, the religion and the institutions which characterized our nation in its infancy. Crude at first was the structure formed of these materials; but they were sound and strong, and the architecture was symmetrical in proportion.

The emigrants, especially those of Germanic lineage, cherished in their minds traditions of local self-government before the crown and the mitre usurped the inalienable rights of man. One principle pervaded the primeval polity of the Goths, namely, "Where the law was administered the law was made." This policy had prevailed in ancient England, manifested by the territorial divisions of tythings, hundreds, boroughs, counties, and shires, in which the body of the inhabitants had a voice in managing their own affairs. These traditions lingered in the minds of the emigrants, and suggested independence controlled by order.

When impatient "strangers"—not Pilgrims proper—on board the "Mayflower" declared that as their charter did not apply to New England, there would be no authority to exercise the powers of government over them, and that when they got on shore they would do as they pleased, Brewster and Bradford and Clark and young Winslow and others determined to effectually repress this riotous spirit. They drew up a covenant which was signed by nearly every man of the little company before they landed—forty-one in number—solemnly combining themselves into a civil body politic. This was the first written constitution of government ever signed by a whole people. It was a pure democracy. It was the germ of American citizenship.

In time a grander idea was developed: that of a republican government of all the municipalities as one—*E Pluribus Unum*—upon the principle of the sovereignty of the people. Mutual protection against the forest barbarians called for combined action, and the New England Confederacy was formed in the seventeenth century, which lasted forty years. That was the germ of the American Republic.

At length mutual protection against the oppression of the imperial government called for combined action, and on the 2d of July, 1776, the assembled representatives of thirteen

English-American provinces *"Resolved,* That these united colonies are, and of right ought to be, free and independent States; that they are absolved from all allegiance to the British crown, and that all political connection between them and the state of Great Britain is, and ought to be, totally dissolved." The colonies assumed the title of " United States of America." That was the birthday of the Republic.

In the summer and early autumn of 1787 a body of fundamental laws of the land was framed by representatives of the States, and ninety-two years ago this week it was signed by them. That Constitution was ratified by the people the next year.

Then our nation was formed, vigorous and powerful; then American citizenship assumed an importance never before known. Every citizen—which term included every person not of Indian or African blood—became a co-equal in the State. This, in brief, is the genesis of this glorious free government of which we are citizens.—*Benson J. Lossing, LL. D.*

THE DUTY OF AMERICAN CITIZENS.

AND now, fellow-citizens, let us not retire from this occasion without a deep and solemn conviction of the duties which have devolved upon us. This lovely land, this glorious liberty, these benign institutions, the dear purchase of our fathers, are ours; ours to enjoy, ours to preserve, ours to transmit. Generations past, and generations to come, hold us responsible for the sacred trust. Our fathers, from behind, admonish us, with their anxious paternal voices—posterity calls out to us, from the bosom of the future—the world turns hither its solicitous eye—all, all, conjure us to act wisely and faithfully, in the relation which we sustain. We can never, indeed, pay the debt which is upon us; but by virtue, by morality, by religion, by the cultivation of every good principle and every good habit, we may hope to enjoy the blessing, through our day, and leave it unimpaired to our children. Let us feel deeply how much, of what we are and of what we possess, we owe to this liberty and these institutions of government. Nature has, indeed, given us a soil, which yields bounteously to the hand of industry; the mighty and fruitful ocean is before us, and the skies over our heads shed health and vigor. But what are lands, and seas, and skies to civilized man without society, without knowledge, without morals, without religious culture; and how can these be enjoyed, in all their extent, and all their excellence, but under the protection of wise institutions and a free government? Fellow-citizens, there is not one of us, there is not one of us here present, who does not, at this moment, and at every moment, experience, in his own condition, and in the condition of those most near and dear to him, the influence and the benefits of this liberty and these institutions. Let us then acknowledge the blessing, let us feel it deeply and powerfully, let us cherish a strong affection for it, and resolve to maintain and perpetuate it. The blood of our fathers, let it not have been shed in vain; the great hope of posterity, let it not be blasted.—*Daniel Webster*.

What the ark was to Israel the ballot should be to the American people, and their love of liberty should act like a divine presence to palsy the hand that profanes it.

—*Rev. R. A. Holland.*

DUTY TO THE STATE.

OUR country is a whole, my Publius,
Of which we all are parts: nor should a citizen
Regard his interest as distinct from hers:
No hopes or fears should touch his patriot soul,
But what affects her honor or her shame.
E'en when in hostile field he bleeds to save,
'Tis not his blood he loses, 'tis his country's;
He only pays her back a debt he owes.
To her he's bound for birth and education;
Her laws secure him from domestic feuds,
And from the foreign foe her arms protect him.
She lends him honors, dignity, and rank,
His wrongs revenges, and his merit pays;
And, like a tender and indulgent mother,
Loads him with comforts, and would make his state
As blessed as nature and the gods designed it.
Such gifts, my son, have their alloy of pain;
And let the unworthy wretch, who will not bear
His portion of the public burden, lose
The advantages it yields; let him retire
From the dear blessings of a social life,
And from the sacred laws which guard those blessings,
Renounce the civilized abodes of man,
With kindred brutes one common shelter seek
In horrid wilds, and dens, and dreary caves,
And with their shaggy tenants share the spoil;
Or, if the shaggy hunters miss their prey,
From scattered acorns pick a scanty meal;
Far from the sweet civilities of life,
There let him live and vaunt his wretched freedom,
While we, obedient to the laws that guard us,
Guard them, and live or die, as they decree.

—Hannah More.

THE BALLOT-BOX.

I AM aware that the ballot-box is not everywhere a consistent symbol; but to a large degree it is so. I know what miserable associations cluster around this instrument of popular power. I know that the arena in which it stands is trodden into mire by the feet of reckless ambition and selfish greed. The wire-pulling and the bribing, the pitiful truckling and the grotesque compromises, the exaggeration and the detraction, the melodramatic issues and the sham patriotism, the party watchwords and the party nicknames, the schemes of the few paraded as the will of the many, the elevation of men whose only worth is in the votes they command—*vile* men whose hands you would not grasp in friendship, whose presence you would not tolerate by your fireside—incompetent men, whose fitness is not in their capacity as functionaries, or legislators, but as organ-pipes; the snatching at the slices and offal of office, the intemperance and the violence, the finesse and the falsehood, the gin and the glory; *these* are indeed but too closely identified with that political agitation which circles around the ballot-box.

But, after all, they are not *essential* to it. They are only the masks of a genuine grandeur and importance. For it *is* a grand thing—something which involves profound doctrines of right; something which has cost ages of effort and sacrifice; it is a grand thing that here, at last, each voter has just the weight of one man; no more, no less; and the *weakest*, by virtue of his recognized manhood, is as *strong* as the *mightiest*. And consider, for a moment, what it is to cast a vote. It is the token of inestimable privileges, and involves the responsibilities of an hereditary trust. It has passed into your hands as a right, reaped from fields of suffering and blood. The grandeur of history is represented in your act. Men have wrought with pen and tongue, and pined in dungeons, and died on scaffolds that you might obtain this symbol of freedom, and enjoy this consciousness of a sacred individuality. To the ballot have been transmitted, as it were, the dignity of the sceptre and the potency of the sword.

And that which is so potent as a *right* is also pregnant as a *duty;* a duty for the present and for the future. If you will, that folded leaf becomes a tongue of justice, a voice of order, a force of imperial law; securing rights, abolishing abuses, erecting new institutions of truth and love. And, however you will, it is the expression of a solemn responsibility, the exercise of an immeasurable power for good or for evil, now and hereafter. It is the medium through which you act upon your country—the organic nerve which incorporates you with its life and welfare. There is no agent with which the possibilities of the republic are more intimately involved, none upon which we can fall back with more *confidence* than the ballot-box.—*E. H. Chapin.*

God sifted a whole nation that he might send choice grain over into this wilderness.—*Stoughton.*

A FREE ballot is the safeguard of republican institutions.
—*James G. Blaine.*

THE POOR VOTER ON ELECTION DAY.

THE proudest now is but my peer,
  The highest not more high;
To-day, of all the weary year,
  A king of men am I.
To-day alike are great and small,
  The nameless and the known;
My palace is the people's hall,
  The ballot-box my throne.

Who serves to-day upon the list
  Besides the served shall stand;
Alike the brown and wrinkled fist,
  The gloved and dainty hand.
The rich is level with the poor,
  The weak is strong to-day;
And sleekest broadcloth counts no more
  Than homespun frock of gray.

To-day let pomp and vain pretence
  My stubborn right abide;
I set a plain man's common sense
  Against the pedant's pride.
To-day shall simple manhood try
  The strength of gold and land;
The wide world has not wealth to buy
  The power in my right hand.

While there's a grief to seek redress,
  Or balance to adjust,—

Where weighs our living manhood less
  Than Mammon's vilest dust,—
While there's a right to need my vote,
  A wrong to sweep away,
Up! clouted knee and ragged coat,
  A man's a man to-day.
                —*John G. Whittier.*

CHANGES OF A CENTURY.

WHAT mighty changes have these one hundred years witnessed! The seed of liberty sown by our fathers has germinated and flourished even in the monarchies of Europe. Napoleon made all tremble with his hostile legions. Forty centuries looked down on his conquering armies from the pyramids of Egypt. France, the scene of so many revolutions, has become enrolled in the list of republics. Other nations, catching the shouts of freemen, have compelled the loosening of the reins of power. Thrones that have stood firmly for ages have been made to tremble upon their foundations. Austria, the land of tyranny and oppression, has compelled her emperor to abdicate. The Pope, whose election was hailed by the whole civilized world as the harbinger of a better administration, was hardly seated upon the throne before he fled in disguise from his pontifical halls, and St. Peter and the Vatican resounded with the triumphal shouts of an awakened nation. Hungary struggled for independence as a nation, and practically achieved it, so that to-day it lives under laws enacted by its own parliament, and accepts the emperor of Austria as king. Russia has emancipated her serfs and taken vast strides in her progress as a nation. China is no longer a walled nation, shut up from the rest of the world; with Japan she has opened her gates to the commerce of the world, and civilization has begun to loosen the scales from the eyes of hundreds of millions of people in these two nations, whose origin, as well as their knowledge in the arts and sciences, is lost in the dim ages of antiquity.

On the Western Continent we have in the war of 1812-15 asserted our right against England to travel the highways of the seas unmolested. The Saxons have conquered and dismembered Mexico. The most gigantic rebellion the world ever saw has been suppressed, and with it fell the institution of slavery. That foul blot upon the otherwise fair face of our constitution, less than a score of years ago, seemed firmly and irreversibly fastened upon the body politic. So steadily was it entrenched behind constitutional guarantees that there seemed no way by which it could be cured; and hence it was endured. But God in his mysterious providence permitted those whose rights were thus protected by constitutional guarantees to make war upon the government which protected them, and in the fratricidal struggle the shackles fell from the limbs of every slave. To-day the sun does not shine in all this mighty republic upon a single bondman. The same constitution and the same laws alike declare the equality of all men before the law without reference to previous condition of servitude, race or color.

In the physical world the progress in the arts and sciences has surpassed any conception which we were able to form. California outshines the wealth of India. We traverse the ocean in ships propelled by steam. The vast expanse of our land is covered by a net-work of iron rails reaching out in every direction. The hourly rate of speed has increased from five miles to thirty, and even to sixty. The world has been girdled with the electric wire. It reposes in safety on the bed of the great deep. On the wings of the lightning it conveys from land to land and shore to shore every moment the intelligence of man's thoughts and man's actions. Each new year has opened up some new improvement or discovery in the world of inventions, which fails me even to enumerate. And who shall say that a century hence the historian of that day will not be called upon to record the further discovery of wonders far surpassing any conception which we are able to form!

—*Judge Isaac W. Smith.*

A CENTURY'S PROGRESS.

AN American statesman travelling in Europe met a large company of distinguished Englishmen at a dinner party. "How many States are there in the Union?" one inquired of him across the table. The guests listened for his answer. With perfect calmness he replied, "I do not know." There was a moment of silence in contemplating such inexplicable ignorance. After the pause of a moment, which gave dramatic effect to his words, he added, "I have been absent for six months in a tour up the Nile. When I left home there were thirty-four States in the Union. How many have since been added I cannot tell." It is safe to say that not one-half who read this page can state with confidence how many stars there are now in our political constellation. It is like remembering the number of asteroids in the solar system.

When this government was established there were thirteen States; now we number, I think, thirty-eight States and ten Territories. Then our territory comprehended 820,680 square miles. Now there are embraced within our majestic realms 3,559,091 square miles—a fourfold increase.

The single State of Texas is larger than the whole empire of France. Mr. Emerson says that we could sink several of the monarchies of Europe in one of our lakes, and scarcely impede the navigation. A sturdy, wealthy backwoodsman, whose home was amid the boundless prairies of the far West, and who had returned from a tour of Europe, chanced to meet Thackeray, who was on a hunting trip upon the plains. To the inquiry of the illustrious novelist of how he liked England, the tourist replied: "Very well in the daytime, but I never dared to go out after dark from fear that I should step off."

The whole of our motherly little island, from whose arms we so rudely rushed one hundred years ago, could be laid down upon the State of Texas, leaving a border all around sixty miles broad.

We were, less than a hundred years ago, quite insignificant. Our pride was often mortified by questions put to us in Europe. The Pope, a third of a century ago, inquired of a distinguished New York clergyman, "What proportion of the inhabitants of the city of New York are native Indians?" A professor at Oxford, England, inquired of an American literary gentleman who had borne letters of introduction to him, "Can the Rocky Mountains be seen from the steeples of New York?" Twenty-five years ago the writer met a gentleman in one of the most aristocratic mansions of England. In the course of conversation the fact was alluded to that he was from America; the portly

Englishman raised both hands in astonishment, exclaiming: "From Hameriky! from Hameriky! God bless my soul! why you speak very good English!"

The first census was taken in the year 1790. The population then numbered 3,929,328. Of these 697,696 were slaves. The last census announces the population to have been then, six years ago, 38,580,371. Not a slave now treads our soil.

It has long been said that our government was but an experiment which would infallibly fail. It has emerged triumphantly from as severe an ordeal as any nation can be exposed to. It is now the strongest nation on this globe. There is not a throne in Europe which is not to-day menaced with perils far greater than any which we have to contemplate.

One hundred years ago Maine was an almost unbroken solitude. A few log-huts were scattered here and there along its rugged shores, and Indian tribes, silent, sullen and despairing, were passing away, amid her craggy coves and the glooms of her forests.

Nearly the whole of the interior of New York was the hunting-ground of savage tribes, numerous and ferocious, often perpetrating deeds of cruelty too horrible to be narrated. Pittsburg was a military post far away beyond the mountains. The morning sun, rising over the Alleghenies, spread its rays over the boundless and uninhabited realms beyond. But scarcely one ray of civilization had yet penetrated those glooms where States of imperial grandeur are now thriving. The largest part of Virginia was a dense forest, which the white man's foot had never yet explored. It required the toilsome journey of a fortnight to traverse the distance between Baltimore and Pittsburg.

Even the imagination of men had hardly travelled so far as to the regions beyond the Mississippi. Even as late as 1803 it was written: "The Missouri has been navigated for twenty-five hundred miles. There appears a probability of communication, by this channel, with the Western Ocean."

In November, 1776, according to the general statement, the illustrious Paul Jones, whose merit and achievements have never been adequately appreciated, raised our first naval flag, under a salute of thirteen guns. It consisted of thirteen stripes and of a rattlesnake coiled at the roots of a pine tree, with the motto in Latin, "Do not tread upon me." The naval fleet of the United States then consisted of but five small vessels. With this armament Paul Jones set sail to encounter the squadrons of England, then consisting of a thousand vessels, bearing armaments of many thousand guns.

France, in 1778, was the first nation which recognized the independence of the United States. Our beautiful banner of stars and stripes, a flag in whose folds are enshrined the dearest rights of humanity, was first honored by a national salute by a French fleet in Quiberon bay. It was on the 22d of February, 1778, that the heroic Paul Jones brought about this result.

In the year 1807 Fulton astonished the dwellers on the banks of the Hudson by driving his newly constructed steamboat, commonly called "Fulton's Folly," against the current at the rate of four or five miles an hour. This strange-looking craft was of one hundred and sixty tons burden. After a long voyage he succeeded in reaching Albany; but it was confidently asserted that he could never accomplish the feat again.

We need not here enter upon the vexed question of the origin of steamboats. In the childhood of the writer they were unknown. Somewhere about the year 1820, Captain Porter commenced running a little bug of a steamboat from Portland to Boston. As I remember the voyage occupied about twenty-four hours. Six passengers were considered a success. Probably some of the ancient men of Portland can give more accurate and interesting details.

In 1811 the steamboat "Orleans" was launched at Pittsburg, and descended to New Orleans in fourteen days. This was the first steamer that ever floated upon the waters of the Mississippi. But who can now count our floating palaces? Who can describe their palatial grandeur? Who can estimate the numbers who now, on the ocean and on the river, crowd their magnificent saloons? There is no other nation which can rival the United States in the number, grandeur and splendor of its steam-propelled marine.

—*John S. C. Abbott*, 1876.

INTELLECTUAL PROGRESS OF THE CENTURY.

WHILE in material progress our country has, in the last century, surpassed all nations, we can also, with justice say, our people have advanced more rapidly in general intelligence than those of any other country. The high tone of the masses may well be the honest boast of Americans. In general diffusion of knowledge, in moral and social rectitude, in domestic purity and comfort, the common people of our country stand in the foremost rank. If much of this is due to the emigration from Europe of the better and not the worst classes of its laboring population, and to the facility with which in the United States comfortable homes may be had, much, too, is due to our admirable system of common schools, our large circulation of newspapers and periodical literature, and our widely diffused and liberal religious teaching. The general intelligence is likewise cultivated by our political institutions. The public discussion on the hustings of political issues, the broad basis of suffrage, and the distribution to the very extremities of the nation of the powers of local government; and perhaps still more than all, the educating process of trial by jury, makes the government a popular school-master. All sexes and ages, through the workings of our system, are receiving instruction by the administration of the laws, and this is not the least of the merits of that administration. The citizen is not only made to feel that the government and the law are sacred, because created and administered by and for the people, but the sense of individual responsibility is cultivated and the range of popular thinking enlarged. So, too, the manifold forms and instruments of our industry promote popular culture. The omnipresence of the railroad, telegraph, printing-press, steam-engine, agricultural and mechanical implements and the myriad magic fingers of machinery, teach the people practical knowledge, and excite that wonder and curiosity which lead to many an advance in physical science; while fairs and expositions, social festivals, and public concerts and amusements give aid to the hearthstone, the school-room and the church, in that general culture which is the surest basis of public virtue, and the indispensable bulwark of free government.—*General Durbin Ward.*

THE EMBLEM OF OUR COUNTRY.

THIS distinguished bird, as he is the most beautiful of his tribe in this part of the world, and the adopted emblem of our country, is entitled to particular notice. The celebrated cataract of Niagara is a noted place of resort for the bald eagle, as well on account of the fish procured there as for the numerous carcasses of squirrels, deer, bears, and various other animals that, in their attempts to cross the river above the falls, have been dragged into the current and precipitated down that tremendous gulf, where, among the rocks that bound the rapids below, they furnish a rich repast for the vulture, the raven, and the bald eagle, the subject of the present account. He has been long known to naturalists, being common to both continents, and occasionally met with from very high northern latitudes to the borders of the torrid zone, but chiefly in the vicinity of the sea, and along the shores and cliffs of our lakes and large rivers. Formed by nature for braving the severest cold, feeding equally on the produce of the sea and of the land, possessing powers of flight capable of outstripping even the tempests themselves, unawed by anything but man, and from the ethereal heights to which he soars looking abroad at one glance on an immeasurable expanse of forests, fields, lakes, and ocean deep below him, he appears indifferent to the little localities of winter, from the lower to the higher regions of the atmosphere, the abode of eternal cold, and from thence descends at will to the torrid or the arctic regions of the earth. He is, therefore, found at all seasons in the countries he inhabits,

THE HISTORICAL WAR EAGLE,
"OLD ABE,"
AFTER THE BATTLE.

Used through the kindness of THEO. J. HARBACH.

but prefers such places as have been mentioned above, from the great partiality he has for fish.

In procuring these, he displays in a very singular manner the genius and energy of his character, which is contemplative, daring, and tyrannical; attributes not exerted but on particular occasions, but, when put forth, overpowering all opposition. Elevated on the high, dead limb of some gigantic tree that commands a wide view of the neighboring shore and ocean, he seems calmly to contemplate the motions of the feathered tribes that pursue their busy avocations below; the snow-white gulls slowly winnowing the air; the busy tringæ coursing along the sands; trains of ducks streaming over the surface; silent and watchful cranes, intent and wading; clamorous crows; and all the winged multitudes that subsist by the bounty of this vast liquid magazine of nature. High above these hovers one whose action instantly arrests his whole attention. By his wide curvature of wing, and sudden suspension in air, he knows him to be a fish-hawk, settling over some devoted victim of the deep. His eye kindles at the sight, and, balancing himself with half-opened wings on the branch, he watches the result. Down, rapid as an arrow from heaven, descends the distant object of his attention, the roar of its wings reaching the ear as it disappears in the deep, making the surges foam around! At this moment the eager looks of the eagle are all ardor, and, levelling his neck for flight, he sees the fish-hawk once more emerge, struggling with his prey, and mounting into the air with screams of exultation. These are the signals for our hero, who, launching into the air, instantly gives chase and soon gains on the fish-hawk; each exerts his utmost to mount above the other, displaying in these rencounters the most elegant and sublime aerial evolutions. The unencumbered eagle rapidly advances, and is just on the point of reaching his opponent, when, with a sudden scream, probably of despair and honest execration, the latter drops his fish; the eagle, poising himself for a moment as if to take a more certain aim, descends like a whirlwind, snatches it in his grasp ere it reaches the water, and bears his ill-gotten booty silently away to the woods.

These predatory attacks and defensive manœuvres of the eagle and the fish-hawk are matters of daily observation along the whole of our seaboard from Georgia to New England, and frequently excite great interest in the spectators. Sympathy, however, on this as on most other occasions, generally sides with the honest and laborious sufferer, in opposition to the attacks of power, injustice, and rapacity, qualities for which our hero is so generally notorious, and which in his superior, *man*, are certainly detestable. As for the feelings of the poor fish, they seem altogether out of the question.

When driven, as he sometimes is, by the combined courage and perseverance of the fish-hawks from their neighborhood, and forced to hunt for himself, he retires more inland, in search of young pigs, of which he destroys great numbers. In the lower parts of Virginia and North Carolina, where the inhabitants raise vast herds of those animals, complaints of this kind are very general against him. He also destroys young lambs in the early part of spring, and will sometimes attack old, sickly sheep, aiming furiously at their eyes.

—*Wilson.*

HE who survives the freedom and dignity of his country has already lived too long.—*De Tocqueville.*

THE AMERICAN EAGLE.

BIRD of the cliff! thou art soaring on high;
Thou hast swept the dense cloud from thy path in the sky;
Thou hast braved the keen flash of the lightning in sport,
And poised thy strong wing where the thunders resort;
Thou hast follow'd the stars in their pathways above,
And chased the wild meteors wherever they rove.

Bird of the forest! thou lov'st the deep shade,
Where the oak spreads its boughs in the mountain and glade,
Where the thick-cluster'd ivy encircles the pine,
And the proud elm is wreath'd by the close-clinging vine;
Thou hast tasted the dew of the untrodden plain,
And follow'd the streams as they roll to the main;
Thou hast dipp'd thy swift wing in the feathery spray,
Where the earth-quaking cataract roars on its way.

Bird of free skies! thou hast sail'd on the cloud,
Where the battle raged fierce, and the cannon roar'd loud;
Thou hast stoop'd to the earth when the foeman was slain,
And waved thy wide wing o'er the blood-sprinkled plain;
Thou hast soar'd where the banner of freedom was borne:
Thou hast gazed at the far dreaded lion in scorn,
Thy beak has been wet in the blood of our foes,
When the home of the brave has been left to repose.

Bird of the clime in which liberty dwells,
Nurse the free soul in thy cliff-shelter'd dells!
Hover above the strong heart in its pride,
Whisper of those who for freedom have died!
Bear up the free-nurtured spirit of man,
Till it soar like thine own, through its earth-bounded span!

Waft it above, o'er the mountain and wave—
Spread thy free wing o'er the patriot's grave.
—*Southern Religious Telegraph.*

AMERICAN HISTORY.

THE study of the history of most other nations fills the mind with sentiments, not unlike those which the American traveller feels, on entering the venerable and lofty cathedral of some proud old city of Europe. Its solemn grandeur, its vastness, and its obscurity, strike awe to his heart. From the richly painted windows, filled with sacred emblems and strange antique forms, a dim religious light falls around. A thousand recollections of romance, poetry and legendary story come thronging in upon him. He is surrounded by the tombs of the mighty dead, rich with the labors of ancient art, and emblazoned with the pomp of heraldry.

What names does he read upon them? Those of princes and nobles who are now remembered only for their vices; and of sovereigns, at whose death no tears were shed, and whose memories lived not an hour in the affection of their people. There, too, he sees other names, long familiar to him for their guilty or ambiguous fame. There rest the blood-stained soldier of fortune, the orator who was ever the ready apologist of tyranny—great scholars who were the pensioned flatterers of power—and poets who profaned the high gift of genius, to pamper the vices of a corrupted court.

Our own history, on the contrary, like that poetical temple of fame, reared by the imagination of Chaucer, and decorated by the taste of Pope, is almost exclusively dedicated to the memory of the truly great. Or rather, like the Pantheon of Rome, it stands in calm and severe beauty amid the ruins of ancient magnificence and "the toys of modern state." Within, no idle ornament encumbers its simplicity. The pure light of heaven enters from above and sheds an equal radiance around. As the eye wanders about its extent it beholds the unadorned monuments of brave and good men who have bled or toiled for their country, or it rests on votive tablets inscribed with the names of the best benefactors of mankind.

> "Patriots are here, in Freedom's battle slain;
> Priests, whose long lives were closed without a stain;
> Bards worthy him who breathed the poet's mind;
> Founders of arts that dignify mankind;
> And lovers of our race, whose labors gave
> Their names a memory that defies the grave."

If Europe has hitherto been wilfully blind to the value of our example and the exploits of our sagacity, courage, invention and freedom, the blame must rest with her, and not with America. Is it nothing for the universal good of mankind to have carried into successful operation a system of self-government, uniting personal liberty, freedom of opinion and equality of rights, with national power and dignity, such as had before existed only in the Utopian dreams of philosophers? Is it nothing in moral science to have anticipated in sober reality numerous plans of reform in civil and criminal jurisprudence, which are, but now, received as plausible theories by the politicians and economists of Europe?

Is it nothing to have been able to call forth on every emergency, either in war or peace, a body of talents always equal to the difficulty? Is it nothing to have, in less than a half century, exceedingly improved the sciences of political economy, of law, and of medicine, with all their auxiliary branches; to have enriched human knowledge by the accumulation of a great mass of useful facts and observations, and to have augmented the power and the comforts of civilized man by miracles of mechanical invention? Is it nothing to have given the world examples of disinterested patriotism, of political wisdom, of public virtue, of learning, eloquence and valor, never exerted, save for some praiseworthy end?

Land of Liberty! thy children have no cause to blush for thee. What though the arts have reared few monuments among us, and scarce a trace of the Muse's footstep is found in the paths of our forests, or along the banks of our rivers, yet our soil has been consecrated by the blood of heroes and by great and holy deeds of peace. Its wide extent has become one vast temple and hallowed asylum, sanctified by the prayers and blessings of the persecuted of every sect, and the wretched of all nations.

Land of Refuge! Land of Benedictions! Those prayers still arise and they still are heard: "May peace be within thy walls, and plenteousness within thy palaces!" "May there be no decay, nor leading into captivity, and no complaining in thy streets!" "May truth flourish out of the earth, and righteousness look down from heaven."—*Gulian C. Verplanck.*

THERE is no country on the globe—not even excepting Britain—which contains more happy and cultured homes than our own.—*T. L. Cuyler.*

AMERICA THE LAND.

THE name of Commonwealth is past and gone,
Over three fractions of the groaning globe:
Venice is crushed, and Holland deigns to own
A sceptre, and endures a purple robe.
If the free Switzer yet bestrides alone
His chainless mountains, 'tis but for a time:
For tyranny of late has cunning grown,
And, in its own good season, tramples down
The sparkles of our ashes. One great clime,
Whose vigorous offspring by dividing ocean
Are kept apart, and nursed in the devotion
Of Freedom, which their fathers fought for, and
Bequeathed—a heritage of heart and hand;
And proud distinction from each other land,
Whose sons must bow them at a monarch's motion,
As if his senseless sceptre were a wand
Full of the magic of exploded science—
Still one great clime, in full and free defiance,
Yet rears her crest, unconquered and sublime,
Above the far Atlantic! She has taught
Her Esau-brethren that the haughty flag,
The floating fence of Albion's feebler crag,
May strike to those whose red right hands have
Rights cheaply earned with blood still, still forever bought,
Better, though each man's life-blood were a river
That it should flow and overflow, than creep
Through thousand lazy channels in our veins,
Dammed, like the dull canal, with lock and chains,
And moving, as a sick man in his sleep,
Three paces, and then faltering: better be
Where the extinguished Spartans still are free,

In their proud charnel of Thermopylæ,
Than stagnate in our marsh; or o'er the deep
Fly, and one current to the ocean add,
One spirit to the souls our fathers had,
One freeman more. America, to thee!

—Lord Byron.

AMERICAN SCENERY.

IT strikes the European traveller, at the first burst of the scenery of America on his eye, that the New World of Columbus is also a new world from the hand of the Creator. In comparison with the old countries of Europe, the vegetation is so wondrously lavish, the outlines and minor features struck out with so bold a freshness, and the lakes and rivers so even in their fulness and flow, yet so vast and powerful, that he may well imagine it an Eden newly sprung from the ocean. The Minerva-like birth of the Republic of the United States, its sudden rise to independence, wealth, and power, and its continued and marvellous increase in population and prosperity, strike him with the same surprise, and leave the same impression of a new scale of existence, and a fresher and faster law of growth and accomplishment. The interest, with regard to both the natural and civilized features of America, has very much increased within a few years; and travellers, who have exhausted the unchanging countries of Europe, now turn their steps in great numbers to the novel scenery and ever-shifting aspects of this.

The picturesque views of the United States suggest a

train of thought directly opposite to that of similar objects of interest in other lands. There, the soul and centre of attraction in every picture is some ruin of the *past*. The wandering artist avoids everything that is modern, and selects his point of view so as to bring prominently into his sketch the castle, or the cathedral, which history or antiquity has hallowed. The traveller visits each spot in the same spirit—ridding himself, as far as possible, of common and present associations, to feed his mind on the historical and legendary. The objects and habits of reflection in both traveller and artist undergo in America a direct revolution. He who journeys here, if he would not have the eternal succession of lovely natural objects

"Lie like a load on the weary eye,"

must feed his imagination on the *future*. The American does so. His mind, as he tracks the broad rivers of his own country, is perpetually reaching forward. Instead of looking through a valley which has presented the same aspect for hundreds of years—in which live lords and tenants whose hearths have been surrounded by the same names through ages of tranquil descent, and whose fields have never changed landmark or mode of culture since the memory of men—he sees a valley laden down like a harvest wagon with a virgin vegetation, untrodden and luxuriant, and his first thought is of the villages that will soon sparkle on the hillsides, the axes that will ring from the woodlands, and the mills, bridges, canals, and railroads that will span and border the stream that now runs through sedge and wild flowers. The towns he passes through on his route are not recognizable by prints done by artists long ago dead, with houses of low-browed architecture, and immemorial;

but a town which has perhaps doubled its inhabitants and dwellings since he last saw it, and will again double them before he returns. Instead of inquiring into its antiquity, he sits over the fire with his paper and pencil, and calculates what the population will be in ten years, how far they will spread, what the value of the neighboring land will become, and whether the stock of some canal or railroad that seems more visionary than Symmes's expedition to the centre of the earth, will, in consequence, be a good investment. He looks upon all external objects as exponents of the future. In Europe they only are exponents of the past.

There is a field for the artist in this country which surpasses every other in richness of picturesque. The great difficulty at present is, where to choose. Every mill upon the rivers, every hollow in the landscape, every turn in the innumerable mountain streams, arrests the painter's eye, and offers him some untouched and peculiar variety of an exhaustless nature. It is in *river scenery*, however, that America excels all other lands; and here the artist's labor is not, as in Europe, to embellish and idealize the reality: he finds it difficult to come up to it. How represent the excessive richness of the foliage! How draw the vanishing lines which mark the swells in the forest ground, the round heaps of the chestnut-tops, the greener belts through the wilderness which betray the wanderings of the watercourses! How give in so small a space the evasive swiftness of the rapid, the terrific plunge of the precipice, or the airy wheel of the eagle, as his diminished form shoots off from the sharp line of the summit and cuts a circle on the sky!

The general architecture of the United States cannot pretend, of course, to vie with that of older countries; yet, taken in connection with the beautiful positions of towns, no drawing will be found deficient in beauty, while many of the public buildings especially are, as works of art, well worthy the draughtsman's notice. The curiosity now generally excited with regard to this country, by its own progress, and by the late numerous books of travels, will throw a sufficient interest around every point that the pencil could present.

. . " The green land of groves, the beautiful waste,
Nurse of full streams, and lifter up of proud
Sky-mingling mountains that o'erlook the cloud.
　　Ere while, where yon gay spires their brightness rear,
Trees waved, and the brown hunter's shouts were loud
　　　　Amid the forest; and the bounding deer
Fled at the glancing plume, and the gaunt wolf yell'd near.

" And where his willing waves yon bright blue bay
　　Sends up, to kiss his decorated brim,
And cradles, in his soft embrace, the gay
　　Young group of grassy islands born of him,
And, crowding nigh, or in the distance dim,
　　Lifts the white throng of sails, that bear or bring
The commerce of the world; with tawny limb,
　　And belt and beads in sunlight glistening,
The savage urged his skiff like wild bird on the wing.

. . . .
" Look now abroad—another race has fill'd
　　These populous borders—wide the world recedes,
And towns shoot up, and fertile realms are till'd;
　　The land is full of harvests and green meads;
Streams numberless, that many a fountain feeds,
　　Shine, disembower'd, and give to sun and breeze
Their virgin waters; the full region leads
　　New colonies forth, that toward the western seas
Spread, like a rapid flame, among the autumnal trees.

. . . .
" But thou, my country, thou shalt never fall,
  But with thy children—thy maternal care,
Thy lavish love, thy blessing shower'd on all—
  These are thy fetters—seas and stormy air
Are the wide barrier of thy borders, where,
  Among thy gallant sons that guard thee well,
Thou laugh'st at enemies: who shall then declare
  The date of thy deep-founded strength, or tell
How happy, in thy lap, the sons of men shall dwell."

—*N. P. Willis.*

THE PRAIRIES.

THESE are the gardens of the desert. These
  The unshorn fields, boundless and beautiful,
  For which the speech of England has no name—
  The prairies. I behold them for the first,
  And my heart swells, while the dilated sight
  Takes in the encircling vastness. Lo! they stretch
  In airy undulations, far away,
  As if the ocean, in his gentlest swell,
Stood still, with all his rounded billows fix'd
And motionless forever.—Motionless?
No—they are all unchained again. The clouds
Sweep over with their shadows, and, beneath,
The surface rolls and fluctuates to the eye;
Dark hollows seem to glide along and chase
The sunny ridges. Breezes of the South!
Who toss the golden and the flame-like flowers,
And pass the prairie-hawk that, poised on high,
Flaps his broad wings, yet moves not—ye have play'd
Among the palms of Mexico and vines
Of Texas, and have crisp'd the limpid brooks

That from the fountains of Sonora glide
Into the calm Pacific—have ye faun'd
A nobler or a lovelier scene than this?
Man hath no part in all this glorious work:
The hand that built the firmament hath heaved
And smoothed these verdant swells, and sown their slopes
With herbage, planted them with island groves,
And hedged them round with forests. Fitting floor
For this magnificent temple of the sky—
With flowers whose glory and whose multitude
Rival the constellations! The great heavens
Seem to stoop down upon the scene in love,—
A nearer vault, and of a tenderer blue,
Than that which bends above the eastern hills.

    As o'er the verdant waste I guide my steed
Among the high, rank grass that sweeps his sides,
The hollow beating of his footstep seems
A sacrilegious sound. I think of those
Upon whose rest he tramples. Are they here—
The dead of other days?—and did the dust
Of these fair solitudes once stir with life
And burn with passion? Let the mighty mounds
That overlook the rivers, or that rise
In the dim forest, crowded with old oaks,
Answer. A race, that long has pass'd away,
Built them; a disciplined and populous race
Heap'd, with long toil, the earth, while yet the Greek
Was hewing the Pentelicus to forms
Of symmetry, and rearing on its rock
The glittering Parthenon. These ample fields
Nourish'd their harvests; here their herds were fed,
When haply by their stalls the bison low'd,
And bow'd his maned shoulder to the yoke.
All day this desert murmur'd with their toils,
Till twilight blush'd and lovers walk'd, and woo'd
In a forgotten language, and old tunes,

From instruments of unremember'd form,
Gave the soft winds a voice. The red man came—
The roaming hunter tribes, warlike and fierce,
And the mound-builders vanish'd from the earth.
The solitude of centuries untold
Has settled where they dwelt. The prairie-wolf
Hunts in their meadows, and his fresh-dug den
Yawns by my path. The gopher mines the ground
Where stood their swarming cities. All is gone—
All—save the piles of earth that hold their bones—
The platforms where they worshipp'd unknown gods—
The barriers which they builded from the soil
To keep the foe at bay—till o'er the walls
The wild beleaguerers broke, and, one by one,
The strongholds of the plain were forced, and heap'd
With corpses. The brown vultures of the wood
Flock'd to those vast, uncover'd sepulchres,
And sat, unscared and silent, at their feast.
Haply some solitary fugitive,
Lurking in marsh and forest, till the sense
Of desolation and of fear became
Bitterer than death, yielded himself to die.
Man's better nature triumph'd. Kindly words
Welcomed and soothed him; the rude conquerors
Seated the captive with their chiefs; he chose
A bride among their maidens, and at length
Seemed to forget—yet ne'er forgot—the wife
Of his first love, and her sweet little ones
Butcher'd amid their shrieks, with all his race.

  Thus change the forms of being. Thus arise
Races of living things, glorious in strength,
And perish, as the quickening breath of God
Fills them, or is withdrawn. The red man, too,
Has left the blooming wilds he ranged so long,
And nearer to the Rocky Mountains, sought
A wider hunting-ground. The beaver builds

No longer by these streams, but far away,
On waters whose blue surface ne'er gave back
The white man's face—among Missouri's springs
And pools whose issues swell the Oregon,
He rears his little Venice. In these plains
The bison feeds no more. Twice twenty leagues
Beyond remotest smoke of hunter's camp
Roams the majestic brute, in herds that shake
The earth with thundering steps—yet here I meet
His ancient footprints stamp'd beside the pool.

    Still this great solitude is quick with life.
Myriads of insects, gaudy as the flowers
They flutter over, gentle quadrupeds,
And birds, that scarce have learn'd the fear of man,
Are here, and sliding reptiles of the ground,
Startlingly beautiful. The graceful deer
Bounds to the wood at my approach. The bee,
A more adventurous colonist than man,
With whom he came across the eastern deep,
Fills the savannas with his murmurings,
And hides his sweets, as in the golden age,
Within the hollow oak. I listen long
To his domestic hum, and think I hear
The sound of that advancing multitude
Which soon shall fill these deserts. From the ground
Comes up the laugh of children, the soft voice
Of maidens, and the sweet and solemn hymn
Of Sabbath worshippers. The low of herds
Blends with the rustling of the heavy grain
Over the dark-brown furrows. All at once
A fresher wind sweeps by, and breaks my dream,
And I am in the wilderness alone.
                —*William Cullen Bryant.*

ONE country, one constitution, one destiny.—*D. Webster.*

A VISIT TO THE YOSEMITE.

TWICE has it been my privilege and my joy to visit the Yosemite Valley. Had it been seven times instead of twice, the seventh visit had been more instructive and ennobling than the sixth. With each return to spot and scene the wonder grows, the admiration kindles into flame more ardent, and the satisfaction waxes in intensity and depth. No description—be it by poet, painter, writer, orator —can be thought of as approaching the reality. "The half was not told," must be the exclamation of the entranced beholder and listener.

We start, say, from the Palace Hotel; cross the San Francisco bay; enter the cars for Merced City; and, if the mosquitoes will but condescend to permit us, enjoy a good night's sleep in preparation for the day's staging. Twelve hours at least are spent before reaching Clark's Hotel; and, having rested and slept a second night, we either move on to the valley the day following, or remain to spend that day in visiting the Mariposa trees. Upon the third day, if we choose, we reach the valley by one o'clock, and become the guests of Black or Hutchings.

There are at least three modes of entrance to the valley; that by which I entered passes "Inspiration Point." This is the point from whence one gains the first view of the glorious spot. We halted and gazed with bated breath and brimming eye. What an impertinence is language in presence of such a scene! I thought of Moses as, from Nebo's crest, "God showed him all the land," from Hermon's snowy helmet to where the desert of the south touches Immanuel's soil; from where Jordan winds its tortuous way to where the waves of the Great Sea lave the foot of Carmel; from where Engedi's groves of spice lade the breezes, to where Sharon's roses bloom and Gilead's forests bleed their balm. There we caught, indeed, the inspiration which has never left us or forsaken us since.

On we dashed, by zigzag but well-constructed road—down, round, back, on, round, backward, onward, downward—until the level of the Merced river was safely reached; thence through shrubbery and o'er sand and streamlet, until we landed in presence of the "Eagle's Nest," and within the musical thunder of the Yosemite Falls.

The valley is about nine miles long, and one mile and a half wide. It is forty-one hundred feet above the level of the sea. Through it flows the Merced river. The walls of the valley are gray granite, nearly vertical, and from three thousand to six thousand feet above the level of the valley, thus from seven thousand to ten thousand feet above the level of the ocean.

The highest fall in the Yosemite is two thousand six hundred and thirty-four feet high. This cataract is composed of three falls: the first, one thousand six hundred feet; the second, five hundred and thirty-four feet; the third, five hundred feet high. The Nevada fall is the most massive; there the main body of the Merced, fresh from the eternal snow and ice of the Sierras, leaps six hundred feet, or nearly four times as high as Niagara; it is sixty feet wide. From thence the river rushes with resistless impetuosity through a narrow gorge over the huge *débris* of boulders with a noise "as of many waters," forming one of the grandest and wildest scenes of the valley.

We climbed, partly on foot and partly on horseback, to Glacier Point. The travel is perfectly safe, the horses are well trained, the road is broad and well defended. On horseback there is but little fatigue experienced. And even were the fatigue fourfold greater, one is well repaid for the toil by the "visions splendid" which greet him from the projecting table which, three thousand two hundred feet above the level of the valley, and seven thousand four hundred feet above the ocean, permits him to look—out, up, down—on one of the most superbly sublime panoramas of this or any other orb.

The cloudless blue is above us; the far-roaming snow-robed plateaus of the Sierra beyond us; the Cap of Liberty and Cloud's Rest to our right; Starr King and Mt. Whitney, South Dome and North, rounded and polished by the gigantic glacier's chisel and plane; El Capitan to our left; the Three Brothers and the Cathedral Spires on either side of the valley; the river but a thread of moving water; the Yosemite with its threefold plunge; far off the subdued thunder of the Nevada and Vernal Falls.

Immensity, almightiness, age, time, eternity, the littleness and the grandeur of man, the glory and the vanity of earth, the self-sufficiency and the incessant activity of Deity, all in turn seize the spirit, move, awe, subdue, yet elevate and inspire the heart. I could not speak amid such magnificence. Even thought seemed paralyzed in the presence of such symbols of the majesty of nature and the surpassing greatness of Him who, through ages innumerable, and by agencies Titanic, had upheaved and sculptured, dispread and massed, consolidated and embellished this august and sacred shrine in earth's far-spanning temple!

You are impressed with the thought that here all zones

and climates, all forms and colors, all aspects and motions, all elements of strength and beauty, of sternness and repose, conspire and combine. There is the valley and the gorge; there is the still radiance of the lake and the glad motion of the rushing river; there is the meek wild flower and the stately pine; there is the gleam of the many-tinted butterfly and the majestic movement of the soaring eagle; there is eternal winter on the summit, there are the luxuries of tropic summer in the dell; there is mountain and there is water; there is beauty and there is sublimity. Dew sparkles; timely rains descend; zephyrs glide or loiter; wild winds swell and sigh; thunder crashes, and lightnings blaze their banner o'er the dusky sky. The eye is regaled; the ear soothed. Now serenity broods within you; and now exhilarating ecstasy flashes and flushes and flows over in eye and cheek and lip. The adventurous is dared, the explorer challenged, the studious wooed, the observing rewarded. Earth's dreary noises are unheard, and man's Mammon worship is forgotten. The cares and fretfulness of life, the strife and rivalry of time, depart. Nature in her divinest forms alone takes possession of the spirit, and man, hushed and reverent, bends to catch the speech of God.

One ought to be very much better for a trip like this. One's threefold being—spirit, soul, body—should return largely benefited. And it is almost a sin if any one go and return unimproved. When such is the case there must be some deep-seated unhealthiness, both in body and in soul.

What do you need to take with you so that you may make the most of a visit? No one ought to go there who does not take with him clear, open eyes, a wakeful, thoughtful mind, an honest, pure, tender heart, and a soul in sympathy with **the great and benignant Creator, Father, and Friend of man.**

I will not stop to say that you need a good, well-filled purse. Nor will I stop to say that you need a friend or two, full of enthusiasm, of vigor, and of susceptibilities. But I will say in one word what you cannot do without, what you must take with you, so as to return most weightily laden with most worthy benefit. That word is health; health of body, so that you can climb and ride without pain and faintness, and laugh and cry in turn; health of heart, purity, love, meekness, docility, reverence, wonder, admiration, gratitude; health of intellect, the clear thought, the keen vision, the quick ear, the elastic nerve of soul-health; health of your entire manhood or womanhood.

Sympathy is essential to the full, remunerative enjoyment of the Valley and its wonders. There are ears, I believe, incapable of distinguishing one note from another. There are eyes positively color-blind. There are men who see nothing in Milton's "Paradise Lost," because it does not mathematically demonstrate any problem. There are natures so thoroughly petrified by sordidness and sensualism that, for their delectation, the Yosemite exists in vain. There are self-conceited, self-idolizing creatures who see nothing to admire in nature. Over the Mirror Lake they sail, and into its depths they glance; it is the only spot in the Valley they enjoy. And why? Because it is the only spot in which, as in a glass, they can look upon themselves reflected! Such as they have reached a stage of culture in which the faculty of admiration works not, for it is not. The wonder of ingenuous and self-forgetting youth has given place to the hard, cruel unfeelingness of a blasted, cinder-like muscle once called a heart.

Sourness and bitterness of spirit disqualify for the Valley. Meekness and humility, simple faith and fervent adoration largely equip for its due and keen appreciation. The clearer the understanding, the tenderer the heart, so much the more is it likely "thine eye shall see the beauty of the Great King" in such a spot as this. You must go with fibre of your being tremulous and strung; with every sense awake and vigorous; with all of memory in play, and all of imagination in lofty mood and tone. You must go with your soul having, as it were, "a look southward, and open to the whole noon of nature." As seen through the lenses of some atrabilarious natures, there is neither form nor comeliness in the loveliest landscapes.

Nor may you hope for success in your visit if you take with you only the Peter-Bell-like spirit:

"A primrose by the river's brim,
 A yellow primrose was to him;
 And it was nothing more."

Rather take the spirit of him who wrote of the "Daisy;" of him who, placing the Orient seashell to his ear, heard through the convolutions of the smooth-lipped conch the cadence of the ocean in whose depths the lovely thing was fashioned; of him who followed the skylark beyond the cloud and heard him carol at the bars of the gate of gold, till seraphs ceased to harp and learned to sing, taught by the frail denizen of the clover and the sod; the spirit of him who, having looked upon a pond margined by daffodils, sat down and wrote:

"I wander'd lonely as a cloud
   That floats on high o'er vales and hills,
 When all at once I saw a crowd,
   A host of golden daffodils;
 Beside the lake, beneath the trees,
 Fluttering and dancing in the breeze,

"Continuous as the stars that shine
 And twinkle on the milky way,
They stretched in never-ending line
 Along the margin of a bay;
Ten thousand saw I at a glance,
Tossing their heads in sprightly dance.
The waves beside them danced, but they
 Outdid the sparkling waves in glee:
A poet could not but be gay,
 In such a jocund company!
I gazed—and gazed—but little thought
What wealth the show to me had brought:
For oft, when on my couch I lie,
 In vacant or in pensive mood,
They flash upon that inward eye
 Which is the bliss of solitude,
And then my heart with pleasure fills,
 And dances with the daffodils."

And, last of all, take that state of heart which voiced itself in the well-known lines:

"Not to the domes, whose crumbling arch and column
 Attest the feebleness of mortal hand;
But to the fane, most catholic and solemn,
 Which God hath planned;

"To that cathedral, boundless as our wonder,
 Whose quenchless lamps the sun and moon supply,
Its music, winds and waves—its organ, thunder;
 Its dome, the sky;

"There, amidst solitude and shade, to wander
 Through the green aisles, or, stretched upon the sod,
And by the silence, reverently ponder
 The ways of God."

—Thomas Guard.

DESCRIPTION OF NIAGARA FALLS.

AT the point where the river issues from Lake Erie, it assumes the name of Niagara. It is something more than three-quarters of a mile in width, and the broad and powerful current embosoms two islands; one of them, Grand Isle, containing 11,000 acres, and the other, Navy Island, opposite to the British village of Chippeway. Below this island the river again becomes an unbroken sheet, a mile in width. For half a mile below, it seems to be waxing in wrath and power. Were this rapid in any other place, itself would be noted as one of the sublimest features of river scenery. Along this rapid, the broad and irresistible mass of rolling waters is not entirely whitened, for it is too deep to become so. But it has something of that curling and angry aspect which the sea exhibits when swept by the first blasts of a tempest. The momentum may be conceived when we are instructed that in half a mile the river has a descent of fifty feet. A column of water, a mile broad, twenty-five feet deep, and propelled onward by the weight of the surplus waters of the whole prodigious basin of the lakes, rolling down this rapid declivity, at length pours over the cataract, as if falling to the central depths of the earth.

Instead of sublimity, the first feeling excited by this stupendous cataract is amazement. The mind accustomed only to ordinary phenomena and common exhibitions of power, feels a revulsion and recoils from the new train of thought and feeling forced in an instant upon it. There is hardly sufficient coolness for distinct impressions, much less for calculations. We witness the white and terrific sheets—for an island on the very verge of the cataract divides the fall—descending more than 150 feet into the abyss below. We feel the earth trembling under our feet. The deafening roar fills our ears. The spray, painted with rainbows, envelops us. We imagine the fathomless caverns, which such an impetus, continued for ages, has worn. Nature arrays herself before us, in this spectacle, as an angry and irresistible power, that has broken away from the beneficent control of Providence.

When we have gazed upon the spectacle and heard the roar until the mind has recovered from its amazement, we believe the first obvious thought in most minds is a shrinking comparison of the littleness and helplessness of man and the insignificance of his pigmy efforts when measuring strength with nature. Take it all in all, it is one of the most sublime and astonishing spectacles seen on our globe. The eye distinctly measures the amount of the mass, and we can hardly avoid thinking with the peasant that the waters of the upper world must shortly be drained down the cataract. But the stream continues to pour down, and this concentrated and impressive symbol of the power of Omnipotence proclaims his majesty through the forest from age to age.

An earthquake, the eruption of a volcanic mountain, the conflagration of a city, are all spectacles in which terror is the first and predominant emotion. The most impressive exertion of human power is only seen in the murderous and sickening horrors of a conflict between two mighty armies. These, too, are transient and contingent exhibitions of sublimity. But after we have stood an hour at the foot of these falls, after the eye has been accustomed to look upon them without blanching, after the ear has become familiarized with the deafening and incessant roar, when the mind begins to calculate the grandeur of the scale of operations upon which nature acts, then it is that the entire and unmingled feeling of sublimity rushes upon it, and this is, probably, the place on the whole globe where it is felt in its most unmixed simplicity.

PAUL JONES AND THE NAVY OF THE REVOLUTION.

COMMODORE PAUL JONES was born in Scotland. His father, a respectable man in the lower walks of life, could only afford him a moderate education for a boy twelve years old. Having fed his roving fancy with tales of adventure gleaned from the old sailors who frequented the ship-yards and lounged in the nautical haunts along the shores of Solway Frith, near his home, he resolved at that age to visit America. Circumstances favored his intentions; and here he passed several years of his life. He became engaged in commerce, and studied navigation. This he carried into practical experience during two or three voyages to the coast of Africa; and, after holding several important commands in the commercial marine, he tendered his services to the infant navy of the colonies—satisfied that their cause was the cause of justice and of right, and anxious to distinguish himself as a defender of that which his conscience approved and to which his generous and heroic sympathies directed him. We first find him commanding the "Ariel," one of the two ships that constituted the navy of Congress at that time. Jones was now twenty-eight years of age. The historian claims for him the honor of raising, with his own hands, the flag of independent America on board the "Ariel," in the Delaware river—the first time it was ever displayed on board a regular American vessel of war. From the "Ariel" he was transferred to the "Ranger," and bore in her to France despatches of the victory of Saratoga. While in a French port, he received from the French commander the first salute that was ever given to the American flag in a foreign port.

In 1778 he made a descent on the English coast, surprising a garrison and capturing a fort, destroying shipping, and taking a king's ship, called the "Drake," in Carrickfergus Bay, throwing the coasts of Ireland and Scotland into consternation, and causing the British Government great expenditure in fortifying their harbors. We now approach the most daring exploit of this truly great character. In company with a fleet of vessels fitted out in France, by the assistance of the French Government, aided by the exertions of Benjamin Franklin, we find him at sea, preying on the English commerce, and boldly attacking the ships of the enemy wherever met.

September 2, 1776, Paul Jones, in the "Bonhomme Richard," in company with the "Pallas" and the "Alliance," fell in with the returning Baltic fleet of merchantmen, under convoy of the king's ships, the "Serapis," forty-four guns, and the "Countess of Scarborough," twenty-two guns. These ships at once signalled the merchantmen to keep on their course, while they boldly stood out to sea, inviting an action. The battle was fought on the eastern coast of England, off Flamborough Head, at night, the moon occasionally lighting the combatants. Paul Jones, in the "Bonhomme Richard," fought the "Serapis," while the "Pallas" engaged the "Scarborough." The "Alliance," frigate, under the command of Captain Landais, a Frenchman, who, from his record, must have been either a madman or a traitor to the cause he had espoused, kept aloof during the greater part of the fight, only coming in towards its close to fire broadside after broadside in such a direction as to injure the "Bonhomme Richard" as much, if not more, than the enemy—in fact, leaving it doubtful against which vessel he had aimed his guns. After a severe fight, the "Scarborough" struck her flag to the "Pallas."

Paul Jones, who had maintained a desperate conflict with his antagonist, despairing of conquering him at long range, on account of the disabled condition of many of his guns, and of the inferior calibre of the remainder, now determined to run the "Serapis" aboard. This bold manœuvre was successfully accomplished, and, lashing his ship to that of his foe, he continued the fight, as sailors say, "yard-arm to yard-arm," the gunners on the lower decks of both vessels actually fighting through the port-holes to prevent one another from ramming home the charges of their guns.

Some of the lower deck cannon on board the "Richard" burst in the earlier part of the action, tearing up the decks above in a frightful manner. During a momentary lull in the firing, occasioned by this accident, the British commander hailed, and demanded whether the "Richard" had surrendered, to which Paul Jones replied, "No: we have not yet begun to fight." Striding from point to point, the hero might then be seen, now on the deck slippery with blood, now in the shrouds, trumpet in hand, calling away his boarders to hurl them on the deck of the enemy, stimulating his crew to renewed efforts by words of fiery courage, and leading in the van of every danger. Let us here imagine the commodore turning suddenly at a cry for quarter, uttered by some craven souls who thought the vessel was sinking. The flag-staff was shot away, the ensign was trailing in the water over the stern; voices cry from out the smoke and darkness, "Quarter for God's sake! we are sinking." Pistols flash, and a stentorian voice is heard shouting, "Who are those rascals? Shoot them! Kill them!" The rushing of hurrying feet across the deck, the dash of heavy bodies leaping through the hatchways, tell, in unmistakable terms, that the speaker there is more to be dreaded than the terrors of the sinking ship.

From all accounts, the conflict at this juncture must have been terrible beyond description. While the sides of the ship were being literally pounded to pieces by cannon actually fired within a few feet of the timbers they were crushing, the men, maddened to fury by wounds, flame, and smoke, were fighting with hatchets, pikes, and every other weapon at hand, including even the rammers of the guns; and while this was going on below the decks, the rigging and round-tops presented a still more frightful picture. The vessels were both now on fire, the flames pouring up through the gaps in the deck, licking up the tarry ropes and tackle, and throwing around all a lurid light of terror. The yard-arms of the contending ships crossed each other's decks, entangled and enveloped in smoke, crowded with sailors, cutting and hacking at each other, more like devils than men, while some exploded hand grenades on the heads of those below. The musketry of the marines rattling from the decks and blending with the sullen roar of cannon, the sharpshooters in the tops, dealing death from above, the shouts of the commanders, the cries of the combatants, of pain or of defiance, the crackling shooting through enshrouding smoke, the decks all ablaze with fire or enveloped in Egyptian darkness—these separate horrors all combined to render that midnight death-struggle on the ocean more like a picture of fiends and furies, conjured up to delight the hellish fancies of infernal spectators, realizing the words of Shakespeare, " Hell is empty, and all the devils are here."

And yet such are the scenes from which we draw our inspirations of heroism, and in which we see our cherished types of valor, daring, and patriotism. How truly these gallant combatants realize that fierce pleasure Sir Walter Scott speaks of—

> "The stern joy that clansmen feel,
> In foemen worthy of their steel!"

This terrible and obstinate conflict lasted three and a half hours; and when the Englishman surrendered, his vessel was found to be anchored, and the flag nailed to the mast. Some time, therefore, elapsed before the usual token of submission could be made manifest; while our vessel was only kept afloat by the almost superhuman efforts of a body of prisoners, who had been confined below decks, and had been during the latter part of the action set at liberty by the officer in charge. Had it not been for this circumstance, the "Bonhomme Richard" would have sunk along side her enemy before his flag had been struck.

Thus ended one of the most sanguinary battles ever fought on the ocean. The "Bonhomme Richard" sank the next morning—the officers and crew being first transferred on board the English ship, which was almost as badly disabled as the "Richard." She, however, was kept afloat, but with great difficulty, and finally made the Texel, to which port Paul Jones had been ordered for repairs.

The "Alliance" now became the flag-ship of our hero, and in her he made another of those voyages which called forth the eulogy of the nation, and during which the enemy's gazettes had, as usual, matter enough for comment on the movements and doings of the "Bold Buccaneer," as they termed him.

During the next year we find Commodore Jones in America once more, where he received a vote of thanks from Congress and the appointment to the command of an American seventy-four; but, the war terminating soon after, he did not get into active service again. The king of France presented him with a gold-mounted sword, and requested Congress to decorate him with the "Order of Merit." This was done, the badge, etc., having been sent over for the purpose. Congress also presented him with a gold medal, in consideration of the zeal, prudence and intrepidity with which he had sustained the honor of the American flag. He was now the Chevalier Paul Jones, and, having returned to Paris on a mission for the United States, he was honored by the Empress of Russia with an appointment as rear admiral of the Russian fleet. He served with distinction, and was invested with the "Order of St. Anna." He retired for the last time to Paris, and died there, much honored and respected. His funeral was marked by public ceremonies befitting a hero and a good man, which there is no doubt he was. "That Paul Jones was a remarkable man," says Cooper, the naval historian, "cannot justly be questioned. In his enterprises are to be discovered much of that boldness of conception that marks a great naval captain; though his most celebrated battle is probably the one in which he evinced no other very high quality than that of invincible resolution to conquer. The expedient of running the 'Serapis' aboard was like him; and it was the only chance of victory that was left."

It will be remembered that the lamented Lawrence intended to accomplish the same result with the "Shannon." But accident frustrated his plan and gave the enemy an advantage, which resulted in the capture of our ship and the death of her commander. In all bold and daring departures from custom or orders, success throws a halo of glory around the master spirit of innovation, while failure is attended with obloquy and oblivion.

Frost, in his "Naval Memoirs," pays this tribute to the memory of the man the nation honored: "It is but just to place him among the first of our naval commanders; for his splendid career exhibited a degree of courage and ability which have been surpassed by none of those who have succeeded him in the brilliant line of our naval heroes."

—*James E. Murdoch.*

HAIL, COLUMBIA.

HAIL, Columbia! happy land!
Hail, ye heroes! heaven-born band!
  Who fought and bled in Freedom's cause,
  Who fought and bled in Freedom's cause,
And when the storm of war was gone,
Enjoy'd the peace your valor won.
  Let Independence be our boast,
  Ever mindful what it cost;
  Ever grateful for the prize,
  Let its altar reach the skies.

Firm—united—let us be,
Rallying round our Liberty;
As a band of brothers join'd,
Peace and safety we shall find.

Immortal patriots! rise once more;
Defend your rights, defend your shore;
Let no rude foe, with impious hand,
Let no rude foe, with impious hand,
Invade the shrine where sacred lies
Of toil and blood the well-earn'd prize.
While offering peace sincere and just,
In heaven we place a manly trust,
That truth and justice will prevail,
And every scheme of bondage fail.
Firm—united, etc.

Sound, sound the trump of Fame!
Let Washington's great name
Ring through the world with loud applause,
Ring through the world with loud applause,
Let every clime to Freedom dear
Listen with a joyful ear.
With equal skill, and god-like power,
He governs in the fearful hour
Of horrid war; or guides, with ease,
The happier times of honest peace.
Firm—united, etc.

Behold the Chief who now commands,
Once more to serve his country, stands—
The rock on which the storm will beat,
The rock on which the storm will beat,
But, arm'd in virtue, firm and true,
His hopes are fix'd on heaven and you.

When hope was sinking in dismay,
And glooms obscured Columbia's day,
His steady mind, from changes free,
Resolved on death or liberty.
    Firm—united, etc.

—*Joseph Hopkinson.*

OUR COUNTRY'S GREATEST GLORY.

THE true glory of a nation is in an intelligent, honest, industrious Christian people. The civilization of a nation depends on their individual character; a constitution which is not the outgrowth of this is not worth the parchment on which it is written. You look in vain in the past for a single instance where the people have preserved their liberties after their individual character was lost. The ruler represents the people, and laws and institutions are the simple outgrowth of domestic character. It is not in the magnificence of the home of the ruler, not in the beautiful creations of art lavished on public edifices, not in costly cabinets of pictures or public libraries, not in proud monuments of achievements in battle, not in the number or wealth of its cities, that we find pledges of national glory. The ruler may gather around his palace the treasures of the world, amid a brutalized people; the senate chamber may retain its faultless proportions long after the voice of patriotism is hushed within its walls: the marble may commemorate a glory which has forever departed. Art and letters may bring no lesson to a people whose heart is dead; the only glory of a nation is in the living temple of a loyal, industrious and upright people. The busy click of machinery, the merry ring of the anvil, the lowing of peaceful herds, and the song of the harvest home, are sweeter music than pæans of departed glory or songs of triumph in war. The vine-clad cottage of the hill-side, the cabin of the woodsman, and the rural home of the farmer are the true citadels of any country. There is a dignity in honest toil which belongs not to the display of wealth or the luxury of fashion. The man who drives the plow, or swings his ax in the forest, or with cunning fingers plies the tools of his craft, is as truly the servant of his country, as the statesman in the senate or the soldier in battle. The safety of a nation depends not on the wisdom of its statesmen or the bravery of its generals; the tongue of eloquence never saved a nation tottering to its fall; the sword of a warrior never stayed its destruction. There is a surer defence in every Christian home. I say Christian home, for I know of no glory to manhood which comes not from the cross. I know of no rights wrung from tyranny, no truth rescued from darkness and bigotry, which has not waited on a Christian civilization. Would you see the image of true glory, I would show you villages where the crown and glory of the people was in purity of character, where the children were gathered in Christian schools, where the voice of prayer goes heavenward, where the people have that most priceless gift—*faith in God*. With this as the basis, and leavened as it will be with brotherly love, there will be no danger in grappling with any evils which exist in our midst; we shall feel that we may work and bide our time, and die knowing that God will bring the victory.—*Bishop Whipple*.

IDEAS THE LIFE OF A PEOPLE.

THE leaders of our Revolution were men of whom the simple truth is the highest praise. Of every condition in life, they were singularly sagacious, sober and thoughtful. Lord Chatham spoke only the truth when he said to Franklin, of the men who composed the colonial Congress: "The Congress is the most honorable assembly of statesmen since those of the ancient Greeks and Romans in the most virtuous times." Given to grave reflection, they were neither dreamers nor visionaries, and they were much too earnest to be rhetoricians. It is a curious fact that they were generally men of so calm a temper that they lived to extreme age. With the exception of Patrick Henry and Samuel Adams, they were most of them profound scholars, and studied the history of mankind that they might know men. They were so familiar with the lives and thoughts of the wisest and best minds of the past that a classic aroma hangs about their writings and their speech; and they were profoundly convinced of what statesmen always know, and the adroit tests mere politicians never perceive—that ideas are the life of a people; that the conscience, not the pocket, is the real citadel of a nation, and that when you have debauched and demoralized that conscience by teaching that there are no natural rights, and that therefore there is no moral right or wrong in political action, you have poisoned the wells and rotted the crops in the ground.

The greatest living statesmen of England knew this also. Edmund Burke knew it, and Charles James Fox, and William Pitt, Earl of Chatham. But they did not speak for the king, or Parliament, or the English nation. Lord Gower spoke for them when he said in Parliament, "Let the Americans talk about their national and divine rights; their rights as men and citizens; their rights from God and nature! I am for enforcing these measures." My lord was contemptuous, and the king hired the Hessians, but the truth remained true. The fathers saw the scarlet soldiers swarming over the sea, but more steadily they saw that national progress had been secure only in the degree that the political system had conformed to natural justice. They knew the coming wreck of property and trade, but they knew more surely that Rome was never so rich as when she was dying, and, on the other hand, the Netherlands never so powerful as when they were poorest. Farther away, they read the names of Assyria, Greece, Egypt. They had art, opulence, splendor. Corn enough grew in the valley of the Nile. The Syrian sword was as sharp as any. They were merchant princes, and the clouds in the sky were rivalled by their sails upon the sea. They were soldiers, and their frown frightened the world.

"Soul, take thine ease" those empires said, languid with excess of luxury and life. Yes; but you remember the king who had built his grandest palace, and was to occupy it upon the morrow; but when the morrow came the palace was a pile of ruins. "Woe is me!" cried the king, "who is guilty of this crime?" "There is no crime," replied the sage at his side; "but the mortar was made of sand and water only, and the builders forgot to put in the lime." So fell the old empires, because the governors forgot to put justice into their governments.—*George W. Curtis.*

INTELLIGENCE THE TRUE BASIS OF LIBERTY.

HOW well said Washington—who said all things, as he did all things, well—" that in proportion as governments rest on public opinion, that opinion must be enlightened. There then must be intelligence at the foundation. But what intelligence? Not that which puffeth up, I fancy, not flippancy, not smartness, not sciolism, whose fruits, whose expression, are vanity, restlessness, insubordination, hate, irreverence, unbelief, incapacity to combine ideas, and great capacity to overwork a single one. Not quite this. This is that little intelligence and little learning which are dangerous. These are the characteristics, I have read, which pave the way for the downfall of States; not those on which a long glory and a long strength have towered. These, more than the general of Macedon, gave the poison to Demosthenes in the Island Temple. These, not the triumvirate alone, closed the eloquent lips of Cicero. These, before the populous North had done it, spread beneath Gibraltar to the Lybian sands in the downward age; these, not Christianity, not Goth, not Lombard, not Norman, rent that fair one, Italy, asunder, and turned the garden and the mistress of the earth into a school, into a hiding-place of assassins—of spies from Austria, of spies from France, with gold to buy and ears to catch and punish the dreams of liberty whispered in sleep, and shamed the memories and hopes of Machiavel and Mazzini, and gave for that joy and that beauty, mourning and heaviness. This is not the intelligence our Constitution means, Washington meant, our country needs. It is intelligence which, however it begins, ends with belief, with humility, with obedience, with veneration, with admiration, with truth; which recognizes and then learns and then teaches the duties of a comprehensive citizenship; which hopes for a future on earth and beyond earth, but turns habitually, thoughtfully, to the old paths, the great men, the hallowed graves of the fathers; which binds in one bundle of love the kindred and mighty legend of revolution and liberty, the life of Christ in the Evangelists, and the Constitution in its plain text; which can read with Lord Chatham, Thucydides and the stories of master statesmen of antiquity; yet holds with him that the papers of the Congress of 1776 were better; whose patriotism grows warm at Marathon, but warmer at Monmouth, at Yorktown, at Bunker Hill, at Saratoga; which reforms by persevering, serves by standing and waiting, fears God and honors America.—*Rufus Choate.*

OUR NATION STARTED RIGHT.

THE men of the Revolution started without a State Church; but they started with an Open Bible, with a heaven-planted conscience, and with the blessing of the God of heaven. These three were enough of capital, I dare say. These men had too firm a faith in conscience, in truth, in God, to think of leaning upon human government for support in the maintenance of that which they esteemed more precious than ease, than profit, than love of country; aye, than love of life. The men who fled from Louis XIV., as Huguenots, might not they be trusted to feed the fires of piety? The men who fled from the hills and gorges of the Waldenses from Sardinian tyrants, might not they be trusted to keep their piety pure? The men who fled from the crooked-hearted Stuarts of England, for conscience sake, might not they be trusted with the holy art of godly worship?

—*Thomas Guard.*

THE SEED CORN OF THE REPUBLIC.

THE real seed corn whence our republic sprang was the Christian households, which stepped forth from the cabin of the "Mayflower," or which set up the family altar of the Hollander and the Huguenot on Manhattan Island or in the sunny South. All our best characters, best legislation, best institutions, and best church life were cradled in those early homes. They were the tap-root of the republic, and of the American churches.

For one, I care but little for the government which presides at Washington in comparison with the government which rules the eight or ten millions of American homes. No administration can seriously harm us if our home life is pure, frugal, and godly. No statesmanship or legislation can save us, if once our homes become the abodes of ignorance or the nestling places of profligacy. The home rules the nation. If the home is demoralized it will ruin it.—*T. L. Cuyler, D.D.*

WITH malice towards none, with charity for all.—*Abraham Lincoln.*

MISSION OF AMERICA.

COLUMBIA, Columbia, to glory arise,
The queen of the world, and child of the skies!
Thy genius commands thee; with rapture behold,
While ages on ages thy splendors unfold.
Thy reign is the last and the noblest of time,
Most fruitful thy soil, most inviting thy clime;
Let the crimes of the East ne'er encrimson thy name,
Be freedom and science and virtue thy fame.

To conquest and slaughter let Europe aspire;
Whelm nations in blood, and wrap cities in fire;
Thy heroes the rights of mankind shall defend,
And triumph pursue them, and glory attend.
A world is thy realm; for a world be thy laws,
Enlarged as thine empire, and just as thy cause;
On Freedom's broad basis that empires shall rise,
Extend with the main, and dissolve with the skies.

Fair science her gates to thy sons shall unbar,
And the east see thy morn hide the beams of her star,
New bards and new sages unrivalled shall soar
To fame unextinguished when time is no more;
To thee, the last refuge of virtue designed,
Shall fly from all nations the best of mankind;
Here grateful to heaven, with transports shall bring
Their incense, more fragrant than odors of spring.

Nor less shall thy fair ones to glory ascend,
And genius and beauty in harmony blend;
The graces of form shall awake pure desire,
And the charms of the soul ever cherish the fire;

Their sweetness unmingled, their manners refined,
And virtue's bright image, enstamped on the mind,
With peace and soft rapture shall teach life to glow,
And light up a smile on the aspect of woe.

Thy fleets to all regions thy power shall display,
The nations admire, and the ocean obey;
Each shore to thy glory its tribute unfold,
And the east and the south yield their spices and gold.
As the day spring unbounded thy splendor shall flow,
And earth's little kingdoms before thee shall bow,
While the ensigns of union, in triumph unfurled,
Hush the tumult of war, and give peace to the world.

Thus, as down a lone valley, with cedars o'erspread,
From war's dread confusion, I pensively strayed—
The gloom from the face of fair heaven retired;
The winds ceased to murmur, the thunders expired ·
Perfumes, as of Eden, flowed sweetly along,
And a voice, as of angels, enchantingly sung:
"Columbia, Columbia, to glory arise,
The queen of the world, and the child of the skies."
—*Timothy Dwight.*

OPENING OF THE CENTENNIAL EXPOSITION.

THE day of opening came. Philadelphia was thronged with strangers from all parts of the world. Every line of travel contributed its multitude. The morning of the 10th of May broke heavily with clouds and rain. But patriotism made gloom impossible in the Quaker city, and enthusiasm supplied the place of sunshine. A thousand flags fluttered in every street, and more than ten times ten thousand people, cheering as they went, pressed their way towards Fairmount Park. A military escort, four thousand strong, conducted the President of the United States to the Centennial grounds. For it was he who should declare the formal opening of the Exposition. The notables of many nations had already preceded him to the scene of the ceremonies. The great open space—traversed by the Avenue of the Republic—between the Main Building and Memorial Hall, had been prepared for the inauguration. There had been assembled the Supreme Court of the United States, Members of the Cabinet and the American Congress, the Governors of many of the States, distinguished officers of the army and navy, the ministers from foreign countries, Dom Pedro II., of Brazil, and his queen, illustrious civilians, statesmen and diplomatists, noblemen with titles and greater men without them, to witness the imposing pageant.

At the appointed hour the splendid orchestra, led by Theodore Thomas, burst forth with the national airs of the various countries participating in the Exhibition. Soon the President ascended the platform and was seated, with the Brazilian Emperor and Empress on his right. Then followed Wagner's celebrated *Centennial Inauguration March*, composed for the occasion. Matthew Simpson, Bishop of the Methodist Episcopal Church, then offered an eloquent and fervent prayer, which was followed by the singing of John G. Whittier's *Centennial Hymn*. When the strains had died away, the Honorable John Welsh, Chairman of the Board of Finance, arose and made a formal presentation of the buildings and grounds to General Hawley, President of the Centennial Commission. The latter, in an appropriate manner, accepted the trust; and then followed the singing of Sidney Lanier's *Centennial Cantata*. General Hawley next delivered an address, recounting briefly the things accomplished by the Centennial Commission, and in the name thereof presenting to the President of the United States the International Exhibition of 1876. The President —most famous of all American chief-magistrates for *not* delivering orations—replied to General Hawley in the following well-chosen address:—

"*My Countrymen:* It has been thought appropriate, upon this Centennial occasion, to bring together in Philadelphia, for popular inspection, specimens of our attainments in the industrial and fine arts, and in literature, science, and philosophy, as well as in the great business of agriculture and commerce. That we may the more thoroughly appreciate the excellencies and deficiencies of our achievements and also give emphatic expression to our earnest desire to cultivate the friendship of our fellow-members of this great family of nations, the enlightened agricultural, commercial, and manufacturing people of the world have been invited to send hither corresponding specimens of their skill to exhibit on equal terms, with friendly competition with our own. For so doing we render them our hearty thanks. The beauty and utility of the contributions will this day be submitted to your inspection. We are glad to know that a view of specimens of the skill of all nations will afford you unalloyed pleasure, as well as yield to you a valuable practical knowledge of so many of the remarkable results of the wonderful skill existing in enlightened communities.

"One hundred years ago our country was new, and but partially settled. Our necessities have compelled us chiefly to expend our means and time in felling forests, subduing prairies, building dwellings, factories, ships, docks, warehouses, roads, canals, and machinery. Most of our schools, churches, libraries, and asylums have been established within a hundred years. Burdened with these great primal works of necessity, which could not be delayed, we yet have done what this Exhibition will show in the direction of rivalling older and more advanced nations in law, medicine, and theology; in science, literature, philosophy, and the fine arts. Whilst proud of what we have done, we regret that we have not done more. Our achievements have been great enough, however, to make it easy for our people to acknowledge superior merit wherever found.

"And now, fellow-citizens, I hope a careful examination of what is about to be exhibited to you will not only inspire you with a profound respect for the skill and taste of our friends from other nations, but also satisfy you with the attainments made by our own people during the past one hundred years. I invoke your generous co-operation with the worthy commissioners, to secure a brilliant success to this International Exhibition, and to make the stay of our foreign visitors—to whom we extend a hearty welcome—both profitable and pleasant to them.

"I declare the International Exhibition now open."

When the President's brief oration was concluded the national ensign was flung out as a signal from the great flag-staff of the main building; the banners of foreign nations were immediately unfurled; cheers rent the air; a salute of a hundred guns from the battery on George's Hill answered to the shout. Memorial Hall, the Main Building, and Machinery Hall were now thrown open to receive the procession of invited guests—four thousand in number, and first to behold the handiwork of the nations. General Grant and Major Alfred T. Goshorn, the able and indefatigable Director-General of the Exhibition, led the way from the Main Building, and down the great isle of Machinery Hall to the centre, where a special work had been reserved for the President and the Brazilian Emperor. This honorable duty was to open the valves of the mighty Corliss Engine, whose tremendous pistons were to start into life and motion the infinite machinery of the hall. At twenty minutes past one o'clock the signal was given by George H. Corliss, the maker of the iron giant. The President and the Emperor, standing upon the raised platform, opened the valves; the ponderous fly-wheel started on its tireless rounds, and the multitudinous engines of the hall began their varied work. The Centennial Exhibition was fairly inaugurated under the most auspicious omens.—*John Clark Ridpath.*

CENTENNIAL HYMN.

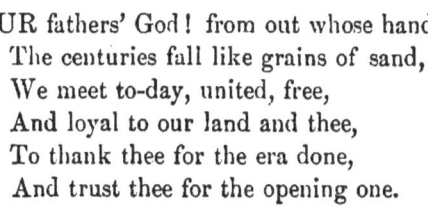

OUR fathers' God! from out whose hand
The centuries fall like grains of sand,
We meet to-day, united, free,
And loyal to our land and thee,
To thank thee for the era done,
And trust thee for the opening one.

Here, where of old, by thy design
The fathers spake that word of thine,
Whose echo is the glad refrain
Of rended bolt and falling chain,
To grace our festal time, from all
The zones of earth our guests we call.

Be with us while the new world greets
The old world thronging all its streets,

Unveiling all the triumphs won
By art or toil beneath the sun;
And unto common good ordain
This rivalship of hand and brain.

Thou, who hast here in concord furled
The war flags of a gathered world,
Beneath our Western skies fulfil
The Orient's mission of good-will,
And, freighted with love's golden fleece,
Send back the argonauts of peace.
—*John G. Whittier.*

GREETING TO AMERICA.

Land of promise, fair and free,
   Earth's opening morning glory,
Columbia, hail! Fame tells of thee
   A short but wondrous story.
From Vasa's land to Washington's,
The way is far, but freedom's songs
From land to land, o'er rolling sea,
   Ring with true heroes' glory.

I see thy peaceful dwellings rise
   O'er boundless territories;
I hear thy children, good and wise,
   Proclaim thy future glories,
That "blessed are the rich in peace,
The merciful!" they will increase,
So says the prophet, they will rise
   To rule earth's territories.

In gold and silver rich thou art,
   Thy crops are great and growing;

But richer still I know thy heart,
    Its treasures overflowing.
To the oppressed thou callest, come!
To homeless ones thou giv'st a home,
To hopeless hearts a hopeful heart,
    To every growth a growing.

So mayest thou grow more strong and free,
    America, forever,
A blessing to all people be,
    A blighted hope—O, never.
But may thy eagles farther fly,
With cries for light and liberty,
Till hearts and thoughts, as eagles free,
    Thy glory hail forever.

—*Frederica Brehmer.*

OUR FUTURE GREATNESS.

GRAND as the past has been, the future shall far surpass it. The best days are all before, not behind. The populations of the earth are but a handful compared with what they shall be. The productions of the soil are but a handful compared with what they shall be. The resources of the hills are but a handful compared with what they shall be. The knowledge gained by science is but a boy's primer compared with what shall be the mastery over nature's forces wielded by man; but child's play compared with what shall be. The spread of virtue is but narrow compared with what shall be. The enlightenment of man is but unlight compared with what shall be. This nation is destined to live, not die; live, not droop; live, not shrivel; live, not drivel; live a deeper life in thought, a purer life in morals, a calmer life in effort, a rounder life in culture, a diviner life in charity, in love.

Why should the mother of the seas be still young, active, advancing, though a thousand years old, and her daughter die? Progress is the law of history, of God. Let the fulness of Christian principle be assimilated by our nation, and we are sure of conservation with progression. Christianity is the salt which repels corruption and disintegration, and conserves in vigorous vitality. Whatever it touches it immortalizes; whatever it controls it preserves; whatever it transforms it imbues with immutability. For it is "the word of our God which abideth forever."

The nation lives by morality. Morality flows from piety. Morality is never purer than its source. Morality never rises higher than its fountain. Pagan nations owned not divine religion; their gods were monsters and their morals foul. What is left for this nation to choose? To which of the saints shall she turn? To none of them—to none of them; but to Him who is the King of saints and the King of nations. And as it was in the beginning, so is it now and ever shall be. O God! to thy care she commits herself for another century. God of her fathers! be the God of their succeeding race. Make us true, upright, just, pure, humble, generous, grateful. Hallow our joys; sanctify our sorrows; chasten us when haughty; guard us when imperiled, and crown us with such glory as we are able to bear.—*Dr. Thomas Guard.*

The word of our nation must be as good as its bond.—*Charles Sumner.*

THE AMERICAN NATION HAS A FUTURE.

I verily believe this nation has a destiny and a history yet to be. I think it probable it is a favored nation and a chosen people; as the Egyptians were once a chosen people, and the Hebrews after them a favored nation. I think we are bound to attain the maximum of our power. No human hand has led us hither, and no human hand can curb that destiny or arrest its progress. In the morning of youth the American Hercules had strangled the serpents which assailed his cradle! As his strength matures, other and more successful labors invite his imperial glance and arms. The haughty capital of Rome is already rivalled by a more splendid edifice on the Potomac; our population resembles that of the ancient mistress of the world in its admixture of all peoples, derived from every clime, and mingling in the same fierce current the restless elements of the globe. Boundless in its ambition, reckless of dangers and impatient of control, sustained in all its trials and wonderful progress by an omnipotent hand which has been more than once visibly interposed, the vast political system of which America is at once the centre and a nucleus rises grandly up to the utmost of our hopes, moves forward with resistless sweep, as if it were, indeed, a part of the Celestial Economies. Like the Colossus at Rhodes, between whose feet once floated the commerce of the world, it holds a beacon in one hand and an arrow in the other, towers to the zenith with unflinching gaze, Heaven's lightning crest her head. The live thunders sleep among her purple heights and sun-crowned crags. Beaming down with a starry, mild and planetary light, the well-known forms of her Northern States and seas no longer cast across this Southern hemisphere dark and doubtful shadows. They climb up with us together and between the older constellations, walking among them and by them, with majestic port and pride; as though the other planets only marked our footprints on the skies, and the universe was our throne.—*Edward Cantwell.*

DESTINY OF AMERICA.

THE Muse disgusted at an age and clime
    Barren of every glorious theme,
In distant lands now waits a better time
    Producing subjects worthy fame.

In happy climes, where from the genial sun
    And virgin earth, such scenes ensue;
The force of art by nature seems outdone,
    And fancied beauties by the true.

In happy climes, the seat of innocence,
    Where nature guides, and virtue rules;
Where men shall not impose for truth and sense
    The pedantry of courts and schools.

There shall be sung another golden age,
    The rise of empire and of arts,
The good and great inspiring epic rage,
    The wisest heads and noblest hearts.

Not such as Europe breeds in her decay;
    Such as she breeds when fresh and young,

When heavenly flame did animate her clay,
　By future poets shall be sung.

Westward the course of empire takes its way;
　The first four acts already past,
A fifth shall close the drama with the day,
　Time's noblest offspring is the last.
　　　　　　　　　—*George Berkeley.*

FREEDOM'S GRAND REVIEW.

MAN has ever cherished the fond belief that the sacrament of death dissolves none of the attributes of the soul; that the love which thrills his being here, for principles and persons, also embues his spiritual existence. Believing this, the sweet hope follows that the ordinances of a merciful God permit the departed one, whose angel feet tread the emerald fields of Paradise, to watch over his earthly loves and joy with them in their joys.

If this dream be true, in this proud hour, when freedom holds her grand review, upon the alabaster battlements of heaven stand the host of sages and martyrs, who, upon earth, braved and suffered to elevate mankind. Behold the immortal Washington, sage of Mt. Vernon, leading by the hand the martyred Lincoln—Father and Saviour of a common country. The Sage of Monticello, with his folded arms and towering brow, his pen of fire; he who, dying, craved no other boon than that above his grave should be inscribed, "Here lies the author of the Declaration of Independence." There is Henry of Virginia; he who startled a world with his loud cry, "Give me liberty or give me death." That cry yet rings down the aisles of a century as pure and clear as when uttered in the House of Burgesses of Virginia. There is Franklin, King of the Lightning, philosopher and statesman; he who, in plain Quaker garb, stood in the presence of the proudest sovereign and the haughtiest aristocracy of the world, charming and convincing all with his eloquent appeal in behalf of freedom. There is the boyish form of Lafayette, as he bounded from the ease of a court and the dalliances of a bride to the gloom and terrors of Valley Forge. Bold Rupert of Liberty! what joy for thee does this day hold, for not only America but also France is free. There is Allen, bold Green mountain boy, as he looked when he leapt Ticonderoga's battlements and demanded its surrender in the name of the Great Jehovah and of the Continental Congress. And Stark, with the light of battle in his eyes, as when at Bennington he declared that that day victory should be his or Molly Stark should be a widow. And Morgan, with his iron-nerved riflemen—the men of Quebec, Saratoga and Cowpens. Pulaski, as he charged at Brandywine to rescue Washington, and as he looked, folded in the arms of death before the gates of Savannah. Montgomery, hero of Quebec—he who in the darkness of the night, amidst the driving snows and hurtling cannon shot, poured out the libations of his noble heart in the cause of Liberty, cradled in the arms of Aaron Burr.

See the gallant cowboys of the Hudson—Williams, Paulding and Van Wart—whose rugged honesty ill-fated Andre's gold nor promise could not overcome. And there is Mad Anthony as he charged at Germantown and at Stony Point, and Putnam, Knox, Lee, Pickens, Sumter, Marion, Greene, Gates, and all the countless throng of sages and heroes of the Revolution, and with them stands the Murat of the battle-field, Arnold—aye, Benedict Arnold. Death has sanctified his life. God reverses man's judgment; the shadows of a century have forever hidden his faults. We can only see him now as the first to spring to freedom's side; as he appeared when he led his troops through the forests of Maine and Canada; as he appeared on that winter night when planning the assault with Montgomery, or, when lying shattered and wounded, he implored the faithful and gallant Morgan to leave him to his fate; or as at Champlain, when he sank with his burning fleet beneath the wave rather than leave any trophy of victory for the enemy; or as at Saratoga, when the day seemingly was lost, he, like a meteor, alone, without authority or any command, summoned the army to follow him and led their way to victory. Standing there, our fathers behold the fair daughters and brave sons of liberty sporting in the bright valleys that border the river where flows unvexed the sweet waters of peace. Whilst Europe trembles and grows pale with war's affright, here peace stands at the helm, and hope and glory fill our sails. This land, the asylum for the oppressed of all the earth, draws to it representative intellect, genius and blood from every nation, and fusing all, gives to us as a nation the engrossed intelligence, endurance and physique of them all. As the fruits of civil, religious and political liberty, they behold our institutions of learning, and particularly the free schools, pouring yearly into the wondering lap of the world legions of men with cultured intellects, all disciples of the faith that man is capable of self-government, and that all men by nature are born free and equal. These legions form the nucleus that in time of peace chain the elements, outstrip time, bridge space and whirl the myriad wheels of industry; and, in time of war, with every successive effort plant higher and still higher the emblem of the free. They behold the Christian Church; the Jewish Synagogue, the Moslem and Pagan Temple, and the Lyceum for Free Thought, all rise side by side. The myriads of their devotees mingling their currents without a menace or a scowl of hate, proclaim conscience free. They behold the thirteen feeble stars grown into a vast constellation, each an empire in itself, yet revolving around a common centre, bound and attracted thereto by the unseen bonds of constitutional law. That flag which they gave to liberty in the carnage, smoke, and death of rebellion, has grown into the recognized insignia of freedom throughout the world. No nation is so distant or so powerful that it does not there hold its honored place; no ocean that does not mirror it; no desert or mountain land that has not been lighted by its smile. It waves in sovereignty over Alaskan glaciers and amid the leafy bannerets of the tropical everglades; it greets the rising sun from amid the towering forests of the Kennebec and waves him good-night from the pearly shores of the Pacific; and now, unstained by dishonor, unsullied by defeat, it flashes back to heaven the triumph of a century.—*Hon. C. E. Delong.*

By the rivers of America light beams forth to the nations. —*Klopstock.*

Let no American leave his native land for enjoyment when he can view the rugged wildness of her mountains, admire the beauty of her cultured plains, the noble extent of her broad rivers, the expanse of her lakes, and fearful grandeur of her cataracts, or *feel* the rich blessings of her freedom.—*Anonymous.*

DECLARATION OF INDEPENDENCE.

A DECLARATION BY THE REPRESENTATIVES OF THE UNITED STATES OF AMERICA, IN CONGRESS ASSEMBLED.

WHEN, in the course of human events, it becomes necessary for one people to dissolve the political bands which have connected them with another, and to assume, among the powers of the earth, the separate and equal station to which the laws of nature and of nature's God entitle them, a decent respect to the opinions of mankind requires that they should declare the causes which impel them to the separation.

We hold these truths to be self-evident, that all men are created equal; that they are endowed by their Creator with certain unalienable rights; that among these, are life, liberty, and the pursuit of happiness. That, to secure these rights, governments are instituted among men, deriving their just powers from the consent of the governed: that, whenever any form of government becomes destructive of these ends, it is the right of the people to alter or to abolish it, and to institute a new government, laying its foundation on such principles, and organizing its powers in such form, as to them shall seem most likely to effect their safety and happiness. Prudence, indeed, will dictate that governments long established, should not be changed for light and transient causes; and, accordingly, all experience hath shown, that mankind are more disposed to suffer, while evils are sufferable, than to right themselves by abolishing the forms to which they are accustomed. But, when a long train of abuses and usurpations, pursuing invariably the same object, evinces a design to reduce them under absolute despotism, it is their right, it is their duty, to throw off such government, and to provide new guards for their future security. Such has been the patient sufferance of these colonies, and such is now the necessity which constrains them to alter their former systems of government. The history of the present king of Great Britain is a history of repeated injuries and usurpations, all having, in direct object, the establishment of an absolute tyranny over these States. To prove this, let facts be submitted to a candid world:

He has refused his assent to laws the most wholesome and necessary for the public good.

He has forbidden his governors to pass laws of immediate and pressing importance, unless suspended in their operation till his assent should be obtained; and, when so suspended, he has utterly neglected to attend to them.

He has refused to pass other laws for the accommodation of large districts of people, unless those people would relinquish the right of representation in the legislature; a right inestimable to them, and formidable to tyrants only.

He has called together legislative bodies at places unusual, uncomfortable, and distant from the depository of their public records, for the sole purpose of fatiguing them into compliance with his measures.

He has dissolved representative houses repeatedly, for opposing, with manly firmness, his invasions on the rights of the people.

He has refused, for a long time after such dissolutions, to cause others to be elected; whereby the legislative powers, incapable of annihilation, have returned to the people at large for their exercise; the State remaining, in the mean time, exposed to all the danger of invasion from without and convulsions within.

He has endeavored to prevent the population of these States; for that purpose, obstructing the laws for naturalization of foreigners; refusing to pass others to encourage their migration hither, and raising the conditions of new appropriations of lands.

He has obstructed the administration of justice, by refusing his assent to laws for establishing judiciary powers.

He has made judges dependent on his will alone, for the tenure of their offices, and the amount and payment of their salaries.

He has erected a multitude of new offices, and sent hither swarms of officers to harass our people, and eat out their substance.

He has kept among us, in times of peace, standing armies, without the consent of our legislature.

He has affected to render the military independent of, and superior to, the civil power.

He has combined, with others, to subject us to a jurisdiction foreign to our constitution, and unacknowledged by our laws; giving his assent to their acts of pretended legislation:

For quartering large bodies of armed troops among us:

For protecting them, by a mock trial, from punishment, for any murders which they should commit on the inhabitants of these States:

For cutting off our trade with all parts of the world:

For imposing taxes on us without our consent:

For depriving us, in many cases, of the benefits of trial by jury:

For transporting us beyond seas to be tried for pretended offences:

For abolishing the free system of English laws in a neighboring province, establishing therein an arbitrary government, and enlarging its boundaries, so as to render it at once an example and fit instrument for introducing the same absolute rule into these colonies:

For taking away our charters, abolishing our most valuable laws, and altering, fundamentally, the powers of our governments:

For suspending our own legislatures, and declaring themselves invested with power to legislate for us in all cases whatsoever.

He has abdicated government here, by declaring us out of his protection, and waging war against us.

He has plundered our seas, ravaged our coasts, burnt our towns, and destroyed the lives of our people.

He is, at this time, transporting large armies of foreign mercenaries to complete the works of death, desolation, and tyranny, already begun, with circumstances of cruelty and perfidy scarcely paralleled in the most barbarous ages, and totally unworthy the head of a civilized nation.

He has constrained our fellow-citizens, taken captive on the high seas, to bear arms against their country, to become the executioners of their friends and brethren, or to fall themselves by their hands.

He has excited domestic insurrections amongst us, and has endeavored to bring on the inhabitants of our frontiers, the merciless Indian savages, whose known rule of warfare is an undistinguished destruction of all ages, sexes, and conditions.

In every stage of these oppressions, we have petitioned

for redress, in the most humble terms; our repeated petitions have been answered only by repeated injury. A prince, whose character is thus marked by every act which may define a tyrant, is unfit to be the ruler of a free people.

Nor have we been wanting in attention to our British brethren.

We have warned them, from time to time, of attempts made by their legislature to extend an unwarrantable jurisdiction over us. We have reminded them of the circumstances of our emigration and settlement here. We have appealed to their native justice and magnanimity, and we have conjured them, by the ties of our common kindred, to disavow these usurpations, which would inevitably interrupt our connections and correspondence. They, too, have been deaf to the voice of justice and consanguinity. We must, therefore, acquiesce in the necessity which denounces our separation, and hold them as we hold the rest of mankind, enemies in war, in peace, friends.

We, therefore, the representatives of the UNITED STATES OF AMERICA, in GENERAL CONGRESS assembled, appealing to the Supreme Judge of the world for the rectitude of our intentions, do, in the name, and by the authority of the good people of these colonies, solemnly publish and declare, That these United Colonies are, and of right ought to be, *free and independent States;* that they are absolved from all allegiance to the British crown, and that all political connection between them and the state of Great Britain, is, and ought to be, totally dissolved; and that, as FREE AND INDEPENDENT STATES, they have full power to levy war, conclude peace, contract alliances, establish commerce, and to do all other acts and things which INDEPENDENT STATES may of right do. And, for the support of this declaration, with a firm reliance on the protection of DIVINE PROVIDENCE, we mutually pledge to each other, our lives, our fortunes, and our sacred honor.—*John Hancock.*

OUR GOVERNMENT—ITS ADMINISTRATION.

GOVERNMENT is essential for the restraint of evil, for the security of justice, and for the development of peace and purity.

THE NATIONAL GOVERNMENT.

The National Government is triune. One government composed of three co-ordinate departments, independent of each other. 1. *The Legislative.* 2. *The Executive.* 3. *The Judicial.* The first makes the laws; the second enforces the laws; the third interprets the laws and administers justice.

LEGISLATIVE DEPARTMENT.

The legislative power is vested in a Congress composed of the people's representatives. It consists of a Senate and House of Representatives.

The Senate is composed of two senators from each State, elected for a term of six years, by the State Legislatures. The senator must be thirty years of age, nine years a citizen of the United States, and an inhabitant of the State for which he is chosen. The Vice-President of the United States is President of the Senate, but has no vote, except in case of a tie, but when sitting as a high court to try impeachments, the Chief-Justice of the United States presides.

The House is composed of representatives elected directly by the people by ballot, the number from each State depending on the population. In 1792 there was one to each 33,000; in 1883 there was one to each 154,325. A representative must be twenty-five years of age, a citizen of the United States six years, and an inhabitant of the State for which he is chosen. The representatives choose their own presiding officer—the Speaker, and have the sole power of impeachment.

The Senate and House meet at the same time and place, but in separate chambers. A majority in each constitutes a quorum. Neither House can adjourn for more than three days without the consent of the other. Members of both Houses are free from arrest during their attendance at the sessions of their respective Houses, or going to or returning from the same, except in cases of treason, felony, or breach of peace. No person is allowed to hold office while a member of either House. Each Congress is limited to two years.

POWERS OF CONGRESS.

Congress is vested with sovereign power to do business with foreign nations, and regulate commerce among the States. But Congress cannot suspend the privilege of the writ of *habeas corpus*, unless where the public safety may require it, neither can it grant any title of nobility, nor in any way favor one State above another. Its object is to develop the resources of the several States, and protect them as a whole.

HOW LAWS ARE PASSED.

A bill must originate in the House of Representatives. If it passes both Houses it is taken to the President of the United States, who signs it, and it then becomes a law. If he does not approve it, he returns it with his written objections. This is called a *veto*. Then it may be reconsidered, and if passed by a two-thirds vote of each House, it becomes a law without the President's signature.

STATES AND TERRITORIES.

The States are *independent* in a degree, but are not *sovereign*. The National Constitution does not allow them the exercise of the functions of sovereign power. Originally there were thirteen States; there are now forty-two. A State is first a *Territory*. A section of the republic is set apart, and a government organized. The Governor and other officers are appointed by the President of the United States, by and with the consent of the Senate.

The Territory has a Legislature which passes local laws, which may be rejected by Congress. The inhabitants elect a representative to Congress; he tells that body what the Territory needs, but he has no vote, and the people of a Territory do not vote for the President of the United States. When a Territory contains a certain number of inhabitants, a convention may be called, a constitution adopted, and an application for admission into the Union be made to Congress. If the application is accepted, the Territory becomes a State.

EXECUTIVE DEPARTMENT.

The executive power is vested in the President of the United States, whose office is limited to four years, but he may be re-elected indefinitely. His power is co-ordinate but not co-equal with the legislative department. He is the agent to execute the will of the people as expressed by law. He is commander-in-chief of the army and navy, also of the militia of the States when called into actual service. He has power to fill official vacancies during the recess of the Senate, and may be removed from office on impeachment for high crimes.

JUDICIAL DEPARTMENT.

The judicial power is vested in a Supreme Court, sitting at the national capital, with such inferior courts as Congress may establish in various parts of the Union. The judges hold their offices during good behavior. The Supreme Court has original jurisdiction in all cases affecting ambassadors, other public ministers, and consuls, and those in which a State may be a party. In all other cases it has appellate jurisdiction as to law and fact.

ADMINISTRATION OF GOVERNMENT.

The President administers the laws through the advice and assistance of eight cabinet ministers. Each minister is at the head of a separate executive department.

THE EXECUTIVE DEPARTMENTS.

The executive departments are known as State, Treasury, War, Navy, Interior, Post Office, Justice, and Agricultural. The last department has been recently organized. These various departments are divided into different branches, and have competent men in charge. Thus through these executive departments the vast machinery of our government is smoothly run, enabling us to enjoy life, liberty, and the pursuit of happiness. If interested in the facts and figures of America, send ten cents to the publishers of this book for a copy of "The National Scrap-Book or All About Our Country."

THE maturity of the nation is but a continuation of its youth.—*George Bancroft.*

A PARTING WORD.

DEFEND your rights and your freedom, fellow-citizens, by keeping alive the sacred fires of intelligence. Never put off the armor of patriotism. Fling a kiss to liberty. Bare the head and bow submissively to the God of all hearts, that it has been your high privilege to stand in this noon-day light under these beneficent institutions. Remember, all who would rest in the seat of free government, that it is not covered with cushions of luxurious down. It is a rock angular with righteousness, adamantine with justice, and snowy white with purity. Let us fit ourselves to occupy it by lives of blameless rectitude and unselfish devotion to freedom.—*William A. Bartlett, D. D.*

www.ingramcontent.com/pod-product-compliance
Lightning Source LLC
Chambersburg PA
CBHW021418300426
44114CB00010B/549